Edible Plants

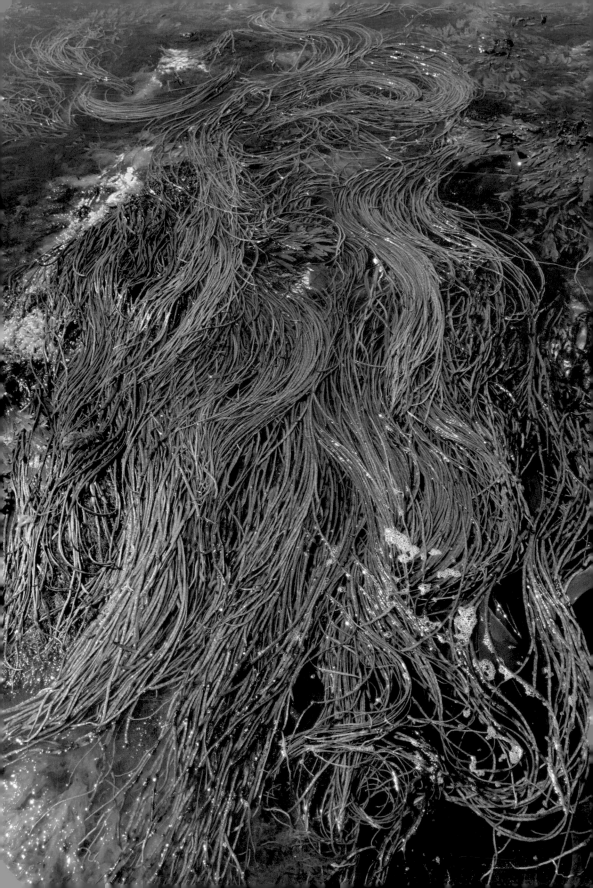

Edible Plants

A forager's guide to the plants and seaweeds of Britain, Ireland and temperate Europe

Geoff Dann

To Dorothy

Front cover photograph: Ramsons.
Back cover photograph: Wild Fennel.

Frontispiece: Sea Spaghetti.

Contents

Acknowledgements

First and foremost I thank my wife and foraging collaborator, Cathy, whose encouragement and practical support made it possible for me to write this book. In particular I am grateful for her editing skills, written contributions (preservation, acorns, chestnuts), and recipe testing.

I would also like to thank:

Plants for a Future for their huge, freely accessible database of recorded plant uses, and the Global Biodiversity Information Facility and the UK's National Biodiversity Network for their distribution data. The Foods of England Project for their hoard of historic recipe books and Dyfed Lloyd Evans, for his enormous collection of traditional recipes at the old celtnet.org.uk website.

Fergus Drennan for feedback on the final draft of the book, David Cracknell and Nick Marsh for a successful Wild Service Tree hunt, Thilaka Hillman for Henbane seedlings (and recipe ideas), James Cross and Danny Clayden for recipe ideas, Ruth Culver for a plant location tip-off, and Prof Paul Cleave for assistance on a reference.

The seaweed nutritional data came from *Seaweeds* by Ole G Mouritsen and *Nutritional Value of Edible Seaweeds* by Paul MacArtain et al.

I must also thank all the people listed at the end of this book, who have given their plant photographs Creative Commons licences. A special mention goes to those of whose images I have used more than one: Stefan Laefnaer (8), H.Zell (6), Anneli Salo (4), Alpsdake, Rasbak, Frank Xaver and Krzysztof Ziarnek (3 each), Jerzy Opiola, Erlend Bjørtvedt, Cillas, Christian Fischer, Krzysztof Golik, Wouter Hagens, Magnus Manske, Kristian Peters, Olivier Pichard, Bjorn S. and GT1976 (2 each). Thanks also to Anne Burgess for use of her Henbit photo.

Designer: Luke Herriott at Studioink.co.uk. Illustration on pages 100-101 by Scott Garrett at www.garrettworld.co.uk.

About the author

Geoff Dann grew up on the North Downs in Surrey, and started foraging as a teenager in the 1980s. He studied philosophy at Sussex University, and has been a professional foraging teacher since 2009. This is his second book. His first – the groundbreaking *Edible Mushrooms* (2016) – is the most comprehensive guide to northern European fungi foraging ever published.

Introduction

A new age of food insecurity is dawning, such that few living Europeans have experienced. Perhaps we sense it somewhere deep inside, for interest in wild food has been growing in recent years – albeit more as a hobby or high-cuisine curiosity than a precaution against famine. But in 2020 our supply chains creaked, our supermarkets showed the strain, and foraging began to re-enter our collective consciousness as a survival skill.

This is the most comprehensive colour-illustrated book ever published on foraging for plants and seaweeds in north-west Europe. Though most of the species covered are wild, it also includes edible ornamentals and agricultural/horticultural escapes.

Foraging books can't be field guides. Field guides need to super-efficiently cover as many species as possible using abbreviated jargon. Foraging books focus on the edible and poisonous, and must also supply information on their culinary uses and/or toxicity. This book includes the most dangerous poisonous species and everything worth eating, and the identification information is provided with foraging safety and usefulness in mind. If you want to identify unfamiliar species in the field, then you need a field guide. I wouldn't advise trusting an app with your life, but perhaps I am old fashioned.

Some foraging books do also delve into herbal medicine. This one occasionally mentions medicinal uses, especially in cases with undisputed scientific evidence of efficacy and no known hazards, but medical herbalism is a large and complicated discipline, and I have no medical training. That said, some illnesses are caused by poor nutrition, many foraged plants and seaweeds are rich in vitamins and minerals, and that is a topic very much within the scope of this book.

Over the past decade, I have attempted to find and photograph in their natural habitat as many of the relevant plants and seaweeds as possible. Inevitably some eluded me, and where possible I tried to grow these in my own garden. Cultivating wild plants has the added benefit of allowing close observation of their whole life cycle, as well as making it considerably easier (both physically and legally) to dig them up and experiment with their subterranean parts.

I have included some recipes, most of which are traditional. A few are more modern, and a handful are sufficiently original to be called my own creations. For the better known wild species, hundreds of recipes can be found online.

It is customary for foraging books to contain a short section on the cultural significance of foraging. Chapter one is an account of how and why human beings originally abandoned hunter-gathering to become farmers, and the long-term consequences of that fateful revolution. Chapter two is about foraging in the 12,000 years since then, the long decline of old traditions and the rapid rise of new ones since the 1970s. It is also about sustainability and long-term food security; this book is intended to be a practical guide for finding and using emergency foods in an uncertain future.

Anthropocene

Homo what? Oh, *sapiens*, yes
Chimpanzee in fancy dress
Then one day it started farming
And ecologically self-harming
Millennia passed, it never learned
Fiddled while the planet burned
Cleverest ape there's ever been
Anthropos of the Anthropocene

Cue battlecries, Silent Springs
Summers of Love and hippy things
Environmentalism's birth
Jonathon Porritt's *Save the Earth*
Save the Earth? Save it from what?
Whatever's in danger, Earth is not
Ah, back in the day when I was a Green
And nobody mentioned the Anthropocene

Times have changed, we have to admit
It's far too late to dodge this shit
Stare the monster in the face
Karma for the human race
There's a whole new era dawning
Old one's over, I'm not mourning
Come to terms, feeling stoic
Not Anthropocene but Anthropozoic

Cleverest Ape there ever was
Caring, sharing Anthropos
Didn't want to read the runes
Sowed the wind and reaped typhoons
Environmentalism? Empty shell
Green-blue planet? Terrestrial hell
Rock and hard place, in-between
Anthropos of the Anthropocene

The domestication of humans

"As the whole world is self, killing a plant or animal is not murder but transformation. Finding food is taken for granted, reinforced by myths telling the hunter to be the animal before presuming to kill and eat it." (Graeme Barker, on animistic hunter-gatherers. From *The Agricultural Revolution in Prehistory: Why did Foragers become Farmers?* 2009.)

Losing Paradise

Humanity is at the end of a transition from tribal hunter-gatherers to techno-industrial dominators of the planet – a process that began with the emergence of the first agricultural technologies, and their promise of new ways to control the wild world. At the time of publication, fewer than 200,000 humans are living as pure hunter-gatherers – 0.0025% of the global population, and still falling. Yet human society today is less secure than it was at the beginning of that process, and after a very long decline, wild food is making a comeback.

This foraging renaissance has nothing to do with people whose own recent ancestors were hunter-gatherers. It is a feature of western societies, especially those furthest removed from that way of life – those which had, until recently, stopped foraging almost entirely. It is dismissed in some quarters as a craze. Nobody, it has been said, needs to forage in the modern world; humans should stick to cultivated food and leave the wild stuff for wildlife. According to this view, today's European foragers are romantic dreamers, pining for a lost way of life that in reality must have been nasty, brutish and short.

But perhaps the notion of a lost paradise is not so crazy. The technological wonders of the 21st century are so familiar that most of us have a hard time imagining living in the world of just decades ago, let alone millennia, while at the same time our civilisation faces existential threats that would have seemed completely alien to our hunter-gatherer ancestors. They were animists, as are 'primitive people' everywhere. They believed the world had always been the way it was, and would always be that way, and that the natural and spiritual realms were one and the same, and would always provide what was needed. They respected it as if it were their own kin.

Their way of life was absolutely sustainable. Ours, regardless of science and technology that would look like magic to them, is absolutely not.

The Neolithic Revolution

The human animal evolved to forage and hunt for a living, just as its ancestral species had done for 540 million years, but in one respect this animal was different to anything that had gone before: it had a brand new survival strategy. Other creatures depend for their survival on things like being able to melt into the background or run very fast, or being very large, or having very sharp teeth, powerful venom or an impenetrable shell. Humans were the first creatures to depend entirely on their wits. For 2.6 million years of 'ice age' (scientifically the Pleistocene epoch) evolution worked on an animal whose bipedal locomotion, dextrous hands and anatomical capability for complex speech, though all of them game-changers in their own right, were mere auxiliary features compared to the revolutionary evolutionary technology of *overwhelming brainpower*. This, in control of those hands and communications, was applied to create weapons for hunting creatures so large and dangerous that an unarmed human would be fortunate to escape unharmed. Lithic technology – the working of stone – advanced at a pace that wasn't even glacial, but it eventually led to the invention of tools for harvesting and processing wild grains and pulses, and even made the felling of large trees possible.

There is a lively debate about the impact anatomically modern humans had on populations of large animals outside their African evolutionary home. Fossils show they first left Africa at least 180,000 years ago, but genetic studies indicate that these early migrants died out.[*] The successful colonisation of the rest of the world started about 60,000 years ago. Megafauna have been disappearing ever since, but we do not know to what extent this was the result of human activity. However, even if these humans *were* responsible for an elevated extinction rate in the late Pleistocene, their impact on the ecosystems they colonised must have been limited by their relatively small numbers.

Then about 12,000 years ago, things started to change more quickly. The ice retreated, and large areas of the northern hemisphere became more attractive for human habitation. Within a few centuries of the start of the next epoch (the Holocene), beginning in south-west Asia, humans started farming. Why here first, rather than somewhere else? The 'Fertile Crescent' had high-quality soil, a reliable water supply, and was home to a disproportionate number of wild species that were particularly suitable ('pre-adapted') for domestication.[†] But that doesn't explain why humans didn't just remain hunter-gatherers.

This first agricultural (or 'Neolithic' – new stone age) revolution has been described by American anthropologist Jared Diamond as "the worst mistake in the history of the human race" and by Israeli historian Yuval Noah Harari as "history's biggest fraud". Studies of 20th century foraging societies[‡] suggest they averaged no more than four hours a day hunting and gathering food, leaving plenty of time for leisure – and this was typically on relatively poor land, rejected by farmers. It is reasonable to assume that Mesolithic (middle stone age) foragers living in a more plentiful environment had at least as much free time.

Neolithic farming was a much harder life, requiring back-breaking work from dawn to dusk, and there's no evidence to suggest those early farmers were any healthier or better fed than their Mesolithic predecessors. The best evidence we have suggests the opposite was true.[§] And even if farming could provide more net calories, it couldn't (and still can't) touch foraging for variety: Mesolithic foragers must have enjoyed a more interesting and balanced diet than Neolithic farmers. This lack of variety persists: globally, today, about 25 cultivated crops comprise 90% of our diet.[¶] Farming also impacted the ecosystem in a fundamental way that foraging does not, causing far bigger changes to the balance of species in the local environment and the genetics of the domesticated species. Additionally, it opened the door to wealth

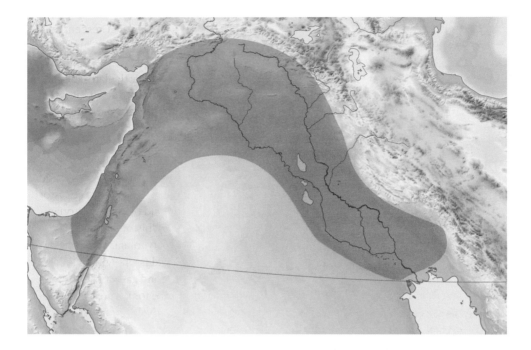

and social inequalities on a scale that had previously been impossible, some of which still plague us today. There should be no myths about noble savages,[#] and analysis of bones suggests that few Mesolithic hunter-gatherers made it to the age of 50, but in many respects it was an easier, healthier and more pleasant way of life than the agricultural one that replaced it. This view of the Neolithic Revolution and its consequences forms the foundational beliefs of the anarchist critique of civilisation known as anarchoprimitivism.

▲ The Fertile Crescent. This is where agriculture first arose, and the first great civilisations flourished a few millennia later. Along with these civilisations came a new sort of spirituality, very different to animism. Animistic belief systems are holistic, inherently mystical-panentheistic, and anathema to mainstream Abrahamic monotheism. The Old Testament (Genesis 1:28) instructs humans to "Be fruitful and increase in number; fill the earth and subdue it. Rule over the fish in the sea and the birds in the sky and over every living creature that moves on the ground." The unstratified and relatively egalitarian world of animistic tribalism was steadily replaced with a rigid hierarchal system: God at the top, humans in the middle (now in a massive hierarchy of their own) and the natural world at the bottom. And instead of there being no beginning and no end, the cosmology of Abrahamic religion starts with humanity being kicked out of Paradise on a path that leads to apocalypse.

* *When did modern humans leave Africa*, Stringer, C, and Galway-Witham, J, Science 359:6374, 2018, pp389-390.

† *Guns, Germs and Steel: A short history of everybody for the last 13,000 years*, Diamond, J, 1998.

‡ *Stone Age Economics*, Sahlins, M, 1972. *Primitive Affluence*, Black, B, 1992.

§ *Early agriculture's toll on human health*, Milner, GR, Proceedings of the National Academy of Sciences of the US 116:28, 2019, pp13721-13723.

¶ *How many plants feed the world?* Prescott-Allen, R, and Prescott-Allen, C, Conservation Biology, 1990.

The Truth About Primitive Life: A Critique of Anarchoprimitivism, Kaczynski, T, 2008.

Exactly how and why foragers became farmers are important questions that archaeologists have been trying to answer for over a century. Many theories have been proposed, mostly based on speculative reasoning, and supported by insufficient or disputed evidence. All the simple answers are inadequate – this was a complex and lengthy process. Initially, the most obvious answer was that farming was a giant technological and cultural leap forwards: 'progress'. Foragers, according to this hypothesis, would obviously have concluded that cultivating plants and keeping livestock is far more reliable and efficient than the lottery of foraging and hunting, right? This sort of thinking projects backwards from our modern perspective instead of understanding what really happened. It involves a concept of progress that is itself a product of modernity and would have been incomprehensible to the first farmers, and almost as meaningless to most medieval Europeans. On a geological-evolutionary timescale, the entire transition from foraging to farming happened in the blink of an eye, but on the timescale of human lives, it took hundreds of generations. It was not a conscious choice – no forager woke up one day and thought: "Why don't we clear the forest, and deliberately grow the plants we need instead of foraging for them!" It happened as the result of countless individual human decisions, each taken because it made sense in the immediate situation, and in the foreseeable, rather than more distant, future.

Foraging as a way of life naturally limits fertility and population density. In most territory available prior to the Neolithic Revolution, the only way to find enough food was to keep moving: Mesolithic hunter-gatherers were almost entirely nomadic (the only permanent settlements to significantly predate the Neolithic Revolution were a few fishing villages). The key to successful foraging, then as now, was to be in the right place at the right time. And if you are continually on the move then there's a limit to how fast you can reproduce – carrying one infant is manageable, but carrying two is not. This practical limitation was reinforced by the later weaning age of children in foraging societies, which has the biological effect of reducing female fertility due to higher levels of the hormone prolactin. Even with a low population density and a slow birth rate, populations in those foraging societies would have steadily risen during years of abundance, but sooner or later there would be leaner years when food was scarce, even for foragers, with their flexible diet. The young, the old and the weak would struggle to survive these hard times, lowering the human population back into balance with the rest of the ecosystem.

Fear of hunger must have been a factor in the development of agriculture. If your foraging territory is limited by the presence of competitors, threatening your ability to feed yourself, you might be tempted to create a clearing, to provide habitat for the kind of plants that are good for foraging, and attract herbivores to hunt. Perhaps you'll selectively hunt the males, leaving the females to reproduce. In these ways humans started to intentionally modify the ecosystem and the genetics of the plant and animal species that they depended on (they had already been doing so unintentionally for millennia).

Towards the end of the Mesolithic period there was an increase in sedentism: abandoning a nomadic way of life is a necessary prerequisite for agriculture as we understand it. The first evidence of humans spending extended periods in fixed settlements dates from about 2,000 years before the start of the Neolithic Revolution, but these people were still foragers. What made them different to the nomadic majority was that they had claimed the most productive territories as exclusively theirs, usually at boundaries between multiple ecosystems, such as where a river meets the coast or passes through the foothills of a mountain range. Such locations would have been able to supply abundant resources at different times of the year, and permanent or semi-permanent settlement would also have allowed people to start preserving and storing some of the glut of food that is available to hunter-gatherers in spring and autumn. Sedentism also led to a step-change in the rate at which humans were modifying the genomes of the species destined to become the first domesticated crops and livestock. For example, the very act of harvesting seeds for storage puts selective pressure on the species involved. It favours the development of larger seeds in more easily harvested configurations on the plant, because those are the ones most likely to end up in a basket and accidentally dropped near a settlement, even if they aren't deliberately planted.

Unfortunately, establishing long-term settlements in productive foraging locations and increasing the amount of edible plants in your immediate vicinity does not solve the problem of food insecurity for very long. It actually makes things worse, because the resulting population increase leaves a greater number of people vulnerable to future shortages. But there was no way back, either for the earliest farmers or for the majority who still foraged. For a while – in some cases for a long while – foragers and farmers co-existed in relative peace, and even traded with each other.* The foraging societies sometimes adopted some elements of the 'Neolithic package' (sedentism, animal husbandry, agriculture and pottery), while foraging remained their primary means of subsistence. The products of farming would have been seen as exotic, high-status goods within foraging societies. This wasn't enough to immediately convert them to a way of life that must have looked as hard as it was, but in almost all cases, eventually, the farmers either displaced the foragers, or the foragers became farmers. Farming then began spreading geographically in fits and starts from south-west Asia north-west into Europe and east into Asia, and other domesticated species spread from other points of origin slightly later.

The vicious circle was complete. Gradual replacement of nomadic foraging with sedentary farming, and incremental improvements in farming technology, drove further increases in human population levels, threatening food security again. Overshoot was followed by famine, but the long-term trend was an inexorable growth of the human operation on Planet Earth, always at the expense of the wider ecosystem.

On a global scale this process continues, for now. At the time of writing, the human population is increasing by well over 200,000 every day – more than the total number of pure hunter-gatherers still

* *Parallel palaeogenomic transects reveal complex genetic history of early European farmers,* Lipson, M, Nature, 2017, DOI: 10.1038/nature24476.

in existence. Food production still needs to meet an ever increasing human demand, and the wild world is being destroyed at a more frightening pace than ever. Both are only made possible by the use of vast amounts of fossil fuels to fertilise farmland and power the industrialised world. Unfortunately for us, those fossil fuels are both non-renewable and irreplaceable. This chapter of our story will not have a happy ending. Overshoot, resource depletion and ecological collapse on a grand scale threaten the biggest food crisis of them all, and a brutal restoration of the long-term balance between humans and the rest of the global ecosystem that was interrupted 12 millennia ago.

The Anthropocene

Some have suggested that the Holocene epoch, which started around the end of the ice age and the beginning of the Neolithic Revolution, has itself recently ended. Depending on whose version you prefer, the end point lay somewhere between the start of the Industrial Revolution in the 18th century and the first man-made nuclear explosions in 1945. 'Anthropocene' refers to a new epoch, the defining character of which is humans having become a key factor determining the content of the Earth's biosphere, and consequently the rocks being formed at the surface. In those rocks, geologists of the distant future (should there be any) will find a massive increase of fossilised humans, the structures we build and our waste products, and a corresponding decrease in the quantity and diversity of fossils of almost everything else. 'Anthropos' is Greek for 'man' or 'human being', 'cene' means 'recent'. The word has been in use since the mid-1970s, but since the turn of the century the Anthropocene

has become an increasingly useful concept for people trying to understand and explain the changes taking place on our planet, and provide proper context in terms of geological history and the long-term future. Anthropogenic phenomena such as human-induced climate change and the current mass extinction may well have become unstoppable, at least without intentional intervention on a global scale ('geoengineering'), which would itself leave an indelible mark on the geology currently being formed.

A minority of the popularisers of the term still hope for a 'Good Anthropocene', where further technological advances allow humans to solve some of these systemic problems, save the day for advanced civilisation and maybe even pave the way for a glorious transhuman future. The majority expect a 'Bad Anthropocene', where the centre does not hold and the question is not so much whether things will fall apart, but how. In the words of Graeme Barker, we differ from our wild foraging ancestors not just in our ways of doing, but in our ways of thinking and being. The Anthropocene is not just a geological concept; it frames important questions about how 21st century humans think about ourselves and our place in the world, and how that differs from the way people thought about those things before and after the emergence of farming, science and industrialisation.

This is the context of the foraging renaissance. Two paradises have been lost – that of the human condition before farming and that of the Holocene ecosystem that techno-industrial civilisation is systematically destroying. We might say that our society has become dangerously disconnected from the natural world, and that foraging helps to re-establish that lost connection, but maybe the view from the Anthropocene should be that we are as connected to the natural world as we ever were, and that civilisation is a natural process, however unnatural it might look.

Perhaps we are not murdering the wild world, but transforming it.

The Anthropozoic

Every now and then in the Earth's long history, something happens that changes everything and changes it forever. An early example was the Great Oxygenation Event, approximately 2.5 billion years ago, caused by the first appearance of a revolutionary evolutionary technology. Cyanobacteria found a new way to acquire food – a new kind of photosynthesis that released free oxygen as a by-product. Oxygen is a highly reactive element that had never previously existed in this form in the Earth's biosphere. For a few hundred million years, the consequences were limited by the vast amount of iron dissolved in the oceans, which precipitated out as iron oxide, forming rich ore deposits that we're still mining. As the oceans ran out of iron, free oxygen started building up, first in the water, then in the atmosphere. Nearly all of the organisms in existence at the time had evolved in an oxygen-free world, and for them, the accumulating oxygen was a death sentence. The entire biosphere had to adapt to a new reality: out with the old ecological order, and in with the new.

▾ Black-banded Ironstone, formed during the Great Oxygenation Event.

It happened again 540 million years ago at the start of the 'Cambrian Explosion', when all the major branches of animal life that exist today suddenly appeared, along with a mind-boggling array of others destined to be failed evolutionary experiments, displacing almost everything that existed before (scientists aren't sure what triggered this process). Some 292 million years later, massive volcanic activity changed the climate and caused the Permian extinction, or 'Great Dying'. About 95% of marine species were wiped out, and almost as many on land. From the ruins of the old ecosystem, a new kind of reptile emerged – the dinosaurs. They ruled Earth unchallenged until their own fate was sealed 65 million years ago when an asteroid slammed into what is now the Yucatán Peninsula in Mexico, setting the planet on fire and poisoning the atmosphere again. Once more life recovered from the shock, and this time it was the turn of the mammals to take over.

These three great revolutions in the course of geological and evolutionary history mark the boundaries between one great geological *era* and the next – the Paleozoic ('old life'), Mesozoic ('middle life') and Cenozoic ('recent life'). These eras are divided into periods (we're in the Quaternary), and the periods are divided into epochs such as the Holocene and Anthropocene.

There is an older term than Anthropocene, coined by Italian geologist Antonio Stoppani (1824-91). Way ahead of his time, Stoppani sensed the enormity of the impact humans were having on the rest of life on Earth, and he tried to warn people. For him, declaring merely a new epoch was an understatement. When Earth's ecosystem eventually arrives at a new equilibrium, following the emergence of the revolutionary evolutionary technology of overwhelming brainpower, the long-term changes may well be comparable to those of the Great Oxygenation Event and the three era-ending cataclysms. If so, then it is time to declare a whole new era: the Anthropozoic.

Further reading

The Emergence of Agriculture, Smith, B, 1995.

Before Farming: Hunter-gatherer society and subsistence, Campana, D, et al, 1995.

Guns, Germs and Steel: A short history of everybody for the last 13,000 years, Diamond, J, 1998, and by the same author *The Third Chimpanzee*, 1993.

The Agricultural Revolution in Prehistory: Why did Foragers become Farmers?, Barker, G, 2009.

Domestication of Plants in the Old World, Zohary, D, et al, latest version 2012.

Foragers, Farmers and Fossil Fuels: How Human Values Evolve, Morris, I, 2015.

The Anthropocene and the Global Environmental Crisis: Rethinking modernity in a new epoch, Hamilton, C, et al, 2015.

Foraging traditions old and new

Old traditions

Humans continued to depend on foraged food long after the development of farming. For the rich, wild food primarily meant hunting game, along with a few prized fungi. For everybody else, but especially the rural poor, foraged plants and seaweeds provided an essential backup for times when access to cultivated food was compromised by famine or conflict. Another element of the old tradition was the appeal of diversification even in non-famine times. In poor rural communities the cultivated food was monotonous, and since a lot of wild food is strongly flavoured, it could, with the help of some creative cookery, be used to liven up an otherwise dull diet. It also increased access to vitamins and minerals, but they probably didn't know that.

By the start of the 20th century, these traditions and the associated knowledge had almost died out in north-west Europe, and were heading that way in the south and east too. A 2012 paper called *Wild food plant use in the 21st century: the disappearance of old traditions and the search for new cuisines involving wild edibles*[*] highlighted the waning of the main motive for keeping the old foraging traditions alive: fear of famine. In 19th century Europe, famine had still been a clear and present danger. Though the potato blight of 1844-49 is most frequently associated with Ireland, it affected much of northern Europe and was the most recent serious European food crisis caused by something other than conflict. As memories of famine began to fade, so did folk knowledge of edible wild plants, and by 2012 only the elders of a few rural communities still retained any at all. Among this oldest generation, knowledge survived of two main categories of emergency food: things that could be used to bulk out flour as grain supplies dwindled, and pot-herbs.

A tradition survives in some places, particularly in southern Europe, of creating dishes containing a blend of an enormous variety of wild plants (40 or perhaps even 50). Ethnobotanist Timothy Johns has theorised that this behaviour was directly linked to the need to preserve knowledge that might prove critical in times of scarcity – even though some plants in the blend were inferior, knowledge of their edibility might one day save lives. Some of these multi-species wild dishes have even evolved into local, modern culinary specialities such as Frankfurter Green Sauce (p75 and p381), Easter Ledger Pudding (p329) and the Italian wild green salad Misticanza. Perhaps the best example is from Dalmatia in Croatia. Mišanca isn't a dish, or even a specific blend of wild plants, though it always includes an Allium such as wild onion. As with Misticanza, the name means 'mixture', and traditionally it included upwards of 20 wild species, including grasses and flowers. It is used in many different dishes, and selecting the perfect mixture for a specific use has become the trademark of a high-quality chef in the region.

---

[*] Vol 81 of *Societatis Botanicorum Poloniae*, Łuczaj, L, et al.

Waning fear of famine wasn't the sole reason for the decline of old traditions. Ecological changes also altered the availability of many types of wild plant, mostly due to an increase in intensive industrial farming methods. More livestock, especially cattle, means more animal waste finding its way into watercourses, and different plants growing there, as well as making the foraging of aquatic plants less attractive and less safe. Modern arable farming has had an even greater effect on wild species. Quite a few traditionally foraged plants are arable weeds that were once manually harvested while the main crop was brought in, but have become rare as a result of the large-scale spraying of herbicides.

Books

The old foraging traditions were oral, passed down directly from one generation to the next, most frequently by women. Before the 20th century, there were very few books whose main subject was foraging for wild food. There were, however, plenty of books about the alleged medicinal properties of plants, both wild and cultivated, some of which included information about food and other uses.

William Turner began his career as a naturalist. He studied at Cambridge University and his groundbreaking 1538 book *Libellus de re Herbaria novus* ('New book about plants') was the result of a great deal of time spent seeking and studying plants in their natural habitat. He went on to study medicine in Italy, and his *A new herball* (published in three parts between 1551 and 1568) was the first book written in English to describe the "uses and vertues" of wild European plants.

John Gerard was a botanist and horticulturalist. His 1597 *Herball, or Generall Historie of Plantes* is both more famous and more controversial than Turner's book. Authoritative writing about wild plants demands that you actually find the plants in question, but your chance of finding all the plants you would like to write about is remote, even if you spend many years searching far and wide. Gerard travelled very little (though he claimed otherwise). Instead, he created a herbal garden, in which he grew interesting plants sent to him as seeds, including many that weren't native to the British Isles.* This allowed at least some original research on new plants, and provided the opportunity to check for himself some of their alleged virtues. He also indulged in quite a lot of plagiarism of the work of Flemish herbalists Rembert Dodoens and Matthias de Lobel, and French horticulturalist Charles de l'Écluse. His book re-used 1,800 botanical woodcuts from other sources (re-using Dodoens' woodcuts would have given the game away). Though hugely successful, Gerard's *Herball* eventually became infamous for its mistakes – some inherited from the works he copied, some the result of borrowed text being wrongly matched with borrowed illustrations, and one a case of wrongly believing he'd seen evidence of a tree that bore geese as fruit.

Two other books deserve a mention here. Botanist and horticulturalist John Parkinson wrote the largest book in this genre ever published (*Theatrum Botanicum,*

* The term 'British Isles' is considered politically problematic by some people. In this context it is purely scientific, referring to an archipelago of over 6,000 islands in north-west Europe, and there is no alternative in common use.

1640), covering 3,800 plants, including kitchen garden plants and orchard trees. Nicholas Culpeper was a pharmacist and astrologer, and his 1652 book *The English Physitian* (later re-titled *The Complete Herbal*), was a bestseller, not least because of its anti-establishment humour and accessibility for the common people. It was written in ordinary language, and sold at a much more affordable price than any of its rival publications.

Some early examples of recipe books quoted in this one are *The Accomplisht Cook, or The Art and Mystery of Cookery* by Robert May (1660), *The Accomplish'd Lady's Delight In Preserving, Physick, Beautifying, And Cookery* by Hannah Woolley (1675), *Acetaria: A Discourse Of Sallets*, by John Evelyn, a friend of Samuel Pepys (1699), and *English Housewifry, Exemplified in Above Four Hundred and Fifty Receipts* by Elizabeth Moxon (1741). These books do not distinguish between wild and cultivated plants, and some that were grown in 17th and 18th century kitchen gardens have since fallen out of favour.

The works of Gerard and of Culpeper remained in use for the next two centuries. It wasn't until 1862 that a recognisably modern book appeared on the uses of British wild plants: *The Useful Plants of Great Britain* by C Pierpoint Johnson. Along with the medical and veterinary information, the book describes many other uses of wild plants – as sources of dyes, textiles and wood for woodworking and fuel, and providing fodder for animals and food for people. It also includes a few seaweeds and fungi, both of which were classed as plants at the time. The book you are reading also contains some quotes from *British Poisonous Plants* (1856), which was written by another Johnson (Charles), not to be confused with C Pierpoint. Notable books about edible and poisonous fungi were published in 1886 (William Delisle Hay's *Elementary Text-book of British Fungi*) and 1891 (MC Cooke's *British Edible Fungi*).

These books did not ignite a popular foraging revival. The zeitgeist of the late Victorian era was of progress and prosperous technological modernity, not the preservation of apparently obsolete folk knowledge. It was the zenith of the British Empire, with all manner of exotic foreign foods on offer, at least for those who could afford them, so there was little motivation for rediscovering the joys of foraging for native wild species. For those without wealth, there was no time for such hobbies, or no access to the countryside. Though a low point for wild food, this was a golden age for British cookery. The eight volumes of *The Encyclopedia of Practical Cookery: A Complete Dictionary of all Pertaining to the Art of Cookery and Table Service* (1892), edited by Theodore Francis Garrett, contain entries for obscure edible plant products from distant corners of the empire, but mention only a tiny fraction of the wild European species in this book. Ramsons didn't make the cut. They do, however, include 68 recipes for chestnuts and 10 for dandelion, and quite a few that made it into this book.

This period of confident abundance came to an abrupt end in 1914. World War I prompted increased British interest in edible/useful wild plants, especially those of medicinal relevance. German pharmaceutical companies had been very dominant in the period before the conflict, so this was a necessity (see *Britain's Green Allies: Medicinal Plants in Wartime* by Peter

Ayres, 2015). In addition to the medicinal plants, horse chestnuts were collected to make soap and sphagnum moss for dressing wounds. Books specifically about wild food made an appearance shortly after. In the preface of *The Wild Foods of Great Britain* (1917) LCR Cameron wrote: "The incidence of war has brought home to its inhabitants that an island like Britain is not self supporting, and that scarcity, if not actual want of food, is daily becoming more possible... " Cameron's 260 kinds of wild food included hedgehogs and frogs (both now protected), but the section on plants is disappointingly small.

Between the wars Florence White, who had founded the English Folk Cookery Association in 1928, wrote two relevant books: a book of traditional recipes called *Good Things in England* (1932), which remains in print, and *Flowers as Food* (1934). Then during World War II things got more serious again. In a 1939 book also called *Wild Foods of Britain*, Jason Hill called for people to "reinforce the national larder". The collection of one particular wild food was even organised by the government: rosehips, which provide the highest concentration of vitamin C of any European wild food, replacing the lost supplies of citrus fruits. The pamphlet on rosehips generated a great deal of interest, and its author – nutritionist Claire Loewenfeld – received thousands of letters requesting information about other types of wild food. Six more pamphlets followed under the name *Britain's Wild Larder*.

When the war was over, Loewenfeld began work on a series of books under the same name, to make available the folk knowledge uncovered by wartime research. The word 'larder' (even after 'wild') conjures visions of domesticity, and these books have a different tone to the foraging guides that came after. There is no romanticising of hunter-gathering and no mention of high cuisine, just practical information about the potential role of wild foods in hard times. The introduction starts with "The world is apprehensive about food shortages", and goes on to warn how overpopulation, soil depletion and potential disruption to food distribution systems "naturally cast a dark shadow on our future without taking into further account the prospects of shortage caused by possible war". The recipe selection was clearly influenced by a decade of post-war austerity and rationing. In the end only the first two books were published: *Fungi* (1956) and *Nuts* (1957). Perhaps by that time people had had their fill of scarcity and were beginning to feel more positive about the future.

New traditions

The wild food culture of 21st century Europe can trace its roots to the hippy movement of the late 1960s and early 1970s, and the iconic *Food for Free* by Richard Mabey (first published in 1972). That the food was free wasn't really the point. For some people it was a move towards healthier, more ethical food: wild is as organic as it gets, and most wild foods are the diametric opposite of the carbohydrate-rich, fibre-poor, highly processed diet of many modern westerners. For others it was a way to search for their inner hunter-gatherer (Mabey described it as "a poke in the eye for domesticity"). But few pioneers of the new tradition had serious concerns about their own food security or that of the western world in general. When Cameron's 1917 book was republished in 1977 the original preface about food scarcity wasn't included, and the new preface was about increasing the variety of fresh, unpackaged food in our diet. And when a single volume version of *Britain's Wild Larder* came out in 1980, having been updated six years after the author's death, all talk of food shortages had been replaced with "interest in the countryside", "fresh air and exercise" and "trying new flavours in our cookery".

By the end of the 1990s a radical new sort of high cuisine was emerging – wild food offers new avenues for culinary adventurers to explore. Probably the most famous restaurant in northern Europe is René Redzepi's *Noma* in Copenhagen, which specialises in re-inventing Nordic cuisine and continually uses foraged food in inventive ways. It is the Neolithic situation reversed: the wild food has become exotic and high status, and the farmed fare taken for granted.

Also part of the new culture are the tales of miraculous escapes from emergency situations, the military-style survivalism of Bear Grylls, and reality TV shows where people compete to survive on remote, uninhabited islands. While these *are* examples of foraging as a response to hunger, they have little to do with the everyday lives of ordinary people; most of us don't anticipate ending up in situations like these.

For half a century, the foraging culture in the western world has been more of a break with the past than a continuation of older traditions.[*]

The future

The search for new cuisines goes on, social media having turned it into a giant collective effort, as chefs and enthusiasts all around the world share their latest wild creations. But what about the longer term future?

Rewilding and regrounding

The term 'rewilding' is usually applied by conservationists to places. It is a process whereby the wild world is allowed to reclaim an area, sometimes helped by the intentional re-introduction of lost species. The term has also been applied by anthropologists to people: learning how to forage for wild food is a way to undo some of our domestication. The mental health crisis isn't going away, and spending time outdoors engaging with the wild world as nature intended is seen as a means of psychological 'regrounding'. It is a way to help cope with the cognitive dissonance caused by knowing resources are finite while trapped in a world of perpetual overconsumption, watching the capitalist machine grinding out ever more 'progress'.

There is a growing trend for doing this with children, as well as adults tired of the rat-race. Teach them in the woods, where it is wilder and muddier, rather than in the sanitised indoor world and the artificial environment of playgrounds. Maybe sow a few mental seeds and hope the next generation is slightly less messed up than we are.

---

[*] This is true not just in Britain and Ireland but also other parts of Europe, such as the Baltic states, where we might assume the culture was more continuous. For example, see: *Changes in the Use of Wild Food Plants in Estonia: 18th – 21st Century*, Sõukand, R, and Kalle, R, 2016.

Some anarchoprimitivists try to take it much further, believing the solution to our problems is a post-civilisation hunter-gatherer 'an-prim society', free from super-tribal power structures. But how could we possibly get from here to there? Wild food, on its own, never supported more than 50 million people globally and there are 8 billion of us now. The Holocene ecosystem is gone, the sixth mass extinction is already underway, and climate change looks unstoppable. Appealing though it may be to some romantics and revolutionaries, going backwards isn't an option. Human rewilding can only be for individuals or small groups, and for most of them only temporarily. As a society, we have to find a way forwards from where we are now.

Collapse

Anarchoprimitivists aren't the only people anticipating a post-industrial-agricultural world. There is a growing fear that civilisation as we know it is already in the early stage of collapse. There is no sign of political or economic change on the scale needed to save it, either globally or nationally. The UK is nowhere near food self-sufficiency, which fell from 78% in 1984 to 64% in 2019* but most of us don't consider this a serious problem. After all, we've been ignoring warnings about overpopulation and food crises since Thomas Malthus wrote about them in 1798. Why listen now? The past isn't a reliable guide to the future. In the spring of 2020, for the first time in the supermarket age, westerners got a shocking taste of empty shelves. In the UK it took just a few days to go from relative normality to full-scale

panic, and a wide range of products became scarce, including long-life dried and canned food. The Covid-19 pandemic exposed the fragility of our supply chains. As the future becomes increasingly uncertain, alternatives to our regular food sources will become more important, especially in shorter-term emergencies.

Unfortunately, in the longer term our wild larder can never replace the vast amount of food we import; there are far too many people and nothing like enough remains of the wild world. If things get tough, the most attractive and less abundant wild foods will quickly be foraged into oblivion, and this worsens as the ratio of human population to available area for foraging increases. This problem was identified as serious in Epping Forest (right next to London) several years ago, and that was without food supply concerns. The response was a total fungi foraging ban that may be a sign of things to come. It is hard to imagine running out of dandelions, blackberries or wracks, and not many people will be bothered if entire stands of non-native species like alexanders are taken for food, but wild food on its own won't be enough. If we want to avoid total collapse while there's still something worth saving and finally create a sustainable civilisation, then a more permanent solution will be needed.

Permaculture?

Is a sustainable post-industrial-agricultural civilisation possible? This was another question being asked in the late 1960s, and the answer that emerged in the early 1970s, along with the fledgling environmental movement and new foraging culture,

* *Agriculture in the United Kingdom*, Defra, 2019, https://www.gov.uk/government/statistics/agriculture-in-the-united-kingdom-2019

was permaculture. It is a philosophy encompassing food production and ecology, with a goal of establishing a new balance between humans and the ecosystems we inhabit: "The conscious design and maintenance of agriculturally productive ecosystems which have the diversity, stability, and resilience of natural ecosystems."* The name means 'permanent agriculture'.

Permaculture and anarchoprimitivism have some important similarities. Both view conventional agriculture as harmful, and seek a new food culture that works in harmony with nature instead of attempting to dominate it. The godfather of permaculture – Bill Mollison – drew deeply on indigenous practices, rather than inventing something entirely new. Permaculture does away with neat domestic vegetable beds and industrial crop monocultures. It creates wild-looking spaces with their own mini-ecosystems designed to produce 'abundance', which is then harvested in a more foraging-like way than traditional crops. A lot of the initial work involves observing the land and then working with it, rather than imposing upon it. Permaculture is a whole system, from sacrificial crops to keep the birds happy, who will also eat the pests, to companion plants that bring up nutrients from deep underground or suck nitrogen from the air, to ducks who eat slugs and chickens who eat insect grubs, both providing manure. If you're going to plant a boundary hedge, why not make it an edible hedge, so it also provides food on both sides? Future foragers will be very grateful.

Permaculture also reaches beyond food production. The intention is to replace conventional agriculture, not merely as a set of procedures, but as a way of life, just as agriculture replaced hunter-gathering. For this to work, the worst mistakes of the past must not be repeated. The three equal foundational ethics of permaculture, as originally proposed by Mollison, were *Care of the Earth*, *Care of people* and *Setting limits to population and consumption*. The first two are relatively unproblematic, but the third has faced stiff resistance from people who want to replace it with principles demanding fair shares or redistribution of surpluses, or hide and water it down in a principle about 'future care'. Fairness is a worthy goal, but will become increasingly unachievable, especially on a global scale, in the context of a deglobalising and collapsing techno-industrial civilisation. Physical limits are an inescapable feature of the world we live in, and our politics must adapt to them, not the other way around.

The unconditional acceptance of limits to growth is necessary as a foundational principle for *any* sustainable system operating in a finite physical space, be it agricultural, social, political, economic or all of these things. Either we choose to set, and abide by, realistic limits to the human operation on Earth, or the rest of the ecosystem will find ways to impose limits whether humans like it or not. The former is a prerequisite for the "conscious design and maintenance of agriculturally productive ecosystems" – it is permaculture on the grandest scale, and our only realistic hope for a Good Anthropocene. The latter entails the unconscious evolution of an ecosystem under intense pressure to counterbalance human dominance: a Bad Anthropocene.

* Generally attributed to Bill Mollison.

Laws and ethics

UK foraging law is fairly straightforward, with some complications in Scotland. In England, Wales and Northern Ireland, it is perfectly legal to take unprotected flowers, fruits (including nuts), foliage and fungi, provided they are growing wild and you are not planning on selling what you pick. If you take cultivated crops then that is theft, but nobody owns wild plants, seaweeds or fungi. If you take anything with an intention to sell, without the permission of the landowner, this is technically theft and the landowner can sue you for damages. Uprooting wild plants is illegal without permission; breaking the soil is viewed as damage to property.

In Scotland, the situation is slightly different after the Land Reform (Scotland) Act 2003 provided people with the right to roam on most private land. This right is qualified by a requirement for people to use that land "responsibly", which is open to interpretation when it comes to foraging. The Nature Conservation Act (Scotland) 2004 also introduced new restrictions on collecting wild plants (presumably this also implies seaweeds) or fungi in National Nature Reserves and Sites of Special Scientific Interest, of which there are quite a lot, especially in some of the places where you might want to go foraging. Foraging in these places in Scotland now requires the permission of Scottish Natural Heritage and the written permission of the landowner. In Ireland there is no legislation specifically governing foraging, though there is protection for certain plants and some regulations about asking for landowner permission.

Obviously we should not be foraging for wild plants that are rare and/or protected, and I make clear in the text in the few examples where this applies. A full list of plants protected under the Wildlife and Countryside Act 1981 can be found on the UK government's website.[*] It should be noted that some species can be internationally or even nationally rare, and yet locally abundant. Sea kale is the perfect example of this, and taking a few leaves for personal use will do no harm if there's a beach full of it ... unless everybody has the same idea.

Outside of personal use the situation is more controversial. Increasing interest in foraging has opened up a market for new commercial enterprises selling wild food, primarily to restaurants, and there have been legal clashes over their activities.

It is particularly frowned upon to pick some sorts of wild flowers, partly because eating flowers is considered a bit strange in our culture, and partly because over-picking in the past led to steep declines in some species. This includes some that were intensively picked by foragers, rather than for decorative purposes, a prime example being primroses and cowslips for wine. A resurgence of large-scale foraging for these would not be a welcome development, but there are plenty of less controversial edible flowers.

Beyond this, and given the predicament we find ourselves in, the legal and ethical aspects of foraging are certain to generate more debate going forwards. There may well be a case for a review of UK law, but it is unlikely to become a priority any time soon.

---

[*] *Wildlife and Countryside Act 1981*, http://www.legislation.gov.uk/ukpga/1981/69/schedule/8

The right place at the right time

A lot of wild food is available only to those who have paid close attention to time and place. As a person who came to wild food via the world of ephemeral and frequently elusive fungi, I was always keenly aware of this. But it is just as true of plants, seaweeds and game animals, and has always been this way for hunter-gathers. You need to carefully observe your own foraging territory, throughout the year, so you can better predict what you will find in a particular place at a particular time. This includes watching plants throughout their life cycle, including times when they aren't providing anything to eat, so you can learn to identify them before flowering, or as seedlings. Your knowledge will eventually build up, helping when you're in unfamiliar territory too. This includes both the intuitive recognition of plants from a distance – their 'gestalt', as Miles Irving puts it – and learning how to pick up clues from the landscape itself. Luck still plays a big part, but knowledge loads the dice.

Places

Many plants are fussy about habitat – and not just the rare ones. Wild plants face fierce competition for space, light, water and nutrients, and many only thrive in precisely the habitat they are best adapted to. Because of this, noting the habitat is important when trying to identify a wild plant, and seeking out a particular habitat matters if you are trying to find a particular plant.

Intertidal
North-west Europe has some of the largest tidal ranges in the world. Tidal flows are funnelled through tight spaces and into dead ends, and slosh around the British Isles in a circular fashion in both directions at the same time. Exactly how these tides operate is complex and arcane, but fortunately it is not necessary to understand it to be in the right place at the right time; that is what tide tables are for.

'Spring tide' refers to the biggest tides (the water level 'springs about'), which occur around the time when the moon is full or new. They also always happen around the same times of day at any particular location, because they are partly driven by the position of the sun with respect to the coastline. The most extreme tides annually happen near equinoxes ('equinoctial tides'), when the sun exerts its strongest pull on the Earth (we call these 'great tides'). The most extreme of all happen when a great tide coincides with the moon at perigee (closest to the Earth).

Nothing demands you to be in the right place at the right time quite like foraging in the intertidal zone. Getting it badly wrong costs lives, so always check the tide tables, especially if you are on a beach you don't know well. In terms of finding food, some can only be found very close to the low tide-line during the most extreme spring tides. Once on a wet, windy February morning, at just about the lowest tide of the twenty-teens, I went to witness a very rare full exposure of the wreck of a 17th century warship. It was covered in whelks – the only time I've ever found live whelks, which are normally sub-tidal, exposed at low tide.

As a general rule, the intertidal zone provides very rich pickings for foragers, and there's quite a lot of intertidal zone available if you happen to live on an island. Even if a beach is nothing but an expanse of sand or mud, shellfish such as cockles and razor clams can be found at low tide, but the best foraging beaches are rocky, with a variety of rock pools and a wide range of edible seaweeds and shellfish.

At and above the high-tide line

Saltmarsh is a special case of intertidal. Historically there were large expanses of saltmarsh in the British Isles, wherever there was flat land close to the sea. Most of this land has since been drained, walled off and used to feed livestock. A few pockets remain, and a similar habitat occurs where the tidal sections of rivers meet the surrounding countryside. Saltmarsh is home to a specialised community of salt-tolerant plants, a disproportionate amount of which make good eating for humans. Sea cliffs, coastal grasslands and the tops of shingle beaches also provide a home for some of the best edible wild plants.

These plants face a different set of threats to most of the other plants in this book. In temperate woodland or grassland, plants face an onslaught of predation from slugs, insects and other invertebrates, as well as herbivorous mammals and birds. Many protect themselves with bad-tasting and/or toxic chemicals, or physical defences such as thorns and stings. Coastal plants are less threatened by these things – most terrestrial invertebrates dislike saline environments, and large herbivores avoid sea cliffs and shingle beaches. Instead, these plants have evolved to cope with living in exposed locations where there is a shortage of freshwater and a lot of salt. They are often fleshy, salty and in some cases highly aromatic – properties that make them attractive to humans.

This category also includes the verges at the sides of busy roads, which often host species adapted to coastal areas, due to salting in winter, though pollution from traffic is a problem here.

Freshwater habitats

Streams, rivers above the tidal zone, canals, lakes and lowland bogs are also productive hunting grounds for a forager, partly because they provide multiple adjacent habitats. Young, fresh growth of aquatic and marginal plants is abundant in spring, and many of the same species have tuberous roots which can be collected in the autumn and winter. This is cold, muddy and hard work, but would have been a valuable emergency food supply for our ancestors.

There are also some hazards you need to be aware of. Especially, you should never eat raw any plant that has been collected in freshwater downstream from places where livestock are present. The risk comes from parasites such as liver flukes, which have complex life cycles involving cattle and aquatic snails. Cooking kills them.

Grassland

Managed grassland (ie lawn) is usually poor for foraging, though some fungi can thrive if chemicals aren't applied. Pasture and unmanaged or wild grassland is home to a much wider variety of wild plants. Grasses themselves are an interesting case. If a group of related plants includes multiple cultivated crop species, it typically includes plenty of good edible wild species as well, but grasses are an exception to this rule. Most wild grasses aren't worth the effort of collecting and processing, and are only good as food for herbivores which have evolved a digestive system to deal with them.

Agricultural land

In the millennia since humans invented agriculture and began domesticating wild plant species as crops, wild plants have adapted to the new ecological niche this created. As a result there are now new species, or subspecies, of plants that have become specialised weeds of agricultural land. Some of these are good edible species in their own right, and in fact some of our crop species (eg oats) originally established themselves as agricultural weeds that were collected along with the main harvest. Other common weeds of agricultural land evolved as early colonisers of disturbed ground, and thrive in the annually disturbed environment of farmed fields. These include common red poppy, the seeds of which are a commercially viable crop in their own right. This habitat also comes with a warning – watch out for evidence of herbicide spraying on the margins of crop fields.

Hedgerows and hedgebanks

Hedges are particularly important, on agricultural land and elsewhere, and for both wildlife and foragers. The older the hedge, the wider the variety of species in residence. This includes both the shrubs and small trees that comprise the hedge itself, many of which produce edible flowers, fruits and nuts, and the herbs that make a home at the base of the hedge. Some fields also have drainage ditches around the edge, providing habitat for aquatic and semi-aquatic/ marginal plants.

Woodland

Foraging for plants in woodland reflects the intensely seasonal nature of that habitat. In deciduous woodland, there is a period in the spring before the canopy closes over, during which certain plants – notably spring-flowering bulbs – complete their whole growth cycle. The tender spring leaves of many deciduous trees are also good to eat, and the young needles of conifers can be used for wines and teas. Later in the year, autumn brings a glut of fruits and nuts, as well as a dazzling array of fungi.

Moors and mountains

Upland areas pose a challenge for most creatures which aren't specifically adapted to that habitat, including humans. For much of the year they do not provide a lot in the way of food. Their most productive time is late summer and autumn, when an abundance of berries can be found. The same can be said of the related habitat of heathland, though this can be lowland and/or dry as well as upland and wet.

▾ Urban salad: Smooth Sowthistle and Hairy Bittercress (bottom right), growing in a pot outside a vacant pub along with poisonous Groundsel (bottom left).

Urban and suburban

Urban and suburban areas aren't just one habitat, but a patchwork of different micro-habitats. Lawns and verges are effectively grassland, equivalent to grazed or non-grazed depending on the mowing regime. Walls and rocky waste ground provide homes for plants naturally adapted to live on cliffs and scree. Untended flower beds provide a home for all manner of weeds, man-made ponds serve much the same purpose as natural bodies of freshwater and anywhere with trees is similar to wild open woodland. Our gardens are a habitat different to anything found in the wild, due to the presence of species that cannot reproduce naturally in northern Europe.

Roundabouts can be surprisingly good places for foraging, provided they aren't too busy traffic-wise. Not many humans ever set foot on them, and they are dog-free. Waste ground, untended or recently disturbed land is usually worth checking, although there is a potential risk of contamination and it is not always easy to find out.

Public parks are of particular interest. Taking food crops that have been deliberately planted as such is an offence under British law, but in some cases, shrubs and trees planted for purely ornamental reasons also happen to be edible. Taking nuts, berries or edible foliage from such plants in parks is a bit of a grey area under UK law, but it is unlikely you will get into trouble for doing it on a small scale. It is also widely, but wrongly, believed that you can forage anything that is growing in a private garden, if the bit you are taking is overhanging a boundary with your land, public land or a footpath. Technically this material still belongs to the owner of the land on which the plant is growing.

Times

Foraging is an intensely seasonal activity (with seasons defined more by weather than calendar). While there are a few things that can be found at any time of year, most are available in a specific window, sometimes very narrow. Foragers cannot help but experience a heightened awareness of the way the natural world changes through the year. Twice a year, a bounty becomes available for foragers in temperate zones. This happens in spring and autumn, typically starting around the equinox and lasting for about a month.

Spring

The peak spring plant foraging season takes off as the day length rapidly increases and the bitter cold of March gives way to the strengthening April sun. It is particularly rich in deciduous woodland, the forest floor carpeted with flowering bulbs in a hurry to complete their annual growth cycle before the leaves reappear in the canopy, shutting off their light source. This is the time for tapping the rising sap of birch and other trees, and edible wild leaf and stem plants produce masses of tender, fresh growth. The very low spring tides around the equinox are also the perfect opportunity for collecting edible seaweeds.

Late winter and early spring were historically difficult times, especially if there had been a poor harvest the previous autumn. April and May were known as the 'hungry gap' for farming communities at northern European latitude – winter brassicas stop producing leaves and bolt, while the frost-tender spring-planted crops aren't yet ready to harvest. Therefore the first lush fresh spring growth of wild plants provided welcome relief. Not as high in calories as grains, fruits and stored tubers, but a variety of fresh food available in bulk for the first time since autumn.

◄ Three-cornered Leek poking through leaves sprouting from the base of a Lime trunk. Together they provide the perfect foundation for a wild spring salad.

▲ Dulse. Seaweeds thrive when light levels are high.

▲ Fat Hen seeds can provide late summer food even in drought conditions.

Summer

Summer is something of a lottery for foraging in north-west Europe, with much depending on our unpredictable weather. If there is an extended period of dry weather then the herbs and smaller shrubs stop growing. Drought-stressed plants are tougher and more bitter. Cooler, damper weather makes it easier to find wild plants in an edible state. There are also some plants which are dependably available to foragers during the summer, such as fat hen. Many of its relatives in the Amaranth family are coastal species, some of which always continue to grow during the summer, since they inhabit saltmarsh, which is invulnerable to drought. Summer is also the prime time for foraging many species of seaweed.

Autumn

Autumn is probably the best time of all for foraging. The majority of fungi are fruiting, and shrubs and trees are producing fruits and nuts. Some herbaceous plants also start growing again with the increased rainfall, while there's still enough light and the temperature is not too cold. This means new, tender growth is available on perennials such as nettles and hops, and there will be a new generation of some fast-growing small annuals like hairy bittercress. Autumn is also a time for harvesting the roots of many biennial plants (eg burdock). They've spent their first year as rosettes, storing energy in their roots in preparation for sending up a flowering shoot in their second.

▲ Chestnut cases about to open in mid-autumn.

▲ Alexanders in late winter.

Winter

Winter is the leanest time for foraging, but there is still some wild food around. One of the best edible stem vegetables (alexanders) is in its prime in late winter. There are some very good edible salad plants that are winter annuals, which usually germinate in the autumn and are at their best in the winter. Notable examples are watercress, chickweed and springbeauty (aka winter purslane). Winter is also a time for digging up edible roots, bulbs, tubers and rhizomes.

For biennial plants, and those perennials that die back over the winter, this is the time when the underground storage organs are most packed with nutrients. It can be a good time for coastal foraging, with the first crop of some seaweeds available, and filter-feeding shellfish such as cockles and mussels in season.

Taxonomic classification

Taxonomic hierarchy and clades

All species are classified scientifically in a hierarchical system, which is referred to in this book. The term 'clade' refers to any group of species that includes all of the descendants of a single common ancestor (they are *monophyletic*). The goal of modern taxonomy is to make sure the entire hierarchy consists of clades (see pp100-101). Genetic testing is providing a wealth of new molecular data showing many taxonomic groups ('taxons') previously thought to be clades are actually *polyphyletic* (they don't all share a common ancestor at the right level) or *paraphyletic* (some descendants of the common ancestor are missing from the group). This results in much taxonomic shuffling and new Latin names. There are intermediate ranks not shown here or mentioned in this book, and there are important clades that have no official rank. A 'species complex' is a closely related, recently diverged group of species that taxonomists are still working on.

Taxonomic ranks:
Kingdom: eg plants, animals, fungi.
Phylum: eg Rhodophyta (red seaweeds), Embryophyta ('land plants').
Class: eg *Angiospermae* (angiosperms or flowering plants), *Phaeophyceae* (brown seaweeds).
Order: eg *Brassicales*. (This level is always subtitled in this book).
Family: eg *Brassicaceae* (Cabbage family). (This level is always subtitled in this book).
Genus: first half of the species name, eg '*Brassica*'.

Species (or 'specific epithet'): second half of the species name eg, '*oleracea*' (Wild Cabbage).

This book is ordered cladistically, and where possible according to evolutionary age. So seaweeds come before plants, because seaweeds (mostly) predate plants in the history of life on Earth, and flowering plants, which were relatively late arrivals, come last – although they occupy three-quarters of the book.

Oxygenic photosynthesisers

Apart from the exception opposite, every species covered in this book is an *oxygenic photosynthesiser* – a living organism that turns water and carbon dioxide into food in the presence of light, releasing oxygen as a by-product. Most are green, and this is because they contain chlorophylls – a group of green pigments that make photosynthesis possible. Categorising these green things in a consistent manner is not as straightforward as you might imagine. Bifurcating them into plants and seaweeds makes sense in terms of both habitat and usefulness to humans, but it is taxonomically incorrect: seaweeds are classed as such because they live in the sea and look like plants, not because they are a clade of related organisms. The term 'algae' also causes confusion. All seaweeds are marine algae, but 'algae' is an informal, non-scientific term.

Slime moulds, fungi, lichens and cyanobacteria

Slime moulds

Despite their name, slime moulds are not fungi, and were not included in my first book, *Edible Mushrooms*. They obviously aren't plants either, don't photosynthesise, and are included here only because it seemed a shame to leave them out. They are a phylum of single-celled organisms related to amoebae (*Amoebozoa*). These cells can congregate together when it is time to reproduce to form a visible mass known as a 'plasmodium'. Nothing is known about the edibility of most slime moulds, and the one best known for being edible has the least marketable name of any wild food: **Dog Vomit Slime Mould (*Fuligo septica*)**. It is a white, grey or, more often, bright yellow spongy plasmodium, usually found on damp, rotting wood, but also on other kinds of organic debris and sometimes living vegetation. You can find it at any time of year, though most frequently in the autumn,

and it is present worldwide. The only thing you are likely to mistake for it is another slime mould, none of which are known to be dangerously poisonous.

Dog Vomit Slime Mould was traditionally eaten in Central America, where the edible slime moulds are called 'Caca de Luna', meaning 'excrement of the moon', presumably because they seem to appear out of nowhere. In Scandinavian folklore it is said to be the saliva, vomit or droppings of beings called 'troll cats' – familiars of witches who suck milk from cows and then deposit it elsewhere. In North America it is known as 'Scrambled Egg Slime Mould', and as well as looking rather like scrambled eggs, that is pretty much what it tastes like. It is usually not worth collecting because there's not enough and it is distributed too thinly, but every now and then you'll come across a nice, big, fat one, and if you've got a suitable receptacle to hand then you're in business.

▼ Dog Vomit Slime Mould

Fungi and lichens

Fungi were classed as plants as recently as the 1960s, regardless of the fact that they do not photosynthesise. They are actually more closely related to animals than to plants, though they do resemble something like a root system: mycelium, which lives in soil or whatever the fungus is decomposing. The fruit bodies we usually encounter have no direct vegetable equivalent. Hundreds of wild European fungi are edible, but foraging for most of them is something of a specialist activity demanding a book with sufficient space to include all their poisonous lookalikes and a detailed explanation of how to identify them.

Lichens

'Lichen' is an informal term, historically and frequently still used to describe a symbiotic relationship between a fungus and an alga. However, since the term 'alga' is itself informal, and the non-fungal component is sometimes a cyanobacterium, lichens are now more formally known as lichenised fungi, since there are always fungi present.

Though many lichens are edible, few are tasty and traditionally they have been

▾ Oakmoss

soaked in water with sodium bicarbonate, or boiled for a long time, sometimes changing the water several times. If you are in the far north and short of food, but have plenty of firewood and water, this could be the key to surviving a difficult winter. Two are known to be poisonous: **Wolf Lichen (*Letharia vulpina*)** and **Powdered Sunshine Lichen (*Vulpicida pinastri*)**. They are both yellowish, the colouration coming from their toxic component vulpinic acid, and they have been used to poison wolves.

A few species have traditionally been eaten in Europe, most notably **Iceland Moss (*Cetraria islandica*)**. This lichen was once used (mainly in Iceland, but it is present in the British Isles and beyond) as a starch substitute in breads and porridge, as well as a medicine for coughs and other ailments. Today it is used for tea, as a bitter flavouring in alcoholic drinks, a component of organic mouthwashes, and to decorate wreaths and flower arrangements. (NB: Iceland Moss is not a type of Moss; mosses are primitive plants.) Other British species that have been eaten are **Rock-tripe Lichen (*Lasallia pustulata*)** and the very common **Oakmoss (*Evernia prunastri*)**. The former was used as a survival food by early North American Arctic explorers, and the latter is much better known for its use in perfumes than as food (the scent is described as sharp, woody and fruity). **Reindeer Lichen (or *Reindeer Moss*)** is the common name of two species of ***Cladonia*** – ***portentosa*** and ***rangiferina***. These, as the name implies, are important food for reindeer. They are used as flavouring in the Scandinavian alcoholic spirit Aquavit, and have traditionally been eaten by Native Alaskans (Dena'ina), after boiling to soften, although are reputed to cause stomach upsets if not sufficiently cooked.

▲ Iceland Moss

▲ Reindeer Moss

Black Stone-flower (*Parmotrema perlatum*)

Black Stone-flower is a leafy, grey-green species, with a black underside, and black cilia (like eye-lashes) especially at the edges. It is common and widespread in southern England, Wales, Ireland and western Scotland, and is rapidly recolonising other parts of the British Isles where it had become rare or absent due to sulphur dioxide pollution. Black Stone-flower is used as a spice in India and China. Odourless raw, when toasted it releases a sweet, earthy smell reminiscent of star anise, which lends a subtle but luxuriant richness to dishes. One leading authority says the species eaten in India is merely 'closely related',* but foraged European specimens have a similar smell. They should be completely dried, and then stored for at least a few weeks in an airtight container before use.

▼ Black Stone-flower

* *Lichens: An Illustrated Guide to the British and Irish Species*, Dobson, F S, 1979.

Cyanobacteria

Cyanobacteria (formerly 'blue-green algae') are a phylum of true bacteria, directly descended from the first photosynthesisers. They include both free-living single cells, and colonies forming filaments and sheets resembling seaweeds. Some fix nitrogen (they have the rare and precious ability to extract nitrogen directly from the atmosphere, making it available to other organisms). A few are seriously toxic to mammals, most notably the 'algal blooms' which can take over freshwater and marine environments, making both the water and anything that grows in it potentially lethal. The toxins involved are stable molecules that build up in shellfish.

The most important cyanobacteria in terms of food are two filamentous (sub-)tropical freshwater species in the genus *Arthrospira*, commonly known by an older Latin name of 'Spirulina', especially when prepared for consumption. The Spanish conquistadores recorded the Aztecs as having foraged for it wild, and there are records from the mid-20th century of foragers harvesting it in Africa.[*] It has become a well-known, highly nutritious food supplement for humans and livestock, and offers a very efficient means of converting raw materials and solar energy into food.

There's another edible cyanobacterium of more cosmopolitan distribution, and common in Europe. ***Nostoc commune***

▲ *Nostoc commune*

goes by several common names that unhelpfully also refer to other things. It starts life as a gelatinous globule on damp ground, which eventually flattens and merges with its neighbours to form a dirty to bright green mass of tissue. Its close relative *N. flagelliforme* is eaten in south-east Asia, dried and cooked in dishes such as bird's nest soup. In China it is known as Fat Choi ('hair vegetable', due to its vermicelli-like appearance when dried) and features in New Year festivities. It is so popular that the authorities have had to introduce restrictions, including an export ban, because over-harvesting is implicated in land erosion. Some recent research[†] suggests health issues – *Nostoc* contains a small amount of a toxin called *ß-N-methylamino-L-alanine* (BMAA), known to cause neurological disease in mice and fish. However, in humans this is only likely to occur after long-term consumption, and other research[‡] has concluded both *Nostoc* and *Arthrospira* are safe to eat.

---

[*] *Spirulina: An Edible Microorganism: A review*, Sánchez, M, et al, 2003 (Universidad de La Salle, Bogotá).
[†] *The Cyanobacteria Derived Toxin Beta-N-Methylamino-L-Alanine and Amyotrophic Lateral Sclerosis*, Banack, S A, et al, 2010 Dec; Toxins (Basel), 2(12): 2837-2850.
[‡] *Safety assessment of edible blue green algae, Nostoc commune var. sphaeroides Kützing and Spirulina plantensis*, Yang, Y, and Lee, J, April 2011, The FASEB Journal vol. 25 no. 1 Supplement 601.7.

Seaweeds (introduction)

Well over 600 seaweeds can be found in the British Isles, most of which are edible one way or another, although many are rare. Taxonomically they are divided into three large clades, called green, red and brown seaweeds, although their colour doesn't always conform to their category. The word 'alga' is the Latin name for 'seaweed', but it is now an informal term for a very large, diverse and polyphyletic group of organisms, which lack some of the defining characteristics of plants. Strictly speaking, the greens are primitive plants, the status of the reds is debatable, and the browns are a much more distant branch of life.

The average relative positions of members of the three groups, from the high-tide line to well below the low-tide line, is determined by the type of light-absorbing pigments they contain, which in turn determine their colours. Green seaweeds are happiest in the higher reaches and become less frequent further down. Red seaweeds can survive in deeper water than the other groups (down to 30m), and are more abundant near the low-tide line. Some fade to dirty green when higher up, where they are more exposed to sunlight. Brown seaweeds can be found throughout the intertidal zone, but individual species prefer specific locations, and tend to occur in a particular sequence.

▾ Red (Dulse), green (Sea Lettuce) and brown (Toothed Wrack) seaweeds.

Seaweed identification

Identifying seaweeds to species level without a microscope is frequently impossible, but this does not pose a major problem for foragers. The important edible species (or groups) can be identified relatively easily, with no need for scientific aids or highly technical language, and even if you get the identification wrong it is very unlikely that you will suffer serious consequences (see p42).

Seaweed structures

Seaweeds are basically composed of three sections: the holdfast, which anchors them, usually to a rock; something which looks like a stem but is called a 'stipe'; and the blade, which performs roughly the same function as the leaves of plants. Not all seaweeds have stipes and a few don't have holdfasts (so float freely). The entire macroscopic structure of all the larger seaweeds is called a 'thallus'.

Not all seaweeds have the same form of growth. In some cases, such as Sea Lettuce, the whole blade grows as a unit (all its cells continually divide). Others grow from the point where the stipe joins the blade, so the tip is the oldest part, while still more, including most red seaweeds, grow from the tip. This means that neither the best part for eating nor most sustainable part to collect is consistent across all species.

Finding and collecting seaweeds

When collecting seaweeds, always avoid ripping off the holdfast, so the seaweed can regrow. Use a pair of scissors or a sharp folding knife. Many are perennial, and one individual who takes quite a lot of seaweed from one place without safeguarding the holdfast can cause extensive damage. As for more general sustainability issues, it is hard to imagine foraging for private use is going to cause any serious ecological damage in most circumstances, but rising popularity and increased commercial activity do have the potential to lead to trouble in places where there isn't much seaweed relative to the number of people interested in foraging for it.

Finding specific seaweeds can be a black art. Why particular species grow in one exact location, but not another seemingly similar habitat just around the corner, is a mystery. The best advice is just to keep trying, although obviously you need to be aware of the geographical range and preferred habitat of what you are looking for. In some cases the only way you can find them on foot is during extremely low spring tides that only occur a few times each year.

'Common', in the species descriptions means 'common where the correct habitat is available'. East Anglia is something of a seaweed desert, for example, because of the lack of rocks for them to hold on to.

Regarding seasonality, most seaweeds start growing in the winter or early spring, are at their best in late spring and are looking a bit ropey by late summer – although a few species remain edible well into the autumn, and some actually start growing again after taking a break during the height of the summer.

Seaweeds as food

Seaweeds have historically been underused as a food source in Europe, although not as underused as they are today. Some species were once important in parts of Wales, Scotland and especially Ireland, although even there they were often regarded as famine or peasant food. Their status is very different in Japan and Korea. Seaweeds are an essential element of Japanese cuisine, contributing up to 10% of the national diet. Research has suggested that Japanese people are better able to digest seaweeds because their bacterial gut fauna include microbes which themselves eat seaweeds – microbes that have not been found in the intestines of westerners.* It is likely that they got there via the consumption of seaweeds, especially raw.

Our relative unfamiliarity with seaweeds as food can make it tough to know where to start – most don't work well as a boiled side vegetable. Some cooking advice can be applied to seaweeds in general. A lot of seaweeds are high in glutamates and valued for their umami flavour. They are used in soups, stews and stocks (especially seafood stocks). Many seaweeds can also be chopped thinly, either raw or blanched, and added to salads – most effectively in south-east Asian sorts of salad. They can also be dried and ground, or flaked, and used like herbs. Traditionally and commercially they have been used as gelling agents and thickeners.

Their potential for future use as food is enormous, although this may require advances in our knowledge of how to cultivate them (we have much to learn from the Japanese). Many would quickly be foraged out in some locations if we attempted to harvest them commercially, but cultivating them is a rare ecological win-win situation. We would be creating new habitat in what would otherwise be open water (of which there is no shortage), and rather than requiring fertiliser they could actually clean up excess human-introduced nitrates and phosphates.

Seaweeds rank very highly in terms of nutritional value. By dry weight, they contain roughly 10-25% protein, 5-10% digestible carbohydrate, and 5-10% fibre, along with a wide range of minerals and vitamins (but very little vitamin D or fat). Those that contain vitamin C fresh do tend to lose a lot of it if dried. Their mineral content is typically 10 times higher than any terrestrial plant, and in some cases higher even than meat. This is an unusual property for a wild food, where strong tastes and relatively low nutritional value are the norm, making seaweeds a valuable component of a balanced diet. In times of scarcity they have the capacity to provide ample amounts of nutrients that are hard to acquire on land. Because they are immersed in sea water, they have access to a source of these nutrients that land animals have no direct means of exploiting.

Drying and rehydrating

Seaweeds do not stay fresh for long. If not used very soon after picking, they will start to decay (much more quickly than most plants). They can be frozen, which is best for preserving flavour, but the most common method of preserving seaweeds is to dry them. They can also be partially dried and salted, and then sometimes refrigerated.

* *Transfer of carbohydrate-active enzymes from marine bacteria to Japanese gut microbiota*, Hehemann, J, et al, Nature 464, 2010, pp908-912.

They should be washed before drying, unless they were sourced from an absolutely pristine, rocky habitat. This is best done first in a clean rockpool, to dislodge as much sand, shells and invertebrates as possible. If you are worried about the water quality, they can be washed again in clean, fresh water. If they do come from a sand-free rocky habitat then they can be dried and stored without washing in fresh water, which leaves them with a natural salty coating.

The best method is sun-drying, if the weather conditions are conducive – I just hang them on a washing line using clothes pegs. They can also be dried in an oven at low temperature with the door wedged open, or in a food dehydrator. Rehydration times vary widely between species, taking anything between 5 minutes and 2 hours, but 10-15 minutes in a bowl of cold water will usually do. Don't use more water than is required, to avoid losing nutrients and taste into excess water. Rehydrated seaweeds should be used within a few hours, or they will start to decay.

The water content of fresh seaweeds usually varies between 70% and 90% depending on the species. Most seaweed recipes give weights for dried seaweed, which is unhelpful if you are lucky enough to have fresh seaweed available. As a rough guide, if the recipe calls for 10g of dried seaweed, use 50g of fresh seaweed. Rehydrated seaweeds do not work well in all recipes, because they never fully regain their fresh texture.

Seaweed Crisps

Any flat-bladed seaweeds are candidates, including dulse, laver, sea lettuce and kelps.

Ingredients:
Seaweed of choice, plus sesame or groundnut oil for frying.

Wash the seaweed in fresh water and then allow to dry completely. Chop into 3cm squares and then flash fry in a pan in 2cm of hot oil. Allow to drain on kitchen towel. Use as a naturally salty snack, or with dips. Alternatively, put on a lightly oiled baking tray or roasting dish, spread out, then put in an oven at 220°C (fan 200°C) for between 5 and 20 mins, depending on the type of seaweed.

Furikake

'Furikake' is a general term for various mixes of seasonings which are sprinkled on rice. It was invented in the post-war period, partly to address a malnutrition problem, especially calcium deficiency, and has since become very popular in Japan. Most types of furikake include at least some dried and crumbled seaweeds in the mix.

Ingredients:
All sorts of seaweeds can be used, but the most obvious European contenders are laver, dulse, pepper dulse and sea lettuce. Other typical ingredients are salt, sugar, chilli flakes, dried fish flakes (especially tuna and salmon), egg and black sesame seeds.

Shred your seaweed of choice, add toasted sesame seeds, season with salt and sugar, then mix in any other ingredients to taste. Furikake should be added to meals as they are served; they are at their best when still crisp and dry.

Seaweed Sourdough

This works well with sea lettuce, dulse, or – my personal favourite but an acquired taste – pepper dulse.

Ingredients:
650g strong bread flour, 300ml warm water, starter culture, 3tsp salt, 300g dried seaweed.

Put 300g flour, 300ml water, 1tsp salt and a dollop of starter into a bowl, and mix. Leave for 3 hours or until bubbling. Add the remaining flour and salt, and knead for 10 mins, then rest for 30 mins – repeat this twice. On the final kneading, add the seaweed, then rest the dough for 2 hours. Knock out the air, shape the dough and put in a proving basket (or teatowel-lined bowl) for a further hour. Bake in a casserole dish, covered for 15 mins at 230°C (fan 210°C) then uncovered for a further 30 mins at 200°C (fan 180°C).

Brandied Chocolate-Coated Seaweed

This works best with substantial seaweeds like kelps, and is particularly suited to sugar kelp.

Ingredients:
Seaweed of choice, brandy, dark chocolate.

Start with dried seaweed, cut into squares. Reconstitute in brandy instead of water (you can use a microwave to warm the brandy, perhaps two or three times, stirring in between to ensure the seaweed is covered in warm brandy). Melt the dark chocolate in a small bowl over hot water. Dip the reconstituted seaweed into the melted chocolate and place on greaseproof paper. Leave in the fridge to set, and served chilled.

▲ Winged Kelp or Atlantic Wakame

Seaweed toxicity

Most seaweeds are edible; those that aren't are inedible because they are unpalatable, tough or gritty. No British seaweeds are seriously poisonous, although some members of the genus *Desmarestia* (p50) are very acidic – they can release destructive concentrations of sulphuric acid when damaged or exposed to air, and cause gastric problems if eaten. The primary danger for a seaweed forager is not the seaweeds themselves, but contamination with biological or chemical hazards present in the local environment. Anything collected from polluted water is a potential health hazard, especially if the pollution is human sewage and the seaweed is consumed raw.

Heavy metal and trace element content

Seaweeds are remarkably adept at absorbing metals and trace elements from seawater, which can be both a blessing and a curse. They contain large amounts of all sorts of elements that are required by the human body, including some which can be hard to obtain from other sorts of food. In fact, they contain so much of some of these substances that excessive consumption risks overdose. This is especially true in the case of iodine and people with pre-existing thyroid problems, or those already taking iodine supplements. Seaweeds can also concentrate arsenic, mercury and other toxic elements. Different seaweeds absorb differing levels of the toxins, and though in most cases the levels are well below those which should cause alarm, in some cases there is insufficient research to know how worried we should be. Also see Japanese Wireweed (p54).

Brown seaweeds

The brown seaweeds are not closely related to other seaweeds, and only very distantly related to plants. They are multicellular algae belonging to the taxonomic class *Phaeophyceae*, and genetic evidence suggests that most of them have diverged only quite recently, although the group itself may have been around much longer. Around 200 have been recorded in north-west Europe.

Brown seaweeds contain carbohydrates which are indigestible, and therefore a low-calorie form of dietary fibre. They also have other uses – *alginates* are used extensively both in food production (primarily as a gelling agent) and other manufacturing processes, and *laminarin* can be fermented into alcohol, which is of interest to both industrial chemists and makers of craft beers.

Brown seaweeds are an exceptional source of minerals, and historically used in Europe to produce a mineral-rich salt substitute called 'black salt'. Kelps and Wracks were burned, the ash dissolved in water which was then boiled. Salt crystals could then be skimmed off the surface, while sand and other impurities fell to the bottom. A recent EU project* investigated the potential of Bladder Wrack and Sugar Kelp as a modern healthy salt substitute, though the processes used were a bit too techno-industrial to be of much use to most readers of this book, and the results were inconclusive.

Laminariales
Laminariaceae (Kelp family)

The Kelps include the largest of the brown seaweeds, some of which are very important in east Asian cuisine. It was from a member of this family that glutamic acid, the base molecule of monosodium glutamate (MSG) was first isolated by Japanese chemist Kikunae Ikeda in 1908, and it is for their umami taste that they are best known. All the Kelps can be used in salads, cooked: simmer for 10-20 minutes (the longer the more tender, but they also start to become bitter), then chop or shred them and allow to cool before use. They are used in stocks, soups and casseroles, as a vegetable-like accompaniment to a main dish. They can also be made into tsukudani (p49).

Kelps can also be processed into a flour substitute. To do this they must first be peeled when fresh, to remove the outer membrane (this leads to a higher quality end product). Dry the blades in the sun, then put in a food processor until reduced to a fine powder. The resulting 'flour' can be used to replace 1 part out of 5 in any recipe using wheat flour.

Kelps are a rich source of iodine, potassium, iron, calcium and other minerals, as well as containing 7-18% protein and 1-3% fat, and useful amounts of vitamins B1, 2, 3 and C. Excessive consumption can lead to ingesting more iodine than the daily recommend amount, which in extreme cases can cause gastric and thyroid problems (thyrotoxicosis). Be particularly careful if you also take iodine in tablet form.

* *The Application of Edible Seaweed for Taste Enhancement and Salt Reduction,* The TASTE Project: cordis.europa.eu/project/id/315170.

Oarweed/Cuvie/Tangle (*Laminaria*)

"...eaten in considerably quantity in Scotland, being first boiled. Cattle are very fond of it. The stems are sometimes made into knife handles, said to be as durable as buck-horn."

(C. Pierpoint Johnson, 1862)

Oarweed (*L. digitata*) and **Cuvie (*L. hyperborea*)** are large, brown, leathery, perennial seaweeds growing up to 3m long. Their blades are shaped like a hand with very long fingers that can end up tangled, so both species are known as **Tangle**. Their holdfasts have branched root-like structures ('rhizoids') gripping the rock. The stipe of Cuvie can exceed 1m, is circular in cross-section, tapers towards the blade and is prone to snapping. Oarweed is slightly larger but with a shorter and more oval stipe (to 45cm). These common seaweeds are found in the lowest parts of the intertidal zone. Oarweed is only exposed during very low tides, and Cuvie is usually sub-tidal.

The similar **Golden Kelp (*L. ochroleuca*)** is restricted to the far south west of Great Britain, but moving north in response to climate change. All of these seaweeds can be collected from spring to late summer, and are at their best for eating when young.

They can be used in any non-specific Kelp recipe, and their sheet-like structures mean they can also be used as a substitute for pasta in lasagne. They are also used in obstetrics as a cervical dilator – the dried stipe is inserted and left for several hours, and as it absorbs water it rehydrates and expands, gradually forcing the cervix open.

Furbellows (*Saccorhiza polyschides*) is the largest European seaweed, and also common. It belongs to a different taxonomic order, more closely related to Wracks than Kelps, but is visually similar to these two species, at least superficially. The most obvious differences are its rougher and more transparent blade, its flattened stipe and weird, knobbly, bulbous holdfast. It too is edible, but tougher than Tangle.

▾ Furbellows (top left) and Oarweed (bottom right)

▾ Furbellows holdfast

Chinese-Style Oarweed Salad

Ingredients:

200g fresh oarweed, 2tbsp light soy sauce, 1tbsp balsamic vinegar with a dash of Worcester sauce (or Chinese black vinegar), 3 garlic cloves (chopped), 1-2 fresh red chilli peppers (chopped), 3 ramsons leaves (including stems) and 4 flower buds (or use spring onions), 3tbsp vegetable oil, fresh coriander (optional), salted cucumber (optional), black sesame seeds (optional), very young purple sea kale leaves (optional).

Wash the oarweed in fresh water, then roll and slice into thin shreds. Boil for 3 mins, douse in cold water, drain. Put on a serving plate (with the cucumber if using), then add the soy sauce, vinegar, ramsons, chillies and garlic, in that order. Heat the oil until it is almost smoking, then pour over the garlic, and mix. An alternative method is to use ripped dried red chillies in the oil instead of fresh ones in the salad. Optionally garnish with coriander, black sesame seeds and/or sea kale leaves, and serve immediately.

▾ Oarweed

Sugar Kelp (*Saccharina latissima* syn. *Laminaria saccharina*)

Sugar Kelp is a short-lived perennial consisting of a single, undivided, yellow-brown blade with wavy edges and pairs of linear bumps but no midrib, up to 5m long and 20cm wide, with a short stipe. It is common, found in the intertidal and sub-tidal zones, and available for foraging from late spring to late summer.

Both Latin and common names refer to a slight sweetness due to high levels (up to 14%) of a sugar alcohol called mannitol – an isomer of sorbitol that is poorly absorbed by human digestive processes and used as a sweetener in diabetic products.

This sweetness makes Sugar Kelp suitable for use in baked goods such as bread and cakes. You can also use it as a wrapper, for steaming fish, meat or vegetables. It is more tender than most Kelps, so more agreeable as a side vegetable; in Greenland it was traditionally boiled with shellfish. Flash fried it blisters like potato crisps. Like all brown seaweeds, Sugar Kelp is best sun-dried. In Japan, it is then aged in cellars, typically for two to three years but sometimes for as long as a decade. This has the effect of reducing sliminess and increasing the umami taste. A white dusting of mannitol forms on the surface of Sugar Kelp as it dries.

'Kombu' refers to several very similar members of this genus, which are an important food source in Japan. Most are not present in Europe, but Sugar Kelp can be used in any Kombu recipe. The Japanese have been cultivating it for centuries, and use it to make a stock called 'dashi', which provides the foundation of miso soup – a dish eaten daily by 75% of the Japanese population. Dashi is made with Shiitake mushrooms and dried tuna, along with other small dried fish, though you can make a vegan version without the fish. It couldn't be simpler – you just steep the Kombu in water overnight. Other versions involve simmering, though there is disagreement about whether this impairs the taste.

Kombu was introduced as a cultivated crop in the mid-20th century, in China, where annual dry weight of production still runs into the thousands of tonnes and accounts for 40% of the world production of domesticated seaweed. There it is used both for food (fresh in salads and canned), and in industrial processes. The Chinese and Japanese also make a tea with it: 'kombu cha'. This should not be confused with a completely different drink, tea leaves fermented with a bacterial culture and known as 'kombucha' in the western world since the mid-1990s. This is a misapplied loanword (apparently somebody thought the film that forms on the top of the fermented drink looks a bit like seaweed). The correct Japanese name for fermented tea is 'kocha kinoko', but the drink itself originated in China.

Sugar Kelp has the highest iodine content of any edible European seaweed (150-500mg/100g), though the concentration is variable so it is impossible to measure doses for treatment of iodine deficiency. Most of the iodine is removed by boiling. Too much iodine is hazardous to health, but on average the prolific consumption of closely related species in Japan is found to be beneficial.*

* *Assessment of Japanese iodine intake based on seaweed consumption in Japan: A literature-based analysis,* Zava, T.T., Zava, D.T., Thyroid Research 4, 14 (2011).

Alariaceae
Wakame (*Undaria pinnatifida*)

Wakame is an annual with dark green-brown blades which are flat with a distinct midrib and deeply wavy margins. It grows to about 1.3m long and 4cm across. At the base of the stipe there are convoluted spore-bearing structures ('sporophylls'). It is native to south-east Asia and northern Australasia, but has become a prolific invasive species in temperate waters in many other parts of the world and is present on some north-west European coastlines, including parts of southern England. Though currently restricted to a few marinas and river estuaries, most of which are inaccessible to foragers, some marine ecologists fear it is likely to spread much more widely and pose a threat to native species.

Wakame is arguably the most highly regarded edible seaweed in Japan, where it is cultivated and used as a key ingredient in miso soup. The sporophylls in particular are considered a delicacy ('mekabu'), and usually grilled. The blades are boiled and used in salads, flash fried to make a snack, or dried for later use. They are also sometimes partially dried, then salted and refrigerated, as a means of preserving them without losing structure. When rehydrated for use most of the salt is washed out.

▾ Wakame

Winged Kelp (*Alaria esculenta*)

Winged Kelp or **Atlantic Wakame** is also known as 'Dabberlocks', 'Badderlocks', and historically 'Bladderlocks' (though it has no bladders). It is a perennial consisting of single, unbranched, thin, brown, wavy fronds up to 2m long and 15cm wide, with a yellow midrib and short stipe, which may give rise to sporophylls at the base (straight, flat ones up to 20cm long). Individuals often occur within larger stands of other kelps, so are easily missed, although the golden yellow midrib is very distinctive. It is frequent on exposed, rocky shores on the western and northern coasts of the British Isles, much rarer on eastern and southern coasts and absent between Flamborough (Yorkshire) and Southampton (Hampshire). It starts growing in the winter, and is past its best by July. It is collected for food from early spring to midsummer.

From both a culinary and biological point of view, the midrib is important. It provides structure that other kelps don't have, which means the rest of the blade (the 'wings') don't have to be so tough, making them more attractive as a foodstuff with relatively short cooking. Winged Kelp has a smooth texture and a mildly sweet flavour, and is used in soups, stews and salads (cooked), usually after having been dried. Winged Kelp salads are similar to the Ogonori salad recipe on p59. The midrib and stipe can be chopped and chewed raw, deep fried, or preserved as Tsukudani. The sporophylls are also edible (as Wakame). Winged Kelp can be substituted for Wakame in any recipe, though it requires slightly longer cooking. This species is a particularly rich source of calcium, potassium, phosphorus and vitamin A.

Winged Kelp Tsukudani Onigiri (modified traditional Japanese)

Tsukudani is a Japanese cooking method for preserving a variety of foods in soy sauce and mirin, for serving with sticky rice. Seaweed tsukudani can also be used to make a tea – the seaweed is left in the tea, and eaten as the tea is drunk. This recipe also works well with oarweed, sugar kelp, sea spaghetti and wracks. Onigiri are rice balls – packed lunch finger food in Japan.

Tsukudani ingredients:
60g fresh winged kelp blades, 200ml water, 1tsp rice vinegar. 1½tbsp dark soy sauce, 1½tbsp light soy sauce, 1½tbsp sake or dry sherry, 1½tbsp mirin, 1½tbsp sugar, grated fresh ginger root (optional), dried chilli flakes (optional), 2tsp black sesame seeds.

Onigiri ingredients (makes 6):
250g Japanese rice, 600ml water, 2tsp black sesame seeds.

To make the tsukudani, gently simmer the kelp in the water and rice vinegar for 10 mins. Add the soy sauce, sake, mirin and sugar. If you're including the ginger and/or chilli, add them too at this stage. Simmer until nearly all the liquid has gone, and all that remains is a sticky gloop. Add the sesame seeds and mix, then place in the fridge for later use (will keep for well over a week).

Scrub the rice in a bowl of cold water several times until the water is clear, then soak it for 15 mins, cook it for 15 mins in 600ml water, and cool it for 15 mins. To make onigiri, scoop a small amount of rice into a small bowl, make a hollow, add the tsukudani filling and top with more rice. Wet your hands in a mixture of water and rice vinegar (to stop the rice sticking to you) then shape the ball into a triangle with your palms, making sure the filling is all tucked inside. Sprinkle with sesame seeds.

▾ Winged Kelp showing sporophylls. Also see photo on p42.

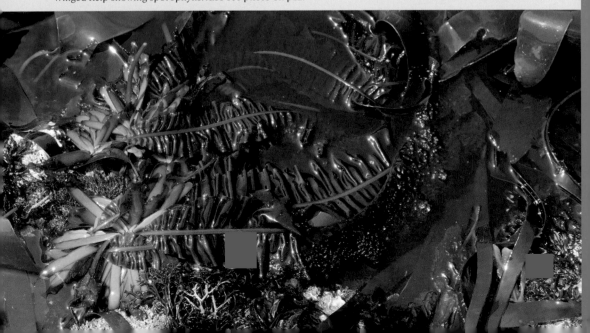

▲ Bootlace Weed

▲ Flattened Acidweed

Chordaceae
Bootlace Weed (*Chorda filum*)

Bootlace Weed or **Dead Man's Rope** is an annual consisting of rubbery or slimy, single, unbranched, hollow filaments that can reach 8m long, and become slightly hairy as they mature. Frequent in suitable habitat and best for eating around midsummer. The rare Furry Rope Weed (*Halosiphon tomentosus*) is similar, but noticeably hairier.

When in prime condition from a pristine environment, Bootlace Weed can be eaten fresh (chopped) in salads or sandwiches, otherwise cooked. It doesn't keep well. Historically it was also used to feed animals, and its name alludes to an archaic use as string, when dried.

Desmarestiales / Desmarestiaceae (Sea Sorrel family)
Sea Sorrels (*Desmarestia*) ⓘ

Sea Sorrels or **Acidweeds** contain sulphuric acid and are capable of damaging other seaweeds if placed in the same container after collection. This is presumably a self-defence mechanism against predation. They have a sour taste, unlike any other seaweeds, and can cause stomach aches if eaten in quantity. There are three British species, though I have only ever found **Flattened Acidweed (*D. ligulata*)**. **Prickly Acidweed (*D. aculeata*)** looks vaguely like Japanese Wireweed (p54), but with 'prickles' rather than 'bobbles'. The prickles detach later in the growth cycle. **Green Acidweed (*D. viridis*)** is smaller, delicate and feathery.

Fucales
Fucaceae (Wrack family)

Wracks are found in a regular sequence from one end of the intertidal zone to the other, with Channelled Wrack at the top and Egg Wrack or Toothed Wrack at the bottom. They are perennial, and dominate in many sheltered intertidal areas. They are all olive-brown. They are all edible, though more frequently used as fodder for livestock than for feeding humans. They were once an important soil improver and fertiliser, especially in Ireland, where they were used in a system called 'Lazy-beds' to grow potatoes before the great famine of the late 1840s. They are also used for skincare and 'detoxification' via the practice of taking hot seaweed baths (the benefits of which are scientifically questionable). As food, they provide a valuable means of increasing the nutritional value of meals, providing calcium and iodine, vitamin B and a wide range of trace elements. They are abundant, and can be dried and then ground into a storable powder to add to stews and stocks. You can also steam fish on them, enhancing the flavour. They can be chopped finely in salads (usually cooked first) and there is an old Welsh tradition of using them very finely chopped in bread sauce. The ends of the fronds are the best bits for eating, and can be collected any time apart from winter, when they stop growing. Dried Wracks are commercially available as a tea (steep for 15 minutes).

▲ Three Wracks (from top – Channelled, Spiral, Egg) in the sequence they are always found in.

Egg Wrack (*Ascophyllum nodosum*)

Egg Wrack is a particularly long-lived species with fronds up to 1m long which have no midrib but many large, egg-shaped air bladders (technically known as 'vesicles') in singletons (not pairs). It is common in the middle of the intertidal zone of various types of beach, usually in relatively sheltered areas. It contains very high levels of calcium and the highest vitamin C content of any European seaweed (38mg/100g) and is commercially marketed as a health supplement.

Bladder Wrack / Spiral Wrack (*Fucus vesiculosus/spiralis*)

Bladder Wrack typically has repeatedly forking fronds up to 2m long, with a prominent midrib and paired spherical air bladders. It is abundant on rocky coastlines in the mid to lower intertidal zone of relatively sheltered beaches. **Spiral Wrack** (photo on previous page) has shorter fronds (up to 35cm), usually lacks the air bladders

and has a very similar range. These two Wracks hybridise with each other and several other relatives, all similarly edible. Bladder Wrack is also known as 'Sea Oak', but this is an unhelpful name which also refers to the bitter *Halidrys siliquosa* (which is itself therefore better referred to by the name 'Podweed'). These species are very rich in iron. The tips can be used in salads; blanched, cooled and marinaded in lemon juice.

Toothed Wrack (*Fucus serratus*)

Toothed or **Serrated Wrack** consists of irregularly branched fronds up to 1.7m long, with serrated edges and a clearly defined midrib. Abundant all around the British Isles and often present where there aren't other Wracks, but plenty of other seaweeds. Best roasted for 15-20 minutes, and works particularly well served with fatty meats like pork or duck after being roasted in the dish with them. Can also be fried, or used in salads (boiled then cooled, or chopped very finely). Makes an excellent Tsukudani (see p49).

▼ Egg Wrack

▼ Bladder Wrack

▼ Toothed Wrack

Channelled Wrack (*Pelvetia canaliculata*)

Channelled Wrack consists of irregularly branched tufts of fronds up to 15cm long, with a deep channel on one side and reproductive receptacles at the end (no midrib or air bladders). This species always occurs in a very specific habitat: a narrow band around the highest point of the lowest high tides. Wherever it is present, it is the highest in the sequence of seaweeds, adapted to survive above the lowest neap high-tide line. It is common on rocky north-west European coasts.

Channelled Wrack is the best Wrack for eating, slightly more delicate and tastier than the rest. It goes well as part of a stir-fry, or briefly boiled then cooled and used as a mixed salad ingredient. It is high in vitamin C and selenium, and particularly high in omega-3 fatty acids, typically found in oily fish and lacking in many people's diets. Channelled Wrack extracts are used in cosmetics and skin creams, and claimed in some quarters to have impressive anti-inflammatory and anti-wrinkle properties as well as aiding recovery from sunburn.

Sargassaceae (Sargassum family)
Japanese Wireweed (*Sargassum muticum*) ⓘ

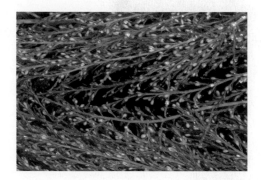

Japanese Wireweed has a perennial holdfast and short structure (a 'main axis'), and many annual light brown, multiply branching fronds ('secondary axes') which come in three types, one of which is covered with tiny air-filled bladders. These can rapidly grow up to 12m long in the spring, although they rarely exceed half that size in northern Europe. Native to south-east Asia, it has become seriously invasive on the southern and western coastlines of the British Isles and is spreading further afield, as far as the Mediterranean.

Wireweed makes a first-class addition to marine-themed salads, chopped and raw. It has a pleasant taste, naturally salty and satisfyingly crunchy. It can also be cooked with various sorts of seafood and works well in stir-fries. It's at its best in summer and feel free to take as much as you like, whenever you see it, because it is a pest. Despite its name, this species and its closest relatives are better known for food use in Korea, where it is known as 'mohm', than in Japan. It was traditionally boiled with pork bones (especially the spine) to make a dish called 'Momguk', served at festivals and family gatherings where a pig had been slaughtered – an example of 'nose to tail' use of a pig carcass.

Japanese Wireweed may contain harmful levels of arsenic if consumed in large quantities. It has been used to remove arsenic from contaminated water. This made me wonder, because a related Asian species – Hijiki (*Sargassum fusiforme*) – is believed to accumulate dangerous levels of arsenic, and is no longer considered safe by some authorities. The Japanese still eat Hijiki, and claim it would need long-term consumption of very large amounts to pose any sort of health threat, but it cannot legally be imported into the EU as food.

I could not find any conclusive scientific data about the potential danger posed by arsenic in Wireweed. Ole Mouritsen's *Seaweeds: Edible, Available, and Sustainable* (2013), which was the most comprehensive and up-to-date book on the food uses of European seaweeds at the time of writing, goes into detail about Hijiki toxicity. Inorganic forms of arsenic are famously toxic, but most of the arsenic in seaweeds is in an organic form, which has not been shown to be unsafe. Mouritsen also tells us that the Japanese may have evolved a more efficient biological mechanism for excreting arsenic, enabling them to safely eat seaweeds that are more dangerous to Europeans. However, he doesn't mention Wireweed at all. I contacted the UK government to ask if Wireweed is officially deemed safe for its citizens to eat. I was told that since there is no history of eating it in Europe, it is classed as a 'novel food', and therefore not authorised for sale, but that they have "no specific advice on this type of seaweed". It is therefore neither banned nor authorised, and I can offer no advice on what is a safe consumption level.

Himanthaleaceae
Sea Spaghetti (*Himanthalia elongata*)

Sea Spaghetti or **Thongweed** begins its life cycle in the autumn as a small, stalked disc up to 3cm in diameter. Through the winter and spring, repeatedly branching flattish 'thongs' grow, eventually reaching up to 2m when they mature in the summer. It can be found in the lower intertidal zone and adjacent sub-tidal area, so is only exposed during very low tides. It is frequent on most north-west European coastlines, but rare/absent on the eastern and south-eastern coast of England, and the south-east coast of Ireland. For foraging it comes into season in late winter, and can be collected until early autumn. Inexperienced collectors sometimes mistake Dead Man's Rope (p50) for Sea Spaghetti, mainly because it looks much more like actual spaghetti.

Sea Spaghetti is often used as a substitute for spaghetti or noodles, either 50/50 or completely. Miles Irving recommends frying it on a high heat, but it can also be marinaded in lemon/vinegar and used in salads, or like the Wracks and Kelps in soups, stews and stocks, and it works well as Tsukudani (p49). Dried Sea Spaghetti can be reconstituted with brandy or kirsch to make an intriguing component of a dessert. This species is very high in magnesium, calcium and zinc, as well as being 10% fibre (higher than almost any plant-based healthy food, and about the same as lentils) and 15% carbohydrate. Sea Spaghetti can be preserved by partially drying and salting. When fully dried (unsalted), it takes 30 minutes to rehydrate. When drying, it is best to keep it straight, which makes it easier to store.

▾ Sea Spaghetti. Also see photo on p2.

Red seaweeds

The red seaweeds (*Rhodophyta*) are a large phylum of multicellular algae. Over 350 species can be found on north-west European coastlines, many of which are impossible to identify to species without microscopy. Recent research[*] suggests that during their early evolution, over a billion years ago, the red seaweeds went through a stage of living in very hostile (hot and acidic) conditions, where their survival depended on being small, simple and able to survive on very little sustenance. As a result, they ended up with a condensed, extremely efficient genome with all non-critical genes selected out. This made it harder for them to diversify later, restricting them almost exclusively to marine environments. According to some definitions, red seaweeds count as very primitive plants, otherwise they are a sister clade to plants. They are also-rans that might have made it big on the land if they hadn't had such a difficult start in life.

Red seaweeds are higher in protein than other seaweeds, high in vitamins, and the most culinarily interesting of the three groups. Of those not covered in detail, known edible species include the westerly distributed **Bonnemaison's Fern-weed (*Bonnemaisonia asparagoides*)** and **Spiny Straggle Weed (*Gelidium spinosum*)**. The general rule is that *any* red seaweed you find growing in abundance can be tested for edibility. Just nibble a bit – if it tastes edible then it is edible, although most are better cooked. This group also includes some common calcified pink 'coral weeds', which are too chalky to eat.

Nemaliales / Nemaliaceae

Sea Noodle (*Nemalion helminthoides*)
Sea Noodle consists of mucilaginous, irregularly branched, red-black noodle-like structures up to 40cm long. It grows on barnacles and limpets, and is widely distributed but uncommon (more common in the south and west of the British Isles). Edible raw or blanched, in salads.

* Genome structure and metabolic features in the red seaweed Chondrus crispus shed light on evolution of the Archaeplastida, Collén, J, et al, *Proceedings of the National Academy of Sciences* 110:13, 2013, pp5247-5252.

Gracilariales / Gracilaceae

Ogonori or Wartweeds
(*Gracilaria/Gracilariopsis*) (!)

Ogonori consists of bunches of thin, red annual strands up to 30cm long, which grow from a perennial holdfast attached to rock or sand, often where saltwater drains off a beach. The females develop 'wart-like' reproductive structures. They are in season for foragers from mid-spring to early autumn, and care should be taken not to damage the holdfast.

The name Ogonori (or just 'Ogo') can refer to various species of *Gracilaria* native to the Pacific Ocean – particularly Japan, but it has traditionally been eaten in many south-east Asian countries. The name can just as well be applied to any members of the genus as well as the very similar *Gracilariopsis*, all of which are edible. There are also other red seaweeds which look rather like *Gracilaria*, most of which are more angular, scruffy and/or branched, such as **Black Scour Weed (*Ahnfeltia plicata*)** and **Dumont's Tubular Weed (*Dumontia contorta*)**. They can be used for food in the same way, though the taste varies.

Rich-flavoured Ogonori is usually eaten cooked in salads in Japan, the Caribbean and also Hawaii, where it is used in a raw fish dish called 'Poke'. It can also be added to soups and stews, pan-fried or roasted. It has a high iron content, and particularly high levels of vitamin C. It has been implicated in poisonings, although not recently. The symptoms were primarily gastric, but there are accounts of more serious cases, including deaths. The seaweed was consumed raw, usually in conjunction with raw fish and investigation has concluded that the most likely culprit is microbial.[*] While there are no known European cases of poisoning involving *Gracilaria*, consuming it raw cannot be recommended, just to be safe, until further information is available.

Gracilaria is commercially important as a source of agar. Agar consists of a pectin and a sugar, and is used as a vegetarian alternative to gelatine, especially in desserts in Asian cookery as a thickener and clarifying agent. It has medical uses as a laxative and appetite suppressant, and has long been used to provide a solid substrate for microbiological research.

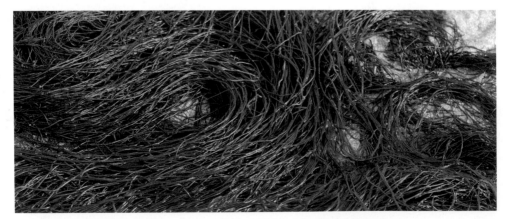

* *Mass Production of Marine Macroalgae*, Pereira, R, and Yarish, C, 2008, Encyclopedia of Ecology.

Ogonori Salad

This is my own invention, in a Japanese-Hawaiian style. It is a favourite on our coastal foraging events.

Ingredients:

80g fresh ogonori, 3 shallots (thinly sliced with a mandoline), ¼ of a cucumber, 3tbsp rice vinegar, 2tbsp light soy sauce, 1tbsp toasted sesame oil, 1tsp honey, 2cm fresh grated root ginger, 1 fresh red chilli (chopped or finely sliced), black sesame seeds.

Slice the cucumber thinly, cover with salt, leave for 20 to 30 mins, then drain and pat off any excess salt. The goal is to get rid of as much water as possible – gently squeezing will help. Mix the rice vinegar, soy sauce, sesame oil and honey to make a dressing. Chop the ogonori into 4-5cm lengths. Blanch the ogonori in boiling water for 40 seconds (it will turn green), then immediately rinse in cold water, to keep it nice and crunchy. Place a layer of salted cucumber and sliced shallots in a circle on a plate. Mix the ogonori with the chilli and ginger, and place in the middle of the circle. Pour the dressing onto the mixture, and garnish with sesame seeds.

Palmariales / Palmariaceae

Dulse (*Palmaria palmata*)

Dulse consists of irregularly split, robust, flat fronds up to 50cm long, attached to a perennial holdfast by a very short stipe. The colour is variable shades of purple-red and dull green, and it is quite tough and chewy. Common on the Atlantic, North Sea and English Channel coasts of temperate Europe in the mid-intertidal zone down to below the low spring tide-line, usually attached to rocks but sometimes other seaweeds. Dulse is collected from late spring to late summer, after which it is past its best. Two species sometimes mistaken for Dulse are **False Dulse** or **Red Rags (*Dilsea carnosa*)** – a tougher species, with wider, shorter, unbranched blades – and **Devil's Tongue Weed (*Grateloupia turuturu*)**, which is much larger, more leathery, less branched, and native to south-east Asia but invading the south coasts of England and Wales, and Brittany. Both are edible.

▲ False Dulse

Dulse is to seaweeds what blackberries are to plants and field mushrooms are to fungi: the one wild edible species the inhabitants of the British Isles never stopped collecting. As a wild edible it is particularly associated with Ireland, but historically Dulse has been the first choice wherever northern Europeans ate seaweed. It packs a serious umami punch with faint spicy overtones, and is good eaten raw, but even better dried, as a snack food – it develops a tasty coating of salt and other nutrients as it dries. It can be chopped into salads, mashed into potato, mixed into butter. Dried Dulse can be crushed and used as a condiment. It can also be prepared by soaking the raw seaweed in fresh water, which tenderises it by bursting its cells. Cooking impairs the taste and eventually disintegrates the structure, although it can be used in soups, incorporated into bread dough, or quickly fried. Dulse can replace the bacon in a vegetarian bacon, lettuce and tomato sandwich, or be made into crisps by roasting for 10-15 minutes (220°C / fan 200°C). Also see recipe for seaweed spread (p69).

Dulse is one of the best seaweeds from a nutritional point of view, with high levels of beta-carotene/vitamin A, all of the B-complex, vitamin C, vitamin E, potassium, zinc, and more iron than sirloin steak.

In recent years Dulse has been successfully cultivated in Spain.

Dulse Litmus Lemonade

This is a traditional cold remedy that can be enjoyed chilled on a warm summer afternoon just as much as hot on cold winter evening. Boil dulse in fresh water for 20 mins. Strain the liquid, which should be red-pink, into a glass and add honey. When ready to serve, add lemon juice and watch it turn blue!

Dulse Coleslaw

Ingredients:
100g fresh dulse (finely chopped), 50g raisins, 200g white cabbage (shredded), 1 carrot (grated), 3 shallots (finely chopped), 5tbsp mayonnaise, 2tbsp white wine vinegar.

Soak the raisins in warm water to make them swell. Put the cabbage, carrot, shallots, raisins and dulse in a mixing bowl, and mix in the mayonnaise and vinegar. Season and mix again, then leave in a fridge to chill before serving.

Soda Bread with Dulse and Stout
(traditional Irish)

Ingredients:
340g wholemeal flour, 340g plain flour, 1tbsp clear honey, 2tbsp baking soda, 1tsp salt, 2tbsp dried dulse (crumbled), 250ml stout, 250ml buttermilk.

Thoroughly mix the dry ingredients in a bowl. Add the stout and buttermilk and stir to make a batter. Grease some loaf tins, pour in the mixture and bake for 45 mins at 200°C / 180°C fan, or however long it takes for the loaves to rise. Remove from the tins to cool, and serve with plenty of butter. Makes a filling bread with a deep umami flavour.

▾ Dulse. Also see photo on p37.

Bangiales / Bangiaceae

"Laver – the true purple laver – [is] wonderfully nutritious, and may be had for the gathering. ... If we had had the business acumen of the French we should have made it as famous as truffles of Perigeux."
(Florence White, 1932)

Laver (*Porphyra*)

Laver are annuals consisting of irregularly shaped, membrane-like fronds up to 30cm long, initially greenish, becoming more brown or purple. They are very thin (only one cell thick) but surprisingly tough. They can be found on rocks anywhere in the intertidal zone, though typically nearer the top than the bottom. The most widely collected species is Tough Laver (*Porphyra umbilicalis*) but at least seven types of Laver grow in European waters, all of which are rather similar and can be used in the same ways. Some species can only be found in the summer, a couple (including Tough Laver) can be found at any time.

Laver is best known in the British Isles for making laverbread – an essential component of a traditional full Welsh breakfast, along with bacon, eggs and cockles. To make it, you first have to wash the seaweed multiple times to remove all the grit and wildlife (don't skimp on this, or you will regret it later) before simmering for 6 hours, which is best done in a slow cooker. It is then combined with olive oil, seasoning and lemon juice or vinegar before serving as a sauce. It can also be rolled in, or combined with, oats or oatmeal, and made into patties and then briefly fried. The taste is rich and satisfying – well worth the wait.

Cooked laver freezes well, provided it is frozen immediately after cooling, and it can be dried and flaked, and then used to thicken dishes and enhance flavour. Nutritionally, it is exceptionally high in both protein (30-35% of its dry mass is digestible protein) and beta-carotene/vitamin A (30,000IU/100g), and is a valuable source of vitamin C, vitamins B, and vitamin E. It is collected from midwinter to late summer, after which it is past its best.

The related and very similar Japanese species, collectively known as Nori, which are used to wrap sushi, have recently been moved from *Porphyra* to *Pyropia* (no European species among them).

Nori is the most economically important cultivated seaweed crop in Asia, and the method is highly technical. This reflects the intriguing life cycle of these algae, which was discovered by a British researcher called Kathleen Mary Drew-Baker in the 1940s. Drew-Baker has a shrine dedicated to her in Japan, where she is known as 'Mother of the Sea', and a festival held in her honour every 14th April.

Gigartinales / Gigartinaceae

Carragheen (*Chondrus crispus*)

Carragheen or **Irish Moss** is a very variable seaweed, with irregularly branching, rubbery annual fronds up to 20cm long, growing from a perennial holdfast. The shape, size and colour all vary, and it can be found everywhere from the mid-intertidal zone to deep water. It is common on British coasts where suitable rocky habits are available, and frequent on the oceanic coastline of continental Europe from Sweden to Portugal.

There is potential for confusion with a large number of similar fan-shaped red seaweeds, none of which are harmful and most of which share similar properties. These include the very common **False Carragheen (*Mastocarpus stellatus*)** of the family *Phyllophoraceae*, which

has twisted and channelled fronds that eventually grow considerably larger. Both are collected as a source of a stabiliser/thickener (carragheenan) used in a variety of processed foods, dairy products and nut milks. Unlike agar, carragheenan can survive an acidic environment, so is the seaweed gelling agent of choice for fruity desserts. Traditionally these seaweeds were used in Scotland and Ireland to produce blancmange or jelly dishes. Carragheen can also be used in soups, and it roasts well (10 minutes), ending up a lot like the 'crispy seaweed' served in British Chinese restaurants (though that is made of cabbage). It is also used as a clarifying/fining agent in home brewing. Carragheen has the highest zinc content of any edible European seaweed (8mg/100g). It is best collected in spring.

See Carragheen Fruit Pudding recipe on p79.

▾ Carragheen

▾ False Carragheen

Furcellariaceae
Black Carragheen (*Furcellaria lumbricalis syn. fastigiata*)

Black Carragheen or **Clawed Fork Weed** is a mass of upright, dark red-brown to black, forking fronds up to 30cm long and 2mm in diameter, originating from a branching holdfast. Frequent on all northern European coastlines, including the Baltic Sea, though less common in some places than it once was due to over-harvesting and eutrophication. It grows both attached to substrate and free-floating. The similar Discoid Fork Weed (*Polyides rotunda*) is redder, has a disc holdfast, and branches more irregularly.

Black Carragheen contains furcellaran, or 'Danish agar'. It came into use in Europe as a substitute for agar when supplies from Asia were cut off during World War II and is now an important gelling agent in commercial food production, and particularly useful since boiling is not required. It is used to make preserves, and in canning meat and fish. Though the process of extracting furcellaran from seaweed is not simple, it can be used as a natural thickener by simply boiling it down. Furcellaran is also used in skin creams.

Carragheen Water (TF Garrett, 1892)

Put 1oz. of Carrageen into a bowl of water, wash it well, put it into another bowl with 1 pint of water, and let it soak for ten minutes. Turn it with the water into a saucepan, add double the quantity more of water, a stick of cinnamon, and 2oz. of sugar, and boil over a moderate fire until the whole has the consistency of cream. Pass it through a fine sieve, add more sugar to moisten if desired, and serve while quite warm.

Carragheen Mould (Jason Hill, 1939)

Simmer for 15 minutes in milk with a flavouring of dried Elderflowers, Bay Laurel leaf or sweet spice, strain it into a basin or mould, sweeten with honey or sugar and allow it to set. The addition of a little cream is a great improvement.

Carragheen Jelly Salad (traditional Irish via Dyfed Lloyd Evans)

Ingredients:
75g fresh carragheen, juice of 3 lemons, one round lettuce, 250g celery (diced), 2 apples (peeled, cored, diced), 3tbsp mayonnaise, walnuts (chopped).

Wash the seaweed in fresh water and place in a bowl of boiling water for 5 mins. Drain, chop, then leave in a small bowl with the strained juice until it has dissolved and the mix has set to a jelly. Chill for 3 hrs, then dice. Mix the celery and apples with mayonnaise. Arrange lettuce leaves on chilled plates, put the jelly in the centre, the celery/apple mix around the edges and sprinkle walnuts over the top.

Ceremiales / Rhodomelaceae

Pepper Dulse (*Osmundea pinnatifida*)

Pepper Dulse has a perennial holdfast and tough, flattened alternately branching annual fronds, of variable size and colour (yellow-green higher up the beach, becoming red, brown or purple where less exposed to sunlight at lower levels). It has a very distinctive strong taste and smell, and a tangled holdfast. Pepper Dulse is common on British coastlines apart from some parts of the eastern and southern coast of England. It can be found on continental European coastlines from southern Sweden all the way down to Gibraltar, but absent in the Baltic. Pepper Dulse is one of the earliest seaweeds, collectable in the early spring when most other species haven't really got going, and is still collectible until early autumn. The less common **Royal Fern-weed** (*O. osmunda* not illustrated) is larger and less branched and **False Pepper Dulse** (*O. hybrida*) has rounded rather than flattened fronds. Both can be used in the same way. The Rounded Fern-weeds (genus *Laurencia*) have branches arranged spirally rather than flat.

Pepper Dulse is used as a spicy, savoury herb, either fresh or dried. The smell coming out of an oven when drying it will make your eyes water (very literally). The taste is variable – peppery, garlicky, becoming less intense and more umami when dried. It goes well as a seasoning on roast chicken, or sprinkled on fried eggs, or with almost any type of fish. We use dried, crumbled Pepper Dulse as a flavouring in sourdough bread (added during the last knead – see p61).

▾ Pepper Dulse

▾ False Pepper Dulse

Green seaweeds

Green seaweeds are a taxonomically unranked paraphyletic group of very primitive plants, of which there are in excess of 100 in northern European waters. They are closely related to, and share important characteristics with, the common ancestor of all land plants.[*] These seaweeds are best collected in spring and autumn, or whenever they are bright green and fresh. All the edible green seaweeds contain high levels of magnesium. The single-celled *Chlorella*, which turns the water of ponds and aquaria green, is believed to be related to green seaweeds, though the taxonomy is currently uncertain. It was once considered to have potential to feed humans on a huge scale, very much like Spirulina – see p36.

Cladophorales / Cladophoraceae

Green Hair-weed (*Chaetomorpha linum*)

Green Hair-weed consists of fine, unbranched threads, somewhat resembling tangled hair. It can be distinguished from similar-looking green seaweeds by the soft, rather than wire-like, feel of the threads. Inhabits the upper half of the intertidal zone, often in locations where the salinity is relatively low due to the presence of freshwater coming down the beach.

Frequent to common on most European coastlines. **Ligurian Sea Brick Weed** (**C. ligustica**) is similar and common, and also edible.

Green Hair-weed can be eaten fresh in salads, or dried and used as a condiment. It contains high levels of vitamin C, and is best for eating in the spring. It is popular with marine aquarium enthusiasts, because it is effective at removing nitrates from the water. Unfortunately, irresponsible dumping of water from these aquaria has resulted in Green Hair-weed becoming a problematic invasive species.

* *Origin of land plants: Do conjugating green algae hold the key?* Wodniok, S, et al, 2010, BMC Evolutionary Biology.

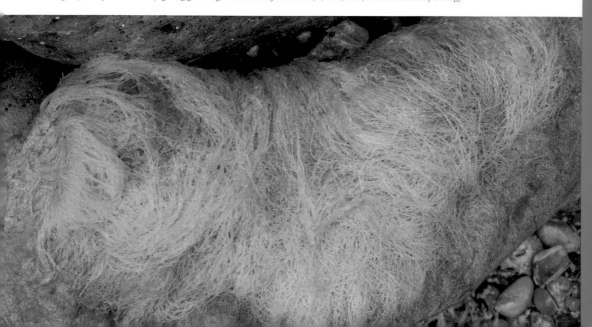

Ulvales / Ulvaceae ⓘ

Ulvaceae is a large family of green seaweeds that are very hard to identify to species level. Broadly, there are two types – sheets (Sea Lettuces) and tubular fronds (Gutweeds). The genus *Ulva* includes many species previously called *Enteromorpha*. All of these species can be a bit hazardous for foragers due to their tendency to grow abundantly in areas polluted by high levels of organic nutrients (including sewage), and also because they absorb inorganic pollutants, such as toxic heavy metals, from their environment. They should be carefully washed.

Sea Lettuce (*Ulva lactuca*)

Sea Lettuces are annuals consisting of irregularly shaped, bright green (can be yellowish to dark) sheets, sometimes with holes, up to 40cm long. There are quite a few species, two of which are common on all British and northern European coastlines and frequent further south – found anywhere from near the high-tide line to below the low-tide line, usually on rocks, sometimes on timber. The most common species is *U. lactuca*, but there are several other sheet-forming varieties of *Ulva*, all of which can be used in similar ways. **Rigid Sea Lettuce (*U. rigida*)** is tougher, without the holes, and more likely to be found year round. **Californian Sea Lettuce (*U. californica*)** is smaller (native to North America, apparently spreading in the north of the British Isles). **Broad Sea Lettuce (*U. gigantea*)** is much larger, and only found in western Ireland. There are more sheet-like Ulva species, *any* of which could be confused with **Greville's Mattress Weed (*Monostroma greveillei*)**, which is lighter coloured and more fragile.

The flavour is quite strong. Use in Asian-style salads (raw if in very good condition, from a very clean environment, otherwise briefly blanched or fried), also in soups and casseroles, or as a side dish to accompany fish. Seaweed cookery writer Prannie Rhatigan's suggestion of putting it in an omelette also works well. Can be roasted into delicious 'crisps' (spray first with a little oil, then put in a medium oven for 5-10 minutes). Also works well dried, crushed and sprinkled on rice.

Sea Lettuce has a strong claim to be a seaweed superfood, containing up to 25% protein, high levels of vitamins A, B3, B12, and especially C, as well as significant amounts of all of the trace elements found in other seaweeds, especially iodine and manganese, and the highest iron content of any European seaweed (100mg/100g).

Sea Lettuce and Dulse Spread/Sauce

Ingredients:
50g fresh sea lettuce, 50g fresh dulse, 2 pickled onions, 2 pickled gherkins, 2tsp capers, juice of 1 lemon, 50ml olive oil, 1tsp wholegrain mustard, 1tbsp balsamic vinegar, 1 small onion, salt and pepper to taste.

Wash the sea lettuce in fresh water and drain well. Combine all the ingredients and blitz until finely chopped, but not quite smooth.

To make a savoury spread, stir in 50ml olive oil, chill for 2 hours and serve with buttered toast. Or to make a sauce, mix 50/50 with mayonnaise, and serve with white fish. Both will keep in the fridge for a couple of days.

▼ Sea Lettuce

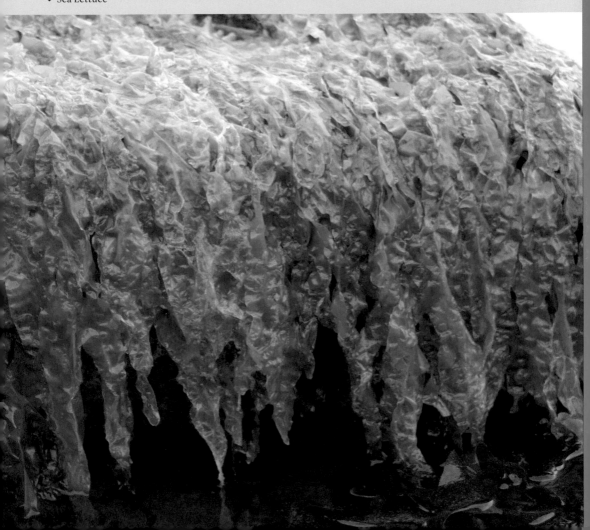

Gutweeds (*Ulva spp.*)

Gutweed consists of green, crinkly, tubular, annual fronds up to 60cm long (max 3cm wide, usually less) and grow almost anywhere on beaches from the splash zone downwards, including in brackish water in estuaries. There are at least five very similar species, several of which are common on European coasts. They can be chopped and used in salads, roasted (5-10 minutes), or dried, chopped and fried until crispy with a little soy sauce and brown sugar. These have the highest iodine levels of any seaweed covered here – twice that of Laminaria. They are best collected from a non-sandy environment, to avoid the extended washing required to rid them of sand.

Proliferous Gutweed (*U. prolifera*), aka Branched String Lettuce and also referred to in English as 'Green Tide', is similar to Gutweed, but with finer tubes that look like fine string or ribbons. It can multiply to plague proportions in the right conditions (high nutrient levels and warm water), forming mats several metres long. It is eaten in China, usually roasted. Other common Gutweeds include **Flexuous Gutweed (*U. flexuosa*)**, which has narrow tubes (<1mm), **Tape Weed (*U. compressa*)**, which has flattened, branching tubes, **Spiky Tendrils (*U. clathrata*)**, which has tiny spikes on the fronds and **Double Ribbon Weed (*U. linza*)**, which looks like a long, thin Sea Lettuce.

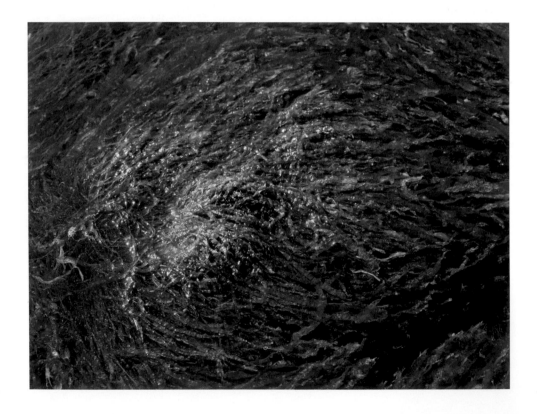

Bryopsidales / Codiaceae

Velvet Horn / Dead Man's Fingers (*Codium tomentosum/fragile*)

Velvet Horn (*C. tomentosum*) has repeatedly forking, dark green, spongy/felty circular annual fronds up to 30cm long, and a holdfast which is either annual or perennial depending on conditions. It is found in deep rock pools in the lower intertidal zone. Frequent on British coasts apart from in eastern England, and European coasts from northern Sweden to Gibraltar. **Dead Man's Fingers (*C. fragile*)** is very similar, but native to south-east Asia and becoming invasive in Europe. ***C. fragile* subsp. *tomentosoides*** is one of the most invasive seaweeds in the world. Both species are in season from spring to summer. The texture is different to other green seaweeds – firm, and velvety. They can be eaten raw if collected in perfect condition from a pristine environment, otherwise briefly fry. They are also used to make skin creams.

▾ Velvet Horn

Plants (introduction)

'Wild' plants

If a plant is planted and/or tended by humans, it is cultivated. If its genome has been changed by humans, then it is domesticated. 'Wild' is the opposite of both. If a domesticated or cultivated species escapes and survives, has it rewilded itself?

Human activity has introduced many plants to parts of the world where they do not naturally occur. A few have gone on the rampage, displacing native species. In Europe, the worst offender is Japanese Knotweed – a plant that is capable of smashing its way through concrete, and extremely hard to eradicate. Himalayan Balsam is another well-known example, often monopolising damp locations where a wide variety of native plants once flourished. Both are good edibles.

Perhaps we need to rethink 'invasive'. Japanese Knotweed and Himalayan Balsam are here to stay. Not satisfied with thoughtlessly moving species about, we're now changing the viable geographical ranges of plants via climate change. These changes are irreversible; a new balance will eventually be established.

▾ Agricultural escapes: Broad Beans and Wheat growing in a riverside meadow, far from fields of either crop. Both were domesticated at the start of the Neolithic. The wild ancestor of Broad Beans has never been found, and may be extinct.

Some definitions

Native: the truest sense of 'wild', though includes native plants deliberately reintroduced by humans.

Naturalised: these are plants introduced from elsewhere by human activity, either intentionally or unintentionally, but now established in the wild. These are sometimes subdivided into 'archeophytes' (already naturalised before 1500CE) and 'neophytes' (more recent introductions).

Casual alien: recent escapes from horticulture, agriculture or rubbish that breed true from seed or reproduce via runners or bulbs but are not yet/fully naturalised, because they usually die out. Historically a lot of waste-ground aliens hitched a ride on unprocessed wool, these days they are more likely to arrive as birdseed.

Wildlings: escapes from cultivation that can reproduce unaided but not true to the cultivated form, having reverted to something closer to an ancestral wild form. (See Crab Apples, p238.)

Hybrids can also occur of any of the above, which may or may not be fertile. Most recognised hybrids aren't covered this book – there are simply too many of them. If nothing is specified in the species guide about the native/introduced status of a plant, then it is native.

Plant parts and what to do with them

Just as with domesticated fruits and vegetables, the same structural part of different plants can be used in very similar ways. This section covers the main components of plants, and their food uses.

Roots, tubers, bulbs and bulbils

Most domesticated root crops have wild ancestors which, though edible, have far less edible roots. Wild Carrots and Parsnips are so weedy and tough that we might wonder how they ever became candidates for domestication in the first place. Others, such as Burdock and Horseradish have big, thick taproots even in their wild form. There are also other wild species whose secondary (non-tap) roots are edible. Rhizomes are a specialised sort of root that grow sideways and give rise to both shoots going upwards and roots going in other directions. Ginger and several related spices are cultivated for their rhizomes. Wild species with edible rhizomes are disproportionately aquatic.

Tubers and bulbs are functionally very similar: they store the energy and nutrients of plants that die back over the winter. Structurally, they differ. Bulbs have a distinct top and bottom, and if you cut them open then you can see their structure. The best-known domesticated bulb is the onion, and the best wild edible bulbs are other Alliums. 'Bulbils' are bulb-like, but form on parts of the plant above the ground, such as flower heads (Alliums again) or leaf axils. Tubers have no structure and more variable shapes, the obvious domesticated example being the potato. Historically the most important has been the Early Purple Orchid, which is now off-limits for conservation reasons.

Pignuts are another example of now-uncommon wild tubers that were once commonly eaten.

Wild greens: stems, shoots and leaves

Stems typically need to be harvested at just the right time; leave them too late and they'll be too tough and/or stringy to eat. Among the best are the Thistles and Alexanders (closely related to Celery).

Shoots are very young stems and leaves, and in many cases they are tastier than more mature parts of the plant. The classic domesticated shoot crop is Asparagus, and its wild relatives are similarly edible. Other first-class forageable shoots include Hogweed, Hops and Bladder Campion.

Leaves make up the bulk of the surface area of most plants and there are lots of wild plant leaves that fall into the category of 'edible, but not great'. They can be tough, hairy, bitter, or employ some other method of deterring animals from eating them. Some of these can be improved by cooking, but there aren't very many edible wild leaves that are really good in a salad. On the other hand, they tend to be nutritious (though low in calories), and more so when raw, and some of them can be extremely abundant in spring. The wild ancestors of domesticated leaf vegetables are among the better of the wild leaf vegetables, although they tend to become bitter with age. Note that 'young leaves' can mean very young, just as with some cultivated leaf vegetables. The needles of conifers also fall into this category, many of which are also edible when very young. Leaves can also be used as herbs, for flavouring, or in teas.

Wild Greens Soup

Ingredients:
1 large potato (diced), 1 large onion (chopped), 300ml double cream, 1 litre vegetable or chicken stock, 400g wild greens (chopped). I suggest 40% ramsons, 40% nettle, 10% cleavers, 5% lady's smock (whole plant, including flowers) and 5% wild fennel.

Fry the potato and onion until the onions are soft, add the stock and the greens and simmer for 15 mins. Blitz, add the cream, and heat back to serving temperature.

▼ Crow Garlic (aka Wild Onion) bulbs exposed at the eroding cliff edge at the top of a beach.

Wild Greens Terrine (traditional Swiss)

Ingredients:
250g wild greens (such as nettles, ramsons, hogweed shoots, ground-elder, wild fennel, bistort and cleavers), 200g cream cheese, 1 heaped tbsp cornflour, fresh grated nutmeg to taste, 4 egg whites, olive oil, salt and pepper.

Fry the greens in the oil until soft. Then blitz with the cheese in a food processor or with a hand blender, transfer to a bowl, stir in the cornflour and grated nutmeg, and season. Whisk the egg whites until stiff, then fold into the greens, and put the resulting mixture into a buttered, floured loaf tin. Put the tin in a roasting dish half filled with hot water, cover loosely with foil and steam in an oven for about 35 mins at 170°C / 150°C fan. When the terrine is set, allow the tin to cool, and turn over before slicing. Serve with tomato salad.

Green Sauce (British World War II version from Jason Hill, 1939)

Chop very finely or pound two or more of the following herbs (according to taste and availability): parsley, chives, fennel, onion, sorrel, [salad] burnet, watercress, lady's smock. Stir in olive oil to the consistency of cream, add vinegar, salt and a pinch of sugar to taste; serve with fish or cold meat.

An 'authentic' German version can be found on p381.

Flowers

Some unopened flower buds can be eaten either raw (eg Ramsons) or pickled (eg Oxeye Daisy), the best-known cultivated example of this being capers (the Caper Bush (*Capparis spinosa*) is a showy-flowered Mediterranean relative of the Cabbage family, commonly growing wild on cliffs and walls as well as being cultivated).

Open flowers can liven up salads, and are used for their aesthetic value, including some that aren't palatable but smell appetising (eg Lilac). There are also many wild and ornamental plants, the flowers of which are the best part for eating (eg wild Sweet Violets). Finally, there are a few where only the nectar is consumed (Honeysuckle being the obvious example). Flowers cultivated for food are less common, but include Day-lilies (which also fall into the category of 'edible ornamental') and saffron (the dried stamens of a species of Crocus). Some catkins (the flowers of wind-pollinated trees) are used as famine foods, to bulk out flour (eg Hazel).

Flowers are also used to make syrups. The basic recipe is usually the same: a 50/50 (by volume) mixture of water and sugar, to which flowers are added. This can be boiled, or just left to steep. Lemon and/or orange juice/peel can also be added, along with other flavourings. The syrup is then stored in the fridge, and used in cocktails and desserts.

Pollen

Edible wild pollen comes from flowers, grasses and their relatives (eg Reedmace), and conifers (eg Pine). It is nutritionally very dense. Just like seeds, pollen has to have everything needed to start growing when it lands in the right place. It contains a very wide range of vitamins, minerals and amino acids, and has many claimed health benefits. It is typically used as an additive, to baked goods, smoothies and salads.

▾ A bee on Borage. Excessive gathering of flowers can deprive bees of their food source.

Flower Fritters

Elderflower, false acacia, meadowsweet and wisteria all make delicious fritters, and you'll find a wealth of recipes online. This one is adapted from a recipe by Dyfed Lloyd Evans.

Ingredients:
180g plain flour, pinch of salt, 1 egg, 400ml flat beer, 300g meadowsweet flower sprays (remove as much of the stems as possible and trim the flowers into small sprays).

Add the flour and salt to a large bowl, make a well in the middle and break the egg into it. Pour in a little beer and start to mix. Gradually add more beer. Mix thoroughly so that there are no lumps and keep adding beer until you have a batter about the consistency of single cream. Cover the bowl with a cloth and rest for 30 mins. Meanwhile trim and rinse the meadowsweet flower sprays. Heat oil in a wok or deep pan and mix your flowers into the batter. Drop spoonfuls of the batter mix into the hot oil and fry until golden, turning once. Lift them onto a plate using a slotted spoon, drizzle with a little honey and serve warm.

Flower Cordials

Elderflower, flowering currant, lilac, meadowsweet and rose can all be used to make floral cordials, for use in drinks or cooking. Recipes vary, but generally follow a theme of boiling or cold steeping the blossoms with sugar or honey, and lemon or orange juice, with optional citric acid if you want to preserve your cordial rather than use it immediately. With citric acid, it will keep for at least a month in the fridge. It can also be frozen.

Ingredients:
20 elderflower heads (stalks trimmed and gently washed in cold water), 1.5l water, 2.5kg sugar, 2 unwaxed lemons, optional 85g citric acid.

Peel the lemon skin with a potato peeler, and slice lemons. Put the sugar and 1.5l of water into a large saucepan, and heat without boiling until sugar dissolves, then bring to the boil, then turn off the heat. Add the flowers, lemon zest and slices and citric acid (if using), cover and leave for 24 hours. Strain through a sieve, and put into sterilised bottles.

Candied Flowers for Cake Decorations

Ingredients:
1 large egg white, 1tsp water, edible flowers with stems removed, icing sugar.

In a small bowl, whisk the egg white and water. Take one flower at a time, held with tweezers, brush whisked egg over the entire surface of flower using a small paintbrush. Sprinkle with sugar. Transfer to a parchment-lined baking tray to crisp flowers. Stand at room temperature for several hours. Sugared flowers can be stored in airtight containers at room temperature for 3 months.

Fruits and cones

Fruits are the one part of a plant whose main purpose is to be eaten, as 'payment' by the plant for distributing its seeds. As with domesticated fruits, they can be preserved either by drying or turning into jam/jelly. Some have to be bletted (starting to rot) or damaged by frost before they become edible. Only flowering plants have fruits – the 'fruits' of Yew are technically a type of cone, but play the same role as true fruits. The cones of most conifers are inedible, but the very young male cones of some species can be eaten (notably Pine).

Most fruits can be made into syrups. Simply cover the berries in water in a saucepan, boil for 10 minutes, strain, add 1kg of sugar to 1 litre of juice, boil for another 5 to 10 minutes, skim and bottle. This works for Elderberries (destalked!), Blackberries, Mulberries, Redcurrants and Blackcurrants.

Kissel is a Baltic / eastern European dish made of crushed or juiced fruit (eg Barberry, Rosehips, Sloe and *Vaccinium* spp.) and potato starch or cornflour, halfway between a jelly and a drink. See p374.

Also see Wild Poppy and Wild Fruit Cake on p149.

Jams, chutneys and fruit leather

Jam needs no introduction, and is an excellent way of preserving fruit. Sugar and pectin combine to create a gel that keeps out water and air, preventing the growth of bacteria, fungi and mould.

The best fruit for jam making is just ripe, when pectin is at its highest. Don't be tempted to try and turn a glut of over-ripe fruit into jam, you'll be disappointed. Different fruits contain different amounts of pectin (Cooking Apples, Quinces, Damsons, Redcurrants and Blackcurrants are high; Blackberries, Strawberries, Rhubarb, Elderberries and Pears are low). So to ensure gelling you can either combine ingredients, or use added pectin.

The basic jam-making formula is equal weights of fruit and sugar. Heat the fruit first, with a little water if needed, bring to the boil, then add the sugar and boil it 'hard' for 10-25 minutes (depending on the fruit) until it reaches 105°C.

To test if it's reached setting point, drop a little jam onto a refrigerated plate, let it cool, then push it with a fingernail. If it wrinkles, it's ready. Pour into warm, sterilised jars, cover the top with a wax disc to prevent mildew, and seal. It should keep for around a year stored in a cool, dark place.

Occupying the space somewhere between jam and pickles, we have chutney. Its combination of vinegar and sugar gives it a long shelf life, perfect for preserving the gluts of autumn for enjoying through the winter. Foraged foods that work well in chutney include Plums, Pears, Apples, Sloes, Crab Apples, Alexanders and Rosehips.

The basic recipe is to chop your ingredients, usually with some onion, garlic, ginger, spices or other strongly flavoured additions, and bring them to a boil in a mixture of vinegar and sugar, and a little salt. Simmer for 15 minutes to 1 hour depending on the ingredients and recipe, then pour into warm, sterilised jars and seal. Stored in a cool, dark place, it should keep for a year or more.

An alternative preservation method is to make fruit leather. Cook fruit gently with a little water and optional lemon and sugar, then blend and spread thinly on trays and dry in a dehydrator, low oven or outdoors.

▲ Mahonia Gin and Mahonia Jelly

Wild Fruit and Carragheen Pudding
(traditional British, with thanks to
Dyfed Lloyd Evans)

Ingredients:
70g dried carragheen (Irish moss), 1kg
wild fruit (eg blackberries) picked over and
washed, 1l water, 2tbsp honey.

Combine the fruit, honey and water in a
saucepan. Bring to a boil then reduce to
a simmer, cover and continue cooking for
1 hour. Strain through a sieve, pulping the
fruit with the back of a spoon to extract
as much juice as possible, then return
the juice to the saucepan and add the
seaweed. Return to a simmer and cook
for about 40 mins, or until the seaweed
has dissolved. Take off the heat and allow
to cool a little then pour into a bowl and
allow to cool completely. Place in the
refrigerator to chill (it will set) and serve
with honey and cream.

The above recipe can be converted for
other fruit and flowers (eg elderflower).

Autumn Pudding (traditional British)

Ingredients:
10 bread slices (can be a little old), milk,
600g mixed autumn wild fruits – eg wild
plum and sloes (stoned), crab apples, wild
berries, 100g honey.

De-crust the bread and moisten with milk,
reserve some for the lid then use the
rest to line the base and sides of a deep
pudding basin. The slices must overlap, or
the pudding will lose its shape. Put the fruit,
honey and a bit of water into a saucepan,
and simmer for 10 mins. Allow to cool
then pour into the pudding case, add the
bread lid and cover with a sheet of buttered
baking paper. Put a saucer on top of the
paper, and refrigerate overnight with a
weight on top of the saucer. To serve, turn
the pudding over onto a plate. Serve with
cream, ice-cream or custard

Seed pods, seeds and nuts

The next stage on from flowers, in some plants, is immature seed pods. A lot of peas and beans are domesticated examples (mange tout are the pods without seeds, garden peas are the immature seeds), and their wild relatives are similarly edible. Other examples of edible immature pods of wild plants include Ramsons and Garlic Mustard.

Mature seeds probably formed a relatively minor part of the diet of mesolithic foragers, but were a critically important part of the Neolithic Revolution. All of the earliest domesticated crops were seeds, belonging to two groups – legumes (Pea family) and grasses (starting with Wheats and Barleys). These domesticated varieties had larger seeds than their wild ancestors, making them much more attractive as food. Harvesting the wild seeds was usually fiddly hard work, and both cultivated and wild forms require processing (separating seed from chaff, then grinding into flour) before they can be cooked and eaten. In a few cases the seeds just happen to occur in a form that makes their collection relatively easy.

There are also quite a lot of seeds whose primary use is as spices rather than to provide nutrition, and of particular interest in this respect is the Carrot family, both in terms of domesticated and wild varieties. Most members of this family have relatively large and easily collected seeds, and they tend to be aromatic as a protection against predation (which doesn't work very well on humans, although this hasn't done those species harm in terms of their survival).

As a general rule, seeds are best left to ripen and dry on the plant, as this is when they are most nutritious and flavourful, but again there are exceptions (eg green Hogweed seeds). Some seeds have to be soaked before they are eaten, and there's just a handful which are eaten as they start sprouting. Beansprouts and Alfalfa are the most obvious domesticated examples, and some of their wild relatives are also edible as sprouts (eg Clover). Other wild seeds eaten in this way include various members of the Cabbage family, and Buckwheat (which is related to Docks, not Wheat).

Nuts are a special case within the category of seeds, providing impressive amounts of protein and fat for the amount of work required to collect them (according to Claire Loewenfeld, we should think of them as 'miniature eggs') – although cracking or shelling them to get access to the edible parts can be a challenge. They fit in the same nutritional space as meat, fish and eggs, and the only other vegetable foods that can compete are pulses. Nuts can often be eaten raw, otherwise roasted, ground into flour, or pressed to make edible oils.

Trees: bark, sap and gum

Some trees have edible inner bark ('cambium'). This should only be used in an emergency, or if the tree is being cut down anyway, because stripping the cambium causes long-term damage to the tree, and could kill it. It can be chewed raw but is better boiled, fried, or ground into a flour substitute. It should be used in moderation – eating too much is likely to cause bowel upsets. The outer bark of some trees can also be used to make tea, but be aware that some trees have poisonous bark. Certain trees can be tapped in spring to collect the rising sap, which is a very dilute sugar solution, also rich in other nutrients. The most famous of these are Birch and Maples (including Sycamore). A few plants, mainly trees, exude an edible gum (see p232).

Preservation techniques

Lactofermenting

Lactofermenting uses 'good' bacteria such as Lactobacillus to break down sugars in food and make lactic acid. This creates an acidic, low-oxygen environment, which combined with the addition of salt, discourages bad bacteria and mould. There are two main kinds of lactofermenting: self-brining, where you shred and rub leaves with salt until the juice comes out (eg sauerkraut); and brine-based, where you submerge roots, bulbs or stems in a salt brine (eg dill pickles).

The simplest ferment is sauerkraut, made by massaging cabbage leaves with salt and packing them into sterilised jars. It's easy to add herbs, wild greens or seaweed to the cabbage to create your own blend – Garlic Mustard, Nettles and Wild Garlic all work well, and the possibilities are endless. For more solid items you'll need to make a salt brine (proportions vary from 2% to 5%).

How long to ferment your creation at room temperature is a matter of taste, climate and debate – anything from 2 days to a month. You'll definitely want to follow a recipe to start with, which will come with a recommended fermentation period. It can then be kept in a fridge (or root cellar) for several months.

Pickling

Pickling works by submerging food in vinegar, creating an acidic environment where few bacteria can survive. Many vinegars can be used – apple cider, white wine and rice vinegars are popular choices. Pickled foods can be stored in a fridge for up to two months. For longer storage at room temperature, you need to process them using a water bath or pressure canner.

There are thousands of recipes out there, to be explored and adapted. Many of these work along a similar theme: arrange your food in clean jars, often with herbs and flavourings; make a brine of vinegar, water, salt and sugar; bring it to a boil; then pour it into the jars and seal them.

Pickling provides an opportunity to create interesting mixtures. A mixed wild spring pickle could include flower buds (Gorse, Ramsons, Dandelion), stems (Sea Kale, Alexanders), roots (Burdock) and tubers (Lesser Celandine), in vinegar flavoured with aromatic wild seeds stored from the previous autumn (Fennel, Hogweed, Alexanders, Mustards), leaves (Bay) and even roots (Wood Avens).

Drying

There are various methods of drying plants, and often the most appropriate depends on how juicy your foraged fare is, and the time of year. Whatever method you use, make sure your food is completely dry before storing it in clean jars. For herbs that means they will be brittle, for fruits, slightly pliable.

Dehydrators are widely available and give reliable results. You can also dry things with your oven on low heat (50°C or below), in an airing cupboard or above a wood burner. In hot, sunny weather, many items can be sun-dried – hang seaweed from your washing line or spread leaves out on screens. You may need to use mesh or cheesecloth to keep flies off.

Poisonous plants

If you're collecting wild plants for food then it is important to also know the most poisonous ones – it is the best way to avoid making a dangerous mistake. Some plants are of variable toxicity. In some cases they become toxic as a defence mechanism when under attack (from specific pests). Others vary according to season, or local genetic differences, and sometimes there is no known reason for the variability. The effect of toxic plants on non-human animals is often variable. It is also the case that some of the most poisonous species are also the most effective medicines. In such cases, dosage is absolutely critical. Effective medical herbalism also requires extensive and detailed knowledge of human physiology and ailments, and is outside the scope of my expertise and this book.

Common plant toxins

The largest group of plant toxins/medicines are the **alkaloids**. These are nitrogen compounds, mostly bases (compounds that can neutralise acids). The most important in terms of plant toxicity are the **pyrrolizidine alkaloids**, many of which are hepatotoxins, causing liver cancer and other diseases. Other types of alkaloids include drugs such as nicotine and cocaine. Plants produce these substances as a defence against predation by herbivores.

Glycosides are compounds consisting of a sugar and something else – usually something chemically active. They are used by plants as a means of storing the non-sugar component in an inactive form. The sugar can be broken off, releasing the active component, many of which are important medicines. There are two important groups in terms of plant toxicity. The first are the cardiac glycosides, which are used as heart medicines but cause heart failure if the dose is too large. The second are the cyanogenic glycosides, which are metabolised into potentially deadly cyanide.

Tannins are a class of large organic molecules which are reactive and flexible enough to form molecular complexes with other types of large organic molecule, including starch and cellulose, but especially with proteins, which they can bind. They are generally detrimental to food quality (though not always, such as in the case of red wines), and many are toxic, though generally not dangerous unless consumed in great quantity.

Oxalic acid ($C_2H_2O_4$) is a strong acid. It occurs in many plants, and ingestion causes weakness, breathing difficulties, gastrointestinal problems, potentially coma and death in extreme cases. Oxalates (which are derived from Oxalic Acid) are an 'anti-nutrient' (they bind to other nutrients, thus depriving the body of them). Oxalates can be reduced by cooking, especially boiling (steaming is less effective, roasting least effective of all).

Coumarin ($C_9H_6O_2$) is an aromatic, benzene-like compound, structurally similar to the potent drug warfarin. It tastes bitter, and is an appetite suppressant, both of which are deterrents to herbivores, but it also has a sweet and pleasant vanilla-like odour which has led to many plants that contain it being used as flavouring as well as air-fresheners. Coumarin also inhibits vitamin K synthesis.

DEADLY PLANTS

Autumn Crocus or Meadow Saffron (*Colchicum autumnale*): contains colchicine, capable of causing severe gastric symptoms, followed by multiple organ failure (p82).

Bracken (*Pteridium aquilinum*): contains carcinogenic ptaquiloside (p88).

Castor Oil Plant (*Ricinus communis*): beans contain ricin – an extremely toxic protein synthesis inhibitor (p176).

Cowbane (*Cicuta virosa*): roots contain cicutoxin – a potentially lethal nervous system stimulant, structrually related to oenanthotoxin (p469).

Daffodil (*Narcissus*): bulbs cause severe gastric symptoms and occasionally death (p126).

Daphne (**Spurge Laurel** and **Mezereon**) berries cause burning to the soft tissues of mouth and throat, followed by coma and death (p310).

Deadly Nightshade (*Atropa belladonna*) and related members of the *Solanaceae*, including *Datura*: contain tropane alkaloids. All parts are toxic, causing a long list of unpleasant symptoms including cardiac and respiratory failure (p419).

False Hellebore (*Veratrum species*): contains powerful steroidal alkaloids capable of causing cardiac arrest (p116).

Foxglove (*Digitalis purpurea*): all parts contain glycosides capable of causing cardiac arrest (p394).

Goat's Rue (*Galega officinalis):* historically used as food for both humans and animals, but now known to contain toxins that interfere with blood sugar levels and can cause a variety of unpleasant symptoms. It was once used as a herbal treatment for diabetes (p186).

Hemlock (*Conium maculatum*): contains coniine, which causes paralysis and death by respiratory failure (p470).

Hemlock Water-dropwort (*Oenanthe crocata*): contains oenanthotoxin, especially in the roots (one root can kill a cow) (p468).

Henbane (*Hyoscyamus niger*): contains tropane alkaloids (see Deadly Nightshade), though not usually fatal (p417).

Herb-paris (*Paris quadrifolia*): contains skin and gastric irritants, but at least one death is recorded (p116).

Laburnum **species:** all parts are poisonous, especially the seeds. Causes a long list of symptoms, including potentially coma and death (p185).

Larkspur (*Delphinium/Consolida* species): contain alkaloids that cause gastric symptoms, and paralysis leading to death by respiratory failure (p150).

Lily of the Valley (*Convallaria majalis*): contains glycosides capable of causing cardiac arrest (p122).

Monk's-hood, Wolfsbane and other *Aconitum* species: contain aconitine, which cause burning, vomiting and nerve disruption, leading to cardiac arrest (p152).

Privet (*Ligustrum* species): berries and leaves contain syringin, causing gastric and nervous symptoms, and potentially death (p415).

Rhubarb (*Rheum* spp.): green parts cause nervous disorders, coma and potentially death (p318).

Spindle (*Euonymus europaeus*): contains various alkaloids (including caffeine), and causes liver and kidney damage, and potentially death (p174).

White Bryony (*Bryonia alba*): 40 berries will kill a human, causing respiratory failure (p263).

Yew (*Taxus baccata*): all parts apart from the soft, red bits of the 'berries' contain potentially lethal taxine (p98).

Ferns

Ferns (taxonomic class *Polypodiopsida*) are non-flowering vascular plants that produce spores. 'Vascular' means they are composed of types of tissue called xylem (for structure) and phloem (for nutrient and water transportation), which allows them to grow much larger than algae and mosses. Modern-looking versions had appeared by 150 million years ago, and there are currently over 9,000 species globally.

Ferns have been very widely used as a food source in the past, and in some parts of the world they still are, although there are safety concerns. These first came to light in 1860-61 when a group of explorers in Australia died after repeatedly consuming a fern called Nardoo (*Marsilea drummondii*), although the precise cause of their death is a matter of historical and scientific dispute. The Aboriginal people prepared these Ferns by grinding them in water to make a flour paste, which was left to soak for at least a day before being made into soup or bread. The explorers failed to realise that this process was leaching out a chemical belonging to a class of anti-nutrients now known as thiaminases – enzymes which break down vitamin B1. Consumption of significant quantities leads to vitamin B1 deficiency, and the potentially fatal disease beriberi. Thiaminases are present in the Ferns as a deterrent to predation, especially by insects. Some thiaminases are broken down by heating, so raw Ferns should definitely be avoided.

▾ Field Horsetail spore-bearing shoots

Equisitales
Equisitaceae (Horsetail family)

Horsetails are relatives of the most ancient plants that ever stood upright on the Earth's surface. Many of them produce their spores at the end of specialised non-photosynthetic shoots that appear before any of the main, photosynthetic growth. They do not resemble other Ferns, but have grooved, upright stems and smaller stem-like structures in place of leaves.

Horsetails (*Equisetem*)

Field Horsetail (*E. arvense*) is a perennial spore-bearing cryptophyte (it dies back to the ground each winter). It is rather variable, with segmented stems up to 90cm tall and 5mm in diameter, and whorls of single-veined side shoots in place of normal leaves. It produces non-photosynthetic spore-bearing stems in early spring, which are usually gone before the appearance of the vegetative shoots, which in turn can be found until the first frosts. Native, inhabiting woodland, grassland, gardens (can be hard to eradicate), disturbed ground and roadsides, usually in damp or wet locations. Common throughout the British Isles and most of the northern temperate zone.

Nearly all parts of Horsetails are poisonous raw, due to their thiaminase content. Cooked, they have been widely used as food, although the only parts that are really worth collecting are the very young spore-bearing shoots and unopened vegetative buds (peeled, in both cases). The spores themselves soon become bitter, but these are easy to scrape off with a knife. The rest of the young shoot is sweet.

In Japan, these young spore-bearing shoots are used to make Tsukudani (p49). The roots are a famine food and Norwegian and Faroese children traditionally collected and ate (raw) the nodules attached to the rhizomes of this species (which aren't always present – I couldn't find any). It is inadvisable to eat large quantities of Horsetails, though they are all considerably more dangerous to cattle, horses and other herbivores than they are to humans. Horsetails contain up to 10% silicates, and so can be used as a sort of natural scourer, to polish hardwoods, brass and pewter (a historic name is 'pewterwort'). They are also claimed to have anti-fungal properties, but by far their most popular use has been, and still is, as a medicinal tea or tincture, claimed to be effective for a wide range for disorders.

▾ Field Horsetail vegetative shoots

Polypodiales

Polypodiales is the largest order of modern Ferns, most of which have 'fiddleheads' – which is the name of the unfurled frond. The fiddleheads of some species have been traditionally eaten, especially in south-east Asia and North America. They are collected when the head is still tightly curled, attached to about 5cm of uncurled stem, and the papery brown 'chaff' should be removed before cooking. They will keep for two weeks in a fridge, but are best used fresh, and should remain crisp even after cooking.

Ferns in this order can be confused with deadly umbellifers (p468). The main difference, apart from the fact that umbellifers have flowers and seeds, is that fern fronds all sprout from the base of the plant, whereas umbellifers have shoots and leaves branching sideways from upright or arching stems. Ferns also have brown spore cases (large brown dots) on the underside of their fronds.

Maidenhair Fern (*Adiantum capillus-veneris*), of the family *Pteridaceae*, is much more common in the southern hemisphere, and tropical/Mediterranean climates than in temperate Europe, where it is better known as a houseplant. It has traditionally been used to make a tea that is reputed to be a uterine stimulant, and therefore should be avoided by pregnant women.

Hart's-tongue Fern (*Asplenium scolopendrium*), of the family *Aspleniaceae*, is easily recognised by its undivided fronds. Common in temperate Europe (and often planted in gardens), its fiddleheads are eaten, boiled and buttered, by foraging professionals Marcus Harrison and Robin Harford, on the grounds that there was historical food use and no evidence of poisoning. They may well be correct to believe it is edible, but personally I don't eat these ferns or recommend their consumption.

▾ Maidenhair Fern

▾ Hartstongue Fern

Polypodiaceae
Common Polypody (*Polypodium vulgare*)

Common Polypody has a horizontal rhizome from which individual evergreen fronds extend 10-50cm. The fronds are divided into up to 20 leaflets, which become much shorter at the end of the frond, and wider at their base, usually touching. They are asymmetrical, one side slightly offset from the other. It is frequent throughout western Europe, in damp, shady places. Hard Fern (*Blechnum spicant*) looks rather similar, and is of unknown edibility, but is easily distinguished by the bland-tasting root. This fern has an intensely sweet-tasting root that contains significant amounts of sucrose and glucose, as well as a saponin called osladin, which is 500 times sweeter than sucrose. It also has a slightly nauseating smell. It is reminiscent of liquorice, and sweetest in the spring. It can be chewed either fresh or dried, though the taste is overpowering and lingers for hours. These Ferns have typically been used more medicinally (for cold and flu symptoms) than as food, like a sort of natural cough lozenge. Polypody makes a first-class flavouring for vodka. Just peel and chop up some root, and leave it in the vodka for a couple of weeks, turning it over every now and then. Miles Irving's suggestion of chopping and using to flavour ice-cream also works well. I can find no information on the edibility of the roots of the very similar Western and Southern Polypody (*P. interjectum* and *cambricum*) and have never found them. The fiddleheads of these species are not edible.

Dennstaedtiaceae
Common Bracken (*Pteridium aquilinum*) ☠

"The writer can bear testimony to the
nutritive qualities of the rhizomes of our
native Brake, having frequently eaten them
in considerable quantities. They should first
be roasted over a fire until the outer skin
is charred, and then the fibres separated
by beating; the starchy substance that
remains tastes much like oat cake, but with
a slight astringency that is not unpleasant.
Few substances will keep off hunger during
violent exertion than the underground
stem of the Brake thus prepared, a fact
worth remembering by the rambler in
uninhabited districts."
(C Pierpoint Johnson, 1862)

Bracken is a perennial cryptophyte with
large, feathery fronds up to 250cm tall,
becoming hollow, and whorls of single-
veined side shoots in place of normal
leaves. Inhabits moorland, open woodland
and other places below 600m. Common
throughout Europe, apart from northern
Scandinavia, and abundant everywhere in
the British Isles. 'Bracken' properly refers to
the whole genus *Pteridium*, which contains
at least 10 species previously just known as
P. aquilinum. From a foraging point of view
they are all the same.

As well as being traditionally consumed
in the western world, noodles made from
Bracken roots are commercially available in
China. There is growing concern over their
safety. Consumption causes a decline in
bone marrow activity, leading to anaemia,
and along with thiaminase Bracken contains
another toxin called ptaquiloside. This
is now known to cause cancers of the
digestive system, and is believed to be the

▲ Bracken fiddleheads

explanation for the high incidence of those
cancers in Japan, where bracken fiddleheads
are a popular food. Ptaquiloside originating
in Bracken and ending up in water supplies
and cow's milk is now also suspected to be
responsible for cancer hotspots in the UK.

Dryopteridaceae (Buckler-fern family)
Male Ferns (*Dryopteris*)   (!)

Male Fern (*D. filix-mas*) is a semi-deciduous perennial with bipinnate leaves up to 1.5m, and tapering at both ends (so the leaflets are longest in the centre of the leaves). The stalks have rust-coloured scales. It is common throughout temperate Europe, usually in damp woodland, sometimes on rocks or roadsides. It has many relatives, and distinguishing them isn't easy.

Edibility information for this species is conflicting. Several sources quoted by Plants for a Future describe both the fiddleheads and rhizomes as edible, Edmund Launert[*] tells us that Bracken (now confirmed as toxic) is the only edible European fern, and that Male Fern is an effective treatment for tapeworms, but that great care must be taken when using it because "even a small overdose can lead to poisoning or blindness". I can find reliable evidence[†] that Male Fern has caused blindness in cattle, but not humans. The Ministry of Agriculture, Fisheries and Food[‡] tells us that the toxins in this plant are found in the stem bases and rhizomes (not the fiddleheads), but poisoning is only recorded in cattle. If you are going to eat this species, it should be blanched for a couple of minutes then served with butter.

Male Fern hybridises with the very similar **Scaly Male Fern (*D. oreades*)** and **Mountain Male Fern (*D. affinis*)**. **Lady Fern (*Athyrium filix-femina*)** was once thought to be the 'female version' of Male Fern (it is smaller and a paler green). There is no clear, reliable information about the edibility of any of them.

▲ Scaly Male Fern fiddleheads

[*] *Edible and Medicinal Plants of Britain and Europe*, Launert, E, 1981, Hamlyn.
[†] *Food Animal Practice*, Anderson, D, and Rings, M, 2009. Section by Miller, P E, pp441-445.
[‡] *Poisonous Plants and Fungi*, UK Ministry of Agriculture, Fisheries and Food, 1988.

Onocleaceae
Ostrich Fern (*Matteuccia struthiopteris*) ⚠

Ostrich Fern is a perennial cryptophye with sterile fronds to 1.8m that taper short to the tip and long to the base, and so resembling ostrich feathers. The fertile fronds are much shorter, brown when mature, and overwinter to release spores in spring. The smooth stems are distinctively grooved and covered by a papery substance that easily rubs off. The plant is colony-forming, and is usually found on riverbanks and other locations liable to flooding. Native and common in much of central and northern Europe, but not to western Europe. Introduced to Britain as an ornamental in 1760, naturalised since 1834, but still more likely to be planted in the British Isles than growing wild. Populations are present in Wales, Scotland and north-west England.

This species is a favourite of North American foragers, and considered a delicacy in Japan ('kogomi'). The fiddleheads are in season in the middle of spring. It causes gastric problems if insufficiently cooked, and should be steamed for 15 minutes.

Gymnosperms

The unranked clade of gymnosperms were the first plants to have seeds. The name means 'naked seed', and they characteristically lack both flowers and fruits. The descendants of these early seed-bearing plants are today's conifers and cycads, along with a group of strange tropical/southern plants called gnetophytes, and the oddity below.

Ginkgoales / Ginkgoaceae

Maidenhair Tree (*Ginkgo biloba*)

The **Maidenhair Tree** is a true 'living fossil' (from 270mya), and the only species in its phylum (*Ginkgophyta*). It is a deciduous tree with very distinctive leaves, and can grow to over 40m. The oldest individuals are claimed to be 2,500 years old, and the tree is now believed to have no built-in senescence – it continually renews itself, and its biological systems will just keep going. No existing population is confirmed to be wild, so its native range is unknown (though includes parts of China), but its future is secure due to its ornamental popularity. It is dioecious and males are preferred, grown from cuttings so their sex is known. This is because the female trees produce fruit-like structures ('sarcotesta') which stink (think concentrated artificial cheese flavouring), presumably to attract some long extinct animal to disperse the seeds. Unfortunately for foragers, it's the sarcotesta that we're after. The seeds, once safely removed from their malodorous fleshy coating (which must be done carefully, because it can also cause skin irritation), are much esteemed in China and Japan. Always cooked, they are used like nuts – fried or roasted they are a popular street food used in both savoury dishes and desserts. The taste is rich and almost fatty, and the texture silky smooth but slightly chewy. However, Ginkgo seeds are also slightly poisonous (more so when raw), containing cyanogenic glycosides that cause gastrointestinal symptoms, confusion and convulsions, so they should not be consumed in large quantities. The leaves are also commercially available for their alleged medicinal qualities. Ginkgo is used in alternative western medicine as a treatment for blood circulation, dementia and erectile dysfunction, although the scientific evidence of efficacy is sketchy.

Pinales

Order *Pinales* contains all the extant true conifers, as well as the yews, which used to be classed in their own order.

Araucariaceae (Monkey Puzzle family)

The *Araucariaceae* are a small and very old family of tall trees, mainly found in isolated locations and hostile conditions in the southern hemisphere.

Monkey Puzzle (*Araucaria araucana*)

Monkey Puzzle is a large tree (can exceed 40m) native to the lower slopes of the Chilean Andes but very popular in cultivation and capable of surviving in surprisingly cold and wet conditions in north-west Europe. Unmistakable and familiar, with sharp, succulent, dark green, triangular leaves, which overlap on its branches and stems to produce a near-complete covering. The species is dioecious.

The cones of mature female trees, where males are also present, contain large edible nuts. Only very rarely does a single tree carry both types of cone, but the pollen can travel several kilometres on the wind. Though it may take several decades for female trees to reach maturity, when they do their potential as a food-producing plant should not be underestimated, because yields can be enormous.

Pinaceae (Pine family) ⚠

The *Pinaceae* are a family of trees that includes most of our familiar Conifers: Pines, Spruces, Firs, Douglas Firs, Larches, Hemlocks and Cedars. The only species native to Britain is Scots Pine, but many others have been planted for ornamental and forestry purposes. Distinguishing between different species is very difficult and even figuring out which genus a Conifer belongs to isn't always easy. The only potentially serious mistake involves Yew (p98).

A syrup can be made from the young needles of all species of Pine, Fir and especially Spruce, used in drinks, jellies and sorbets, or to glaze game and other red meat. All three make good teas (both the new growth and young cones), and can be used to flavour beer and wine, such as the Greek 'retsina', and all have edible pollen, which is used as a 'superfood' additive. Foraging experimentalist Fergus Drennan particularly recommends the pollen of **Atlantic Cedar** (**Cedrus atlantica**), which he adds to honey and tahini to make a sort of halva. The cambium of most species (particularly Pines) is edible fresh, dried, roasted and ground into flour, or even fried. It doesn't taste great, but is sufficiently nutritious to warrant collecting in an emergency – rich in starch and vitamins A and C, and at its best in the spring, collected from the lower part of the trunk.

There are concerns that consumption of Conifers and some non-native Pines can cause problems during pregnancy, although the evidence comes mostly from cows rather than humans. For maximum safety avoid the whole Pine family if you are pregnant.

▸ Western Hemlock (*Tsuga heterophylla*), a popular forestry tree.

Conifer Tip Syrup

The soft young tips should be used, older growth gets a bit too resinous. Mix 1 part sugar and 1 part water (by volume) and bring to the boil, stirring to dissolve the sugar. Take off the heat (so steep rather than boil), then add 1 part conifer needles (by volume), and leave to stand for between 1 and 24 hours, depending on desired strength. Strain through a cheesecloth and optionally add lemon juice to taste. Use in cocktails (goes well with gin).

Conifer Tip Tea

Take the fresh branch tips (from the tree, never the ground), chop them up and add an optional bit of cinnamon stick. Pour on boiling water, then allow to steep for 3 or 4 mins and serve with honey. I don't add lemon, as it masks the natural lemon-like flavour of the needles.

Pines (*Pinus*)

Pines are evergreen coniferous trees up to 80m tall, becoming conical as they mature, with whorled branches and clusters of long (to 8cm), paired, blue-green needles and cones that take two years to ripen. They are particularly fond of acidic soil, and native to the northern hemisphere (though widely introduced in the south). **Scots Pine (*P. sylvestris*)** is the only species native to the British Isles, but over 40 are grown here. In lowland southern/eastern Britain **Corsican Pine (*P. nigra*)** is widely planted (it has longer needles, and no blue tinge).

The seeds of all Pine trees are edible (though the Chinese White Pine, *p. armandii*, causes an allergic reaction – 'pine mouth' – in some), but only those with particularly large seeds are of any commercial importance. None of these grow well in the temperate zones of Europe but **Stone Pine (*P. pinea*)** is common/naturalised throughout the Mediterranean south. Pines produce both male and female cones, both of which provide food. The very young male cones are edible raw when they first emerge, and work well in a salad with tomatoes and cucumber. They soon become too spongey and dry to eat, but they then produce vast amounts of pollen, though you need to get the timing right. If the cones are still green then the pollen isn't ready yet, and if they are brown then you are too late. It is easily collected by shaking the cones inside a bag or large tupperware, without removing them from the tree. It must then be finely sieved. This is touted as a superfood, although insufficient research has been done to establish how nutritious or medicinally valuable it actually is. The immature (still green and slightly flexible) female cones are used to make jams and syrups. These female cones are considerably harder to get hold of than the male ones. There are fewer of them, and they grow higher on the tree (minimising self-pollination). If you're after female cones then try a young tree, or one growing on a steep slope.

Pine has many reputed medical properties. It is antiseptic, used in baths for healing cuts, but especially used to make cough remedies. In Russia and Georgia this medicine takes the form of 'jam' (actually more like honey), and the recipe also works for Spruce and Fir.

Pine Cone Syrup/Jam (traditional eastern European)

This is perhaps best described as pine cone honey, after its consistency – it does not set. If you want to make it into something more jammy and nutritious then add some carragheen (p64) along with the sugar. It is delicious – unlike anything else I've tasted and certainly not some foul-tasting 'medicine'. Best served on white toast. Our daughter went mad for it aged 2, not just devouring the toast but sucking and chewing the cones too. The recipe also works with larch cones, which taste very similar but have a richer colour.

Ingredients:

Female pine cones, sugar, optional carragheen (seaweed), water.

Wash the cones in cold water, then place in a saucepan and fill with water so it covers the cones with 2cm to spare (they float, so the 2cm is at the bottom). Bring to the boil, then reduce the heat, cover and simmer for 30 mins. Then leave in a dark place for at least 12 hours to infuse. Strain the liquid. Set aside a few of the best looking cones, then squeeze the others to extract as much flavour-rich liquid as possible. Mix the liquid 1:1 with sugar (so if you have 1 litre of liquid, add 1kg of sugar), and 20g dried carragheen per 1 litre of liquid if you want it to set. Then cook the syrup over a low heat until it goes dark red and has the consistency of a thick, runny honey. Finally add the reserved cones and simmer for another 5 mins, and pour into sterilised jars.

▸ Young female (left) and male (top) pine cones, at the stage where they can be used in jam and salad respectively.

Pine Pollen Biscuits

Use a basic shortbread recipe and substitute in pine pollen for some of the flour – you can use it in the icing, too.

Ingredients:

125g butter, 55g caster sugar, 160g flour, 20g pine pollen. If icing: 125g icing sugar, 15ml warm water, pine pollen to dust.

Beat the butter and sugar together, add the flour and pollen, roll it out and cut into shapes. Chill in the fridge for 20 mins then bake at 180°C / fan 160°C for 15 mins. Mix icing ingredients together, and when biscuits are cool, add a thin layer of icing then sprinkle on pine pollen before it sets.

Spruce (*Picea spp.*) ⓘ

Spruce are coniferous trees up to 60m tall, becoming conical as they mature, with whorled branches, needles arranged in spirals around the shoots/branches, and hanging cones. The species most frequently planted in the British Isles are the **Norway Spruce (*P. abies*)** – the traditional British 'Christmas Tree' – and the **Sitka Spruce (*P. sitchensis*)**. Over 20 species are grown in northern Europe.

Various parts of Spruce have been used as food, but none of them have ever been very popular in Europe, and are better known as famine foods. The young shoots are the best parts, nibbled raw, pickled, or used to decorate cakes and make tea or beer. They can be used in place of rosemary in any recipe, as a herb in salad dressings, or finely chopped into a crumble topping. The seeds can be pressed for their oil and the roasted insides of the female cones have been used for food, but provide scant reward for the effort required. The very young cones can be eaten in an emergency, but the taste is overpowering. The cambium (inner bark) is used to make cheese moulds (strips of it are tied around a runny ripening cheese, holding it together).

There are reports that some people have a strong allergic reaction to Spruce.

Larches (*Larix*) ⓘ

Larch are deciduous conifers to 45m tall, with dense clusters of very short, fine needles and small, erect cones. They dominate parts of the boreal north, but are restricted in the wild to high altitudes further south. The young shoots are edible in salads, and the young female cones can be used to make jam (see p95). Contains galactose, which can cause problems for people with lactose intolerance.

▾ Spruce tips

▲ Fresh Larch shoots and young red cones

Pickled Spruce Tips

Ingredients:
230ml cider vinegar, 3 heaped tbsp honey, ½ tsp salt, ¼ tsp ground black pepper, 2 dried chillies, 60ml water, 120g rinsed spruce tips.

Pack the spruce tips in a sterilised jar. Put all the other ingredients in a saucepan and bring to the boil, then pour into the jar. Stir 3 or 4 times while it cools, making sure all the tips are submerged. Seal and store in a fridge or cellar. Use in salad dressings.

Spruce Tip Crumble Topping

Ingredients:
100g plain flour, 100g butter, 100g sugar, 50g chopped spruce tips.

Combine the plain flour, sugar and spruce tips in a bowl. Add the diced butter and rub into the flour mix with your fingertips, until the mixture resembles coarse crumbs. Refrigerate for 30 mins before using as a crumble topping.

▼ Young (green) and old Larch cones

Taxaceae (Yew family)
Yew (*Taxus baccata*)

Yew is an evergreen tree up to 20m with flattened, needle-like leaves and modified cones that look like red berries (on female trees only). They are native to most of Europe and reasonably common in the British Isles apart from highland areas, and particularly at home on the steep chalk slopes and limestone cliffs in England. The most similar species are other types of *Taxus*, most of which aren't present in Europe, and those that do occur are of the same foraging relevance as *T. baccata*. Some other conifers have superficially similar leaves.

Nearly the entire tree is extremely toxic, including the dried foliage. Early symptoms of taxine poisoning include vomiting, dizziness and seizures, followed by cardiac and respiratory problems which can be fatal. Worryingly, sometimes the more serious effects, including death, can occur without any previous symptoms. Many other animals are similarly affected.

The flesh of the 'berries', which are actually part of a modified cone known as an 'aril', are edible (usually appearing in autumn). They are sweet and sticky, and make an excellent topping for a pie, tart or cheesecake, or wayside treat. However, great care must be taken to remove (or spit out) the toxic seeds. Some birds are able to safely eat the whole berries, but this is only possible because they cannot digest the seeds. The human digestive system *can* break down the seed coating, so they must not be eaten, even if they are not chewed.

Cupressales
Cupressaceae (Cypress family)

The *Cupressaceae* are a family of coniferous shrubs and trees that include the junipers and redwoods. Common Juniper, one of only three native British conifers, is the only European species of foraging interest.

Juniper (*Juniperus communis*)

Juniper is a coniferous shrub or small tree, sometimes spreading across the ground but capable of growing to 10m. It has needle-like leaves in triplets and inhabits rocky moorland, chalk downland, and old Pine woodland. Also grown as an ornamental. The blue-black cones resemble, and are usually referred to as, berries. It is not as common in Britain as it once was, and is now hard to find in the wild outside its strongholds in the northern half of Scotland, the far north of England and some parts of central southern England. Also present throughout northern temperate and boreal zones. There are no similar species in Europe.

Juniper berries can be nibbled raw, but are best known as the flavouring for gin (the name of which comes from the French for Juniper: 'genievre'). They also work as a spice, or in a sauce, sauerkraut or marinade, with strong-flavoured meats, especially game. You can just rub them into joints of lamb and other meats before roasting. They should only be used when ripe (purplish-blue), as they are unpleasantly bitter when unripe (green). Juniper wood is used in meat smoking/curing.

Juniper is not safe for pregnant or breastfeeding women.

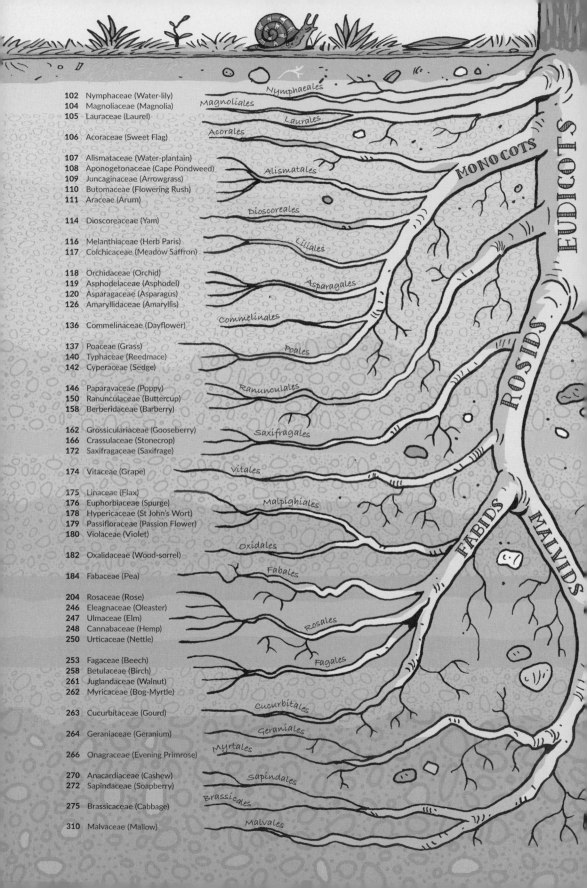

Nymphaeales
Magnoliales
Laurales
Acorales
Alismatales
Dioscoreales
Liliales
Asparagales
Commelinales
Poales
Ranunculales
Saxifragales
Vitales
Malpighiales
Oxidales
Fabales
Rosales
Fagales
Cucurbitales
Geraniales
Myrtales
Sapindales
Brassicales
Malvales

MONOCOTS
EUDICOTS
ROSIDS
FABIDS
MALVIDS

Flowering Plants (Angiosperms)

The angiosperms are a diverse group of over 300,000 (mostly) terrestrial plants, distinguished by their flowers, fruits and endosperm within their seeds. All three of these structures are important food-wise – it is the endosperm that contains most of the nutritional value in seed crops. The group contains the overwhelming majority of plants cultivated to feed humans and livestock, the most important being the grasses (*Poaceae*) and legumes (*Fabaceae*), followed by the Rose (*Rosaceae*), Cabbage (*Brassicaceae*) and Carrot (*Apiaceae*) families, plus two families with few native European members: Nightshade (*Solanaceae*) and Gourd (*Cucurbitaceae*).

Until quite recently, they were split into two large groups: monocotyledons, with one seed leaf, and dicotyledons, with two. Genetics proved the monocots were a clade. They typically have long, thin leaves, frequently have no stem, and include grasses, palms and many familiar bulbs, although the oldest lineages are aquatic. The dicots turned out to be paraphyletic, and some very ancient groups were removed to leave a clade called 'eudicots'.

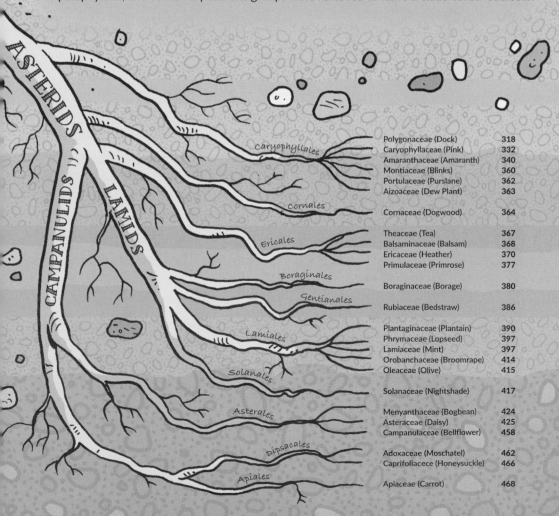

Caryophyllales	
Polygonaceae (Dock)	318
Caryophyllaceae (Pink)	332
Amaranthaceae (Amaranth)	340
Montiaceae (Blinks)	360
Portulaceae (Purslane)	362
Aizoaceae (Dew Plant)	363
Cornales	
Cornaceae (Dogwood)	364
Ericales	
Theaceae (Tea)	367
Balsaminaceae (Balsam)	368
Ericaceae (Heather)	370
Primulaceae (Primrose)	377
Boraginales	
Boraginaceae (Borage)	380
Gentianales	
Rubiaceae (Bedstraw)	386
Lamiales	
Plantaginaceae (Plantain)	390
Phrymaceae (Lopseed)	397
Lamiaceae (Mint)	397
Orobanchaceae (Broomrape)	414
Oleaceae (Olive)	415
Solanales	
Solanaceae (Nightshade)	417
Asterales	
Menyanthaceae (Bogbean)	424
Asteraceae (Daisy)	425
Campanulaceae (Bellflower)	458
Dipsacales	
Adoxaceae (Moschatel)	462
Caprifoliacece (Honeysuckle)	466
Apiales	
Apiaceae (Carrot)	468

ASTERIDS

CAMPANULIDS

LAMIIDS

Nymphaeales

A Water-lily-like plant called Watershield (*Brasenia schreberi*), grown for food in China, is the only other notable member of this order, which is the most ancient group of angiosperms.

Nymphaeaceae (Water-lily family)
The *Nymphaeaceae* are a family of rhizomatous aquatic plants with large floating leaves, and solitary blooms of flowers, widespread in temperate and tropical zones globally.

Yellow Water-lily (*Nuphar lutea*)

Yellow Water-lily is an aquatic herb, rooted in submerged soil, with radially notched sub-circular floating leaves and yellow flowers. The leaves appear in the spring, the flowers in early summer, the seeds ripening in late summer and early autumn. It inhabits still or slow-moving fresh water, sometimes over 1m deep, present throughout temperate Europe and common in the British Isles. **Least Water-lily (*N. pumila*)** is closely related, but rare outside the northern half of Scotland. Fringed Water-lily (p424) is an unrelated edible plant, most easily distinguished by the different leaf veins.

Most parts of Yellow Water-lily can be eaten at some point in its life cycle, and it was once an important food source for Native Americans. The unripe yellow seeds are very bitter, becoming less so as they mature. They were traditionally roasted, winnowed and ground into a powder for thickening soups. The pods were left in water to rot for three weeks, releasing enzymes that allegedly removed all traces of bitterness. The fleshy roots have also been described as edible, but they are loaded with bitter tannins.

White Water-lily (*Nymphaea alba*)

White Water-lily is similar to Yellow Water-lily, but with white flowers and a preference for slightly deeper water, and only unpolluted and boat-free habitats. Frequent across temperate Europe, including most of Britain, though less so in the far north of England, and parts of southern and eastern Scotland.

The edible uses are very similar to Yellow Water-lily. The seeds are smaller, but just as edible, and can be popped like corn. Traditionally in Bangladesh they are fried in ghee. They taste like barley with a hint of pepper. The unopened flower buds are edible, and allegedly nutritious, but bitter. The thick underwater stems, connecting the roots to floating leaves and flowers, can be up to 2m long.

These stems are considered something of a delicacy in some parts of northern Europe. The fibrous skin must be removed before cooking, by making a slit and peeling. In India (especially Bengal) and Bangladesh, Water-lily ('Shapla') flower stems are made into fritters or curried, usually with prawns.

**Shapla Fritters
(adapted from traditional Bengali)**

Ingredients:
Water-lily stems, 6tbsp gram flour (or half rice flour), pinch of turmeric, one chopped onion, 2 garlic cloves chopped (or paste), 1 green chilli and/or 1tsp chilli powder/paste, ¼tsp baking soda, ground cumin, nigella seeds and salt to taste.

Peel the stems and chop into 2-3cm sections. Mix the rest of the ingredients well then coat the stems and fry clumps of 3-4 sections, each side is done when it goes golden brown.

Magnoliales

Nutmeg, Pawpaw and Custard Apples belong to this ancient order of flowering plants, the members of which are typically found in tropical and subtropical lowland forests.

Magnoliaceae (Magnolia family)

Along with the Magnolias, this family includes Tulip Trees (*Liriodendron*), which were traditionally used by Native Americans for making dug-out canoes.

Magnolia

Magnolia is a genus of over 200 shrubs and small trees that are native to south-east Asia and the Americas, but widely planted as ornamentals. Their flowers, which appear in spring, usually before the leaves, have a sour, peppery, ginger-cardamom flavour, which varies proportional to the depth of colour – white varieties are milder tasting. They are eaten raw in salads, infused in vinegar, pickled, made into syrup or added to honey or desserts. The leaves and bark can also be used to make a tea, or as a flavouring, like a bay leaf – especially **Sweetbay Magnolia (*M. virginiana*)**. Their strange seed pods look like they might be edible (and make nutritious bird food) but they taste bad and are slightly poisonous to humans. I can find no records of toxicity for flowers or leaves of any Magnolia. Species recorded as edible include *grandiflora*, *denudata*, *hypoleuca*, *kobus*, *mexicana*, *pterocarpa* and *soulangeana*, as well as *virginiana*.

▾ Chinese Magnolia (*M. soulangeana*) – the most frequently planted Magnolia in the British Isles.

Laurales
Lauraceae (Bay Laurel family)

The *Lauraceae* are a family of mainly tropical/subtropical plants which include among their number Cinnamon (*Cinnamomum*) and Avocado (*Persea americana*).

Bay Laurel (*Laurus nobilis*)

Bay Laurel (or just 'Bay') is an evergreen tree to 18m, with smooth, hairless leaves, tiny yellow flowers and shiny black berries. It is native to the Mediterranean region, but widely planted elsewhere as an ornamental and a source of spices. Naturalised in parts of the British Isles, especially on coastal scrub and cliffs, but usually found planted.

Whole Bay leaves need no introduction as a cooking ingredient, and last more than a year dried. They can also be ground and used in stocks and soups, and an essential oil can be made from young leaves and stems. The berries might be better described as nuts. What looks like flesh is really a thin casing, inside which is something resembling a peanut. The related California Bay Laurel (*Umbellularia californica*) has a larger, fleshier version of this fruit, more like a miniature avocado. The seed was traditionally dried, then roasted and eaten, the flavour resembling coffee or dark chocolate. Long-roasted (European) Bay Laurel nuts taste something like unsweetened peanut-textured extra strong mints, with notes of coffee and nutmeg. They make a punchy, flavoursome coffee substitute, when finely ground and pressed through a cafetière. They are inedible raw.

This species is reputed to have narcotic effects if consumed in large quantities.

Acorales
Acoraceae (Sweet Flag family)

The *Acoraceae* are the oldest extant lineage of monocots, of which *Acorus* is the only surviving genus.

Sweet Flag (*Acorus calamus*)   (!)

Sweet Flag is a robust, aromatic, aquatic, rhizomatous perennial to 1.2m with dark green, wrinkled, grass-like leaves, a clearly defined midrib and undulating margins, which release a spicy odour when damaged. The flowers emerge between 45 and 90 degrees to the stem (like a flag). Plants in the British Isles do not develop fruits, due to a genetic problem, so only reproduce asexually. Inhabits shallow fresh water, especially near the edge of water bodies with a fluctuating level. Native to Asia, but common in northern continental Europe and southern Scandinavia. Frequent in much of England, especially Lancashire and Norfolk (where it was introduced over 400 years ago), but absent in south-west England and rare in other parts of the British Isles. What was until recently known as *A. calamus* is now known to be at least four subspecies, some of which are more widely distributed than the 'true' *A. calamus.*

The rhizome is spicy, aromatic and bitter, and can be used like ginger, or candied, chewed as a breath-freshener or roasted. It's a too much raw. The flowers and young leaves are also edible (usually raw), and Polish children traditionally ate the peeled stalks of this plant. The raw root of Asian strains is reputed to have hallucinogenic effects when chewed. 'Sweet' refers to its pleasant aroma, and it can be used to make an essential oil that has been traded for centuries, and is even mentioned in the Bible (Exodus 30:23). It has been used to flavour wine, beer and other alcoholic drinks, and also bread.

There are serious safety worries. Products derived from Sweet Flag were banned in the United States in 1968, after being found to contain a carcinogenic compound called ß-asarone, but it is not clear whether all the subspecies or strains contain this chemical, or how much. Ironically, the plant also has a long history of usage for a variety of medicinal uses.

Grass-leaved Sweet Flag (*A. gramineus*) is an Asian relative with slender, grass-like leaves, naturalised in a few parts of the British Isles, but more often found in Europe as an ornamental. It has the same edibility status.

Alismatales

The Alismatales are aquatic or semi-aquatic, and include the only angiosperms to grow fully submerged in a marine environment – the Seagrasses. They also include several types of Pondweed (*Potamogeton*) claimed to have edible starch-rich roots, but the ones I've tried didn't seem very edible to me. Some might be more edible than others.

Alismataceae (Water-plantain family)

Water-plantain (*Alisma plantago-aquatica*) is a common European species (apart from the far north) with a starch-rich root used as an emergency food, but only edible after long boiling.

Arrowhead (*Sagittaria sagittifolia*)

Arrowhead is a perennial aquatic herb with arrow-shaped leaves up to 25cm long on stalks up to 50cm above the water, elliptic floating leaves and linear submerged leaves. It has small flowers with three white petals and purple anthers, and is found in shallow, still or slow-moving water. Native and frequent in much of temperate Europe including England, rarer in the rest of the British Isles and absent in the far north. Do not confuse with the unrelated houseplant *Syngonium podophyllum*, with which it shares a common name.

Arrowhead was a food plant for Native Americans, and is still cultivated in some parts of the world, notably south-east Asia. The tubers are too bitter to eat raw but can be boiled for 20 minutes, or fried or roasted, and taste similar to potatoes. The leaves and stems are also edible, also better cooked than raw.

Two relatives, both North American natives, are grown ornamentally and naturalised in parts of the British Isles. **Duck-potato (*S. latifolia*)** is very similar, but with yellow anthers and a similarly edible tuber. **Canadian Arrowhead (*S. rigida*)** has elliptic leaves, stalkless female flowers and an edible tuber that is inferior to that of Arrowhead and Duck-potato.

Aponogetonaceae
(Cape Pondweed family)

The *Aponogetonaceae* are a family of mainly tropical and subtropical aquatic plants, many of which are popular aquarium species.

Cape Pondweed (*Aponogeton distachyos*)

Cape Pondweed is an aquatic perennial with a buried tuber, elongated oval, long-stalked leaves and forked spikes of white flowers. Found in ponds, lakes and slow-moving fresh water, this is an African native, introduced elsewhere as an ornamental pond plant and naturalised (or at least persistent) in various parts of Europe, particularly France and southern England. Rare in Scotland and Ireland. Many other aquatic species have similar leaves, but the flower spikes are very distinctive.

Cape Pondweed is cultivated in South Africa for its edible buds and flowers, which are sold both fresh and canned. They taste of vanilla and are used to make a sort of lamb stew called *waterblommetjie bredie* – literally 'water flower stew' (plenty of recipes for this can be found on the internet). They are also edible raw as a salad vegetable, as are the shoots and foliage. The tubers were traditionally eaten in southern Africa (cooked).

▲ Sea Arrowgrass

Juncaginaceae (Arrowgrass family)
Arrowgrasses (*Triglochin*)

**Marsh Arrowgrass (*T. palustris*, syn
T. palustre)** is a hairless perennial herb with
linear leaves (all basal) 15-60cm tall, deeply
grooved and distinctively aromatic when
bruised, with a spike of small, purple-and-
white flowers and club-shaped fruits. No
stolons (runners). Inhabits ponds, marshes
and wet meadows, often in upland areas
and especially on calcareous soils, also
sometimes coastal. Common in temperate
Europe, including much of the British Isles,
particularly the north, but easily missed
because it looks so much like a grass. Rarer
in southern England.

Sea Arrowgrass (*T. maritimum*) is a
robust, rhizomatous perennial or annual
herb with linear leaves (all basal), the same
height but stouter than its non-maritime
relative, fleshy rather than grooved, less
aromatic, with stolons. Inhabits marshes,
sometimes including freshwater marshes
and boggy grassland, but much more
common in saline, coastal areas. Common in
temperate coastal areas of Europe, including
the south coast of France, and present in
much of the northern hemisphere. Perhaps
more likely to be confused with Sea Plantain
(p393) than Marsh Arrowgrass.

The white base of the stems of both
species are edible, raw or cooked, and taste
like coriander. The seeds are also edible,
cooked and made into a flour or used as a
substitute for coffee.

The green parts of the plants are toxic
(containing hydrogen cyanide), especially
after droughts. It is thought that this toxicity
is also climate-related, as in more northerly
and damper areas they are less likely to
be poisonous.

Butomaceae (Flowering Rush family)

Flowering Rush (*Butomus umbellatus*)

Flowering Rush is a rhizomatous perennial aquatic herb to 1.5m with upright, unbranched stems, and twisted, pointed, linear leaves (all basal) up to 80cm long. The leafless, cylindrical flower stem is topped with a loose cluster of pink, three-petalled flowers, and the fruit is a capsule containing many seeds. Inhabits the margins of still and slow-moving water. Native, frequent and locally abundant in England and Ireland, rarer in Scotland and Wales. Frequent in most of Europe, but rare/absent in Norway and central Sweden. Could be confused with true Rushes when not flowering.

The crunchy, starchy, mucilaginous rhizome is edible after peeling and cooking, or drying and powdering to make a flour. It was historically important as a famine food, and is still collected for food in parts of Russia. It can either be peeled and boiled, changing the water once to reduce bitterness, or roasted and ground into flour.

▾ Flowering Rush

Araceae (Arum family)

The *Araceae* are primarily tropical perennials, many of which use foul odours to attract flies and other insects as pollinators. Most are poisonous and have distinctive flowers, with a large spike (the 'spadix'), surrounded by a bract (the 'spathe'). In addition to the species covered here, **Bog Arum (*Calla palustris*)** is an aquatic plant which is very toxic in its raw state, but has a rhizome that can serve as a famine food after extensive preparation (dry, grind, leach, boil). This species is common in parts of Scandinavia and north-eastern temperate Europe, but very rare in the British Isles. Several poisonous family members are popular houseplants, the most dangerous being Dumb Cane (*Dieffenbachia* spp.), which is of a similar toxicity to Lords and Ladies. It is so called because if you try eating it you will be silenced by the pain in your mouth. *Philodendron* spp., Arum Lily (*Zantedeschia* spp.) and Cheeseplant (*Monstera deliciosa*) have a similar, though less severe, effect.

▼ Fat and Rootless Duckweeds growing together.

Duckweeds (*Lemna and Wolffia*)

Duckweeds are tiny perennial floating plants, all of which are edible, though most are of minimal interest. Their appearance gives no clue they belong to this family.

Fat Duckweed (*Lemna gibba*) consists of a simple thallus up to 5mm across, swollen underside, with a single root. Inhabits still or slow-moving fresh/brackish water. Frequent in temperate Europe apart from Scandinavia, where only present in the south. Frequent in England, uncommon in Wales and Ireland, absent in Scotland apart from the Union and Forth & Clyde canals. Fat Duckweed is grown as food for both humans and livestock. The thallus is edible either raw in salads, or as a cooked vegetable. It offers a very efficient means of producing edible vegetable material.

Common Duckweed (*L. minor*) is flat.

Rootless Duckweed (*Wolffia arrhiza*) has a spherical thallus about 1mm across, with a flattish top and swollen underside, and no roots. It inhabits still fresh water such as ponds and lakes. Frequent in northern France and northern Germany and present further south in Europe, but absent further north; England only in the British Isles, native but rare, though locally common in south-east England and Somerset. This is the smallest vascular plant in the world. It contains significant amounts of carbohydrate and protein, as well as fats and a range of vitamins. It grows rapidly in the right conditions, and is used (mainly in south-east Asia) as food for humans (cooked) as well as commercially farmed shrimps, fish and chickens. It is so good at soaking up trace elements, it has even been used to clean up polluted water.

Lords and Ladies (*Arum maculatum*) ⚠

"In Switzerland, the fresh roots are used as a substitute for soap."
(C Pierpoint Johnson, 1862)

Lords and Ladies is a tuberous perennial herb, with dark green (often spotted deep purple) arrow-shaped leaves in spring, followed by a poker-shaped spike or 'spadix', inside a hood or 'spathe', which between them resemble male and female genitalia, leading to all manner of sex-related common names. Later in the year the spike is covered by a dense cluster of red berries. Inhabits woodland and other shady places; native and common in the British Isles apart from northern Scotland and far north-west Ireland; common in warmer temperate areas of Europe, rare in southern Scandinavia and the Mediterranean south. Mature leaves and flowering parts could only be confused with its larger relative **Italian Lords and Ladies (*A. italicum*)**, which is an introduced/naturalised ornamental plant in northern Europe, native to the Mediterranean region, and similarly toxic.

All parts of this plant are poisonous, and the leaves and berries contain microscopic needle-like crystals of calcium oxalate which, upon contact with the soft tissue of mouth and throat, cause immediate and intense pain and irritation. You are unlikely to swallow more than one mouthful, but by then it is already too late. Repeatedly washing your mouth with milk slightly relieves the pain, but ultimately you just have to wait a couple of days for the swelling to go away. Very young leaves, which sometimes grow in grass, can easily be mistaken for Common Sorrel (p322). Both plants have lobed leaf bases, but those of Sorrel are more pointed, and

▲ Tubers

those of Lords and Ladies are more rounded. They've also been picked by mistake when growing next to Ramsons (p132), ended up blended in the same dish, leading to the hospitalisation of the victims, who ate a considerable amount before realising their mistake. The starch-rich root can be rendered edible by long roasting, and was once even sold as 'Portland Sago', but processing this plant requires much effort for little reward, and isn't safe unless you know exactly what you are doing. It was used in Ireland during the potato famine.

As for the use of the roots as soap, they do not produce a lather, and although they are effective at cleaning your hands, they also leave them itching like a mild nettle sting (presumably caused by the same crystals that make this species so dangerous if eaten). It is not exactly a luxurious experience.

▲ Flowers

▲ Fruits

▼ Lords and Ladies (large) and Sorrel (small) growing together.

Dioscoreales
Dioscoreaceae (Yam family)

The *Dioscoreaceae* are family of tropical lianas (jungle climbers), by far the most well-known of which are the Yams (*Dioscorea*), which are cultivated for their starchy tubers.

Black Bryony (*Tamus communis*) (!)

"They are furious martial plants: roots of briony purge the belly with great violence, troubling the stomach, and burning the liver, and are therefore not rashly to be taken ..."
(Nicholas Culpeper, 1652)

Black Bryony is a climbing perennial herb with an irregular, branching blackish tuber (which is where 'black' in the name comes from) and unbranched, clockwise-twining stems up to 5m long/tall. Leaves are shaped like a playing-card spade, up to 10cm long. The small greenish-white flowers are followed by glossy red berries, which often appear to grow on the leaves of other plants. Found in woodland, hedgerows and waste ground, especially on fences. Native in the British Isles, but absent in Scotland, rare in Ireland, becoming more frequent the further south you go. Common in western and southern Europe. The berries can be confused with those of the unrelated White Bryony (p263).

Most parts of the plant are both poisonous and severe skin irritants, especially the tubers and berries, which contain calcium oxalate crystals (see previous page). Do not touch the berries

with bare hands. According to original research[*] by Ray Mears and Gordon Hillman, attempts to render the tubers edible (like yams) lose so much starch that it is nutritionally not worth the effort. Some older sources[†] claim that all you have to do is boil them! Only the young shoot tips (which are variably copper-coloured) are sufficiently free of crystals to be edible (no more than the top 15cm), and these should be well cooked. They are sold in Turkey and in some rural Spanish markets. Turkish tradition is to cook them in olive oil with spring onions, and then add eggs. In Crete they are served with béchamel sauce.

[*] *Wild Food*, Mears, R, and Hillman, G, 2008, Hodder & Stoughton.
[†] *Field Guide to the Wild Flowers of Britain*, 1981, Reader's Digest.

Liliales

There are very few edible species in the Liliales, but plenty of toxic ones. Like the lilies themselves (which are poisonous, especially to cats) their main human use is ornamental. The two families featured here have recently been moved out of the Lily family (*Liliaceae*). No European member of that family is worth eating, although the Asian native *Lilium davidii* is cultivated for its edible bulb, and tulip bulbs were eaten in the Netherlands as a famine food in 1944. They caused stomach aches, though Roger Phillips* tells us this was because they were old and shrivelled, and that the widely held belief they are toxic is a myth. Tulip flowers are edible, the darker colours having the stonger flavours.

* *The Worldwide Forager*, Phillips, R, 2020.

Melanthiaceae (Herb-paris family)

False Hellebore (*Veratrum*), which is usually found planted rather than wild in northern Europe, contains powerful steroidal alkaloids capable of causing cardiac arrest.

Herb-paris (*Paris quadrifolia*)

Herb-paris is a rhizomatous perennial herb, easily identified by its pointed-tipped, oval leaves at the top of a stem (to 40cm) that carries no other leaves (though contrary to its name, there aren't always four of these). It has a single green flower above the leaves, which develops into a black berry. Native, but mostly restricted to ancient woodlands, especially on calcareous soil in western England. Frequent in Europe, especially the west and north, but unlikely to be confused with any edible species, given its unpleasant smell and very distinctive one-berry-per-plant fruiting regime – although this berry does look a bit like a Bilberry (p373) on its own. It too contains dangerous steroidal alkaloids.

▼ Herb Paris

▼ False Hellebore

Colchicaceae (Meadow Saffron family)
Meadow Saffron (*Colchicum autumnale*) ☠

Meadow Saffron or **Autumn Crocus** is a corm-bearing perennial herb with glossy, lanceolate leaves (spring) to 30cm long and magenta to pale purple flowers produced in autumn (unlike true crocuses, which flower in spring). Native to most of Europe, but rare and protected in the British Isles. Naturally inhabits damp locations in open woodland or meadows, but also widely cultivated. Do not confuse with Saffron Crocus (*Crocus sativus*) – a Mediterranean species and the source of the spice saffron, which is sometimes also given the common name 'Autumn Crocus'.

All parts are potentially lethal, especially the seeds, which rattle in the seed head, making them attractive to children, and the corms, which have been mistaken for onions by gardeners and other edible Alliums (p126-131) by foragers. There are also cases of humans being poisoned by drinking milk from cattle that have eaten this plant. The toxins are alkaloids including colchicine, which is a useful modern drug for the treatment of gout and other conditions. Dosage is crucial and overdoses cause severe gastric symptoms, potentially followed by multiple organ failure.

▼ Saffron Crocus

▼ Autumn Crocus

Asparagales

The Irises (family *Iridaceae*) are members of this order. They are generally poisonous or inedible, although the Saffron Crocus (see previous page) is one exception and ornamental *Gladiolus* have edible flowers. Some older texts say that the seeds of Yellow Flag Iris (*Iris pseudoacorus*) can be used to make a coffee substitute, but they are also poisonous (symptoms are gastrointestinal).

Orchidaceae (Orchid family)

Orchids don't come to mind as obvious candidates for eating, given the status of many as rare and beautiful plants of conservation importance, but this huge family (upwards of 28,000 species) includes vanilla, and many other non-European species have been used as food sources.

Early Purple Orchid (*Orchis mascula*)

Early Purple Orchid is a tuberous perennial herb with green and purple stems up to 65cm high, lanceolate leaves with very obvious purple spots and splodges, and spikes of red/pink/purple flowers. Inhabits woods, grassland and other habitats, usually on calcareous soil. Frequent in western Europe, becoming rarer further east, but absent in colder parts of Scandinavia. There are many pink-purple orchids in northern Europe, but they are protected in the UK and many other European countries, so there is no foraging reason to learn how to distinguish them.

This species has tubers that occur in pairs and have been compared to testicles.

They, and the tubers of other orchids, have traditionally been used to produce a fine, pale yellow powder called Salep. This powder is used to make drinks and desserts that are still popular in Turkey and other parts of south-east Asia, to the extent that wild orchid populations there are under threat. Before the rise in popularity and affordability of imported tea and coffee, 'Saloop' was also a popular drink in England.

Asphodelaceae (Asphodel family)

This is a relatively new family comprised of genera thrown out of several other older families after DNA testing. Its name has also been changed, 'Xanthorrhoeaceae' having been deemed unpronounceable. Human uses are mainly ornamental, the best-known plants being the Red-hot Pokers (*Kniphofia*), as well the Aloes. The leaves and seeds of Aloes have sometimes been eaten when nothing else was available, though they are known to irritate the mouth and digestive system. They are much more useful for the external treatment of burns and other skin conditions.

Orange Day-lily (*Hemerocallis fulva*)

Day-lilies are perennial herbs which die back in the winter, with stems up to 1.5m tall, linear leaves up to 90cm and flowers that each last for just a single day. They naturally inhabit damp areas, especially ditches, but are capable of establishing themselves elsewhere. **Orange Day-lily** is the best known as an edible species, about 1m tall with dull orange flowers, frequent in much of temperate Europe, absent in northern Scandinavia. Frequent in southern England, particularly the south west, rarer in colder parts of the British Isles. Native to Asia but introduced widely, with invasive potential. Easily mistaken for a true Lily if you just look at the flowers, but the leaves are completely different.

The cooked young shoots, stems and leaves are a first-class alternative to asparagus. The flowers and flower buds are edible raw in salads, but are at their best fried, either as they come or as fritters in a lightly flavoured batter (you don't want to overpower the taste of the flowers).

Commercially they are dried and used in soups, especially in Chinese cuisine. The young tubers are edible raw or cooked, but not particularly tasty. Other species of Day-lily are similarly edible.

▾ Orange Day-lily

Asparagaceae (Asparagus family)

The *Asparagaceae* are a large and recently expanded family including many popular ornamental plants, as well as a few edibles. These include the American *Agave* plants, the nectar and sap of which is used to produce tequila, and a sugar substitute. The bulbs of the common Bluebell (*Hyacinthoides non-scripta*) are occasionally mistaken for wild Alliums by foragers, but they cause nothing worse than abdominal pain. I have seen claims that Grape Hyacinth (*Muscari* sp.) bulbs and flowers are edible, but they certainly aren't palatable. The edible white-flowered species in this family share a distinct flavour, and should be cooked.

Butcher's Broom (*Ruscus aculeatus*)

Butcher's Broom is a small, evergreen, rhizomatous shrub with spiny leaf-like shoots known as 'cladodes'. It has single, small, green flowers in the centre of the cladodes, followed by a red berry. Inhabits woodland and hedgerows, tolerating deep shade, but also found on coastal cliffs. Native to the west and south of Europe, frequent in the south of the British Isles, becoming rare in the colder north and east. Also used ornamentally for its winter colour. The boiled, roasted/toasted then ground berries are used as a coffee substitute, especially in Turkey. Also has multiple claimed medicinal uses (especially the root), and apparently really was once used as a broom.

Solomon's-seals (*Polygonatum*) (!)

"The roots [of *P. multiflorum*], macerated for some time in water, yield a substance capable of being used as food, and consisting principally of starch. The young shoots form an excellent vegetable when boiled and eaten like asparagus, and are largely consumed in Turkey. The curious name of this herb is said to be derived from the section of the root exhibiting marks resembling Hebrew characters."
(C Pierpoint Johnson, 1862)

▾ (escaped) Garden Solomon's-seal

Solomon's-seal (*Polygonatum multiflorum*)
is a patch-forming, rhizomatous, perennial
herb up to 90cm with arching, leafy,
rounded stems, alternate ovate-elliptic
leaves, white-and-green flowers that hang
from the stems at the base of each leaf, and
black berries. Locally common in the British
Isles apart from colder parts of Scotland, in
shady areas, especially ancient woodland
over chalk and limestone. Native and
frequent in temperate areas of Europe, apart
from colder parts of Scandinavia. **Scented**
or **Angular Solomon's-seal (*P. odoratum*)**
is very similar (shorter and more angular
stems, longer and more fragrant flowers that
don't narrow in the middle), and edible in
the same ways. It is more common in much
of Europe than Solomon's-seal, but less
so in the British Isles, though very locally
common in northern England. There is also
a common hybrid between *multiflorum* and
odoratum known as **Garden Solomon's-
seal (*P. x hybridum*)**, which is taller and
more robust. The rare and protected native
Whorled Solomon's-seal (*P. verticillatum*),
which has upright stems, much thinner,
whorled leaves, and red berries, is also
edible. Much more common in northern/
mountainous continental Europe, especially
Scandinavia. See quote above for usage (of
all species). Macerating the roots is intended
to reduce bitterness.

The berries of all Solomon's-seals are
poisonous, causing vomiting. The seeds
contain saponins and shouldn't be eaten.

▲ (Cultivated) Solomon's-seal

▼ Solomon's-seal fruits

Lily of the Valley (*Convallaria majalis*) ☠

Lily of the Valley is a colony-forming rhizomatous perennial herb, with stems up to 30cm tall bearing one or two broad, long-stemmed, leathery leaves up to 25cm long, and flowering stems bearing drooping racemes of strongly sweet-scented white, bell-shaped flowers (late spring) and small orange to deep red berries. Locally common as a native wild plant in England and Wales, especially in deciduous woodland clearings on dry, calcareous soil. More frequently it is an escape from cultivation. Rarer in Scotland and very rare in Ireland. Common in temperate areas of Europe but less so near coasts, and rare/absent in the far north and Mediterranean south.

Both the leaves and the flowers have been confused with Alliums (p126), wild and cultivated.

All parts of this plant contain saponins and potentially deadly cardiac glycosides, but most cases of human poisoning involve children eating the berries and result in nothing worse than severe vomiting. It has been used medicinally for heart complaints, but the dosage is critical. The flowers are used in perfumes and soap.

Bath Asparagus (*Ornithogalum pyrenaicum*) ⓘ

Bath Asparagus or **Spiked Star-of-Bethlehem** is a perennial herb with basal leaves up to 60cm long, which die back before the emergence of a dense spike of up to 20 white-and-green, star-shaped flowers on a stem up to 80cm (late spring). Inhabits roadsides, grass verges and woodland. Frequent as a native wild plant in a few strongholds in southern England, particularly around Bath, rare or absent elsewhere in the British Isles apart from as a garden escape. More common in warm, temperate and Mediterranean Europe, and rare/absent further north. The leaves could be confused with all sorts of things, but the flowers are distinctive. The young leaves, stems and unopened flower spikes are delicately onion-flavoured. They were once commercially collected and cooked like Asparagus. The bulbs can cause skin irritation and should not be eaten.

▾ Lily of the Valley

The bulbs of **Star-of-Bethlehem (*O. angustifolum*)** were once eaten but all parts of that plant are now known to contain toxins similar to those in Foxglove (p394). It has flowers arranged more like an umbel than raceme, and a white stripe on the leaves.

Garden Star-of-Bethlehem (*O. umbellatum*) and **Drooping Star-of-Bethlehem (*O. nutans*)** are ornamental introductions from southern Europe, now locally common naturalised in rough grassland but more often a recent garden escape. Both should be assumed to be toxic.

▲ Star-of-Bethlehem

▼ Bath Asparagus

Yucca

Yuccas or **Spanish Daggers** are perennial shrubs or small trees with tough, sharp, sword-like leaves and spectacular panicles of large, white flowers, followed by fleshy fruits. They are native to the hotter parts of the Americas; some species (notably *Y. gloriosa*) can survive outside in the warmer parts of the British Isles, others are grown as houseplants or conservatory plants.

    Yuccas have been confused with Cassava (otherwise known as 'Yuca', see p176) since before scientific naming began, which has led people to mistakenly believe that Yucca roots are good for eating (they aren't poisonous, but are not as edible as Cassava). It is the flowers and fruit that are eaten, the strong-flavoured petals are best cooked for a few minutes, and the bitter fruits of some species are peeled and slowly baked or roasted.

Hosta

Hostas are rhizomatous perennial herbs, mostly with broad, oval leaves, and large white or purple flowers. They are native to eastern Asia, but widely cultivated elsewhere as ornamentals.

    The leaves and stems are edible, cooked. The best part is the 'hoston' – the rolled-up emerging leaf – which is a popular vegetable in Japan, where they are known as 'urui' or 'giboshi'. These should be stir-fried or steamed and buttered. Raw, some varieties have an unpleasant aftertaste. Older leaves need longer cooking, and are better boiled. The flowers are edible raw, slightly bitter and sweet. All hostas are edible, but *H. montana* and *H. sieboldiana* are those recommended as food.

Asparagus (!)

(Garden) Asparagus (*A. officinalis*) is a perennial herb with thick, upright stems to 1.8m, multiply branching feathery foliage (technically all just stems, with nothing identifiable as leaves), and bell-shaped flowers that can be green, yellow or white, and small, red berries. Usually found in sandy coastal areas of the British Isles (where it is not native), but also inhabits a variety of other sorts of places (riverbanks, cliffs, heaths, churchyards). Common and native in Europe, apart from northern Scandinavia. Common in England, rarer in Wales, rare/absent in Ireland and Scotland. Wild-growing plants are often garden escapes. This is the ancestor of domesticated Asparagus. The young shoots are edible, but they must be cooked – they are poisonous raw and become more so as they mature, as are the berries (causing vomiting).

Wild Asparagus (*A. prostratus* syn. *Asparagus officinalis* subsp. *prostratus*) is a low-growing or prostrate version of this plant. It is internationally rare and should not be picked: only present in southern and western coastal areas of England and Wales, and south-east Ireland (where it is legally protected).

▾ Garden Asparagus with unripe berries

▾ Wild Asparagus

Amaryllidaceae (Amaryllis family)

Allium is the genus of Onions, Garlic and countless ornamental garden plants, and by far the biggest genus in this family. A great many of these bulbous perennial herbs are edible to some extent, although a lot of the ornamental varieties are tough or don't taste great. Poisonous (but not deadly unless consumed in extreme quantities) members of this family include Daffodils (*Narcissus*) and Snowdrops (*Galanthus*).

There is a long list of edible European Allium species which are only available to British foragers as ornamentals. You can experiment with eating any part of them. **Golden Garlic (*A. moly*)** is a bright yellow member of the genus, native to rocky habitats in the Pyrenees, usually ornamental in the British Isles but naturalised in

some places. Another Allium native to European mountains is the white **Victory Onion (*A. victorialis*)**. **Neapolitan Garlic (*A. neapolitanum*)** is a Mediterranean species with a large, white flower head, usually ornamental in the British Isles, but naturalised in south-west England. **Keeled Garlic (*A. carinatum*)** is native to continental Europe. Has spectacular bright pink flowers and is naturalised in places, especially Scotland. **Round-headed Garlic/Leek (*A. sphaerocephalon*)** has grooved leaves and dense purple umbels. Very rare and protected as a wild plant in the UK, but grown ornamentally. Common in dry and rocky places throughout southern Europe, and as far north as northern France, where its native range abruptly ends. Traditionally foraged around Lake Baikal.

▾ Golden Garlic

▾ Victory Onion

▾ Neapolitan Garlic

▴ Keeled Garlic

▴ Round-headed Garlic

Wild Leek (*A. ampeloprasum*)

Wild Leek has a stout cylindrical stem up to 2m, flat leaves and a sub-spherical, white, pink or purple flower cluster which has no visible bulbils. Inhabits field edges and paths, especially in sandy/rocky and/ or coastal areas. Wild plants are common in Mediterranean areas, but rare in most temperate areas, present as far north as southern Sweden. Probably an ancient introduction to the British Isles, most common in south-west England, south Wales, and some parts of western Ireland, rare or absent elsewhere.

This species is the wild ancestor of domesticated Leeks and Elephant Garlic. All parts are edible. The bulbs and leaves are cooked like a smaller, more pungent version of domesticated Leek. A bit overpowering raw.

Babington's Leek (*A. ampeloprasum var. babingtonii*, not pictured) is very similar, but with irregular umbels – many large bulbils, and fewer flowers, all sterile and some on long-stalked secondary umbels. It is common near the Cornish coast, but rare everywhere else, or only present as an escape from cultivation.

▲ Wild Leek flower

▼ Wild Leek

Rosy Garlic (*A. roseum*)

Rosy Garlic is a bulbous perennial herb up to 75cm, with long, thin, smooth-edged leaves with no keel on the back, and umbels of bright pink flowers, usually mixed with purple bulbils. Inhabits grassland, dunes, roadsides and hedgerows, preferring well-drained soils. Native to the Mediterranean, naturalised as far north as southern England.

Common in Cornwall and near the south coasts of England and Wales and the coast of East Anglia, rarer inland in England and Wales, and rare or absent in Scotland and Ireland.

The flower heads, with bulbils, make an interesting and attractive addition to a salad, or garnish for grilled fish. The bulbils on their own can be used whole, cooked, like miniature cloves of garlic. A personal favourite.

Wild Onion (*A. vineale*)

Wild Onion or **Crow Garlic** is a very variable perennial to 1.2m, with stiff, upright, round stems, half-cylindrical (channelled on one side) hollow leaves, and very variable purple flower heads. These are sometimes entirely composed of bulbils, sometimes entirely of flowers, but typically both, enclosed in a single bract. It is found on roadsides, dry grassland and dunes, especially near the sea, and often found as a weed among cultivated crops. Common in the south of the British Isles, becoming less so further north and absent in the Scottish Highlands. Frequent to common in most of Europe, as far north as southern coastal areas of Scandinavia. Further afield, this has become a problem invasive species.

The young leaves, bulbs and bulbils are all edible, though slightly bitter. The bulbs are the highlight (cooked). They have a very strong aroma, and are best used to flavour casseroled meat dishes, although they also work on a pizza. Raw, they are about as edible as raw garlic.

Field Garlic (*A. oleraceum*) is similar to Wild Onion, with round, slightly ridged stems, half-cylindrical hollow leaves, and variable flower heads with a mix of flowers and bulbils (very rarely only bulbils) and two very long bracts, which are persistent. It prefers dry to slightly moist fields, slopes and calcareous soil. Frequent to locally common in England, particularly in the north, but absent in northern Scotland, and rare in the rest of the British Isles. Frequent to common in most of Europe, but absent in the far north. Edibility as Wild Onion.

▲ Wild Onion. See photo of bulbs on p75.
▼ Field Garlic

Sand Leek (*A. scorodoprasum*)

Sand Leek or **Rocambole** is a perennial herb to 80cm and with flat, solid, slightly keeled, rough-edged leaves, a cylindrical flowering stem and a globular cluster of purple flowers and bulbils enclosed by two short bracts. Its habitat is very varied, including riverbanks, damp broadleaved woodland and saltmarsh. Common in parts of northern England (particularly Cumbria and Yorkshire) but occasional to rare in the rest of the British Isles. Frequent in Germany and central Europe and present from the south coast of Scandinavia to southern Spain. The whole plant is edible, and one of the best Alliums. This plant was grown for food from the middle ages until at least the early 19th century, and cultivars are now grown as ornamentals.

> **A pretty sauce for woodcock, or any wild fowl** (Mary Kettilby, 1728)
>
> Take a quarter of a Pint of Claret, and as much Water, some grated bread, two or three Heads of Rocambole, or a Shallot, a little whole Pepper, Mace, and flic'd [presumably 'sliced', meaning grated] Nutmeg and Salt; let this stew very well over the Fire, then beat it up with Butter and put it under the Wild-Fowl, which being under-roasted, will afford Gravy to mix with this Sauce.

▲ Wild Chives

Wild Chives (*A. schoenprasum*)

Wild Chives grow in packed clumps. They have cylindrical, hollow leaves to 50cm tall and dense, circular umbels of pink-purple flowers and no bulbils. Habitat is varied, from rocky areas near coasts to damp meadows and open woodland. Frequent in most of Europe, including England and Wales (though thought to be native only in the south west of Britain) but rarer in Scotland and Ireland. Edibility as domesticated Chives. This species has been cultivated for at least 4,000 years. All parts are edible. See recipes on p75 and p381.

▲ Mouse Garlic

Mouse Garlic (*A. angulosum*) is a good edible species resembling Chives, native to much of central Europe, where it is found in wet meadows and other damp places. In the British Isles it is only present as an ornamental. All parts are edible.

Ramsons (*A. ursinum*)

Ramsons or **Wild Garlic** is a strong-scented perennial herb with bright green, near-flat (slightly ridged-triangular), elliptical, hairless leaves up to 40cm long, with long, twisting stalks. It has circular or flat-topped umbels of white flowers (no bulbils) on leafless stalks up to 45cm high, followed by three-lobed capsules. Common in the British Isles, apart from the Scottish mountains, in damp woodland, especially the ancient sort, and particularly in valley bottoms. Common everywhere in temperate Europe apart from Scandinavia, where it is only found in southern coastal areas.

This plant starts producing leaves in late winter, and has completed its cycle and died back by midsummer. Take care when picking – there are too many cases of people grabbing handfuls contaminated with poisonous species. The poisonous Lily of the Valley (p122) is regularly mistaken for Ramsons, and although it lacks the garlic smell the two species can grow in proximity and the scent can remain on your hands. Lily of the Valley has paired leaves, Ramsons does not. Lords and Ladies (p112) has also been mistaken for Ramsons, although the leaves of that plant are darker, more shiny and have lateral veins and irregular edges. Could also be confused with other wide-leaved *Allium* species.

The whole plant is edible, including the bulbs, which are prized by wild boar and brown bears (hence the specific epithet, which means 'bear'). Though it is illegal to uproot plants in the UK, this one often grows near streams and is occasionally exposed by spring floodwater, allowing collection without digging, and use whole. Leaves, stems and flowers (avoid washing these before use, as it will diminish the taste) are used in salads, often combined with eggs – Ramsons egg salad is a traditional dish made by adding fresh chopped leaves to egg mayonnaise. The leaves can also be made into pesto or soup (often partnered with nettles, countless recipes online), or used to flavour cheeses. They can be chopped and stirred into risotto when cooked or served with boiled new potatoes and butter, or in omelettes, or as part of savoury pie fillings. As a side vegetable they can get a bit stringy – the best part to use for this purpose is the thick, white bases of the stem leaves, just as the plant starts sending up flowering shoots. Steamed for three minutes, they are sweet, crunchy and mildly garlicky. In Russian tradition, the stems are preserved in salt, and Ramsons salt made from the leaves has become very popular in recent years. The unopened flower buds pack quite a punch, and are good pickled, either on their own (like cocktail onions) or mixed with other things. The immature seed pods can be eaten raw in salads, cooked in a stir-fry, or added to mixed pickles.

Ramsons Flower Fritters

Ingredients:
Ramsons flower heads (about 50), 1 egg, 250ml milk, 150g plain flour, 1tbsp mixed herbs, salt and pepper to taste, 50g butter.

Clean the flower heads and chop. Whisk the egg, then add the milk and flour and beat into a batter, and then add the flowers, herbs and seasoning. Leave to stand for 30 mins before using. Then fry the batter-flower mix in butter, flipping at half-time so each side is golden brown when done. Drain on kitchen towel, and serve with a drizzle of honey.

Ramsons Salt

Ingredients:
Ramsons leaves (usually not stems) and a good quality of coarse salt, in proportions of 1:9 by weight.

Wash, dry and chop the leaves (usually not the stems), add the same weight of salt to the leaves, and then grind in a pestle and mortar, or blend, to make a paste. This paste is then mixed with the rest of the salt, which is then spread out and dried in the sun or a low oven. The attractive green salt is then used to finish other dishes.

Ramsons Pesto

Ingredients:
1 litre ramsons leaves, 1 garlic clove (chopped), 300ml olive oil, 100g pine nuts (chopped), 100g parmesan cheese, salt to taste.

Blitz the leaves and garlic in the oil. Add the nuts and blitz again. Add the cheese and salt and blitz again.

▲ Whole Ramsons

▲ Ramsons salt

▲ Ramsons seed pods

Three-cornered Leek (*A. triquetrum*)

Three-cornered Leek is a perennial herb to 50cm, with flat leaves and a loose umbel of Bluebell-like, green-lined, white flowers on a triangular-profiled stem, and no bulbils. The whole plant smells of garlic/onion when crushed. Inhabits woodland, roadsides, riverbanks. Common in southern England (esp. the south west) and southern Ireland, rare/coastal further north and absent from northern Scotland. Common within 30 miles of the coast in southern and western Europe, but not present in Scandinavia or Germany, and rare inland elsewhere. This species is typically available in great abundance where it does occur. It is an invasive species in the British Isles, and causing it to grow in the wild is illegal. Giant Snowdrop (*Galanthus woronowii*), Spring Snowflake (*Leucojum vernum*) and white forms of Bluebells (*Hyacinthoides non-scripta*) could be mistaken for Three-cornered Leek, but they don't smell of onions/garlic, nor do they have three-cornered stems. All are poisonous.

The whole of this plant is good to eat, from bulb to flowers. Three-cornered Leek is a first-class spring salad plant (occasionally appearing at the end of autumn), mild enough to be used as the base for a mixed salad including other species with stronger flavours, and the white flowers provide visual appeal and a slight peppery note. Can also be used to make a pesto, or as a cooked green vegetable or part of a mixed wild greens soup.

Few-flowered Garlic (*A. paradoxum*)

Few-flowered Garlic is similar to Three-cornered Leek, but with only one leaf per flower stalk, far fewer flowers per stalk (often just one), but many bulbils. Victorian introduction from south-west Asia, now occasional in the lowland British Isles, but unevenly distributed and often a recent garden escape. Frequent in central areas of temperate Europe (Germany, France, Poland), but absent in the south and very rare in Scandinavia. Edible but poor by the standards of this family (bitter undertones).

▲ Few-flowered Garlic

▲ Three-cornered Leek

▼ Whole Three-cornered Leek makes the perfect wild salad onion.

Commelinales

This is the sister order to the Zingiberales, home to Ginger and Banana.

Commelinaceae (Dayflower family)
The popular houseplants in the genus Tradescantia belong to this family.

Pickerelweed (*Pontederia cordata*)

Pickerelweed is a semi-aquatic perennial to 80cm. The leaves are oval, with cordate bases and pointed tips, and the flowers are violet-blue (rarely white). It is native to North America but grown as an ornamental plant in European ponds and lakes, where it can become very well established.

The whole plant is edible, though the rhizomes aren't exactly a culinary delight. Young shoots and leaves can be eaten raw, though better cooked like spinach. The flowers are tasty, and the seeds can be used like rice.

Poales

"Sedges have edges, rushes are round, grasses are hollow, what have you found?" (anon)

True sedges belong to the *Cyperaceae*, a family of grass-like plants mainly associated with nutrient-poor wetlands. Few have food uses, the most historically important sedge being the Papyrus Sedge (*Cyperus papyrus*), used in ancient Egypt to make paper. True rushes belong to the *Juncaceae*, none of which were worth including, though the far-northern Baltic Rush (*Juncus balticus*) exudes an edible sugar. 'Reed' refers technically to grasses of the genus *Phragmites*, but informally to various other water-loving members of the *Poaceae* – the true grasses, which have flat leaves and stems that can be flat as well as hollow.

Poaceae (Grass family)

The domestication of Wheats (see picture on p73), Barley, Rice and Maize made the first civilisations possible, and along with Rye, Oats, Sorghum, Millet and Sugarcanes they've kept humans and our livestock fed ever since. Though every other agriculturally important plant family is also of major interest to modern foragers, grasses are little more than a curiosity. The domesticated forms are primarily grown for their seeds, and while the seeds of all wild grasses are just as edible, very few have been regularly eaten. This is because the amount of food they deliver is a poor reward for the work needed to harvest and process them. Milling cereals is a time-consuming, energy-intensive business, and most wild grasses have small and/or fiddly seeds.

The wild ancestors of the grass crops that early European civilisations depended upon were mostly native to south-west Asia. As agriculture moved north into colder climates, these domesticated crops adapted to the new conditions. With the notable exceptions of Oats, native grasses of the north were not domesticated. Domesticated cereal crops are genetically more distant from their wild ancestors than, for example, most domesticated fruits. They reproduce sexually and are grown from seed rather than cuttings and grafts, so there have been thousands of cultivated generations with considerable human-induced alteration. It was often a single mutation or hybridisation event which got the ball rolling, but it took a lot of small steps to turn wild grasses into high-yield crops.

If the prospect of hard work doesn't deter you from experimenting with dehusking, grinding and eating wild grass seeds, there is one important safety issue. The small, black fruit bodies of Ergot (*Claviceps purpurea*) and various other members of its genus, which are parasitic on Rye, Wheat and other grasses, cause a range of extremely unpleasant symptoms. These include vomiting, uterine contractions, fever, seizures and hallucinations (the alkaloids responsible are structurally related to LSD) and even gangrene.

Grasses were also used by Neolithic people when boiling meat. Stones were heated red-hot, and then dropped into a pot and left until the water boiled. Then meat covered with a lattice of grasses was added, and more red-hot stones placed on top. The grass served to protect the meat from burning, as well as adding flavour and colour. The lower stems of many species are eaten by children as a snack.

Bamboos (Bambusoideae) (!)

Bamboos are a large unranked clade of primitive grasses, none of which are native to Europe, though many species are grown here as ornamentals. Most types of Bamboo are edible. The newly emerged young shoots are collected in the spring, cut in half lengthways and peeled to reveal their white centres. After stripping away any fibrous tissue from the base, and slicing into strips, they must then be boiled in slightly salted water, to remove a cyanogenic glycoside called taxiphyllin. The boiling process can take anything from 10 minutes to 2 hours, depending on whose tradition you consult. The boiled shoots are then used in soups, stews and stir-fries.

▾ Bamboo

▴ Couch Grass

Couch Grass (*Elymus repens*)

Couch Grass is a rhizomatous perennial to 1.5m, with roughly hairy leaves and upright flower/seed spikes. A persistent weed that is almost impossible to eradicate by physical removal alone, because it regrows from the tiniest root fragments. It has nevertheless been deliberately introduced in some places as food for animals, and medicine, usually for kidney and bladder complaints. The rhizomes are also edible, and have proven to be a valuable source of carbohydrate during famine. They can be cooked and eaten as they come, or dried and ground as a flour extender.

Common Reed (*Phragmites australis*)

Common Reed is a perennial grass, with tough, hollow, unbranched stems that can exceed 4m (the tallest British grass), flat leaves up to 70cm long, large, soft, feathery flower heads and an extensive rhizome system. Inhabits shallow fresh water. Common in Europe and present worldwide. This plant has one of the better wild roots for eating. They were historically ground and used like oats or flour, though they become too tough to eat as they mature. The cores of the young shoots also make nutritious eating, just after they emerge in spring, like Reedmace (next page). The stems are allegedly high in sugars which can be extracted by chopping and boiling until reduced to a syrup (my own attempts failed).

▲ Common Reed

Manna Grass (*Glyceria fluitans*)

Manna Grass or **Floating Sweet-grass** is a perennial grass with stems to 1m, and rough, pale green leaves, folded at the keel, which often lies on the water surface. It is found in ponds, rivers and ditches, on acidic soils, and is present throughout the temperate zone of Europe, apart from the far north. The seeds of this species were historically important in eastern Europe, especially Poland. They were an expensive, high-status food, collected by peasants in late autumn as tribute to landowners.

▲ Manna Grass

Typhaceae (Reedmace family)
Reedmaces (*Typha*)

"It is called Dunch-down, because, if the down thereof happens to get into the ears, it causes deafness. The leaves of it are called mat-weed, because mats are made therewith."
(Nicholas Culpeper, 1652)

"The leaves of this plant are used largely by coopers to place between the staves of casks and tubs, to render them watertight. The pollen from the sterile flowers is extremely inflammable, and is employed by the makers of fire-works as a substitute for that of the club-moss."
(C Pierpoint Johnson, 1862)

Reedmace is widely but wrongly called 'Bulrush', an error that originated with various 19th century illustrations of Moses in the Nile, surrounded by both true Bulrushes and Reedmace. Some people believe this battle has been lost and 'Bulrush' should be accepted as a valid name. I have no idea how the 'dunch-down' would get into people's ears, and the pollen is no longer used in the production of fireworks, but the flower spikes can be dipped in animal fat and used as torches.

Greater Reedmace (*T. latifolia*) is a robust, grass-like, rhizomatous perennial herb to 3m, with grey-green leaves (greyer than Yellow Flag Iris, p118) and flower heads that look like black sausages. The 'sausage' contains the female flowers, the male flowers are above. It is usually found in nutrient-rich shallow water, and tends to dominate. Common throughout Europe, apart from northern Scandinavia. **Lesser Reedmace (*T. angustifolia*)** is similar but smaller, paler and with narrower leaves, and has a section of stem between the male and female flowers. It is found in similar places and has the same uses. In the British Isles it is more common in the south, the lowlands and coastal areas generally.

The spring shoots can be peeled and the hard, white centres can be eaten raw or cooked. Boil for 5-6 minutes in slightly salted water, then sautée in olive oil. The female flowering spike is edible before it matures – 'Reedmace-on-the-cob' – fresh-tasting and crunchy raw, or cooked and served with butter. The pollen can be used in cakes and crêpes, imparting a sweetcorn-like flavour (use 50/50 with wheat flour). The seeds have also been eaten, ground into flour or pressed to make an oil. In winter, the rhizomes are rich in starch, sugars and protein, and can eaten whole (peeled and boiled), or processed into a high-quality flour. The best time to harvest the roots is just after they've started shooting in early spring. The starch is found in the hard centre of the rhizome, and this central zone thickens towards the shoot. You need to peel off the papery skin and foamy outer layer to harvest the starch-rich centre. The richest part is just below the base of the shoot – you will find a hard lump where it meets the rhizome, which can be levered out. The rest of the rhizome core can then be pulled apart and pounded or blended in water to release the starch, and the starch allowed to settle out of the water. The resulting gloopy paste evaporates into a cornflour-like powder.

▸ Top row – immature flower spike and pollen, Reedmace-on-the-cob, 'dunch-down'.

Middle row – mature female flower head, rhizomes and spring shoots.

Bottom row – cross-section of rhizome, flour.

Cyperaceae (Sedge family)

The seeds of most true Sedges (*Carex*) are covered by an extra layer of husk, their foliage is tough and there is little history of people collecting their roots for food, but there are a couple worthy of a forager's attention.

Great Fen Sedge (*Cladium mariscus*)

Great Fen Sedge is a stout, tough perennial up to 3m, with tough, grass-like leaves and clumps of large seeds. Found in fens and other boggy habitats. Native and frequent in temperate Europe, but unevenly distributed in the British Isles. More common in East Anglia and the western coasts.

This Sedge has plentiful seeds which lack the extra husk, and it has been suggested that this species was an important source of food for mesolithic foragers in northern Europe.[*] The young shoots are also just about edible. Historically used for thatching.

Pendulous Sedge (*Carex pendula*)

Pendulous Sedge is a perennial to 2.4m, with long, smooth, triangular (in cross-section) leaves that are yellow-green on the upper surface and greyer on the lower. It has catkin-like flowers (early summer) and long, drooping seed heads which can be collected into the autumn. Typically grows in dense stands. Common in temperate Europe apart from Scandinavia, where it is restricted to southern coastal areas.

▲ Great Fen Sedge

This plant is extremely common in some areas, and the seeds are easily collected by running your fingers along the seed head. They must then be processed, which is a time-consuming business. The first step is to parch them in a dry frying pan for a couple of minutes, stirring all the time, to open the outer husks. Then you need to rub them between your hands or fingers, to loosen and dislodge the seeds from their papery casing. Then comes the tricky bit – winnowing them. You need to use wind, or your own breath, and gravity, to separate the grains from the chaff. This process is hard to do perfectly – it is up to you how much effort you want to put into improving the quality. You might want to stand on a plastic sheet, so you can collect what comes out of the winnowing container and try to extract more seeds from it. The seeds can then be ground and used as flour, or partly ground to make Sedge Snaps.

---

[*] *Wild Food*, Mears, R, and Hillman, G, 2008, Hodder & Stoughton.

Pendulous Sedge Snaps

Ingredients:

100g winnowed pendulous sedge seeds, 50g sugar (or partially replace with honey), 20g butter, pinch of salt.

Grind the seeds briefly in a pestle and mortar, then toast for 2 mins. Mix all the ingredients well and spread thickly onto the centre of a tray covered with baking paper. Cook at 180°C / fan 160°C for 5 mins until the mixture liquefies, then remove from the oven and use a spatula to spread more thinly. Return to the oven for another 5-10 mins, making sure it doesn't burn. Allow to cool and then break into pieces.

▲ Pendulous Sedge seed head

▲ Unprocessed seeds

▲ Parched and (imperfectly) winnowed seeds

▲ Common Club-rush

Club-rushes (*Schoenoplectus*)

Common Club-rush (*Schoenoplectus lacustris*) is an aquatic perennial herb with stems to 3.5m, leaves usually reduced to sheaths around the stems and rather dull, nondescript flowering heads. Frequent to common in most of Europe, rare/absent in northern Scandinavia. Common in most of the British Isles in still or slow-moving shallow fresh water, uncommon in the Scottish mountains and in Cornwall. **Grey Club-rush (*S. tabernaemontani*)** is smaller and greyer, and found in a wider variety of habitats (including dune slacks and peat bogs). The roots of both these species are usable like many other plants in this section – dried and ground, or boiled down into a syrup. Club-rushes are thought to have been the source plant for the first breads ever baked by humans. It is probable that both the seeds and the rhizomes were used for this purpose. The pollen can be used like Reedmace pollen (p140). This plant was also traditionally used to make thatching for roofs and seats for chairs, and the pith was made into paper.

Sea Club-rush (*Bolboschoenus maritimus*)

Sea Club-rush is a perennial herb to 1m, with strong, upright, triangular stems, rough-edged leaves and brown spikelet flowers. Native and common in coastal areas of the British Isles apart from the far north, and inland along major waterways. Frequent in most of Europe, particularly in the south and in coastal areas further north; absent inland in Scandinavia. The tubers and young roots are edible in the same way as the other aquatic grasses in this section, and the leaves used to make baskets, mats, shoes and clothing. The seeds are also edible, more abundant than *Schoenoplectus* species, and often found at archaeological sites.

▾ Sea Club-rush, by a river estuary.

Sweet Galingale (*Cyperus longus*)

Sweet Galingale is a rhizomatous aquatic perennial herb to 1m, with triangular stems that terminate in a flower head. It is naturally found in shallow water, especially at pond edges, and also on permanently damp ground. Common in southern and western Europe, particularly Greece, Spain, Portugal and France, rare/absent further north and east. Frequent to locally common in England, less so in Wales and absent in Scotland and Ireland. Widely grown as an ornamental plant.

The tubers were a popular medieval spice, used in soups and stews, pies, and also desserts. It was an essential ingredient in a traditional sweet called 'Pokerounce', which was a sort of spiced toast. It was also once used in perfumes. The etymology links it to Galangal (a spice related to and similar to Ginger), but the taste is much milder and sweeter. It is fibrous, so needs fine chopping or processing.

Galyntyne
(from 'The Forme of Cury' by the Chief Master-Cook of King Richard II, 1390)

Take crusts of Bread and grind them small, do thereto powder of galyngale, of cinnamon, of ginger and salt it, temper it with vinegar and draw it though a strainer & present it forth

In modern English: Take breadcrumbs and vinegar, galingale, cinnamon, ginger and salt. Blend into a sauce.

Ranunculales

This order is home to numerous plants in the family *Menispermaceae* that produce the lethal toxin curare, once widely used by Native South Americans to tip their poison darts, as well as the most poisonous European species, some of which have been used for similar purposes.

Papaveraceae (Poppy family)

The Poppy family are herbs with white/yellow latex or watery sap. **Greater Celandine (*Chelidonium majus*)** is a foul-tasting, poisonous and medicinal member, not closely related to Lesser Celandine (p154). It contains isoquinoline alkaloids which have been used medically, but dosage is difficult to judge, and also causes eye irritation, dermatitis and suppression of the nervous system. The Fumitories (*Fumaria*) have been widely used in traditional herbal medicine, but their only known food use is as a plant-milk curdling agent. Ornamental members of the genus *Dicentra* ('Bleeding Heart') have leaves and roots which cause convulsions, but aren't deadly.

Yellow-horned Poppy (*Glaucium flavum*)

Yellow-horned Poppy is a biennial or perennial herb with branching stems, thick, lobed, grey-green leaves, yellow flowers (summer) and large horn or sickle-shaped seed pods (autumn). Frequent on shingle beaches around much of the British coastline, especially the south east, but absent from the north of Scotland. Protected in the UK under the Wildlife and Countryside Act 1981.

The edibility of the seeds of this species is disputed, with some sources claiming an edible oil can be extracted and others claiming that all parts of the plant, including the seeds, are poisonous. Given its protected status, the seeds should not be collected by UK foragers anyway. The root is the most seriously poisonous part of the plant. The main toxin, glaucine, has been used as a recreational drug, and if a historical record from 1698 is to be believed, the plant is hallucinogenic. Apparently a man who ate a pie made from the roots, having mistaken them for Sea Holly (p493), became convinced that his porcelain chamber pot was made of solid gold.*

* *Field Guide to the Wild Flowers of Britain*, 1981, Reader's Digest.

Common Red Poppy (*Papaver rhoeas*)

Common Red Poppy is an annual herb up to 80cm, with upright hairy stems, divided leaves on long stalks, and large, solitary red flowers (late spring and early autumn), also on very long stalks, followed by distinctive 'obovoid' seed capsules. It inhabits recently disturbed ground, such as fields, paths and waste ground. The seeds can lie dormant for decades, waiting until the ground is disturbed before germinating (which is why they are associated with battlefields). Historically best known as an agricultural weed, especially in wheat fields (Pierpoint Johnson calls it 'Corn Poppy', and accuses farmers of 'carelessness' in allowing it to grow, since the seeds are small enough to be sifted from the wheat). Common in most of the British Isles, but much less so in northern Scotland. Native to Europe but not the British Isles, where it is a Neolithic introduction. **Long-headed Poppy (*P. dubium*)** is very similar, and there are other, rarer, British red poppy species. The precise shape of their seed capsules is important for determining the species, but beyond the scope of this book.

The seeds of all European red poppy species are edible raw or cooked, usually used as a flavouring in bakery, and can also be processed to make an oil, or just boiled. There is conflicting information about the edibility of the leaves and flowers, with some sources advising that all parts are poisonous, but others saying that the leaves are edible when cooked, at least before the plant has flowered, or that the flowers can be used to make a syrup or to flavour wine. The ambiguous edibility information also extends to other poppy species such as Welsh Poppy (*Meconopsis cambrica*) and the naturalised Californian Poppy (*Escholzia californica*).

Opium Poppy (*P. somniferum*)

"The seed of this plant was offered, fried, at the beginning of the second course, and eaten with honey. Sometimes it was sprinkled on the crust of a kind of household bread, covered with white of eggs. Some of it was also put into the panada, or pap, intended for children – perhaps to make them sleep the sooner."

*(**The Pantropheon; Or, History of Food, Its Preparation, from the Earliest Ages of the World**, Alexis Soyer, 1853)*

Opium or **Breadsead Poppy** is an annual herb to 1m, with a slightly hairy stem, large, lobed leaves, and large flowers (to 18cm diameter) which are usually lilac, but sometimes white, purple or red, with large dark blotches near the base. The stem and leaves are grey-green and waxy, and all parts of the plant exude white latex when damaged. Not native, but an occasional escape, mainly found close to human habitation, and more common in England than Scotland and Wales.

This species is easily distinguished from its closest relatives by the impressive size of its flowers. Most varieties not grown for their opiate content do not contain large amounts, especially in cooler climates, although this species was once cultivated in England on a small scale for medical purposes. The seeds are used whole for human food, and were historically pressed to make a high-quality oil. Other parts of the plant have caused poisoning in animals.

Note: the Poppy Drops recipe opposite is included for historical interest only; following this recipe is now illegal in the UK.

Wild Poppy Seed and Fruit Cake
(traditional Eastern European)

Ingredients:
360g wild poppy seeds, 6 eggs, 250ml honey, 130g wild fruit (eg blackberries).

Grind the poppy seed into flour, and place in a bowl. Separate the egg yolks and whites, beat the yolks until they thicken, then add the honey slowly, continuing to beat. Then add the fruit and poppy flour and mix. Finally, beat the whites until they stiffen, and fold into the cake mixture. Then put into a greased, floured cake tin and bake at 170°C / fan 150°C for 50 mins. When cool, serve sliced with cream and wild mint.

Poppy Drops (TF Garrett, 1892)

However beautiful the flowers of the plant (*Papaver somniferum*) may be, and however serviceable for table decoration, they are not suitable for culinary purposes, because of their somniferous influence, due to the opium contained in the juice. Medicinal drops are sometimes made of them as follows: Put some Poppy flowers (wild ones for preference) in a basin with boiling water to cover them, to extract the essence. Put some sugar in a sugar-boiler, boil it to the ball degree [about 120°C], add the essence of Poppies, and boil the syrup mixture to the crack [about 150°C]. Pour it all out on to a well-oiled tin sheet, and put it in a warm place so that it will keep pliable. Pull off a small piece, roll it out to about the thickness of a clay-pipe stem, cut this up into equal-sized small pieces, roll them into balls, and put them on a board well sprinkled with caster sugar, covering them with it. Put them on a sieve, roll them about a little, then put them into boxes, and they are ready for use.

Ranunculaceae (Buttercup family)

The *Ranunculaceae* are a large family of herbaceous plants and woody climbers, most of which are foul-tasting and poisonous, including all of the common Buttercups (*Ranunculus*) and Wood Anemones (*Anemone*). A lot of them contain protoanemonin – a bitter and acrid-tasting irritant of the skin and mucous membranes, which causes vomiting, dizziness, jaundice and hepatitis if consumed. It is heat-unstable, so cooking helps to some degree. A few are extremely dangerous, the worst of which belong to the genus *Aconitum* (Monk's-hood). Other potentially lethal species belong to the genera **Delphinium** and **Consolida** (both commonly known as 'Larkspur', and both normally encountered as ornamentals in the British Isles). **Pasque Flower (*Pulsatilla vulgaris*)**, a rare and protected native, mainly found in the chalk downland of south-east England, is also dangerously poisonous, though historically important as medicine.

Stinking and **Green Hellebore** (***Hellebore foetidus and viridus***) can cause violent vomiting, although both were once used as a treatment for intestinal worms. All other Hellebores are also poisonous to some degree. One notable edible group is **Nigella (Love-in-a-mist)**, only found as ornamentals in northern Europe and used as a spice in Indian cookery under the name 'Black Onion Seeds'.

Baneberry (*A. spicata*)

'Baneberry' is the name of both the genus and a perennial herb also known as **Eurasian Baneberry (*A. spicata*)**, which grows to 60cm tall, and has small, crowded white flowers (early to midsummer) and shiny black berries (late summer and autumn) up to 11mm long. The leaves are up to 40cm long, toothed, bipinnate and compound. It inhabits limestone pavements and woodland, and is frequent in much of temperate Europe, especially the north and east. In the British Isles it is found mainly in northern England, where it is localised and rare. The berries have been known to cause heart failure, especially in livestock, but are rarely fatal to humans. The rest of the plant is also toxic, but to a lesser degree. The leaves vaguely resemble Blackberry, but the flowers and berries are very different.

Columbine (*Aquilegia vulgaris*)

Columbine is a perennial herb with branching stems to over 1m tall, with leaves divided into three leaflets which are subdivided again into three, and large, spurred flowers which are usually blue in wild plants, but can be purple, pink, white or brown. Native and frequent to common throughout Europe in wood, scrub and roadsides, especially on alkaline soil, and widely cultivated. It is easily confused with ornamental *Columbine* cultivars. The flowers are a little similar to the deadly poisonous *Aconitum* species (p152), but the leaves are completely different.

The flowers (early summer) and leaves contains toxins that are broken down by cooking/drying, but both can be eaten raw in small quantities. The flowers in particular are used in salads, and to make a tea. The roots and seeds are more seriously toxic, and must not be eaten (causing gastroenteritis and heart problems).

▲ Baneberry   ▼ Columbine   ▼ *Delphinium elatum*

▼ Pasque Flower

Monk's-hood (*Aconitum*)

"The plants are ... of a martial venomous quality; if they be inwardly taken, they inflame the heart, burn the inward parts, and destroy life itself. Dodonaeus reports of some men at Antwerp, who unawares did eat some of the monk's-hood in a salad, instead of some other herb, and died forthwith: this I write that people who have it in their gardens might be aware of it. ... The reason this herb goes by the name wolf-bane was this: men in former ages hunting for wolves used to poison pieces of raw flesh with the juice of this herb and lay them as baits, on which the wolves died presently."

(Nicholas Culpeper, 1652)

Monk's-hood (*A. napellus*) is a perennial herb up to 1.5m tall, with deeply cut leaves up to 10cm across, dark purple/blue flowers on hairy stalks, and thick black roots. It naturally inhabits woodland and stream sides, and is sometimes found on waste ground. Native to (and frequent in) Wales and south-west England, and much of central and western Europe. Widely grown as a temperate garden plant and occasionally escapes.

This plant contains an alkaloid called aconitine which causes severe gastrointestinal symptoms, paralysis, coma and death by heart or respiratory failure, sometimes within two hours of contact. This sap has been known to kill people after entering their bodies through cuts on their hands, so use gloves when handling it. It is the most dangerous poisonous plant in the British Isles, all parts being toxic, especially the roots. These have been mistaken for those of several unrelated edible plants, including Horseradish, Jerusalem Artichoke and Alexanders, leading to numerous fatalities. In this case the foul taste doesn't save people, because such a small quantity can prove lethal. The foliage is also deadly, young leaves having been confused for edible members of the Carrot family (although again they taste very different – Monk's-hood is bitter). Canadian actor Andre Noble died after consuming leaves while hiking in Newfoundland in 2004.

Monk's-hood was used as a medicine in medieval Europe, and was still in use in Germany and France in the mid-19th century for the treatment of gout and rheumatism. It is sometimes referred to in English as '**Wolfsbane**', but that name should probably be kept for its cousin **A. lycoctonum**, which is the most poisonous European plant of them all, used traditionally to make poison arrows and bullets, as well as poisoning wolves. It also grows up to 1m tall, with palmate-lobed, deeply cut leaves, and yellow or dark violet flowers, and inhabits damp woodland in mountainous areas, particularly in the Alps and Scandinavian mountains.

"The whole herb has powerful acrid-narcotic qualities, that have rendered it long celebrated both as a medicine and a poison. When the leaves or root are chewed, they cause a slightly acrid taste and pungent sensation in the mouth, followed by numbness and then a general tremor of the whole body. If the amount swallowed is sufficient, these symptoms are succeeded by vomiting and diarrhoea, accompanied usually by much pain in the abdomen, and a sort of contraction of the throat, and often attended by convulsive movements and clenching of the hands and jaws. Delirium sometimes occurs, and great dimness of sight."

(C Pierpoint Johnson, 1862)

▲ Monk's-hood   ▼ Wolfsbane

Lesser Celandine (*Ficaria verna* syn. *Ranunculus ficaria*) (!)

Lesser Celandine is a small perennial herb (to 25cm) with fleshy, glossy, long-stalked, cordate leaves, some of which develop dark markings, and solitary yellow flowers. On some plants, there are small bulbils in the leaf axils. Found in damp woodland, scrub, meadows, grass verges and hedgerows, common in temperate areas of Europe as far north as southern Sweden, frequent in the Mediterranean south, and abundant throughout the British Isles. The leaves could be confused with a number of other plants, including Ivy-leaved Toadflax (p394).

The raw leaves, which are rich in vitamin C, are edible before the plant has flowered (winter and early spring), and are used as a mild component of a mixed salad, or cooked. The flower buds can be eaten, and pickled like capers or Marsh-marigolds (overleaf). The leaves and flowers become increasingly laden with protoanemonin after the plant has flowered, but the later leaves can be used as a cooked leaf vegetable. The bulbils are also edible cooked.

The plant has a cluster of small tubers (it was historically known as 'Pilewort') which are edible (cooked). They are at their best as the above-ground parts of the plant begin to die off, and though a high-quality food, I am yet to find a way to clean them that isn't a lot of work. You will need to detach the tubers from the stem, and then clean off all the mud, stones and dead tubers (the roots are edible). Repeated washing and use of a sieve eventually leaves you with just the edible bits. They should be sautéed in butter, with a little cornflour added to thicken, then seasoned and served – crunchy, tasty and nutritious. Alternatively, they can be boiled in salt water then stored in vinegar, and used as an accompaniment to cured meats. Preserved in this way, they last for over a year.

Charred Lesser Celandine tubers have been found at several Neolithic archaeological sites in northern Europe, including the British Isles. It is possible our ancestors didn't even have to dig them up. Historical European sources describe large amounts of the tubers being washed out of soil by heavy rain as 'rain of potatoes' or 'heaven's barley'.*

* *Charred root tubers of lesser celandine in plant macro remain assemblages from Northern, Central and Western Europe*, Klooss, S, et al, Quaternary International Volume 404, Part A, June 2016.

Marsh-marigold (*Caltha palustris*) ⚠

Marsh-marigold is a stout, hairless perennial herb with usually solitary flowers like large buttercups, long-stalked cordate leaves and hollow stems, which can be upright (to 80cm) or horizontal. It inhabits marginal areas of ponds and streams, ditches, and other boggy places in grassland and woodland. Frequent throughout temperate areas of Europe, including mountains and the extreme north, and could be confused with Yellow Water-lily (p102), although this grows in deeper water.

The flower buds are pickled like capers. Young shoots, leaves and stems can be boiled, changing the water a couple of times to reduce bitterness, and served with butter or vinegar. Causes typical symptoms of protoanemonin poisoning if consumed raw, particularly the roots. The flowers were also once used to decorate churches at Easter, as tribute to the Virgin Mary, which is why it shares the name 'Marigold' with at least two unrelated plants ('Mary's Gold').

Pickled Marsh Marigold Buds

Take only fully closed buds, and boil them twice, discarding the water, then drain and place in a sterilised jar. Take 4 parts vinegar, 2 parts water and 1 part sugar, plus salt and mustard seeds to taste, bring to the boil, then pour into the jar. Seal and leave for at least a month before use.

Old Man's Beard Omelette

Wash the shoots, and boil in lightly salted water for 2-3 mins, until they become soft but not mushy. Drain, and squeeze as much water out as possible. Then fry in olive oil with a little garlic. When all the water has been cooked off, add some beaten eggs and make into an omelette.

Old Man's Beard (*Clematis vitalba*) ⓘ

Old Man's Beard or **Traveller's Joy** is a woody, deciduous climbing shrub with tendrils, pinnate leaves with slightly toothed leaflets, fragrant green-white flowers (with only a calyx, no petals) and characteristic 'hairy' seed heads. The name Traveller's Joy comes from the pleasant fragrance of the flowers. It is common all over the southern half of the British Isles, preferring chalk, on wood edges and many other places, especially urban. Rarer further north. Common in southern Europe, becoming rarer in the north. Easily confused with cultivated *Clematis* species, all of which should be considered toxic to some degree. Some other climbing plants are very poisonous, but they do not resemble this species.

The shoots are traditional fare in Italy and Spain, where they are *carefully broken off just below the first two leaves*, and then cooked and sometimes pickled. They can be bitter/acrid, and quickly become more so below the tip, the unpleasant taste indicating the presence of protoanemonin. This plant has alleged medicinal and other uses, including as tinder, string, rope and baskets.

Berberidaceae (Barberry family) $(!)$

Barberries are medium-sized shrubs with nasty spines, small, oval leaves and edible, acidic berries. It is probable that none are native to Britain, but some are very ancient introductions. Trying to figure out which species you've got can be tricky, especially if you only have the berries. These berries vary in culinary value, though none are poisonous to adults unless consumed in large quantities, especially when raw. All members of this family contain berberine, which is used as medicine for diabetes, high cholesterol and bacterial dysentery, and also sold as a weight-loss product, but is potentially harmful to infants, and pregnant or breastfeeding women.

Barberry (*Berberis*)

(Common) Barberry (*B. vulgaris*) is a deciduous shrub up to 3m, with elliptic green leaves, sometimes flushed purple, up to 5cm long and 2cm wide, with a minutely serrated margin. The stems bear three-forked spines at the base of the leaf stalks, drooping bunches of yellow flowers (spring), and scarlet, oblong-oval berries up to 1cm long (late summer and autumn). Inhabits hedgerows and wood edges, preferring chalk. Native to central and southern Europe, it is probably an ancient introduction in the British Isles. Once very common, this plant was systematically destroyed in Europe because it acts as a host for a fungus called 'wheat stem rust'. It is now occasional at best, though more common in remote non-wheat-growing areas, and because modern wheat varieties are resistant, Barberry could make a comeback.

The young leaves can be used in salads, or dried and used to make a refreshing tea. The very acidic/sour berries are edible raw or cooked, and are rich in vitamin C. They can also be used to make a drink, in preserves (especially jellies for meats) and pies. They can be candied, were historically used like citrus peel, and are still commonly consumed in Iran, where they are known as 'zereshk', in rice, poultry and lamb dishes.

The seeds are toxic, so must not be crushed when making juice, and must be discarded before consumption. When foraging, be aware that the smaller fruits will contain smaller or undeveloped seeds. (Domesticated Barberries are seedless.) The bark is also toxic, which makes the spines more dangerous, blistering the skin. Barberry is suspected of being an abortifacient (so avoid if pregnant). Traditionally this plant was also used to make a yellow dye.

The non-naturalised but widely planted ornamental **Japanese Barberry (*B. thunbergii*)** is similar, but with smaller leaves (purple in most cultivars), and berries that are more bitter. It is reported to cause minor gastric upsets, especially if consumed in quantity. There are also numerous other ornamental Berberis species, some of which naturalise.

▾ Japanese Barberry

"In Egypt a drink, prepared by macerating the crushed berries in about twelve times their quantity of water, with the addition of a little Fennel seed, is largely used as a cooling draught in fevers, especially those of a malignant character, this fruit having strong antiseptic qualities. When boiled with sugar, it forms a good substitute for tamarinds."
(C Pierpoint Johnson, 1862)

Barberry, Lamb and Nut Stew (Khoresht-e Zereshk)

This is a traditional wedding dish from western Iran. The contrasting textures and sweet and sour flavours symbolise the ups and downs of marriage. Exotic, delicious and very filling.

Ingredients:
500g diced lean lamb, 2 finely sliced medium onions and 1 crushed garlic clove, 250g sliced almonds, 250g sliced or chopped pistachios, ½tsp crushed cinnamon, 120g dried barberries, 60g sugar, 2 pinches saffron in 4tsp warm water, salt and pepper.

Soak the lamb in cold water for a few mins, fry garlic and onions until browned (but not burned), drain lamb, add lamb and cinnamon to the pan and stir-fry until browned all over. Add water to cover, put on a lid and simmer gently for 40 mins. Put the almonds and pistachios in a separate pan, cover with cold water and bring to the boil, drain immediately and add to the stew. Simmer for another 15 mins. Briefly stir-fry the barberries in oil (do not burn). Add the sugar, mix well, then add to the stew. Reduce to the desired thickness, season to taste and add the rosewater and saffron water directly before serving with white rice.

Darwin's Barberry (*B. darwinii*) is an evergreen shrub to 4m, with lots of branches and spiny, oval leaves up to 25mm long and 12mm wide. The stems bear three-branched spines, orange flowers (spring), and dark purple to black berries (summer), up to 7mm in diameter. Native to South America and usually found as an ornamental in Europe, though occasionally naturalises in hedgerows. The leaves and berries can be used as Barberry, and the berries in muesli (raw, dried).

The name 'Holly-leaf Barberry' can refer to **B. ilicifolia**, which has the same edible uses as other Barberries, and is rather similar. They are easier to tell apart when in flower (*ilicifolia* has yellower flowers, *darwinii* more orange). The name can also refer to *Mahonia aquifolium* (next page).

Wilson's Barberry (*B. wilsoniae*) is a semi-evergreen shrub to 1.5m with very spiny stems, small leaves, yellow flowers (spring) and beautiful pink to scarlet berries (late summer and early autumn) up to 6mm long. Native to China, where it inhabits hedgerows and wood edges. In Europe usually found as an ornamental, but occasionally a garden escape or bird-sown, particularly in England. The leaves and berries are used as Barberry. The raw berries are very sour, but more enjoyable raw than some other members of this genus, if you like that sort of thing. Just watch out for the thorns.

▲ Darwin's Barberry flowers

▲ Darwin's Barberry berries

▲ Wilson's Barberry

Oregon Grapes (*Mahonia*)

Mahonia is a genus of evergreen shrubs or small trees (to 2.5m), most of which have spiny compound leaves up 30cm long, yellow (or sometimes orange or red) flowers borne in dense clusters (midwinter to spring), and dark blue berries (early summer). Natives of eastern Asia and North America, they naturally inhabit open woodland and brushland, but several species and hybrids are planted as ornamentals or cover for game birds, and they sometimes escape. The species most frequently found growing wild in northern Europe are **M. aquifolium** and **japonica.**

The acidic berries can be eaten in moderation raw, dried, added to muesli, and used in preserves or to make wine. They go well with game, as a jelly, or to flavour a sauce, or just as a garnish. They also work well in a crumble with Japanese Knotweed (p326) and they make a superb liqueur (follow the recipe for sloe gin on p228, berries should be pricked before use). The flowers can be nibbled off the plant, or used in salads, but please remember that they are very important as a source of nectar at a time of year when not much is available for insects. The very young leaves can also be eaten, briefly cooked.

▲ Paeony

Saxifragales

Witch-hazel (*Hamamelis*) has edible seeds (native to North America but sometimes planted as an ornamental in Europe). **Ornamental Paeonies (*Paeonia* of the *Paeioniaceae*)** have edible flowers, used to float in punches and flavour teas (p269).

Grossiculariaceae (Gooseberry family)
Apart from a few Andean species, the deciduous shrubs of *Ribes* (the only genus in this family) are native to colder temperate areas of the northern hemisphere. The cultivated varieties are relatively recent domesticates compared to most fruit crops, with no English references to them earlier than the 16ᵗʰ century.

Wild Gooseberry (*Ribes uva-crispa*)

Wild Gooseberry is a perennial shrub to 1.3m with spiny, branching stems and three or five-lobed leaves, small bell-shaped green/pink flowers and bristly green, yellow or purple berries that are somewhat smaller than in the domesticated forms. It can be found in hedgerows, copses and open deciduous woodland, and is occasional in the British Isles. It is native to most of northern Europe but probably not Britain.

This is the wild ancestor of domesticated gooseberries, which were first grown in continental Europe and became popular in England around the time of Henry VIII. Since then they have become a British speciality. The fruits of the naturalised plant are usable in exactly the same way and the young leaves are also edible, and sometimes used in Easter Ledger Pudding (p329). The related and similar but darker-berried North American native **Coast Gooseberry (*R. divaricatum*)** is grown as an ornamental in Europe, and occasionally escapes.

▼ Gooseberry

Flowering Currant (*R. sanguineum*)

Flowering Currant is a perennial shrub to 2.5m with hairy, fruity-scented leaves, large bunches of drooping pink or red (rarely white) flowers, and purple-black berries with a white bloom. A North American native introduced to the British Isles in 1826 and now frequent in hedgerows and on waste ground.

The flowers are used in salads, syrups and cordials. Raw, they taste sweet with a bitter aftertaste. The berries are perfectly edible, but have a slightly bitter taste and lots of seeds. Best dried and used in muesli. This plant is useful as edible hedging.

Flowering Currant Cordial

Ingredients:
Equal amounts of flowers (packed), sugar and water.

Bring the water and sugar to the boil, add half the flowers, simmer for 15 mins, strain and cool. Add the remaining flowers and steep for 24 hours, strain and put in a sterilised bottle. Serve chilled with a sprig of fresh mint (p400).

Wild Redcurrant (*R. rubrum*)

Wild Redcurrant is a perennial shrub to 2m with three- or five-lobed palmate leaves with a slightly wavy margin, green-yellow flowers (spring) produced in racemes, and bright red, slightly translucent berries (mid to late summer). It is frequent in damp, shady woodland throughout temperature Europe, including all parts of the British Isles (where it is probably native) except northern Scotland. The berries are used as the domesticated crop, and the flowers make a decent herbal tea.

There are several other red-berried European species of *Ribes*. The very similar, but larger-fruited **R. sativum** can be found in much of western Europe (this Latin name is also sometimes used to describe domesticated Whitecurrants). **Rock Redcurrant (R. petraeum)** is restricted to mountainous areas of western Europe. Both *sativum* and *petraeum* had arrived in the British Isles by the late 16th century. All three were grown together, and some hybridisation occurred, but *sativum* is the primary ancestor of modern domesticated varieties of both Redcurrants and Whitecurrants.* **Mountain Currant (R. alpinum)** is similar to these species, but usually only has three-lobed leaves. It is common in the continental mountains of Europe, and southern Scandinavia, but very rare in the British Isles and the red berries are not worth collecting anyway. Two other very similar northern European species are the **Downy** or **Nordic Currant (R. spicatum)** and **R. schlechtendalii**.

To Pickle Red and White Currans (Hannah Woolley, 1675)

Take Vinegar and White-Wine, with so much Sugar as will make it pretty sweet, then take your Red and White Currans, being not fully Ripe, and give them one walm, so cover them over with the said Pickle, keeping them always under Liquor.

(Note: 'Walm' is an archaic word meaning 'bring to a rolling boil and then let it drop back down'.)

---

* *Cabbages and Kings: The Origins of Fruit and Vegetables*, Roberts, J, 2001.

Wild Blackcurrant (*R. nigrum*)

Wild Blackcurrant is a perennial shrub to 2m with alternate, strongly scented three- or five-lobed palmate leaves, larger and more pointed than Redcurrant and with a more clearly serrated margin. It has white flowers (spring) in drooping racemes of up to 20 individual flowers, and dark purple berries (late summer). It is locally common in hedges and woodland in temperate areas of Europe, including most parts of the British Isles, though less so in the Scottish mountains, and present throughout the northern temperate zones. Be aware, if collecting from the wild, of potential confusion with the extremely poisonous Baneberry (p150). **Buffalo Currant (*R. odoratum*)** is another species with tasty black berries, grown as an ornamental in Europe and occasionally escaping in the British Isles.

This is the wild ancestor of the familiar domesticated Blackcurrant, and if you are lucky enough to get to its berries before the local wildlife does, they can be used in exactly the same ways: in preserves and pies, to make a drink, or a wine. High levels of vitamin C. The leaves are as aromatic as the berries, and can be used as a flavouring when salt-pickling wild mushrooms as well as for making tea. They can also be used to spice up an Easter Ledger Pudding (p329).

▾ Wild Blackcurrant

Crassulaceae (Stonecrop family)

The *Crassulaceae* are primarily a family of small, fleshy, evergreen herbs, but there are also a few deciduous and aquatic members, and larger tree-like species. They are better known as ornamental garden and house plants, including the mildly poisonous Money Tree (*Crassula ovata*) and Flaming Katy (*Kalanchoe blossfeldiana*), although most of them *are* edible.

House-leeks (*Sempervivum*)

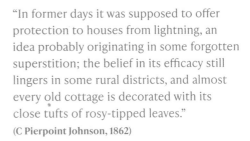

"In former days it was supposed to offer protection to houses from lightning, an idea probably originating in some forgotten superstition; the belief in its efficacy still lingers in some rural districts, and almost every old cottage is decorated with its close tufts of rosy-tipped leaves."
(C Pierpoint Johnson, 1862)

Common House-leek (*S. tectorum*) is a robust succulent perennial herb with a packed basal rosette (3cm wide or more) of fleshy, green and purple-red leaves and an upright stalk (to 50cm) bearing clusters of white-and-pink/purple/red flowers (summer). It is native to mountainous areas of southern Europe but widely cultivated and occasionally escaped elsewhere.

Humans have grown this species for thousands of years, traditionally on roofs, and mainly for medicinal and magical reasons. The leaves are edible, raw or cooked, tasting slightly astringent but mild and pleasant. They can also be juiced, but this juice is purgative if consumed in large quantity.

Other members of the genus, grown as ornamentals, seem to be similarly edible and I can find no records of serious toxicity to humans, though all will cause gastric problems if consumed in quantity.

◄ Common House-leek

Wall Pennywort (*Umbilicus rupestris*)

Wall Pennywort or **Navelwort** is a succulent perennial herb up to 25cm with smooth, fleshy, shiny, circular, centrally depressed ('umbilicate') green leaves, and spikes of bell-shaped greenish-pink, cream or white flowers (late spring and early summer). Inhabits walls, rocky crevices, steep banks and stumps. Very common in Wales, Ireland and south-west England, absent from much of the rest of the British Isles. Common in southern and western Europe, particularly Spain, Portugal, southern and western France. Absent in Scandinavia and eastern Europe. Could be confused with the superficially similar but unrelated (and non-toxic) Marsh Pennywort (p468).

    The leaves are edible – raw or cooked. Good in salads, especially when young, in the spring and early summer. A nice crunchy texture, but the flavour tends to become a bit too much later in the year, and they do vary quite a bit from plant to plant. Traditionally claimed to have many medicinal uses, though scientific evidence is lacking.

"A curious plant of this order...the Navel-wort, remarkable for its circular, fleshy leaves, concave on the upper surface, and with the footstalk attached to the centre beneath a small depression, is applied by the peasantry in Wales to the eyes, in certain disorders of those organs. In the west of England it is used by herb doctors as a remedy for epilepsy. Its medicinal properties are not very well established."
(C Pierpoint Johnson, 1862)

▸ Wall Pennywort with Ivy (see p468)

Stonecrops (*Sedum* and *Petrosedum*) (!)

"Trick-Madame, *Sedum minus*, Stone-Crop; is cooling and moist, grateful to the Stomach. The *Cimata* and Tops, when young and tender, dress'd as *Purselane*, is a frequent Ingredient in our cold *Sallet*."
(John Evelyn, 1699)

"Pliny gravely recommends [Common Stonecrop] as a means of producing sleep, for which purpose, he says, it must be wrapped in a black cloth and placed under the pillow of the patient without him knowing it; otherwise it will be ineffectual."
(C Pierpoint Johnson, 1862)

The Stonecrops are succulent perennial herbs with leaves of varying and somewhat disputed edibility – raw, cooked or pickled. They are slightly bitter/acrid, more so after flowering, but pleasantly crunchy and variably sour. Some stonecrops, especially Biting Stonecrop, are reported to cause skin irritation, and also gastric problems, which are less likely if they are cooked.

Reflexed Stonecrop (*Petrosedum rupestre* syn. *Sedum rupestre, S. reflexum*) grows up to 35cm, with stiff, brittle, fleshy blue/grey/green leaves and yellow flowers on straggly, upright stems. Inhabits dry, rocky places, especially old walls. Introduced in the British Isles, widely naturalised in England and Wales, much less so in Scotland. Frequent in temperate areas of Europe, apart from northern Scandinavia. The best edible species in the group, and least likely to cause nausea. Used in salads. It is probably this species that John Evelyn referred to as 'Trick-Madame'.

The similar **Rock Stonecrop (*P. forsterianum* syn. *Sedum forsterianum*)**, which in Britain occurs mainly in its native south-west England and Wales, is also described as edible by some authorities, but known to cause stomach upsets. It has tighter, shorter, denser foliage spikes.

White Stonecrop (*Sedum album*) forms mats or cushions (to 20cm) of bright green fleshy leaves, alternate and ovoid to cylindrical, green with pinkish tints, and large clusters of small white flowers, sometimes tinged pink. Inhabits dry rocks, walls and cliffs, and is often found in gutters and on man-made paths. Common in Europe, apart from northern Scandinavia, and frequent to common in most of the British Isles, though rarer in Scotland.

English Stonecrop (*S. anglicum*) is very similar to White Stonecrop, but lower-growing (mat-forming, to 5cm), with smaller flower clusters and red-tinged, grey-green leaves. It is almost entirely restricted to the far west of the British Isles (so poorly named, since apart from Cornwall, those far western places are in Ireland, Scotland and Wales, rather than England).

Common or **Biting Stonecrop / Wall Pepper (*S. acre*)** is similar but smaller (to 10cm), but with yellow flowers and found especially in coastal areas. Native and frequent to common throughout Europe, including the British Isles, apart from mountainous areas of Scotland. This species is the most likely of the group to cause nausea, so is only usable very sparingly as a spice.

Tasteless Stonecrop (*S. sexangulare*) is taller (to 25cm) and relatively tasteless, but otherwise very similar. It is an ornamental, naturalised in a few places in the British Isles.

▲ Biting Stonecrop   ▼ Reflexed Stonecrop   ▼ White Stonecrop

Pickled Stonecrop

Put 250ml cider vinegar, 250ml water, 1tsp salt, 1tsp mustard seeds, 1tsp dill seeds and 1 clove of garlic into a saucepan, and bring to the boil. Pour over the stonecrop shoots/leaves in jars, seal and leave to cool. Put in the fridge, and it will be ready to eat in a week.

Orpine (*Hylotelephium telephioides* syn. *Sedum telephium*)

Orpine is a succulent, hairless perennial that dies back in winter. It has an upright but rather limp stem to 70cm and fleshy green/blue oval leaves. The stems and leaves can be reddish, and the flowers can be white or yellow, but are typically pinkish-red. Habitat is varied, but usually woodland, inland and lowland. Common in temperate areas of Europe, apart from the far north. Widespread and locally common in the British Isles, native everywhere but Ireland, absent in north-east Scotland. This is a complex species. Unlikely to be confused with anything poisonous, but there are other related species sometimes found as garden escapes and naturalised in a few locations (notably *Sedum spectabile* and *spurium*, both of which are edible). A variety of this plant is also cultivated as an ornamental.

The leaves are edible raw or cooked, and the fresh, young leaves were commonly used in medieval England as a salad plant. The taste is rather like pea pods. Older leaves need cooking, best sautéed. The knobbly, fleshy roots are easy to dig up, but take some effort to clean. They are slightly bitter and not recommended raw, but the bitterness diminishes on cooking. They can be fried, or boiled for a few minutes and mashed.

▼ Orpine in spring, when the leaves are eaten.

▼ Orpine flowering in late September.

Roseroot (*Rhodiola rosea* syn. *Sedum rhodiola*)

Roseroot is a succulent, hairless perennial herb to 40cm, with dense whorls of fleshy grey-green stem and leaves, multiple stems growing from thick, scaly rhizomes that smell of roses when damaged, and clusters of yellow flowers in the summer (up to 35mm long) at the tips of the shoots. Inhabits mountains and sea cliffs, on calcareous soils. Native and common in the Scottish Highlands, rare/absent elsewhere in the British Isles. Present in the Arctic, mountainous and cold temperate zones of the northern hemisphere.

The whole plant can be eaten, raw or cooked. Traditionally used as food in North America, especially the stem and leaves. The roots have a history of medical use in Scandinavia, Russia and China. Reputed to be effective against depression (particularly seasonal affective disorder, which is most prevalent at the northerly latitudes where this plant grows wild). The Federal Drug Administration in the US has banned the sale of Roseroot products due to lack of evidence of safety and efficacy.

Saxifragaceae (Saxifrage family)

'Saxifrage' means 'rock breaker', which refers not to the rocky habitat in which many saxifrages are found, but to their historical use to treat kidney stones. Many are cultivated ornamental plants. In addition to those mentioned below, another edible species is Strawberry Saxifrage (*Saxifraga stolonifera*) – native to Asia but introduced to Europe for ornamental use – the leaves of which are used in Japanese cuisine.

Golden-saxifrages (*Chrysosplenium*)

Opposite-leaved Golden-saxifrage (*C. oppositifolium*) is a creeping, low-growing (to 15cm), mat-forming, evergreen perennial, with opposite leaves and tiny yellow-green flowers (late spring). It is common in the British Isles apart from eastern central England, in damp, shady woodland, by springs and streams, and on cliffs. It is also present in western and central Europe from Norway to northern Spain, east to Germany and northern Italy. The leaves could be confused with Ground-ivy (p408), but that grows in drier habitats. The leaves are edible; raw in salads or cooked in soups.

The similar (but non-mat-forming) **Alternate-leaved Golden-saxifrage (*C. alternifolium*)** is also edible, but declining across its whole range in the colder and wetter parts of Europe, and too rare to justify picking.

▲ Opposite-leaved Golden-saxifrage
▼ Alternate-leaved Golden-saxifrage

Purple (Mountain) Saxifrage
(*Saxifraga oppositifolia*)

Purple Saxifrage is a creeping, low-growing, mat-forming perennial, with opposite, rounded leaves and a dense covering of purple flowers that can change the colour of the desert landscapes it often inhabits. It particularly likes rocks and cliffs, but can be found in many other habitats, though always cold. It is abundant in the northern Arctic, and at high altitudes further south. In the British Isles present only in northern mountains. Unlikely to be confused with anything else (three other members of the genus live on British mountains, but they have white or yellow flowers).

The flowers are bitter immediately after you put them in your mouth, soon becoming sweet. This species is an extreme psychrophile – capable of surviving in environments so cold that no other flowering plants can live there. It holds records for both the highest flowering plant in Europe and the most northerly flowering plant in the world.

▾ Purple (Mountain) Saxifrage

Vitales / Vitaceae (Grape family)

Grape (*Vitis vinifera*)

Grape is a perennial liana to 30m tall, with alternate, palmate-lobed leaves up to 20cm across and red, purple or green berries (grapes) up to 6mm in diameter. Inhabits damp/humid forests, and stream sides. The wild plant (the ancestor of all domesticated Grapes) is native in southern Europe and common as far north as southern Germany, becoming rarer further north, though it is now naturalised in parts of England. Discarded cultivated Grapes also occasionally germinate and survive in hedgerows in the south of the British Isles. Both are likely to become more common. Berries and leaves are edible.

Malpighiales

The Malpighiales are a very large order of flowering plants, which include the Coca plants that are the source of cocaine (*Erythroxylum*) and Willows (*Salix*), the bark of which was the original source of aspirin. White Willow (*S. alba*) and Crack Willow (*S. fragilis*) both contain the active ingredient salicin. Cambium or leaves are either chewed unprocessed or dried and made into tea, but dosage is hard to control and stomach problems are possible.

Spindle (*Euonymus europaeus*) belongs to the sister order Celastrales. This species has rather odd-shaped pink berries which contain various alkaloids (including caffeine), and cause liver and kidney damage, and potentially death.

▾ Wild Grape

▾ Spindle

Linaceae (Flax family)
Flax (*Linum*) (!)

▲ Perennial Flax

"At the period when the gods did not exact much, but were contented with humble offerings, men placed on the altars loaves made of Linseed meal; a treat the immortals gratefully accepted, though certainly it would not much tempt us of the present day. The Asiatics afterwards thought of pounding the linseed, frying it, and mixing it with honey; these cakes seemed to them too good for their divinities, so they ate them themselves. In the time of Pliny, the Lombards and Piedmontese ate this miserable bread of the gods, and even found in it a most agreeable flavour. These nations have since improved their taste."

(Alexis Soyer, 1853)

Flax has been used by humans to make textiles for 30,000 years, and domesticated for at least 9,000. The domesticated form is considered a species in its own right. **Cultivated Flax (*L. usitatissimum*)** is an annual herb to 90cm with thin leaves and pale blue flowers. It escapes from agricultural fields or birdseed mixes, and is usually found on waste ground or grass verges. Its Latin name means 'much used', for this was an extremely important crop until the start of the 20th century, grown for both fibres and seeds, from which linseed oil is extracted to leave a protein-rich 'cake' used as horse feed. The oil has many uses in addition to food, primarily in paint, varnish and putty. Flax seeds have been re-popularised as a healthy 'superfood'. The wild ancestor is believed to be the smaller **Pale Flax (*L. bienne*)**, a biennial or perennial herb to 60cm with narrow, lanceolate leaves and pale blue five-petalled flowers, a rare native in Europe as far north as England, inhabiting dry grasslands, especially near the sea. The smaller and much more common **Fairy Flax (*L. catharticum*)** is also known as 'Purging Flax' and was used as a laxative. From a foraging point of view, the most important species is **Perennial Flax (*L. perenne*)** – a herb to 60cm with lanceolate leaves and pale blue flowers, native to the Alps and central northern Europe. It also occurs in English chalk grasslands and a few other scattered locations, probably as an introduced species, and is planted as an ornamental. The mildly spicy seeds can be eaten as they are, or used to produce a nutritious and tasty oil, though there is some question about toxicity, with some sources claiming both seeds and oil must be cooked before eating, because they contain cyanide raw.

Euphorbiaceae (Spurge family)

There are very few edible members of this family, with the notable exception of the South American staple tuber crop Cassava (*Manihot esculenta*), from which tapioca is made. Even this must be properly prepared to render it edible, and there are varieties which are potentially lethal. There is no shortage of other poisonous members, including the Castor Oil Plant (*Ricinus communis*), the raw seeds of which contain one of the most dangerous toxins known to science (ricin). One chewed seed can kill a human. It is a southern European plant, but cultivated further north and not to be confused with another ornamental – the unrelated False Castor Oil Plant (*Fatsia japonica*), which looks very similar indeed. I can find no reliable information on the toxicity of *Fatsia* berries, most sources describing them as 'inedible'.

▲ Caper Spurge fruits

Spurges (*Euphorbia*)

"[Caper Spurge (*E. lathyris*)] has long been cultivated in gardens on account of its fruit, which is often pickled as a substitute for capers, resembling them in size and appearance, and somewhat in their pungent flavour. In a fresh state it is highly acrid; but the process of long steeping in salt and water, and afterwards in vinegar, neutralizes the active principle, or so far lessens its virulence, as to render it inert in the quantity of such condiment usually eaten." (Charles Johnson, 1856)

Caper Spurge is not safe to eat, no matter how long it is steeped. Some people believe it deters moles, and cultivate it for that purpose.

Euphorbia is a huge genus (over 2,000 species), including 13 in the British Isles, all of which have poisonous sap and very poisonous seeds. Their sap causes skin irritation, so even handling them can cause problems, and in some species a single seed could kill a child if consumed. The key identifying feature is their distinctive green flowers, which lack both petals and sepals. They are sometimes misidentified as the fused leaves of edible Springbeauty (p361).

▼ Sea Spurge flowers, typical of the genus *Euphorbia*.

Mercurys (*Mercurialis*) ☠

Both British Mercury species are poisonous, mainly causing gastric symptoms but potentially lethal if eaten in large quantities. They are well known for poisoning dogs and livestock.

Annual Mercury (*M. annua*) is a hairless annual herb with branching stems to 50cm, with shiny leaves and tiny green flowers. This is an ancient introduction which is common in southern England in disturbed habitats such as gardens and arable land, and slowly spreading northwards. There are no obvious edible lookalikes, the closest being Chickweed (p336) or a Goosefoot (p177).

▾ Annual Mercury

▴ Dog's Mercury

Dog's Mercury (*M. perennis*) is a hairy, rhizomatous perennial herb to 50cm with unbranched stems, opposite pointed, oval, toothed leaves, and spikes of small green flowers. It has an unpleasant smell, reminiscent of rotting fish. Typically found in deciduous woodland (especially with Beech) in the lowlands of the south and east of England, rarer elsewhere in the British Isles and often in rocky habitats further north. This species is native, and an indicator of ancient woodland, and produces a beautiful blue dye. Dog's Mercury is definitely known to kill cattle, and the only recent human poisoning was the result of mistaking the plant for Brooklime (p393). It might also be confused with Ground-elder (p177). The leaves are different, but it is a similar size and colour, and can be found in the same places.

Hypericaceae (St John's Wort family)
St John's Wort (*Hypericum*) (!)

Perforate St John's Wort (*H. perforatum*)
is a rhizomatous perennial herb with round stems to 90cm with two opposite raised ridges. Leaves are opposite, stalkless, narrow oblong-oval with translucent spots visible when held to the light. Bright yellow flowers followed by a capsule fruit. Common in the British Isles apart from the far north, on roadsides, open grassland, scrub and wood edges, particularly on chalk/limestone. Native and abundant throughout Europe, apart from northern Scandinavia. There are many other small St John's Worts, similar apart from the perforations and the medicinal properties.

This plant is much more important as medicine than food. The flowers and flowering shoots are an anti-depressant.* The leaves and fruit are used to make a tea, the flowers for flavouring mead and the leaves were also once used to wrap cheese, supposedly helping to preserve it during transportation.

St John's Wort can act as a photosensitising agent when eaten by fair-skinned people.

Tutsan (*H. androsaemum*) is a hairless upright perennial shrub to 1m, with branching red stems, oval, stalkless leaves, bright yellow flowers and black berries. It is locally abundant, especially in the south and west of the British Isles, usually in damp woodland. The name comes from the French 'Toute saine' ('all healthy/wholesome'), indicating its historical importance as a herbal medicine, though the berries are poisonous (producing mainly gastric symptoms). The leaves are believed to have antiseptic and anti-depressant properties.

There are several other shrubby non-native members members of this genus, the best known of which is **Rose of Sharon (*H. calycinum*)**. All have poisonous berries.

▼ Perforate St John's Wort

▼ Translucent spots

▼ Tutsan

* *Herbal Medicine: Biomolecular and Clinical Aspects*, 2nd edition, edited by Benzie, IFF, and Wachtel-Galor, S, 2011.

▲ Common Passionflower (fruits not quite ripe)

Passifloraceae (Passionflower family)

The *Passifloraceae* are native to Central and South America, but many species are cultivated elsewhere for their flowers or fruit, or both, most importantly Passionfruit (*Passiflora edulis*).

Common Passionflower
(*P. caerulea*)   (!)

Common Passionflower is a perennial climber up to 20m with alternate, palmate, five-lobed dark green leaves, tendrils, complex blue flowers up to 10cm across and orange fruits. Native to South America, but introduced widely elsewhere and can be invasive in warmer parts of Europe, including southern Britain.

Contrary to some sources that describe this fruit as inedible, it is perfectly edible and some people rather like it. It invades my own garden from both sides, through as well as over the old stone walls. The leaves and roots are toxic (contain cyanide precursors).

Violaceae (Violet family)

Violaceae includes quite a few trees and shrubs, but the largest group, and the only one of any interest to European foragers, is made up of much smaller plants.

Violets and Pansies (*Viola*) ⓘ

Sweet Violet (*V. odorata*) is a small perennial with no stem, heart-shaped, hairy, finely toothed leaves on long stalks, creeping runners and **strongly scented**, solitary violet or grey-white flowers, also on long stalks. It is common in England in open woodland, roadsides, hedgebanks, parks and churchyards, becoming much rarer as you go further north and absent from the north of Scotland. Native to Europe and Asia. Introduced in North America and Australia. There are many other European violets, all of which lack the aromatic flowers, and all are edible. **Hairy Violet (*V. hirta*)** is the most similar and sometimes considered to be a subspecies.

The young leaves are edible raw or cooked, and are available during the winter. They have a mild taste, and their mucilaginous properties make them useful for thickening soups and stews. Older leaves become unpleasantly tough. The flowers can be used in a similar way, and are also available from late winter (this species is the first violet to flower). The slightly bitter bases should be removed. The fresh flowers are particularly useful as an aromatic addition to salads and desserts, and used to make confectionery and as a flavouring in baking. The flowers make a lovely infused vinegar (use a high-quality vinegar, many recipes available online). Leaves and flowers are also used to make a herbal tea.

The roots and rhizomes are poisonous (strongly emetic) and medicinal, used in the treatments of coughs, bronchitis and other mouth/throat inflammations.

Common Dog-violet (*V. riviniana*) has hairless leaves and violet flowers. It inhabits open woodland, hedgerows and gardens, and is the most common violet in the British Isles. Abundant almost everywhere.

All other *Viola* species (at least 13 in the British Isles, some of which are known as 'Pansies') can be used in the same way, although they lack the sweet smell, and **Hairy Violet (*V. hirta*)** is a bit hairy.

▼ Common Dog-violet

These recipes are included for historical interest only; please don't pick violets on this scale.

Violet Pudding (Medieval English from Harleian MS279)

Ingredients:

450g trimmed, rinsed violet petals (heaven knows how long these would take to collect), 350ml (unstrained) almond milk, 230ml water, 4tsp sugar, 2tbsp rice flour ¼tsp saffron.

Boil water in a pan, add violets (bases trimmed), return to the boil and stir continuously for 1 minute. Drain petals, mince and mash into paste. Bring the almond milk to the boil, reduce heat, simmer and stir for 2 mins, then add the paste and slowly add the rice flour, still stirring. Then add the sugar and saffron, and simmer and stir for 5 more mins. Serve immediately.

Paste of Violets (Hannah Woolley, 1675)

You must take Violets ready pickt, and bruise them in a Marble Mortar, and wring the Juice from them into a Porringer [shallow bowl], and put as much hard Sugar in fine Powder, as the Juice will cover, dry it, and then pouder it again; then take as much Gum-dragant [tragacanth gum] steeped in Rose water as will bring this Sugar into a perfect Paste, then take it up & print it with your Moulds, and so dry it in your Stove.

▾ Sweet Violet

Oxalidales / Oxalidaceae
(Wood-sorrel family)

Wood-sorrels (*Oxalis*) (!)

"The Wood-sorrel forms a very pleasant and wholesome salad plant in small quantity, and is used much in France for that purpose; but it should be remembered that though agreeable in flavour, the salt it contains is in large quantities poisonous, and therefore it should be eaten only in moderation."
(C Pierpoint Johnson, 1862)

Wood-sorrels contain oxalic acid and so should be avoided by people with kidney problems (especially kidney stones) or calcium deficiency. However, they are also rich in vitamin C, and were historically used to treat scurvy.

Wood-sorrel (*O. acetosella*) is a low-growing, rhizomatous perennial herb with green (sometimes flushed purple below) trifoliate compound leaves (each untoothed leaflet heart-shaped) on long stalks, and white-and-pink flowers (spring and early summer), also on long stalks. Locally abundant in the British Isles, in damp woodland, heaths and hedgerows, and also in more open rocky places in the north. It is common on acid soils in temperate areas of Europe, apart from the extreme north, and rare/absent in the Mediterranean south. Wood-sorrel was once cultivated in the British Isles before being displaced by French Sorrel (p320).

The leaves and their stalks are available all year round, taste of lemon and can be eaten raw in salads (they go well in potato salad), or cooked and used to flavour other foods, or to make a sauce to serve with fish. Wood-sorrel butter goes well with seafood and freshwater fish. Can also be used to make a cold drink (add to hot water, then chill). The flowers can also be eaten raw or used to decorate and flavour cakes.

Procumbent Yellow-sorrel or **Creeping Wood-sorrel (*O. corniculata*)** is a small annual or short-lived perennial herb with trailing or ascending stems, green to purple-red trifoliate compound leaves on long stalks, and yellow flowers (spring and early summer). An older name is 'Sleeping Beauty', because of the way its three leaflets fold down at night. This is a persistent weed of gardens and agricultural land. Common in south-east England, becoming much rarer as you go north and west. Claims that this plant contains dangerous levels of oxalic acid are wrong – it can be used exactly like Wood-sorrel. Seed pods are also edible. **Pink Wood-sorrel (*O. articulata*)** is similar, but with deep pink flowers, and larger, thicker, paler, slightly furry leaves. Introduced from South America as an ornamental but naturalised in many locations. Eaten in India as a green vegetable, and more substantial (and therefore attractive as food) than its relatives.

There are several other non-native members of this genus grown ornamentally and naturalised in Europe as garden weeds or in locations close to human activity, all of which are edible.

▾ Procumbent Yellow-sorrel

▲ Wood-sorrel

▼ Pink Wood-sorrel

Fabales / Fabaceae (Pea family)

"Few orders are more diversified in properties, or more dangerous as regards the operation of certain species. ... its wholesome members ought rather to be regarded as exceptions to a very deleterious character."

(Charles Johnson, 1856)

This is a large family of plants, which range in size from tiny herbs to small trees, all of which share a common flower structure. They have five petals: the two at the sides are called 'wings', the two below fused together are called the 'keel' and the single one above is called the 'standard'. In some species the flowers form dense clusters where this structure is hard to see.

Many are grown as crops, ornamentals or both. Their importance as food plants, both historically and in the modern world, can't be overstated: along with grasses, plants from the Pea family fuelled the Neolithic Revolution. They include Soy (the most important protein source for domesticated herbivores), forage crops like Alfalfa and Clover, popular garden vegetables such as Runner Beans, and Lentils (one of the first domesticated crops). Their ability to turn atmospheric nitrogen into usable nitrates, thus increasing soil fertility, means they may become even more important in the future. They are essential to permaculture.

Domesticated Peas and their closest relatives (*Pisum*) are native to the Mediterranean and central Asia, and do not grow wild in northern Europe. The southern European Carob (*Ceratonia siliqua*) also belongs to this family, as do the tropical/subtropical Peanut (*Arachis hypogaea*) and Tamarind (*Tamarindus indica*).

▲ Ornamental Lupin

There are also plenty of toxic members of the Pea family, and there is considerable overlap between toxic and edible groups and species. A general rule is to avoid eating any of them in large quantities, even after cooking, although the type of toxicity is not consistent across the whole family, some being much more dangerous than others. The Birds-foot Trefoils (*Lotus*) are suspected to be carcinogenic, and contain hydrogen cyanide, so should not be eaten. The seeds of some ornamental **Lupins (*Lupinus polyphyllus*)** contain toxic bitter alkaloids; those lacking the bitterness are edible. Soaking in brine reduces toxicity.

Laburnum

Common Laburnum (*L. anagyroides*) and **Scotch Laburnum (*L. alpinum*)** are very similar, small (to 13m) trees, native to the mountains of continental Europe but widely grown as ornamentals. **Voss's Laburnum (*L. x watereri*)** is a popular hybrid of the two. They have trifoliate leaves and drooping racemes of bright yellow flowers, followed by seed pods which turn from green to brown (though not all cultivars set seed).

All parts of the plants are poisonous, especially the seeds, though the foliage is more toxic before flowering. Documented cases of human poisoning are rare, and usually involved children who had eaten either the flowers or the seeds, resulting in persistent vomiting, followed by dizziness, headache and breathing problems. All victims fully recovered, though there are recorded deaths of cattle, horses and one dog. The primary toxin (cytisine) is structurally similar to nicotine and is used as an aid to quit smoking, though the correct dosage is very important, because it can cause coma and potentially death. Laburnum wood is highly valued for making into ornamental items.

Crownvetch (*Securigera varia* syn. *Coronilla varia*) ☠

Crownvetch is a low-growing, straggly perennial herb to 1.2m, with pinnate leaves (up to12 leaflet pairs), no tendrils, pale pink/purple/white flowers in globular clusters, followed by narrow, segmented seed pods. Native to most of Europe, introduced in the British Isles but naturalised and locally abundant in dry grassland, roadsides, railway embankments and wasteland, especially urban brownfield sites. It is quite aggressive, even in poor growing conditions, and has been used to prevent soil erosion, but has become an invasive problem in some places. Crownvetch contains nitroglycerides used to treat cardiac problems, which are lethal in large doses. It is poisonous to most mammals, though some ruminants can safely eat it because their digestive system breaks down the nitroglycerides.

Goat's Rue (*Galega officinalis*) ⚠

Goat's Rue is a robust, upright perennial herb to 1.5m with pinnate leaves (4-8 leaflet pairs) and pale pinkish-purple or white flowers. Native to southern Europe, naturalised and frequent in south-east and central England on grass verges and waste ground, rare or absent elsewhere in the British Isles. Distinguishable from purple-flowered vetches by having a terminal leaflet at the end of the pinnate leaves, rather than a tendril. Might also be confused with White Melitot (also found on waste ground), which only has three leaflets. **Sainfoin (*Onobrychis viciifolia*)** is smaller, with pinker flowers, and found on chalk grassland. Once a widely used fodder plant, it has marginally edible leaves.

Traditionally used as food for both humans and animals, as well as an ornamental and green manure, Goat's Rue is now known to cause a range of unpleasant symptoms, and potentially death. It has been used medically to increase the flow of milk in lactating mothers – humans as well as sheep and goats – and to treat diabetes. The compounds responsible (galegine and guanidine) decrease blood sugar, and were instrumental in the development of modern diabetic drugs.

▼ Crownvetch

▼ Goat's Rue

Restharrows (*Ononis*)

Common Restharrow (*O. repens*) is a sprawling, creeping perennial herb with usually spineless hairy stems to 60cm, small, finely notched, grey-green, hairy, oval leaves and pale pink flowers in the summer (wings same length as keel). It is frequent in most of the British Isles in dry pasture, and on rough grassland, sand dunes, shingle or cliffs, especially on chalk/limestone and in coastal areas. Less common in central Wales and rare in northern and western Scotland, and generally frequent across most of northern temperate Europe. There is a spined variety (var. *horrida*).

The rhizome is edible, raw or cooked. It tastes of liquorice, and can be soaked in water to make a drink. The shoots and flowers can also be eaten raw in salads, cooked or pickled. Liquorice (the confection) is made from the root of a related species (*Glycyrrhiza glabra*), native to southern Europe and also known as 'Liquorice'. Wild Liquorice (*Astragalus glycyphyllos*), which is scarce in the British Isles, can't be used to make liquorice. Restharrows were historically a major problem for farmers. Not only did their tangle of deep roots literally stop horse-drawn ploughs ('harrows'), but if dairy livestock ate the plant, its liquorice flavour would taint the milk.

Spiny Restharrow (*O. spinosa*) is an upright perennial herb to 70cm with spiny, hairy stems, narrower leaves than Common Restharrow and white/pink flowers in summer (wings shorter than keel). Frequent and locally common in much of central and southern England on grassland and rough ground, rare or absent elsewhere in the British Isles, but common in most of Europe apart from the far north. Though it lacks the rhizomes of Common Restharrow, the roots were also once chewed as a liquorice substitute, and the shoots and flowers can be used in salads.

▾ Common Restharrow

False Acacia or Black Locust
(*Robinia pseudoacacia*) ⓘ

False Acacia is a thorny, deciduous tree to
30m with pinnate leaves up to 25cm long,
and thick, furrowed bark. The long racemes
of flowers are usually white, but sometimes
pink/purple, appearing in the spring, and
sometimes again in late summer to early
autumn. They are followed by bean-like
seed pods up to 10cm long. False Acacia can
be found in woodland and scrub, usually
on calcareous soil, and is locally common
in some parts of England, but rare outside
horticulture. It is native to the south-
eastern United States, but widely introduced
elsewhere including temperate zones of
Europe. The poisonous Laburnums (p185)
are smaller, the flowers are yellow and the
leaves are trifoliate.

▾ False Acacia

False Acacia flowers are a highly regarded treat in Italy and elsewhere in Europe, and rightfully so – lightly battered and deep fried they are delicious. You can get away with shallow frying them, but the batter must be on the runny side. They can also be used to fill pancakes, and make jam. See recipes on p77. The boiled seeds are edible, and there is conflicting information about the toxicity of the pods (some sources report that they are an intoxicant, others that they cause gastric complaints). There is also conflicting information about the edibility of all parts of the plant raw – it has certainly been implicated in livestock poisonings and given the characteristics of this family it is probably best to cook them. There is a documented case[*] of a human poisoning after ingestion of the bark. The toxins involved are toxalbumins – a class of compounds that inhibit protein synthesis but are usually rendered inert by digestion, and only seriously poisonous if injected. This tree is an important honey source in North America, and the wood is highly regarded for burning in stoves. True *Acacia* is a large, polyphyletic genus, mostly tropical and/or Australian, with smaller, frillier leaves and yellow flowers.

▼ False Acacia seed pods

▲ Wisteria

Wisteria

Wisteria is a genus of woody climbers to 20m, with pinnate leaves up to 35cm long, hosting up to 19 leaflets, and large racemes of showy flowers (spring), which can be purple, pink, white or yellow. The flowers are edible, and best used raw in salads. They can also be made into fritters like False Acacia, though the large size of the racemes poses a practical problem. If you're thinking of eating the yellow variety, be sure you don't confuse it with *Laburnum* (p185). The pods which follow are also similar to those of *Laburnum. Wisteria* are native to Asia and North America, but widely grown elsewhere as ornamentals. The rest of the plant is toxic, especially the seeds.

[*] *A Rare Ingestion of Black Locust Tree*, Journal of Toxicology: Clinical Toxicology, 42:1, 93-95, Hui, A, et al, 2004. DOI: 10.1081/CLT-120028752.

▲ Broom

Broom (*Cytisus scoparius* syn. *Sarothamnus scoparius*) (!)

Broom is a spineless, deciduous, perennial shrub to 2.2m with stiff, branching, five-sided stems and small trifoliate leaves. The abundant yellow flowers appear in the leaf axils (spring and summer) and are followed by small, dark pods containing black seeds. Frequent to common in most of the British Isles in dry, acidic habitats such as heath and scrub, sometimes grassland. Less common in central Ireland. Native and frequent to common in Europe from southern Scandinavia to the far south.

Do not confuse with **Spanish Broom** (**Spartium junceum**), which has flexible stems, needle-like leaves and toxic flowers. This is a Mediterranean species which is not currently naturalised in the British Isles.

The flower buds can be pickled or used raw as a garnish or in salads (goes well with St George's Mushrooms and tomatoes). The shoots can be used to flavour beer. The seeds and pods are slightly toxic, containing quinolizidine alkaloids, which primarily affect the nervous system and the heart. Some sources also suggest other parts of the plant (twigs, leaves) are toxic, so it is best to use only in moderation, and avoid completely if you are pregnant. Historically, Broom was used to make paper and fibres.

Gorse (*Ulex europaeus*)

Gorse, also known as Furze in parts of southern England and Whin in Scotland, is a perennial shrub to 3m with sharp, rigid, deeply grooved spines in place of leaves. The small, yellow flowers appear from late winter to midsummer, and smell of coconut/vanilla, though only in the sunshine and many people can't detect it at all. Native and abundant almost everywhere in the British Isles, France and northern Spain, especially on heathland, but also open woodland, scrub, dunes and cliffs. **Western Gorse (*U. gallii*)** is smaller, with much less deeply grooved spines, and darker flowers which appear from midsummer to late autumn. It is found in the west of the British Isles, Brittany and north-west Spain. **Dwarf Gorse (*U. minor*)** is even smaller, and more delicate. It is found mainly in the south and east of the British Isles, and western France.

The flower buds are edible raw in salads, but are inferior to Broom, and can be infested with insects. They make one of the best wild flower wines, and can be pickled like Broom buds (see opposite). The dried flowers are commercially available as a tea, and the shoot tips can be used for the same purpose.

▾ Gorse

Gorse Flower Tea

Put two tablespoons of bruised gorse flowers in a mug, fill with boiling water, and steep for 10 mins. Add honey to taste.

Pickled Broom (or Gorse) Buds Preserved in Brined Verjuice

(Sir Hugh Plat's *Delightes for Ladies to adorne their Persons, Tables, Closets, and Distillatories with Beauties, Banquets, Perfumes and Waters*, 1600)

Ingredients:

500ml verjuice or white wine vinegar, 5tbsp fine sea salt, 400ml fresh broom buds (rinsed and dried).

Put the verjuice (or vinegar) and salt in a pan. Bring to the boil and stir until the salt dissolves. Add the broom buds and simmer for 1 minute. Strain buds, but don't discard the pickling liquid. Pack into sterilised jars, pour over the hot liquid, cover with lids and allow to cool. Allow to mature for at least 3 weeks before using to garnish salads or in place of capers.

▾ Broom (left) and Gorse (right)

Vetches (*Vicia*) (!)

Vetches are herbs with pinnate leaves (with opposite leaflets), ending in tendrils in most species, and two leaf-like stipules at the bases of the leaf stalks. Small yellow-flowered plants in other genera but called 'vetches' (eg Kidney and Horseshoe Vetches) are of no foraging interest or mildly toxic.

Vetches are primarily famine foods. Apart from Broad Beans, the seeds of temperate European vetches are poisonous raw but can be made safe by boiling for 20 minutes (Miles Irving recommends pressure cooking), and discarding the water. In normal times this is not worth the effort. The young shoots and leaves are also edible, and they too should be cooked. A few of the flowers can be added to salads.

Common Vetch (*V. sativa*) is an annual with sprawling or climbing stems to 2m, 4-8 leaflet pairs, terminating curly tendrils, and stipules normally with teeth. The purple-pink flowers appear in pairs or singletons (summer) and the pods are very small (late summer and early autumn). Common throughout temperate Europe (with at least four recognised subspecies), especially south-east England. Found on unimproved grassland, waste ground, banks, roadsides and other grassy places. Easily distinguished from other vetches by the pair of flowers at the base of each leaf, which are the best edible part of this plant.

Tufted Vetch (*V. cracca*) is a perennial with climbing stems to 2m, 5-15 leaflet pairs, untoothed stipules and terminating tendrils, drooping racemes of up to 40 dull purple flowers (late spring and summer) and small green pods. Native and common throughout the British Isles and temperate Europe on roadsides, waste ground, tall grassland, disturbed land, woods and hedges, especially where it is damp. Historically a problem weed of arable fields.

Bush Vetch (*V. sepium*) is a climbing/spreading perennial to 50cm, with 3-9 leaflet pairs, half-arrow shaped stipules, branching tendrils, and short racemes of dull pink-purple flowers. Native and very common in temperate Europe in woods, scrub and hedgebanks.

Hairy Tare (*V. hirsuta* syn. *Ervilia hirsuta*) is an annual with stems which crawl and climb to 1m or more, leaves terminating in tendrils, racemes of white, pale blue or mauve flowers and tiny pods. Inhabits grassland and agricultural fields, especially in disturbed areas. Frequent in lowland temperate Europe. Recorded in E Sturtevant's *Edible Plants of the World* (1919) as having been occasionally cultivated as food.

Broad Bean (*V. faba*) (also pictured on p72) is an annual to 1.8m with leaves up to 25cm long, white flowers and large pods containing the familiar beans. This was one of the earliest and most widespread domesticated plants. Its wild ancestor has never been found/identified and is probably extinct. Introduced almost everywhere there are human settlements, from the tropics to cold temperate areas, and usually found as a short-term escape from cultivation. As well as the beans, the leaf tips are edible.

▼ Broad Bean

▲ Common Vetch

▼ Bush Vetch

▲ Tufted Vetch

▼ Hairy Tare

Clovers (*Trifolium*) ⓘ

If you include all the alien species, 30 species of clover have been recorded in the British Isles, many of which are known to be edible to some extent; the two featured here are just the best known. The Medicks (p198) and Wood-sorrels (p182) are regularly confused with Clovers. The Lesser, Hop and Slender Trefoils (*T. dubium*, *campestre* and *micrancanthum*) have similar leaves, but yellow flowers. These have been eaten in the past, but are better known as medicinal plants and should be avoided by foragers.

The leaves and young flowers of Clovers are edible, raw or cooked. They can be used to flavour rice ('Clover Rice'). The dried flowers make a pleasant herbal tea, which should be served with honey and lemon. The sprouted seeds can be used in salads, but raw unsprouted seeds are mildly toxic. There are also reports that diseased plants can be toxic, and it is not always obvious they are diseased, though you should look out for discolouration on the leaves.

White or **Dutch Clover** (*T. repens*) is a perennial herb with creeping, rooting stems to 60cm, alternating trifoliate leaves (shorter and less pointed than Red Clover, and with shorter stalks) and globes of white or cream flowers. It is native and abundant throughout the British Isles and temperate Europe in grassland and waste ground, especially on clay.

The flowers and pods of White Clover were dried and ground into flour in Scotland and Ireland during famines (in Ireland it was called 'Chambroch bread', according to Pierpoint Johnson). The cooked roots are also a famine food.

Spiced White Clover
(with thanks to Dyfed Lloyd Evans)

Ingredients:
300g clover leaves, stems and young flowers, 50g butter, ½tsp coriander seeds, ½tsp fennel seeds, 2 star anise segments or some black stone-flower, salt and pepper.

Toast the spices in a dry frying pan for 1 minute, then grind to a paste. Steam the clover for 3 mins then drain. Fry the paste in butter for 1 minute, then add the clover and fry for another 3 mins, stirring regularly. Serve immediately.

Red Clover (*T. pratense*) is a perennial herb with upright or sprawling stems to 70cm, alternating trifoliate leaves with pale, crescent-shaped splodges near the centre, and globes of pink flowers (can be pale or dark). It is native and abundant throughout Europe on grassland, roadsides and waste ground, especially near the sea.

Red Clover works well in pancakes – just make a normal pancake batter with 50/50 white and wholemeal flour. When it is about the consistency of single cream, and lump-free, add a good measure of red clover florets (individual flowers picked from the flower head). It also makes a potent country wine.

Red Clover Wine

(from *The Secrets of some Wiltshire Housewives*, Edith Oliver/WI, 1927)

Ingredients:
4.5l red clover blossoms, 4.5l boiling water, 3 lemons, 2 oranges, 1.8kg white sugar, 30g compressed yeast, 0.25l cup warm water.

Put the clover blossom into a crock or wooden tub (do not use a metal vessel, or one with a soft glaze). Pour boiling water over the blossoms. Slice the lemons and oranges into it. Add the sugar and let stand until lukewarm. Dissolve the yeast in the water and add that. Let it stand for 5 days, stirring twice a day. Strain off and let stand for 3 days. Bottle it, leaving the corks loose for 10 days, then seal tightly and leave for a month.

Melitots or Sweet Clovers (*Melitotus*) ⓘ

All these species were introduced to the British Isles in the 16th century by medical herbalists, who used them to make ointments for treating bruises and blisters. They have long spikes of yellow or white flowers, and are much more common in England than elsewhere in the British Isles. They should only be used (for food) fresh. When dried, their coumarin content renders them toxic, as well as highly aromatic.

The fresh young shoots, leaves and flowers are edible in salads, though bitter. The leaves and pods can be used in soups and casseroles, going especially well with rabbit. The flowers make a nice cake decoration. The flowering tops can also be used to make a refreshing drink – you need a good handful of tops to 3tbsp of sugar or honey, in 1 litre of water. Leave in a fridge for a few hours and it will be ready to drink.

White Melitot (*M. albus*) is an annual or biennial herb to 1.5m, with alternating trifoliate leaves and long racemes of white flowers (summer), followed by pods containing single seeds. It is frequent in parts of central and south-east England, in fields and on waste ground, on neutral or alkaline soils. Rarer elsewhere in the British Isles, and native to south-east Europe. Historically used to flavour sauces in continental Europe (source: Miles Irving). Also an important nectar plant for honey production, a forage plant for cattle, and used as green manure.

"In Switzerland ... it is much grown and has acquired celebrity from being used to give the peculiar flavour to Gruyère cheese, so highly esteemed in Continental Europe. For this purpose the flowers and seeds are bruised and mixed with the curd before pressing ... "
(C Pierpoint Johnson, 1862)

Ribbed or **Sweet Melilot (*M. officinalis*)** is a hairless biennial herb with a trailing or upright stem up to 1.5m long and trifoliate leaves. The long racemes of yellow flowers are followed by single-seeded pods which are brown when ripe. It is frequent in lowland England on field margins, roadsides and waste ground, rarer in Scotland and Wales, and native to south-east Europe. It was this species that the Swiss used to flavour Gruyère cheese. The roots were eaten by the Kalmuks (Mongol Buddhists of the Russian steppe).

Small Melitot (*M. indicus*) is very similar to Ribbed Melitot, but smaller and rarer. **Tall Melilot (*M. altissimus*)** is also very similar, but with smaller seed pods which are black when ripe. Frequent in central and south-east England, rare elsewhere in the British Isles. Both can be used in the same ways.

Medicks (*Medicago*)

'Medick' has nothing to do with Medicine – it refers to the ancient civilisation of 'Mede', in what is now Iran, and was the Roman name for Lucerne. There are at least 10 species in northern Europe, several of which are naturalised in a few locations in the British Isles, and numerous other smaller members of this family can look similar. The seeds can be sprouted like Alfalfa, or cooked, and the leaves used as a pot-herb (they are bitter raw).

Lucerne or **Alfalfa** (*M. sativa*) is a scrambling perennial herb to 90cm with hairy trifoliate leaves, blue, mauve or yellow flowers (summer) and tightly coiled seed pods. Inhabits field margins, waste ground and grass verges and common in East Anglia, where it is either native or an ancient introduction. Rarer elsewhere in the British Isles, especially Scotland and Ireland, but frequent in continental Europe. **Sickle Medick** (*M. falcata*) is very closely related, with yellow flowers and much straighter seed pods. Lucerne could also be confused with Tufted Vetch (p192), though that plant has one-sided racemes.

Domesticated Lucerne is well known as a health food, and rich in vitamins. The sprouted seeds are used a salad vegetable, and unsprouted can also be ground and used as a flour improver. These seeds are slightly toxic when unsprouted and raw (containing enzyme inhibitors which interfere with protein digestion). Wild, the best edible part is the sweet-tasting flowers. Lucerne can also be dried and used as an appetite-stimulating tea. It has long been an important fodder crop for cattle and sheep (as silage or hay – it causes bloat when used fresh), and has an exceptionally deep root

▲ Lucerne

system, making it drought-resistant as well as nitrogen-fixing.

Black Medick (*M. lupulina*) is a semi-perennial herb with stems to 80cm long, trifoliate compound leaves (with no black blotch in the centre of the leaflets), and a short point at the tip. The small, yellow, clover-like flowers are followed by small, ovoid, black (when mature) seed pods containing a single seed. Black Medick inhabits grassland and disturbed ground, preferring alkaline, nutrient-poor soils, and is common in the British Isles apart from central and north-west Scotland, and throughout Europe apart from the far north. **Spotted Medick** (*M. arabica*) is similar, but with distinctive black blotches in the centre of the leaflets, fewer flowers per head, and green, spiral pods. Lesser Trefoil (*Trifolium dubium*) is the most similar species outside this genus, but lacks the pointed tips to the leaflets.

▲ Black Medick

▲ Spotted Medick

Lathyrus (genus)   ⚠

All members of the pea genus *Lathyrus* are mildly toxic, especially raw, and consumption of excessive quantities can cause a serious disease known as Lathyrism. Symptoms include bone and brain deformities, and muscle wastage, starting with weakened legs and ending with total paralysis below the waist (which can be permanent). The ornamental Sweet Pea (*L. odoratus*), native to southern Europe, is one of the worst offenders. Cooked, and in moderate quantities, the seeds of all species can be safely eaten.

Heath Pea
(*L. linifolius* syn. *montanus*)

"The stems creep underground, and at intervals enlarge into small tubers. These tubers are sweet in taste, and very nutritious, either boiled or in the raw state. In the Highlands of Scotland, where the Bitter-Vetch abounds, they are collected by the people, dried, and used for chewing, like the betel-nut in India, or the coca in Peru, and are said to increase the strength and improve the lungs of those addicted to the habit. They are likewise considered to give a relish to the whiskey so largely consumed in those mountain districts."
(C Pierpoint Johnson, 1862)

Heath Pea or **Bitter Vetch** is a hairless perennial herb with winged stems to 50cm and alternating leaf stalks with 1-4 leaflet pairs, toothed stipules and no tendrils (it does not climb), clusters of 2-6 pink-red flowers turning blue-green (early summer) and bean-like seed pods. Native to the British Isles, and common in open broadleaved woodland, hedgerows, banks, heaths, rocky places, and rough, unimproved grassland, absent from East Anglia to East Midlands. Do not confuse with *Vicia ervilia*, which is also known as 'Bitter Vetch', but does not occur in temperate Europe.

This plant is possibly of medicinal interest as an appetite suppressant, having historically been used to stave off hunger during famines.

▼ Heath Pea

Everlasting Peas (*L. latifolius/grandiflorus/sylvestris*)

Broad-leaved Everlasting Pea (*L. latifolius*) is a perennial herb with sprawling or climbing, winged stems to 2.5m, with tendrils and alternating pairs of blue-green leaves (length:width ratio less than 4:1) on long stalks, and racemes of pink flowers. Native to southern Europe, introduced in northern Europe. In Britain it is usually found on roadsides or as a garden escape, and invasive in some locations in southern England. It is much rarer in other parts of the British Isles. **(Two-flowered) Everlasting Pea (*L. grandiflorus*)** is very similar, apart from having more slender square stems and showier flowers (from light pink to dark magenta on the same bloom, and usually in pairs on a single stalk). Also introduced from the Mediterranean and doesn't usually form pods in the British Isles. **Narrow-leaved Everlasting Pea (*L. sylvestris*)** has longer, narrower leaves (length:width ratio more than 4:1), and slightly smaller and paler flowers. It is a perennial climbing herb to 2m, with floppy, winged stems, alternating pairs of leaves on short, winged stalks, tendrils in sets of three, red-pink flowers and bean-like seed pods. Found in open broadleaved woodland, forest margins, hedgerows and banks (especially railway embankments) and disturbed/waste ground, usually scrambling or climbing over other vegetation. Native to the British Isles, it is occasional, though locally common in much of England and Wales, rarer in the north.

The flowers of all three make a fine addition to a mixed salad, both decoratively and in terms of their sweet pea-like taste, and the pods as well as the peas are also edible in moderation. The young shoots (cooked) make a nice garnish to seafood dishes.

▲ Narrow-leaved Everlasting Pea

▲ Two-flowered Everlasting Pea   ▼ Broad-leaved Everlasting Pea

Tuberous Pea or Earthnut
(*L. tuberosus*)

Tuberous Pea is a climbing perennial herb with wingless stems to 1.2m, alternating pairs of leaflets on short stalks and a terminating tendril, red-pink flowers (summer) and a bean-like seed pod. It is occasional in the British Isles, not fully naturalised in many places, and more frequent in England, in open broadleaved woodland, hedgerows, banks, arable land and rough grassland. Native to south-eastern parts of temperate Europe and western Asia, introduced in western Europe along with cereal cultivation.

This species has been cultivated for its edible tubers. They are delicious, but growth is slow and the tubers are few. The peas are also tasty while green, but small.

Sea Pea (*L. japonicus*)

"The seeds are bitter in taste and very unpalatable, but having proved valuable in times of scarcity, entitle the plant to a place among our useful vegetables. In 1555, the people in the neighbourhood of Aldborough and Orford, in Suffolk, suffering from famine, supported themselves to a great extent by the seeds of this plant, which grew in great abundance in the sandy hills there. It had not been noticed by the inhabitants before, and its supposed sudden growth was very generally regarded by them as a miraculous interposition of providence, though some attributed it to the wreck of a vessel laden with peas on that coast during the previous year, an origin equally improbable, as the Sea Pea is nowhere cultivated for food. It is most likely that the plant had grown there, as suggested by an old writer, for centuries, but the seeds being nauseous in flavour, no one had recollected the circumstance until pressed by famine to seek food among the wild herbs of the neighbouring waste."
(C Pierpoint Johnson, 1862)

Sea Pea is a hairless perennial herb with trailing/sprawling stems to 90cm and alternate grey-green leaves and terminating tendrils, purple (becoming blue) and white flowers (mid to late summer) and bean-like seed pods up to 5cm long. Sea Pea forms mats on beaches, and is generally rare in the British Isles but locally abundant on shingle on the south and east coasts of Great Britain and Ireland. More common in Scandinavia and the north coast of continental Europe.

The seeds, pods and young shoots are edible (all cooked), but should not be consumed in large quantities, and should be left alone in the UK for conservation reasons (protected under the Wildlife and Countryside Act 1981). This species is distributed by sea, able to survive floating in sea water for five years, which explains its large natural range.

Rosales

In addition to the families included here, the Rosales also includes the *Moraceae* (Mulberry family). **Mulberries (*Morus*)** are small trees that produce masses of Blackberry-like fruits (only ripe when dark red). They were once common in the southern half of England, then became almost unheard of, and are now beginning to make a comeback. These fruits are extremely delicate and thus hard to protect during transportation, making them unsuitable for commercial use. Figs (which only very occasionally grow wild in the British Isles) also belong to this order.

Rosaceae (Rose family)

The *Rosaceae* are a large family of flowering plants containing many familiar domesticated fruit crops and ornamentals. A lot of the species most relevant to foragers are the wild ancestors of cultivated varieties. Most of this family falls into two large 'tribes'. The first half of the species covered here (up to Parsley Pierts on p225), are the herbs and smaller shrubs (including Brambles) of tribe *Rosoideae*. The second half, from Blackthorn onwards, are the larger shrubs and trees (including the stone fruits) of tribe *Amygdaloideae*.

The whole family comes with a safety warning, especially the *Amygdaloideae* (see the genus entry for Prunus, p226). The edible fruits of **Quince (*Cydonia oblonga*)**, which is not native to north-west Europe but is grown as far north as Scotland, have particularly toxic pips.

Some familiar ornamental members of this family have berries which are inedible, or almost inedible. These include the shrubs

▲ Firethorn

in the genus *Cotoneaster* and *Photinia*, the berries of which are visually attractive, but taste unpleasant, as well as being dry, full of pips and mildly poisonous. Even the birds only eat these when they've run out of tastier options. The berries of their relatives the **Firethorns (*Pyracantha*)**, which have thorns and leaves with serrated edges, aren't much better – although they can be used to make jam. The pips are slightly poisonous, and must be removed.

Roses (*Rosa*)

Detailed here are four common native species and an abundant alien. There are several rarer natives, and many other aliens and hybrids. All are potential food sources, and a good choice for edible hedging.

The flowers of all Roses can be used for their scent and flavour, in drinks, desserts and preserves, although the bases of the petals are bitter and should be discarded. Rose petal honey is delicious (many recipes available online). The petals can be dried and ground to a powder, then used as a flavouring

▲ Dog Rose

in baked goods. The fruits (hips) are well known to foragers, sometimes left to blet. During World War II they were made into a syrup, providing a valuable source of vitamin C when citrus fruits weren't available. This was still commercially available in the 1970s – I remember being served it as part of my primary school dinners as an accompaniment to ground rice pudding. It is a useful ingredient for creating desserts. Rosehip and Crab Apple jelly is a perennial favourite (plenty of recipes online, and also see recipe on p245). The hips can be used to flavour vodka, brandy or gin, and also to make tea, though this requires the careful removal of the irritating hairs. One way to do this is to dry them, then blitz, then repeatedly sieve to remove the hairs. The young shoots are edible peeled, like Brambles (p208), and the young leaves and shoots make a decent herbal tea.

Dog Rose (*R. canina*) is a very variable deciduous perennial shrub with scrambling/arching stems to 3m, with equal-sized hooked thorns, toothed pinnate leaves and large white or pale pink flowers (summer) followed by orange-red fruits (autumn, see next page). By far the most common wild rose, native to the British Isles and abundant in the south, less so in the north, also common throughout Europe apart from the far north. It has a number of similar relatives and subspecies.

Sweet Briar (*R. rubiginosa*) is similar to Dog Rose, though smaller (to 2m) and with unequal thorns. Native in the British Isles and common on calcareous soils. **Field Rose (*R. arvensis*)** has weaker, trailing stems, narrow-based thorns and white flowers, and is common in England and Wales, but very rare in Scotland and uncommon in Ireland. Frequent across most of temperate Europe. **Burnet Rose (*R. spinosissima*)** is a smaller scrambling species with very dense spines and hairs, cream-white flowers and purple-black hips. Locally common in coastal areas, much rarer inland. Best known for making tea (from the hips and leaves).

▼ Burnet Rose

Rosewater

Put rose petals in pot, add a little water (but not much), simmer for 2 hours without letting it boil, strain through several layers of cheesecloth. For small amounts, just keep in the fridge. To keep larger amounts for a longer time, you will need to boil and put in sterilised jars. For uses, see opposite and p158.

Rosehip Syrup (British World War II recipe)

Ingredients:
1kg rosehips, 450g sugar, water.

Trim and finely chop the hips. Boil 2l of water in a pan, add the hips, return to the boil, remove from heat and leave to infuse for 10 mins. Place in a jelly bag and let the juice drip through. Return pulp to pan, add 1l of water, and repeat the process. Return all the strained juice to the pan, add the sugar and stir over low heat until dissolved. Boil for 5 mins. Remove from heat and pour into sterilised bottles. Seal bottles with sterilised corks. For a long-lasting syrup, bring these bottles slowly to the boil again in a deep saucepan, and simmer for 5 mins before storing.

Wild Rose Jam (Jason Hill, 1939)

To every pound [0.45kg] of hips allow half a pint [0.55l] of water. Boil till the fruit is tender and pass the pulp through a fine sieve to keep back the seeds. Add 1lb of sugar to 1lb of pulp and boil till it jellies. No hips should be used for jam until they have been touched by frost. Either an enamel-lined or glass oven-ware saucepan must be used.

▲ Japanese Rose

Japanese or **Beach Rose** (*R. rugosa*) is a suckering shrub to 1.5m, with densely prickled, upright stems, distinctly corrugated leaves and scented flowers (spring) which are usually dark pink (there is a rarer white form). In early autumn the plants can have both flowers and hips at the same time. Native to eastern Asia, it is a coastal specialist and can become invasive on sea cliffs. Has considerably larger hips than most of its relatives, making it of particular interest to foragers. They are inferior to some other roses for syrup, but the best for jam and cakes and can be nibbled raw, though you need to avoid the hairy insides. Pick when deep red, not orange.

We came up with the recipe on the right because the main ingredients happened to be available at our foraging HQ in Sussex, and it has proved very popular. The flavours and colours work beautifully together.

"The fruit when it is ripe maketh most pleasant meats and banqueting dishes, as tarts and such like; the making whereof I commit to the cunning cooke, and teeth to eate them in the rich mans mouth."
(John Gerard, 1597)

◀ Dog Rose

Japanese Rosehip and Bullace Upside-Down Cake

Ingredients:
Topping: 2tbsp butter, 2tbsp brown sugar, 20 bullaces, 20 Japanese rosehips; Cake: 140g butter, 150g caster sugar, 100g flour, 50g ground almonds, 2 eggs, 1tsp cinnamon, 1tsp rosewater, milk.

Carefully de-seed and de-hair the rosehips (cut them in half and use a teaspoon to remove the insides), and halve and stone the bullaces. Line an 8inch cake tin with baking paper, smear butter across it and sprinkle with the brown sugar. Into this, press the bullaces and rosehips. Be artistic – concentric circles look nice. In a mixing bowl, cream together the sugar and butter, then beat in the eggs and rosewater. Add the flour, almonds and cinnamon and mix well. Spread the mixture over the fruit. If too firm, add a splash of milk until it's spreadable. Bake at 180°C (fan 160°C) for 1 hour or until a knife inserted into the middle of the sponge comes out clean. Flip the cake over on to a cooling rack, carefully peel back the paper from the caramelised fruit, and leave to cool.

Brambles / *Rubus* (genus)

For botanists, the genus *Rubus* is sufficiently large and difficult an area of taxonomy as to warrant its own name: *batology*. These plants typically have prickly, bristly or spiny, woody stems. Their fruits are 'aggregates' of individual 'drupelets'. Domesticated varieties grown for their fruit are known as 'cane fruits'. This page covers the domesticated varieties primarily grown as ornamentals.

Chinese Bramble (*R. tricolor*) is a prostrate or climbing evergreen (usually) shrub with alternate, slightly lobed, glossy, dark green leaves, roughly hairy, but non-prickly, stems, and white flowers followed by red berries. Native to southern China, it is widely grown elsewhere as ornamental ground cover, occasionally escaping, and spreading in the British Isles. The fruits are similar to Raspberries, and used in the same ways.

Japanese Wineberry (*R. phoenicolasius*) is a scrambler which bears bristly (but not very thorny) biennial stems from perennial

▼ Chinese Bramble

roots. These grow unbranched to 3m in the first year, with pinnate leaves (three or five leaflets). Bristly racemes of white flowers are produced in the second year on side shoots, followed by orange-red, sticky-shiny fruits that look halfway between a Blackberry and a Raspberry. This plant has been cultivated for its fruits, though they are not to everybody's taste.

Creeping Raspberry (*R. hayata-koidzumii*, not pictured) is a low-growing species, with crinkly palmate-lobed leaves and orange-yellow berries. It is native to the Taiwanese mountains, and though best known as an ornamental, it has escaped in various parts of Europe, including north-west England. The berries are edible and pleasant-tasting, but small.

Salmonberry (*R. spectabilis*) is an upright species to 2m, with soft spines, showy, vivid pink flowers, and orange fruits. Native to North America, grown as an ornamental and for fruit, and now naturalised in many parts of the British Isles, especially Scotland. Fruits are edible but very sour.

White-stemmed Bramble (*R. cockburnianus*, not pictured) is a scrambler to 5m, with unusual (for this genus) pinnate leaves (a bit like Meadowsweet). The whole plant, including the fruits, is covered in a strong white bloom. Native to China, grown as an ornamental and hedging in the British Isles, and naturalised in many places, especially western England and central Scotland. Fruits are edible but poor.

Cutleaf Blackberry (*R. lacininiatus*) is very similar to Blackberry, apart from its deeply cut leaves. Native to Eurasia, but not the British Isles. Grown as an ornamental, and naturalised in a few places. Fruits are also very like Blackberries.

▲ Salmonberry   ▼ Japanese Wineberry   ▼ Cutleaf Blackberry

Blackberry (*R. fruticosus* agg.)

Blackberries or **Brambles** are very well known thorny perennial shrubs with small white to pale pink flowers in spring and early summer, and black fruits in late summer and early autumn. They are common everywhere in the British Isles except for the highest mountains, and throughout temperate areas of Europe as far north as the southern coast of Scandinavia.

The suffix 'agg.' refers to hundreds of different 'microspecies' which can both hybridise and reproduce asexually. The key identifying feature that distinguishes them from similar species is that the torus of the berry (the end of the stem that runs into the centre of the berry) comes away with the berry, rather than remaining on the plant and leaving the berry with a hollow centre (as in Raspberries). All these microspecies have different characteristics. They fruit at different times, and some produce much tastier, juicier or larger berries than others. You will sometimes find multiple varieties growing right next to each other, at which point their differences can be very obvious.

Blackberries are perhaps the only wild food that the British have always foraged for. They are super-abundant in the wild, and for this reason they were only domesticated in the 19th century (and even then in America, not Europe). Even now the domesticated varieties are generally grown outside their native zone as an export crop, so we can buy them when they aren't in season. The fruit can be eaten raw or made into preserves, pies, wines, syrups, and so on. Young shoots (with soft spines, and that can be easily snapped off) are also edible (peeled and cooked). The leaves make one of the better herbal teas, but they should be dried slowly enough to slightly ferment.

Tradition has it that Blackberries should not be collected after Michaelmas (29th September), because the devil spits on them. The truth is probably worse: they do indeed tend to go a bit squishy around this time, and the culprit is a Flesh Fly (*Sarcophaga carnaria*), which drools saliva on them, predigesting them so it can suck up the juices. Unfortunately, as the name implies, these flies are also attracted to rotting meat. And faeces.

Chilled Blackberry Soup

Makvlis Supi is a traditional Georgian/Polish/Russian dish, served cold with sour cream as a starter. Popular in my own household and very healthy.

Ingredients:
600g fresh blackberries, finely chopped herbs (50g coriander, 5g mint, large sprig of fresh thyme), 1 small onion (finely chopped), 1 garlic clove (finely chopped), 1 small cucumber (peeled, seeds removed and diced/sliced), 1tsp wine vinegar, salt to taste and sour cream to serve.

Put blackberries in bowl and crush and strain to produce a thick pulp. Add water to the pulp until you have 900ml of liquid (you can use this water to extract more liquid from the crushed material) and then add all the other ingredients apart from the sour cream. Add salt to taste and allow to chill for several hours before serving with the sour cream.

Blackberry Cordial (TF Garrett, 1892)

To each pound of Blackberries allow ½ lb (230g) of moist sugar, mix well, and put into large wide-mouthed jars, filling them up with brandy to cover the fruit. Add 1 teaspoonful each of cloves and allspice to each gallon (4.5l) jar, cover, and leave three weeks to macerate. Pour off the liquor, squeeze the fruit thoroughly, filter through a tammy cloth, bottle, and cork. This may be served with water.

Blackberry Pie (TF Garrett, 1892)

Pick the Blackberries clean of stalks and debris, and put them into a flat pie dish lined with a good paste. Grate a little nutmeg over, add the juice of a lemon and its grated rind, and a piled teacupful of moist sugar; then pour in 1 gill (140ml) of water, put on a top crust, and bake in a moderate oven. Sometimes apples to the extent of a third of the fruit are added, and the juice of a lemon is another great improvement.

Blackberry Pudding (TF Garrett, 1892)

Take a sufficient quantity of Blackberries and thinly-sliced apples, mixed, to fill a pudding basin. Turn out the fruit from the basin, and line with a good pudding crust; replace the fruit, add 2lb (0.9kg) of sugar, cover over, and tie up with a cloth. Plunge into boiling water, and let it boil for two hours, or nearly.

▲ Dewberry

Dewberry (*R. caesius*)

Dewberry is a perennial shrub with softish thorns (fewer than Blackberry), scrambling blue-green biennial stems (weaker than Blackberry) up to 2m tall, alternate, hairy, palmate-compound leaves, small white flowers (summer to early autumn) and juicy blue-black berries (smaller than Blackberries, from late summer). Found in a variety of habitats (open woodland, ditches, scrub, rough grassland, dunes) on alkaline soil. Frequent in much of Wales and England although unevenly distributed. Rare in Scotland, absent from the far north. Present throughout Europe, apart from northern Scandinavia. Often mistaken for Blackberry, and often growing alongside it, although Dewberry fruits have a distinctive white bloom.

Uses as Blackberry, and opinions differ on whether they are classier, or inferior. Can hybridise with other members of this genus.

Wild Raspberry (*R. idaeus*)

Wild Raspberry is a suckering, deciduous, perennial shrub with prickly, upright, biennial stems to 1.5m, pinnate compound leaves, small white flowers and red fruits (occasionally yellow). It is common throughout the temperate zone of Eurasia in woods, heaths, scrub and rocky locations, often where it is damp, and particularly in hilly/mountainous regions.

This is the wild ancestor of domesticated raspberry, with more irregular but also more intensely flavoured berries. These are very popular with birds, so it can be a challenge to actually find any. However, they are worth seeking, and should be eaten raw – they are too good for cooking. The leaves make a popular herbal tea, and there is conflicting advice regarding whether this is safe/recommended at various points in pregnancy, or when trying to get pregnant. Folk wisdom has it that raspberry leaf tea, consumed in the third trimester, 'strengthens the uterus', which results in fewer problems during birth. Some medical experts advise against its use, on the grounds that it might 'interfere with labour'. Others claim it can trigger contractions and thus help labour. The leaves are also used in herbal smoking blends.

▼ Wild Raspberry

Stone Bramble (*R. saxatilis*)

Stone Bramble resembles a Blackberry apart from the fruit, which is smaller, irregular and red. It is a perennial shrub with annual stems to 60cm which have more needle-like prickles than Blackberry, alternate compound leaves, and small white flowers. It is locally common in damp woodland, clearings and particularly in rocky areas in Scotland and parts of Wales, rare elsewhere in the British Isles. Present throughout the temperate zones of Eurasia, always more common in northern areas. Uses are as Blackberry and Raspberry, though inferior and with larger pips.

▲ Stone Bramble
▼ Cloudberry

Cloudberry (*R. chamaemorus*)

Cloudberry is a low-growing perennial with non-prickly stems to 20cm, and round, lobed, toothed, alternate leaves. It has five-petalled white flowers and raspberry-like yellow-orange or red fruits. The name 'cloud' is derived from the old English for hill ('clud'), and it is absent from lowland Britain, but locally common in boggy, acidic areas in the far north and upland areas only. Collecting them can be challenging, because they like to grow scattered across the ground in treacherous terrain. Present throughout the more northerly parts of northern temperate zones. This species is highly prized, and used like Raspberry. The fruit rarely forms in Britain, due to an overwhelming prevalence of male plants.

Wild Strawberry (*Fragaria vesca*)

"Wild strawberries may take time to gather, but they are worth the trouble for their excellence with a dash of white wine and sugar or in flans and tartlets. If they are stewed in making kissel their appearance becomes unprepossessing, but the process develops 'the excellent, cordial smell of the strawberry leaves dying', which imparts an interesting and unusual flavour to the sweet."
(Jason Hill, 1939)

See Cranberry on p374 for more on Kissel.

Wild Strawberry is a perennial herb with soft stems to 15cm, and sharp-toothed trifoliate leaves (dark green on the upper side, paler below) on long, hairy stems. The plant has rooting runners, and small, five-petalled white flowers, followed by small red fruits (midsummer to early autumn). Usually found in woodland, or areas where woodland has been cleared, especially on chalk. It is native to south-west Asia but introduced widely elsewhere a long time ago and is now abundant throughout Europe, especially the north. The larger **Green Strawberry (*F. viridis*)** is common in much of temperate Europe, but not present in the British Isles. It is called 'green' because it doesn't fully redden when ripe. **Barren Strawberry (*Potentilla sterilis*)** has smaller, duller leaves (also edible), which have fewer teeth, and usually missing a tooth at the far end of the leaf. It produces fruits which are small, dry and inedible ('achenes').

Wild Strawberries are small, but the strongly flavoured fruit are commercially collected for the production of gourmet jams, sauces and syrups. They can be dried and used in muesli, and make a good wine. The leaves can be eaten in salads or cooked, and can be used (fresh or dried) to make a tea with a high vitamin C content.

This is not the wild ancestor of modern domesticated Strawberries, which are a hybrid between two American species of *Fragaria*. Centuries of attempts to breed larger versions of the tasty European Wild Strawberry ended in failure. It was only when European plant enthusiasts started growing several different types of Strawberry brought back from the New World in the 18th century, which were much larger but also less tasty, that the ancestor hybrid of today's domesticated varieties first appeared.

▾ Barren Strawberry

A Tart of Straw-Berries

(from *A book of fruit and flowers*, Anonymous, 1653)

Pick and wash your *Straw-Berries* clean, and put them in the past one by another, as thick as you can, then take *Sugar*, *Cinamon*, and a little *Ginger* finely beaten, and well mingled together, cast them upon the *Straw Berries*, and cover them with the lid finely cut into Lozenges, and so let them bake a quarter of an houre, then take it out, stewing it with a little *Cinamon*, and *Sugar*, and so serve it.

Pottage without sight of Herbs

(Robert May, 1660)

Mince your herbs and stamp them with your oatmeal, then strain them through a strainer with some of the broth of the pot, boil them among your mutton, & some salt; for your herbs take violet leaves (p180), strawberry leaves, succory [chicory] (p440), spinage, lang de beef [sugary, flaky pastry], scallions, parsley (p477), and marigold flowers, being well boil'd, serve it on sippets [small pieces of bread/toast].

◄ Wild Strawberry

Silverweed (*Argentina anserina* syn. *Potentilla anserina*)

Silverweed is a perennial herb with creeping runners to 80cm, upright pinnate leaves (3-12 leaflet pairs) which are silvery-silky, especially on the underside, and up to 25cm long. It has yellow flowers, followed by a group of achenes (dry fruits). Common throughout the British Isles apart from northern Scotland, on grassland (especially in damp places, but not always), roadsides, waste ground and agricultural land, particularly beside paths and tracks. Also common throughout the northern temperate zones. There are at least 15 other Potentilla species to be found in the British Isles, mostly non-native, but the only other one with pinnate leaves (others are palmate) is **Rock Cinquefoil (*P. rupestris*)**, an Alpine-Pyrenean species also native to Scotland, but very rare. Nearly all of them are recorded as having been used to make herbal teas.

The starch-rich roots are eaten, and have been an important famine food, best collected as the foliage dies back in autumn, and tasty nodules form on the tubers to store the plant's energy. They are good enough to qualify as decent food in non-famine times too, but it seems a shame to dig up such pretty wild plants. Scrub, then boil or roast for 20 minutes, and serve with a blob of butter. Alternatively, dry and grind into flour. The leaves taste pleasant enough, though they are a bit tough for eating. They are used to make a tea with various alleged health benefits.

Cinquefoils (*Potentilla*)

Sulphur or **Rough-fruited Cinquefoil**
(*P. recta*) is a deciduous perennial shrub
with sprawling stems to 1.5m, finely hairy
palmate leaves, five-petalled pale yellow
flowers followed by a cluster of hairy
achenes. Naturally inhabits swamps and
damp rocky areas in the Mediterranean,
grown as an ornamental in the British Isles,
but occasionally escapes and naturalised in
places. The young leaves are edible (raw), as
are the nutty, unripe achenes.

   Tormentil (*P. erecta*) is a creeping or
ascending herb to 10cm, with stalkless,
shiny, dark green leaves which are trifoliate,
but stipules at the leaf base make them
appear to have five leaflets). The four or five-
petalled flowers look more like a buttercup
than a member of the Rose family. Common
throughout Europe including most of the
British Isles, though declining in the south
east. Found in a wide range of habitats. The
roots are very bitter, but have been eaten
in emergencies. They are the key ingredient
of a bitter Bavarian liqueur called Blutwurz,
and can also be used to make a red dye.

   Creeping Cinquefoil (*P. reptans*)
resembles Tormentil, but it has wholly
creeping stems, rooting at the nodes, and
leaves on long stalks. Very common in
grassland and waste ground throughout
lowland temperate Europe. The leaves are
edible, but not recommended unless you
are starving.

▲ Sulphur Cinquefoil

▲ Tormentil

▲ Creeping Cinquefoil

Avens (*Geum*)

"The roots have a mild, woody astringent taste and a small handful infused in a bottle of wine for a week with a piece of orange peel makes a very palatable vermouth. A bunch as thick as a lead pencil and two inches long is roughly equivalent to one clove."
(Jason Hill, 1939)

Wood Avens or **Herb Bennet** (*G. urbanum*) is a hairy, rhizomatous, perennial, upright or spreading evergreen herb to 70cm, with a branching stem and toothed, pinnate leaves and a large terminal leaflet which has three main lobes. The bright yellow five-petalled flowers are held erect, and are followed by burr-like achenes. Naturally inhabits woodland, but also found on waste ground and is a persistent garden weed. Common in the British Isles and throughout Europe, apart from the far north (of both).

'Bennet' is a corruption of 'Benedict', the saint who founded the order of Benedictine monks. This plant was once believed to have powerful magical properties, and was hung over doors to prevent evil spirits from crossing the threshold. It is (or was) used elsewhere in the world during exorcism rituals.

Water Avens (*G. rivale*) is similar, but with darker, more deeply toothed leaves and a circular, unlobed terminal leaflet and drooping white and red flowers. It is found in much damper environments, primarily a species of the mountainous and northerly areas of Europe, and much more common in Wales and Scotland than in England, apart from East Anglia and the New Forest.

The leaves of both species, which are mild tasting and edible (cooked) when young, soon become tough and hairy. Avens are better known to foragers for their roots. These smell and taste like cloves, with a hint of cinnamon, and used to flavour soups and stews (tied in bundles, then removed later). They make an excellent addition to wild pickles – just add a section of carefully cleaned roots to the other spices when boiling the vinegar. Note that the stringy roots are used too, not just the thickest underground stem. To bring out the flavour, dry them first (preferably in the sun). They then become brittle, and are easily powdered. The roots have also been used to flavour beer, and in herbal medicine for treating stomach aches and other digestive disorders.

◀ Water Avens

Wood Avens, Dandelion and Meatball Soup
(Traditional British, with thanks to Dyfed Lloyd Evans)

This soup is best cooked in early spring, when the wild leaves are still relatively non-bitter. Use fresh, young growth.

Ingredients:
200g dandelion leaves, 75g wood avens leaves, 20g wood avens roots (chopped), 100g rice, 2l chicken stock, 450g minced beef, 1 egg, 2tbsp fresh breadcrumbs, 1tbsp freshly minced parsley, 1tbsp minced onion, 1tbsp minced garlic, ¼tsp salt, ¼tsp freshly ground pepper, pinch of nutmeg, 3tbsp Parmesan cheese, 2tbsp sour cream.

Boil the stock, add the wild leaves and roots, simmer for 5 mins, add rice, and leave to simmer for another 20 mins. Mix all of the other ingredients together, shape into meatballs, and place them in the fridge. Bring back to the boil, then add the meatballs and cook for 10 mins. Serve with crusty bread.

▾ Wood Avens

▾ Wood Avens root bundle

Agrimony (*Agrimonia eupatoria*)

(Common) Agrimony is a hairy, deciduous perennial herb to 1m, often red-tinged, with upright, branching stems and serrated, interruptedly pinnate leaves (up to six main pairs). The spikes of five-petalled golden yellow flowers (summer and early autumn) are followed by burr-like achenes. Found in grassland, on hedgebanks, waste ground and roadsides, usually on alkaline soil and in full sun. Common in most of the British Isles, rare in northern Scotland, and common throughout Europe, apart from the far north.

Agrimony tea, made from the leaves and sometimes all of the above-ground parts of this plant, is widely available, and has a distinctive, fresh taste. It is sometimes mixed with standard tea. Historically this was a very important medicinal herb, with a long list of alleged healing properties, but the only active ingredients scientifically known are tannins, which are present in such high quantities that it has been used for tanning leather. The seeds are a famine food. Agrimony was also used in Anglo-Saxon England for flavouring beer, and produces a yellow dye.

The less common **Fragrant Agrimony (*A. procera*)** is very similar, but more robust, lacking the red tinge, with a leafier stem and scented leaves, and found on more acidic soils. It can be used in the same ways.

Salad Burnet (*Poterium sanguisorba* syn. *Sanguisorba minor*)

"A sweet herb, once used in salads and sauces. The following mixture was employed to make a ravigote, or pick-me-up: tarragon, burnet, chives, and chervil."
(TF Garrett, 1892)

Salad Burnet is a perennial herb to 60cm with sharp-toothed, grey-green pinnate leaves (3-12 leaflet pairs) and round clusters of tiny pink and green flowers (summer). Native across Europe, apart from the far north, in unimproved dry grassland, especially on alkaline soils. Frequent in some lowland areas of England and most of Wales, rare in Scotland and central Wales.

This plant was once cultivated, and introduced to America by settlers for this purpose. The young shoots can be eaten, usually boiled. They are slightly bitter with a hint of cucumber, resembling Meadowsweet (next page) but not as overpowering. Goes well with cottage and cream cheeses, or chopped into butter. The youngest leaves are used in salads and dressings, as a decorative garnish to cold drinks, and for flavouring wines, brandy and vinegar. Also as a flavouring for sweet German wine, along with a slice of lemon and optional sugar and soda water. The flowers were once popular for making into a country wine. See recipes on p75 and p381.

There is an uncommon, slightly larger subspecies (**var. *balearicum***) called **Fodder Burnet**, which used to be grown to feed animals, and the even larger **Great Burnet** (***Sanguisorba officinalis***) is usable in similar ways, though not as good.

▲ Salad Burnet
(the froghopper 'cuckoo spit' is harmless).

Salad Burnet Vinegar (Richard Dolby, *The Cook's Dictionary*, 1830)

Fill a wide-mouthed bottle with fresh green burnet leaves, cover them with vinegar and let them stand for ten days. To make it very strong, strain the liquor, put it on fresh leaves to fourteen days longer.

Meadowsweets (*Filipendula*)

"Imagine the fresh, floral aroma of elderflower but backed with deeper, richer almondy notes – like lychee meets marzipan. Why it isn't a more popular dessert flavouring all over the world, I will never know."
(James Wong, from *The Guardian*, 2017)

Meadowsweet (*F. ulmaria*) is a hardy perennial herb to 1.4m with stalked, interruptedly pinnate, toothed leaves. The dark red stems smell strongly of Germolene when broken, and the leaf stalks and lacey greenish-white flowers are also strongly scented. Common throughout the British Isles and temperate Europe, in damp but not permanently waterlogged soils in fens and woodland, also sometimes on roadsides, riverbanks and cliffs. Do not confuse with umbellifers (*Apiaceae*, p468) – the flower heads are different (the stalks don't all branch out from the tip of the stem). The purgative Common Meadow-rue (*Thalictrum flavum*) has similar flowers, but completely different leaves. **Giant Meadowsweet (*F. camtschatica*)** is similar but grows to 3m, and usable in the same ways. Native to eastern Asia, it is grown as an ornamental and naturalised in a few damp Scottish locations.

The name is derived from 'mead sweet', reflecting the use of the flowers as a flavouring in mead, wines, cider and other alcoholic drinks, as well as non-alcoholic fruity drinks, cordials and teas, and in fruit flans and pies, where it offsets tartness. The flowers can replace elderflowers in any recipe, and can be dried for storage. See the flower fritter and cordial recipes on p76. The young leaves are used to flavour soups, and the root is edible (cooked). They make an excellent flavoured vinegar (infuse 20g of Meadowsweet flowers per 250ml of cider vinegar). This plant was used in medieval times as a strewing herb, and is of medicinal importance. It contains aspirin-like salicylic acid, and was an effective traditional remedy for headaches, hangovers and inflammation, as well as plague (see recipe).

Dropwort (*F. vulgaris*) is an upright perennial herb to 70cm, with a stem that smells of Germolene when broken, and interruptedly pinnate leaves (up to 30 main leaflet pairs) and cream-white flowers, followed by achenes. A rather rare native of calcareous grassland, also grown as an ornamental. The roots are edible (cooked), and the young leaves can be eaten in salads.

▼ Dropwort

Four Thieves Vinegar (traditional French, from *Gattefossé's Aromatherapy*, René-Maurice Gattefossé, 1937)

Take three pints of strong white wine vinegar, add a handful of each of wormwood, meadowsweet, wild marjoram and sage, fifty cloves, two ounces of campanula roots, two ounces of angelic[a], rosemary and [white] horehound and three large measures of camphor. Place the mixture in a container for fifteen days, strain and express then bottle. Use by rubbing it on the hands, ears and temples from time to time when approaching a plague victim.

(Note: Various modern versions, for culinary rather than medical use, include Rosemary, Sage, Juniper berries, Thyme, Cloves and Cinnamon, as well as Meadowsweet.)

▾ Meadowsweet

Lady's Mantles (*Alchemilla*) ⓘ

Lady's Mantles are perennial herbs with distinctive palmate or palmate-lobed, grey-green leaves (lobes toothed), and small yellow flowers, followed by a single achene. Their habitat is varied, but they especially like roadsides, and hilly or mountainous areas. The leaves are water-resistant (like a duck's back) and the Latin name for this genus is derived from a belief that the droplets of water from the leaves of the plant could turn base metals into gold. There are many very similar and inter-fertile subspecies of **Lady's Mantle (*A. vulgaris*)** in the British Isles and conflicting information about their edible and medicinal uses.

The larger **Soft Lady's Mantle (*A. mollis*)** is widely grown as an ornamental, and regularly escapes and naturalises.

The youngest leaves are edible and mild-tasting, chopped and added to salads or steamed; older leaves soon become unpalatably leathery. They are one of the possible components of Easter Ledger Pudding (see p329). The peeled roots have been eaten (cooked) as a famine food, though they are bitter and astringent. Some sources advise that consumption of this species should be avoided by pregnant and breastfeeding women, although it is also widely used (usually as tea) as a herbal treatment for various disorders of the female reproductive system, including regulating periods and 'preparing the uterus for birth'.

▾ Lady's Mantle

Parsley Pierts (*Aphanes*)

Parsley Pierts are small annual herbs to 20cm (usually smaller) with tiny, deeply lobed leaves and almost invisible flowers, usually germinating in autumn and maturing the following summer. They inhabit grassland and disturbed dry ground, including lawns and especially stony arable fields. This is a genus of about 20 similar species, and some studies indicate they should be included in Alchemilla, with which they share the water-resistance. Though they can be locally abundant, they are elusive – 'Aphanes' means 'unnoticed'. They can be mistaken for seedlings of Creeping Buttercup or a cut-leaved Geranium species. Parsley Pierts make a good salad ingredient, and were traditionally pickled. The leaves resemble those of Parsley, and they also taste similar. The Latin name is a corruption of the French perce-pierre ('stone piercer'). They often grow in stony ground and can appear between stones, which led medieval herbalists to believe – wrongly – they could be used to treat kidney stones.

▾ Field Parsley Piert

Prunus (genus)

The stones of many members of this genus contain a cyanogenic glycoside called amygdalin, which is metabolised into hydrogen cyanide. This is what gives Apple pips and Bitter Almonds their bitter taste. Some guides describe the kernels inside the stones of various stone fruits to be edible, but consumption of any with high concentrations is potentially fatal – and while this is unlikely, eating any particularly bitter fruit, stone or pip is not advisable. The kernels of Plums, Apricots and other stone fruits can be pressed to make oils with a variety of claimed health benefits, as well as culinary value as salad oils. This too is somewhat controversial, with advice being given to avoid the oil "if it is too bitter". Perhaps such oils are best kept for external use. Wild Almonds contain relatively high concentrations of amygdalin, and are correspondingly so bitter and toxic that it is a wonder they were ever domesticated. Domesticated Almonds are descendants of rare wild forms with low concentrations of hydrogen cyanide, but who was testing them to find out? The blossoms of all *Prunus* species are edible, usually used as a garnish or in salads. Cherry leaves are used to keep pickled cucumbers crisp (3-4 leaves per litre of vinegar).

Edible species not covered here: **Peach (*P. persicaria*)** frequently germinates from discarded stones in northern Europe, but rarely reaches maturity. **Almond (*P. dulcis*)** is another species that grows from rubbish, as well being planted as a street tree. Several non-native species of Cherry, all with edible fruit, are naturalised or at least surviving in the wild in a few locations in the British Isles – including **Pin Cherry (*P. pensylvanica*)**, Japanese Cherry (*P. serrulata*) and **Fuji Cherry (*P. incisa*)**. Also **St Lucie Cherry (*P. mahaleb*)**, the stones of which are used to make a spice (mahaleb).

Cherry Plum (*P. cerasifera*)

Cherry Plum is a deciduous tree to 12m with oval leaves, and white flowers that appear earlier than other plums, scattered along the branches. Fruits are red or yellow, to 3cm diameter, in late summer or early autumn, sometimes missing a year, other times very abundant. Frequent in the wild, and planted as hedging or street trees. Some ornamental varieties have purple leaves and/or pink flowers. Native to south-east Europe, introduced to the British Isles around the 16th century, cultivated for its fruit. Sometimes mistaken for Blackthorn (p228), even though it usually has no thorns, and could also be confused with varieties of *P. domestica* (p229).

The fruit is edible raw, though the flavour is variable. Best used in pies and preserves. Important in Georgian cuisine, where they are used in sauces, soups and stews. Both blossoms and fruits make a good wine.

Blackthorn (Sloe) (*P. spinosa*) ⚠

"...they should be stewed slowly to extract the flavour of their kernels and their juice added to Elderberries or Whortleberries to their great improvement, or used alone to make an excellent kissel."

(Jason Hill, 1939)

See Cranberry on p374 for more on Kissel.

Blackthorn is a deciduous shrub to 5m, with a dense tangle of thorny branches, small, narrow, oval leaves, and abundant white flowers that appear before the leaves in spring. The white-bloomed, dark blue to purple-black fruits ('sloes') are up to 12mm in diameter. Common throughout the British Isles in woodland and hedges and on rocky slopes, apart from the Scottish mountains and outer islands.

Sloes can be eaten raw, but they are very astringent. More often they are used to flavour gin or vodka. For this purpose they were traditionally only picked after a frost, but they can instead be frozen at home or pricked (which can be more challenging than it sounds – the skins are quite tough). The freezing process breaks the skin and makes it easier for the gin to absorb the flavours, though it won't ripen an unripe fruit. Sloes can be used to make preserves (with apple, for a jelly to be served with meat) or pickled (like olives). This shrub is also a natural choice for edible hedging.

There are some hazards. The seeds can be toxic (containing hydrogen cyanide), and care must be taken when collecting sloes. The broken-off spines of Blackthorn are well known for causing severe infections or a similar response due to alkaloid content, especially if they become lodged in joints. If you get spiked, it is important to remove all foreign material quickly, and apply antiseptic.

Sloe Gin/Vodka

Ingredients:
500g sloes, 250g sugar, 1 litre of gin/vodka.

Put in a clip-top jar and shake every day until the sugar dissolves, then store somewhere dark for three months before straining and bottling for storage. Best left to mature for several months.

▲ Black Bullace

Plum (*P. domestica*)

P. domestica is a descendent of wild Cherry Plum (p226), some varieties having hybridised with Blackthorn. Its many variants, wild and domesticated, and their tendency to hybridise, make identification difficult. They grow to a maximum of 10m, and the fruit varies widely in size, shape, colour and taste. All are edible, so how you use them depends on preference. They are usually usable for pies and preserves, at least. An edible gum can be collected from damaged bark.

    P. domestica **subsp.** *domestica* refers to the thornless domesticated plum, which has large fruits with flat stones. **Greengage** (*P. domestica* **subsp.** *x italica*) is oval and usually green. First grown in Iran, it arrived in the British Isles in the 18th century, via France. **Mirabelle (*P. domestica* subsp.** *syriaca*) is a French variety, small, oval and dark yellow, and very sweet. Mainly planted, but sometimes found growing wild, in which case it is very easily confused with a yellow Cherry Plum. **Damsons** and **Bullaces (*P. domestica* subsp.** *institia*) are varieties that originated in the British Isles, though the name 'Damson' is derived from 'Damascene' (plum of Damascus). Damsons are usually planted rather than wild, sometimes have thorns, and bear fruit that are dark blue to nearly black, slightly pear-shaped, and smaller than most other plums, with more rounded stones. Bullaces are the most common wild-growing plums of the British countryside, and an ancestor of domesticated Damsons. They are near spherical and variable in colour (yellow, green, purple or black), slightly smaller, and ripen later than Damsons. Their strong flavour means they are best cooked (recipe p207), or used to flavour gin. 'White Bullace' has yellow-green fruits, flushed red, and is easily confused with Cherry Plum (which has larger fruits). 'Black Bullace' is blue-black with a white bloom and more likely to be confused with a sloe, with which it probably shares more genes than other Damsons.

Cherry Laurel (*P. laurocerasus*) ⓘ

Cherry Laurel is an evergreen shrub or small tree to 15m with glossy, obovate, dark green leaves up to 30cm long with a finely toothed margin and prominent pale green veins, white flower spikes (early spring) and purple-black fruits (late summer) to 2cm diameter. Native to southern Europe but widely used as hedging, naturalised and becoming invasive in the British Isles. **Portugal Laurel (*P. lusitanica*)** has narrower, darker leaves, red stems and berries of a similar edibility.

I regularly read online warnings of how deadly Cherry Laurel is. In fact, the fruits are edible, with caution. Like much of this genus, there is a toxicity associated with bitterness, so particularly bitter fruits should be avoided, and the stones must not be eaten. They should not be consumed unripe or raw, but the cooked ripe fruits make good eating. They are popular in eastern Europe and Turkey, for making jams, cakes and syrups, and flavouring cordials and alcoholic drinks. They make a good fruit leather. The leaves are toxic, and people have mistaken Cherry Laurel for the unrelated Bay Laurel (p105), the leaves of which are used as a herb. Cyanide fumes released from shredded foliage can also be a problem while disposing of hedge clippings, especially in the confined space of a car.

Cherry Laurel Fruit Leather

Ingredients:
500g ripe (black) laurel cherries, juice of half a lemon, 3tbsp sugar, 125ml water.

Simmer the laurel cherries in the water for 5-10 mins, stirring with a wooden spoon to release the stones. Pass the mixture through a colander, then pick out the stones. Return the cherries (skins included) to the pan, add the lemon juice and sugar, and simmer for another 10 mins. Blitz to a fine paste and spread evenly on greaseproof paper on a baking tray. Place in a low oven until the mixture becomes leathery. Some recipes call for several hours at 170°C / fan 150°C but it needn't take quite that long. You can also use a food dehydrator, or sun-dry the leather. However you do it, it needs a few hours of air-drying to finish it off afterwards.

Bird/Rum Cherries (*P. padus/serotina*)

The cambium of both these species is edible. In both cases some sources describe the kernels as edible too, but this cannot be recommended as safe.

Bird Cherry (*P. padus*) is a deciduous tree to 20m with peeling bark with an unpleasant odour, stalked, obovate/elliptical leaves, and drooping racemes of sweet-scented, five-petalled flowers, followed by shiny black fruits. It naturally inhabits damp mountain woodland and is native in the northern half of the British Isles, a garden escape further south. Present in the entire northern European sub-arctic zone.

The fruits are eaten in Siberia, but they are bitter, and not recommended raw. They can be dried, ground into flour and baked into cakes, but are best used to make jam. The young leaves are eaten as a cooked vegetable in south-east Asia. An infusion of the bark is used in herbal medicine as a mild painkiller and sedative.

Wild Black or **Rum Cherry (*P. serotina*)** is similar to Bird Cherry, but an introduced species (from North America) and only naturalised in parts of south-east England, where it is invasive. Larger than Bird Cherry, with longer, shinier, greyer leaves.

The fruits are variably bitter, especially when not quite ripe, although sweeter, juicier ones can be used in preserves and pies. The bark has also been used for smoking foods.

▲ Bird Cherry
▼ Rum Cherry

Wild/Sour Cherries (*P. avium/cerasus*)

Wild Cherry or **Gean** (*P. avium*) is a suckering deciduous tree to 30m, with dark, shiny bark that peels, producing characteristic horizontal lines. The finely toothed, alternate, ovoid leaves have one or two pairs of tiny red glands where the leaves meet their stalks. Flowers in umbels, fruit is usually dark red to almost black, to 2cm diameter. Native and common in hedgerows and woodland edges in the British Isles, apart from the far north of Scotland, widely distributed in Europe, and frequently planted. It is sometimes called 'Bird Cherry', and that is what its Latin name means, but 'Bird Cherry' usually refers to *P. padus* (previous page). Used as edible hedging.

Sour or **Dwarf Cherry** (*P. cerasus*) is a shrubby version of Wild Cherry to 10m, with more cup-shaped flowers arranged in smaller umbels. Occasional in most of the British Isles, rare in Scotland. Native to south-east Europe and south-west Asia, introduced and naturalised in the rest of Europe. Thought to be a hybrid of *P. avium* and the Wild European Ground/Dwarf Cherry (*P. fruticosa*), which is native to central/eastern Europe and has very bitter fruits. Historically, over 50 varieties of Sour Cherry were grown, falling into two broad categories – the darker red Morello Cherry and the lighter red Amarelle Cherry.

The taste of the fruit of both species is variable, sometimes bitter, and more sour in *cerasus*. They are used in pies and preserves, also to make wine or flavour brandy. The leaves are used to flavour syrups. In Japan, the leaves of both domesticated and wild cherries are salted then used to wrap a pink rice cake with a bean paste centre, to make a sweet called 'sakuramochi'. The leaves can also be used to make wine. Other uses are the same as their relatives: salad oil from the kernels (provided it is not too bitter), edible flowers and gum from the bark. The tasteless gum can be used as an edible glue.

▾ Wild Cherry

▾ Edible gum on Wild Cherry bark

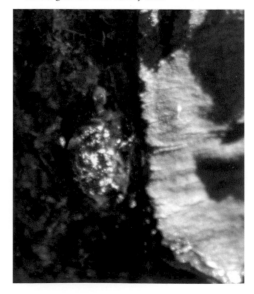

Chokeberry (*Aronia*)

Chokeberries are deciduous shrubs native to eastern North America. **Red Chokeberry (*A. arbutifolia*)** is the largest, growing up to 4m, though usually smaller. It has simple leaves, velvety on the underside, which turn red in the autumn. The flowers are small and white or pale pink, and the berries, which resemble those of Hawthorn, can hang on the branches into the winter. Normally found as an ornamental in Europe, **Black Chokeberry (*A. melanocarpa*)** is significantly smaller, and has black berries. There is also a naturally occuring hybrid known as **Purple Chokeberry (*A. prunifoloia*)**. Though normally found growing as ornamentals, both species and their hybrid are naturalised in the British Isles, currently rare, but expected to increase.*

The name 'Chokeberry' allegedly refers to the astringency of the fruits, and how they make your mouth pucker. The (red) ones I have tried didn't have this effect on me, tasting pleasantly like apple. Chokeberries are cultivated for their fruits on an industrial scale in Russia and Germany. They are used in a wide range of products including jams and other spreads, wines, fruit juices, syrups, tea, salsa, ice cream, beer and confectionery. They can also be eaten raw off the bush, or dried and added to muesli.

▲ Red Chokeberry
▼ Black Chokeberry

* *New Flora of the British Isles*, fourth edition, Stace, C, 2019 (first published 1991).

Hawthorn (*Crataegus monogyna*)

Hawthorn is a deciduous shrub or small tree to 12m with very thorny stems, obovate, deeply lobed leaves (longer than they are wide), and clusters of strongly scented white flowers in late spring, followed by dark red fruits to 12mm diameter. Common in the British Isles in hedgerows, scrub and woodland, apart from northern Scotland, often planted in hedges. Native and common throughout Europe, as far north as southern Scandinavia. **Midland Hawthorn (*C. laevigata*)** is very similar, but less thorny and the leaves are slightly different (wider than they are long).

The berries are used to make jam, ketchup, fruit leather and wine, and in herbal medicine for treating menopause-related anxiety and palpitations. The taste and juiciness is very variable, so it is worth trying a few different trees. The young shoots, flowers and leaves can be eaten raw, and the flowers can also be used to flavour brandy. The roasted seeds have been used as a coffee substitute, but there is a safety issue (cyanide again).

West Country Hawthorn and Kelp Spring Pudding
(traditional British, with thanks to Dyfed Lloyd Evans)

Ingredients:
350g self-raising flour, 175g beef suet, pinch of salt, freshly ground black pepper, 250ml cold water, 150g hawthorn leaf buds, 6 rashers of streaky bacon, 30g dried kelp, rehydrated (or 180g fresh).

Sift flour and salt into a bowl, add the suet and pepper. Steadily add water while mixing, until it becomes a soft dough. Knead until elastic on a floured surface, then roll into a 5mm thick oblong. Scatter the buds onto the pastry, avoiding the edges, then gently press the buds in. Draw out the bacon using the back of a knife, then arrange over the buds, season and place the seaweed on top of the bacon. Put a little water on the edge of the pastry and then roll up like a swiss roll, sealing the edges. Tie up pudding in a muslin and steam for 1 hour 40 mins. Serve thickly sliced with vegetables and gravy.

Juneberry (*Amelanchier lamarckii*)

Juneberry is a deciduous shrub or small tree to 8m with white star-shaped flowers which appear in early spring, sometimes before the leaves, and berries that ripen to deep red or purple between midsummer and early autumn. It is naturalised in parts of south and north-west England and the area between the West Midlands and the Welsh border, rare elsewhere. It is also introduced sporadically across Europe. In its native eastern Canada it is very rare in the wild, and possibly extinct.

The berries are edible and excellent, raw or cooked, tasting a bit like apples.

Medlar (*Mespilus germanica*)

Medlar is a deciduous shrub or small tree to 6m with elliptical-lanceolate leaves, white flowers and red-brown fruits resembling rosehips. The twigs, leaves and flower stalks are all downy. Naturalised in hedgerows and wood edges in a few locations in southern Britain, not present in the north. Native to southern Europe.

Medlars have been cultivated for over 2,500 years, although rarely grown in modern times. In northern Europe, the fruits only become edible after the first frosts have caused them to blet. They are then eaten raw, or made into a jelly. They can also be baked whole, although the seeds should not be eaten.

Medlar Tart (Robert May, 1660)

Take medlers that are rotten, strain them, and set them on a chaffing dish of coals, season them with sugar, cinamon, and ginger, put some yolks of eggs to them, let it boil a little, and lay it in a cut tart; being baked scrape on sugar.

Medlar Cheese (TF Garrett, 1892)

Put some Medlars into an earthenware jar, stand it in a saucepan with boiling water nearly to the top, and keep it boiling gently over a slow fire. When the Medlars are quite soft, pass them through a fine hair sieve, and weigh the pulp, and for every pound allow 1½ breakfastcupfuls of coarsely-crushed loaf sugar and ½ teaspoonful of allspice. Put all the ingredients together in the preserving pan, and stir them over the fire with a wooden spoon until thickly reduced, skimming occasionally. Turn the cheese into moulds, and keep them in a cold place. When ready to serve, turn the cheeses out of the moulds onto a dish.

Apples (*Malus spp.*)

Crab Apples (*M. sylvestris*) are bushy deciduous trees to 10m, with spiny twigs, oval leaves, pink flowers and small yellow-green fruits. Native but only occasional in most of the British Isles at forest edges and in copses, hedgerows and scrub. Rarer in Scotland, especially the north.

The fruits are edible raw, but they are very acidic. They are better cooked, usually to make apple sauce. They also make a nice jelly, on their own for serving with pork, or with Rosemary for serving with lamb. Crab Apples are high in pectin, so are useful in jam-making for helping mixtures of other fruits to set. They also make a decent cider, or wine, a tea can be made from the leaves, and a soft drink ('Crab Apple Tea') can be made by slicing the unpeeled apples, simmering for an hour and sweetening with honey. They make a good fruit leather, for which you will find many recipes online. The flowers of all Apple trees are also edible. This is a good choice for edible hedging. See Rowan and Crab Apple Jelly recipe on p243.

Wild Crab Apples are one of at least two ancestors of domesticated Apples (*M. domestica* or *pumila*), the other and more important one being the Asian *Malus sieversii*. Most 'wild' Apples found in Europe today are the random genetic result of discarded cores – these are known as 'wildlings', and typically they don't have spines. Some wildlings can produce fruits small enough to be confused with rosehips or cherries and though they tend to be small, yellow and sour they are always worth trying, because you never know what might turn up. This is how most Apple cultivars were first discovered. There are also ornamental cultivars called 'Crab Apples', with edible fruit of variable culinary value.

Domesticated descendants of edible wild species fall into two broad categories. The first reproduce sexually and are grown from seed. This means they have gone through a process of hundreds or thousands of generations of artificial selection, during which their characteristics have slowly and steadily been altered to suit the needs of humans. The second are those which arose spontaneously, maybe just one or two generations away from the wild ancestor. These cultivars can only be reproduced by taking cuttings, meaning that in effect every individual is a clone of the first. Apples fall into this category, as do many other fruit trees, and that is why if you grow an Apple tree from seed, it may not resemble either parent. Most will disappoint, but every now and then the genetic lottery will produce something wonderful like a Bramley.

▾ Crab Apple

▲ Ornamental Crab Apple 'John Downie'

Crab Apple Jelly (adapted from Florence White, *Good things in England*, 1927)

Ingredients:

Crab apples, a panful; 1 large lemon; and loaf sugar, 1kg to every litre of liquid.

Rub the apples with a cloth; don't peel them, but they may be cut in halves to see if they are quite sound at the core. Put in preserving pan and cover with water. Boil up and simmer till the fruit is a pulp. Pour into a jelly bag and leave to drain till next day. Measure the liquid. Add 1kg sugar to every litre of liquid, add also the lemon juice.
Put back it into the preserving pan. When the sugar is dissolved, boil it up quickly until it becomes stiff (about 20 to 30 mins). Put into glasses and tie down.

Crab/Wildling Apple Sauce

Ingredients:

1kg apples, at least 250g sugar.

Wash the apples and remove visible bad parts. Put 250ml of water with the apples into the slow cooker and leave on low for 6 hours. The process can be completed in an hour or so in a pan on a hob, but you'll have to watch it in case it needs more water. When the fruit is soft, remove from heat and allow to cool. Then strain through a sieve or food mill, or mash and strain. Transfer to a heavy pan on low heat, add the sugar and stir to dissolve. Taste for sweetness, the required level of which will depend both on the original flavour of the apples and your intended use. As a sauce for meat, it can be more sour and less sweet. If destined for use in a dessert, it may need more sugar.

Pears (*Pyrus*)

Wild Pear (*P. pyraster*) is a deciduous tree to 20m, with thorny branches, ovate leaves with toothed margins, white flowers (spring) and variable fruits to 4cm diameter. They are native to central and southern Europe; most, or maybe all, 'wild' British Pears are escapes from cultivation.

Along with *Pyrus caucasica*, this species is ancestral to domesticated Pears (*P. communis*). It can be hard to distinguish what sort of pear you have found, since both these ancestral species hybridise with domesticated Pears. They are also closely related to Apples and with the 'wild' versions, it can be hard to even tell whether you have an Apple or a Pear, since the shape of both can mislead. Generally, Pears like warmer climates and have white blossom, whereas Apples need cold winters to set fruit, and have blossom flushed pink. Pear trees can also grow much taller than the largest Apples. The closely related **Plymouth Pear (*P. cordata*)** is rare, restricted to the western fringes of Europe, and protected in the UK. **Willow-leaved Pear (*P. salicifolia*)** has narrow willow-like leaves and even smaller, harder fruits, though they can be eaten after bletting. Native to south-east Europe but often planted in the warmer parts of the British Isles.

Wild Pears are hard, acidic and unpalatable raw, but can be processed in various ways: marinated in vinegar to make a sauce for meat, 'pickled' in syrup/wine, fermented into a perry, or cooked and used in sauces and desserts. The flowers are also edible. In Poland, fading traditional interest in Wild Pears was revived when 90% of the cultivated Pear crop was lost in the first winter of World War II. *Gruszczok* is a dish that emerged at the time, made from pears and flour, with the optional addition of eggs, sugar and spices.

Sorbus (genus)

'Sorbus' is the prescientific Latin name of a domesticated southern European tree, the fruits of which were, and still are in some places, called 'sorbs'. 'Sorbus' was anglicised into 'service', and the name 'Service Tree' came to refer also to a wild relative (p244) with similar fruit (though smaller), but very different leaves. Sorbus is now the name of a taxonomically problematic genus that is likely to be broken up. The variation in leaf forms within this genus reveals how pinnate leaves evolved from simple ones – there are a great many microspecies and hybrids, with every intermediate form between the two.

Whitebeams (*S. aria agg.*)

Whitebeams are deciduous trees to 25m, with oval leaves that have toothed/lobed edges and pale undersides. They have cream-white flowers (early summer) and naturally inhabit woodland and scrub, usually dry and calcareous. There are over 40 closely related microspecies and hybrids, which are very hard to tell apart and many of which are rare, though the group as a whole is common. Much planted in urban areas.

The fruit is edible raw, but uninspiring. Like a very dry, mild-tasting apple. Used to make sauces and jellies. Bletting doesn't seem to improve them, and they rot quickly after frost damage.

▲ (True) Service Tree

(True) Service Tree (*S. domestica*)

Service Tree is a deciduous tree to 25m with pinnate leaves to 25cm, formed of 6-8 leaflet pairs, white flowers and green/brown/red apple or pear-shaped fruits up to 3cm long. Very rare in the British Isles (mainly south Wales and the Severn valley), and almost certainly introduced. Native to central and southern Europe and grown for its fruit and wood since antiquity. The fruit is edible raw (bletted) or cooked, mainly used to make jam or alcoholic drinks.

Rowan or Mountain Ash (*S. aucuparia*)

Rowan is a deciduous tree to 20m, with pinnate leaves formed of 4-9 leaflet pairs with a terminal leaflet, dense clusters of cream flowers, and orange to red fruits (late summer and early autumn). Naturally inhabits woodland, usually acidic, especially in dry, scrubby or rocky areas and mountainous regions. Widely planted

as an ornamental, also as edible hedging. It is common throughout temperate areas of Europe, including the extreme north, rarer in the Mediterranean south. Common in the British Isles, particularly in northern areas. The leaves superficially resemble Ash (p416), which has alternating blades in its pinnate leaves, rather than pairs, and completely different fruit.

The berries have a high vitamin C content. Raw, they also contain parasorbic acid, which causes nausea and indigestion. Cooking and freezing both break this down. They are traditionally picked soon after a frost, which makes them sweeter (but leave it too long and they will spoil). Another method is to keep them for 10 weeks in a weak vinegar solution. They can be used to make chutneys and pickles, jellies to accompany meat, a fruit sauce, or in pies. Some recipes work better if the berries are dried before use. They make a very sour sparkling wine, which is something of a personal favourite. The flowers can also be used to make a cordial (see p77).

▲ Rowan or Mountain Ash

Rowan and Crab Apple Jelly

Ingredients:
1kg berries, 1kg crab apples,
1.5kg sugar, water

Destalk and wash the berries. Peel and roughly chopped the apples, leaving in the cores (for pectin). Put the fruit into a large, heavy pan, with enough water to come about halfway to the level of the fruit. Bring to the boil and simmer, occasionally stirring and crushing the fruit, until you have a soft pulp. Strain through a jelly bag or cloth suspended over a bowl, and leave to drain (don't squeeze it if you want a clear jelly). Move to a clean pan and add 750g sugar for every litre of juice. Stir over a low heat to dissolve the sugar, then boil, skimming off the scum as it rises. After 10 mins of boiling, take the pan off the heat and drop a teaspoon of jelly on to a cold surface and push it with your finger. If the surface wrinkles then it is ready, otherwise boil for 5 more mins and repeat. Pour into sterilised jars, cover with waxed paper and lids. The jam will be ready in a few weeks.

Chequer or Wild Service Tree
(*S. torminalis*)

Chequer Tree is a deciduous tree to 25m, with irregular maple-like leaves to 14cm, clusters of white flowers (early summer) and greenish-brown fruits (early autumn) to 15mm diameter. Native but rare, usually occurring as isolated trees (even though it suckers) in old woodland in England and Wales (absent in Scotland). More common in central northern Europe.

The fruits, which are very rich in vitamin C, are best bletted. They can be left on the tree to blet, and make a delicious wayside snack, with a date-like texture and a flavour more like plums or dried peaches. However, the bletted fruits are hard to collect in quantity without squashing, so it is better to pick them as they ripen in mid-autumn, and then store them until they go soft and dark.

The fruits were used in France, both in medieval times and during World War II, to make a flour substitute/extender that doubles as a condiment for desserts. The bletted berries are dried, either in the sun or in a food dehydrator. When completely dry and crumbly, use a coffee grinder or pestle and mortar to grind to a fine powder, which should then be finely sieved.

The chequer-board symbol was traditionally used on pub signs, many of which were also named 'Chequers'. This may be because the fruit was once used in beermaking, but there's also a theory that the name comes from the light and dark pattern produced by bletted and unbletted fruits in the same pot. The wood is dense and attractive, and valued by turners and traditional manufacturers of musical instruments, though now mostly used for high-quality veneers.

Wild Service Tree Vodka

Ingredients:
1.5l ripe wild service berries (stems removed), 700ml vodka.

Wash berries thoroughly, drain and spread on a tray to dry (preferably in the sun). Then freeze for at least 1 week, before placing in a jar with the vodka. Allow to infuse for at least a month in a dark place, shaking/turning the jar every now and then. Then filter the liqueur into bottles, seal tightly and leave to mature for a further two months.

Wild Service and Rosehip Jelly

Ingredients:
Rosehips and fully bletted wild service berries in a ratio of 3:1, water, sugar.

Remove stems and wash the fruit, then place in a saucepan with just enough water to cover the fruit, and bring to the boil. Reduce heat and simmer for 40 mins, then use a muslin or jelly bag to strain (allow this to drip naturally over several hours rather than pressing it through, to keep the jelly clear).
Add 75g of sugar to 100ml of juice, and bring to the boil again, stirring until the sugar has dissolved. Continue to boil for 10 mins and then test to see if it will set: put a spoonful on a chilled plate and if it forms a skin when you push it with your finger, it is ready. If not ready, boil for a few more mins and try again. Skim any scum from the surface, pour into sterilised jars and seal.

Eleagnaceae (Oleaster family)

The *Eleagnaceae* are mainly subtropical/ tropic thorny trees/shrubs of dry/saline habitats with silvery leaves and red/orange/ grey fruits, many of which are edible. The related *Rhamnaceae* (Buckthorn Family) include Purging Buckthorn (*Rhamnus catharticus*) and Alder Buckthorn (*Frangula alnus*), both of which have black berries used medicinally as a laxative, though an overdose will cause vomiting. Fresh Alder Buckthorn bark causes violent vomiting if eaten.

Sea Buckthorn (*Hippophae rhamnoides*)

"The fruit is acid, and, though not very agreeable in flavour, is eaten by children. The Siberians and Tartars make a jelly with the berries, and eat them with milk and cheese, while the inhabitants of the shores of the Gulf of Bothnia prepare from them an agreeable rob, which they use as a condiment to their fish."
(C Pierpoint Johnson, 1862)

Sea Buckthorn is a suckering, deciduous, viciously spiny shrub to 4m (rarely a small tree up to 10m) with multiply branching stems, alternate silvery green linear leaves and rather dry yellow-orange berries (ripening autumn and remaining through winter). Common on temperate European coastlines, particularly on dunes, and also planted inland. Common on most British coastlines, particularly in the south and east, where it is native.

The fruit is edible raw or cooked, but the thorns make it dangerously difficult to collect (as well as first-class edible hedging). It contains very high levels of vitamin C, and can be made into a fruit juice drink, ice cream or sorbet. A 'rob' is the thickened juice of ripe fruit, traditionally obtained by evaporation of the juice over a fire until it acquires the consistency of a syrup, which is then sometimes mixed with honey or sugar. Sea Buckthorn also makes a nice wine, and (ironically, given its vicious thorns) is used in creams for damaged hands.

▾ Note the huge, sharp spine in the lower centre of the picture pointing down and to the left.

Ulmaceae (Elm family)
Elm (*Ulmus*)

English Elm (*U. procera*) is a suckering deciduous tree to 40m, easily recognised by the asymmetrical bases of its short-stemmed, double-toothed, dark green leaves (Lime also has asymmetrical leaf bases, but its leaves are much softer and lime green – p316). This species once dominated large areas of England, but is now only common as large trees in a few strongholds, notably the city of Brighton and Hove. More widespread in hedges in lowland Britain, and present in most of western and southern Europe. **Wych Elm (*U. glabra*)** is a larger tree, with larger, more elliptical leaves than English Elm, and less obviously unsymmetrical at the base. Native everywhere in Europe. **Small-leaved Elm (*U. minor*)** is very similar to English Elm, but with smaller, smoother leaves. Common in lowland England, mainly in hedges. There are numerous other closely related species and hybrids, all usable in the same way.

The newly formed, unripe fruits can be eaten raw (this type of fruit is called a 'samara'). They are soft and sweet, with a slightly bitter aftertaste and were historically used as a breath-freshener. Caught at the right moment they make a perfect salad ingredient. They can also be cooked. They do not keep – even in a fridge they go limp and start to dry out within a few hours. As they ripen they become dry, brittle and bitter.

The cambium can also be eaten, either cooked, or dried and ground into a thickener, and a tea can be made from the leaves.

▸ Elm samaras, on a street tree in Brighton.

Cannabaceae (Hemp family)

"Shall we mention *Hempseed*, the *Cannabis* of the ancients, which was served fried for dessert? That hemp should be spun and made into ropes, well and good; but to regale one's-self with it after dinner, – when the stomach is overloaded with food, and hardly moved from its lethargic quietude by the appearance of the most provoking viands that art can invent – what depravity! What strange perversion of the most simple elements of gastronomy!"

(Alexis Soyer, 1853)

The largest genus in the *Cannabaceae* is *Celtis* – the Hackberries – which primarily inhabit warmer temperate regions. The **European Hackberry** or **Nettle Tree (*C. australis*)**, which is native to Mediterranean Europe but introduced further north as an ornamental, has edible fruits and seeds. **Cannabis** itself, aka **'Hemp' (*Cannabis sativa*)** is native to western Asia but can turn up almost anywhere as an escape from cultivation or birdseed. Its seeds are edible raw, or used to make an oil, and the leaves can be used in soups as well as to make fibre.

found as an escape. Native to Europe and frequent throughout. Do not confuse spring shoots with Black Bryony (p114).

Hops are best known for flavouring and preserving beer, and it is the dried female flowers (or 'cones') that are used for this purpose, as well as making tea. The young leaves and shoots (top 20-30cm) are edible, most abundantly in spring, but the plants can also produce tender new growth in the autumn. Trendy, expensive, commercially available hop shoots are collected from plantations, which is labour-intensive work (though lateral shoots must be cut out anyway). They can be used raw in salads (no bitterness at all, taste similar to pea shoots), and cooked, on their own or in soups, risotto, omelettes and frittatas, quiches, and flans. Briefly boiled, or sautéed in butter, they are delicious. Another option is pickling or lactofermenting. The rhizomes can also be eaten. The main rhizome is too woody, but in spring new ones grow, from the ends of which fresh shoots appear above ground. These rhizomes are white, sweet and crunchy, and usable like beansprouts. Hops are also used in herbal smoking mixtures.

Hop (*Humulus lupulus*)

Hop is a dioecious perennial herb with square stems that can climb to 6m or more ('hoppan' is Anglo-Saxon for 'climb'). The stems have tiny but rough, backward-facing prickles, which cause abrasive injuries to anyone trying to clear them with unprotected hands and forearms. The leaves have 3-7 lobes and toothed edges, and the flowers are green. Locally common in England and Wales in wet woodland and hedgerows, rare in Scotland, frequently

▼ Hop rhizomes (spring)

Hop Shoot Soup (traditional British)

Ingredients:

400g fresh hop shoots, 30g plain flour, 30g butter, 1 small onion (finely chopped), 800ml 50/50 mixture of whole milk and water, flaked sea salt, freshly ground black pepper, ramsons flowers for garnish.

Add the hop shoots to a pan of slightly salted boiling water, return to the boil then simmer for 5 mins, and drain. Meanwhile, cook the onions in butter for 5 mins (so they are softened, but not brown). Gradually add the flour and milk/water mix, stirring all the time, to make a smooth roux. Blend the shoots into a purée, then stir into to the onion/roux mix, season to taste, heat through, garnish and serve immediately with hot toast or fresh crusty bread. This recipe can be adapted for many other wild greens.

▼ Shoots (spring)

▼ Female flower (summer)

▼ Male flower (summer)

Urticaceae (Nettle family)
Stinging Nettles (*Urtica*) (!)

"The common name of the plant, or rather its Saxon equivalent, Netel, appears to be derived from *nœdle*, a needle, from the sharp stings."

(C Pierpoint Johnson, 1862)

(Common) Stinging Nettle (*U. dioica*) is a rhizomatous, dioecious perennial herb to 2m in need of no further description. Widespread and abundant throughout Europe (and almost everywhere else) on nutrient-rich waste ground and roadsides, and in woods, fields and gardens. It is possibly a Roman introduction to the British Isles. **Small Nettle (*U. urens*)**, another ancient introduction from continental Europe, is similar but considerably smaller, though no less ferocious.

Only young leaves and shoots should be eaten, either in spring, before the plant has flowered, or when it sends out fresh growth in the autumn, especially if they have been cut back. In summer, after flowering, nettles become mildly toxic due to the presence of calcium carbonate crystals called cystoliths, which can irritate the urinary tract. One of the most nutritious wild greens, high in vitamins, minerals and protein. Given their widespread availability, this makes them an important potential contributor to the wild larder. Scientific testing* of powdered nettle determined it to be considerably richer in protein and minerals than wheat or barley flour. Nettles are used as a pot-herb or in soups, or simply boiled and served hot with butter (and optionally lemon juice), on toast, or allowed to cool and mixed with cottage cheese. They make a great pesto, for which there are many recipes available online. Nettle kimchi is well worth a try. They are also a choice component of mixed wild green dishes, including boiled spring puddings (see p329). In Georgia, nettles are boiled with walnuts. They work as a pizza topping, or in bread. Traditionally made into beer and wine, as well as tea (both fresh or dried leaves). A personal favourite is nettle crisps, which can be either deep fried or dipped in very hot oil in a small pan, with your chosen selection of spices. They cook in 20-30 seconds. An alternative method is to roast them for a few minutes.

The seeds are reputed to be a 'superfood'. They are available from mid to late summer, and ready when the seed heads of the female plant droop back down towards the stem, while still green, before they go brown. The seedless male plants are visually similar to the females, though there are subtle differences to the inflorescences. The females droop down more, especially if they are loaded with seeds, and the males have a lighter, fluffier look (pictured overleaf). You'll need gloves, obviously – just run your hand up the stem and collect the seed heads. The individual seeds are easily detached, and you can then put them through a colander to remove the stalks. The seeds (which don't sting) are best used fresh, as a crunchy addition to salads, to add variety to soups and stews, make a refreshing tea, or even coat chocolate truffles.

Dried nettle is used in smoking blends, and as recently as the 19th century, table cloths and bed linen were made from nettle fibre.

---

* *Comparison of nutritional properties of Stinging nettle flour with wheat and barley flours*, Adhikari, B, et al, *Food Science & Nutrition*. 7 August 2015; 4(1):119-124, doi:10.1002/fsn3.259.

Sausage and Nettle Soup

There are two traditions of sausage and nettle soup. One is of Italian origin, and derived from sausage and spinach soup, made with de-cased spicy Italian sausage meat and plenty of herbs. The other is from the west country of England, and is also sometimes made with spinach, along with stock and milk and sour cream, or even coconut milk. This is the English version.

Ingredients:
500g nettles, 500g spinach or mixed wild greens, 500ml chicken or vegetable stock, 1½tbsp flour, 30ml cold milk, 3 cooked sausages (chopped into chunks), 1½tbsp sour cream, salt and pepper.

Wash and blanch the nettles in boiling water. Drain the nettles and put back in the pot, with spinach if using. Add the stock, salt and pepper to taste, and simmer for 4 mins, adding more stock if required. Allow to cool, then blend. Make a smooth paste from the flour and milk and mix with the blended greens and sausages, back in the pot. Reheat to serving temperature, and swirl in the sour cream, and serve immediately.

Nettle Kimchi

Ingredients:
250g nettles, 6tbsp salt, 2 litres water, 2 onions finely sliced, 4 cloves crushed garlic, 1tbsp minced ginger, 2tbsp chilli flakes.

In a large bowl, mix the salt and water (unchlorinated if possible). Rinse the nettles then soak them in the brine overnight. Drain the nettles and reserve the liquid. Combine the remaining ingredients, then massage them into the nettles. Pack the mixture into a sterilised clip jar and add enough of the reserved liquid to cover, then weight it down to keep it submerged. Clip the lid down and store at room temperature for two weeks, burping the lid daily. Then move to the fridge, where it will keep for up to a year. The flavour will develop over time, so eat according to taste.

Pellitory-of-the-wall
(*Parietaria judaica* syn. *diffusa*)

Pellitory-of-the-wall is a finely hairy perennial herb to 80cm with a thin, pinkish-red, multiply branching stem. It has stalked, lanceolate to ovate alternate leaves, and tiny white/pink flowers. This species is usually found growing at the base of old, sunny walls, and only rarely in its natural habitat of cliffs and rocky slopes. It is common in England and on the Welsh coast, rare in Scotland and central Wales. Native and common in the southern half of temperate Europe, becoming less so further north. **Eastern** or **Upright Pellitory-of-the-wall (*P. officinalis*)** is native to central and south-east Europe, naturalised but uncommon in the British Isles. It is a larger plant (to 1.6m), with longer-stalked leaves.

The young shoots of both species are edible raw in salads, and taste a bit like cucumber. This taste diminishes on cooking. Italian wild food chef Roberto Gamacchio suggests serving it with pasta, béchamel sauce and chilli. Causes an allergic reaction (itching) in some people.

▲ Stinging Nettle flowers (female top/left, male bottom/right)

Fagales / Fagaceae (Beech family)

The *Fagaceae* are a family of nearly 1,000 species, mainly northern hemisphere trees, over half of which are oaks.

Beech (*Fagus sylvatica*)

Beech is a large deciduous tree to 45m with smooth, grey bark and simple, oval, untoothed, alternate, shiny leaves which can remain after turning brown in the autumn, especially in hedges. The small nuts (autumn) have cases with thick, rough hairs. Native and common in southern Britain, and has been for at least 4,000 years, planted further north more recently. This tree inhabits mountainous areas in the southern end of its European range. There are a variety of ornamental cultivars, the best known of which is the red-leaved Copper Beech. **Oriental Beech (*F. orientalis*)** is a closely related tree, native to Asia and eastern Europe, and usable in the same ways.

The very young leaves can be eaten raw in spring, or used to flavour vinegar. The nuts were historically most important as food for pigs. Nuts with kernels are not produced every year, but are abundant in the right conditions. Baked and salted, they are a decent substitute for almonds. They can be eaten raw or dried, ground and used with cereal flour. They can also be peeled and pressed to make a high-quality oil that can be used like olive oil, both in cooking and salad dressings. The seed husks are slightly toxic, and livestock have been poisoned after eating oil made from pressing the seeds and husks together. Some sources claim that large quantities of

the nuts/oil are poisonous even when the husks are removed, and should therefore be cooked. Two liqueurs are made from beech, both called 'noyau'. The original French version uses the kernels ('noyaux' means 'stones'). A more recent English version (recorded by Dorothy Hartley in 1954) is made with the young leaves, and should probably be called something else.

Oaks (*Quercus*)

"In wartime it was, and is still being used to eke out the precious supply of coffee."
(Clare Loewenfeld, 1957)

Oaks are large trees, sometimes reaching 40m, and most have some sort of variation on the familiar wavy-edged leaf shape. All Oaks can produce acorns - some autumns very few or none at all, and other years thousands. This is called 'mast fruiting' and we're not sure how the trees orchestrate it. Two varieties are native to the British Isles - **Pedunculate Oak (*Q. robur*)** and **Sessile Oak (*Q. petrea*)**. The former is more common in the lowlands and the latter on higher ground, producing sessile (stalkless) acorns.

Acorns have historically been very important as fodder, especially for pigs. A poor year for acorns could threaten meat supplies. Acorns are of particular interest as an emergency back-up food for humans - one that can be collected in mast years with relatively little effort, and stored for up to a decade. They are self-preserving - you simply collect them and keep them dry, and you only go to the bother of shelling and processing them if there's a food shortage.

The acorns of both native Oaks can be eaten, either roasted or as flour, but require careful preparation due to their tannin content, which varies between trees. The leaves can be used to keep pickled cucumbers crunchy (3-4 leaves per litre of vinegar).

Watch your local Oak trees and be ready to gather the acorns when they have just turned from green to brown and started to fall to the ground. Carefully discard any that have tiny holes in, or other damage. Then store them somewhere warm and dry for at least two weeks, after which the shells will be easier to remove. If any inner skins remain, store for another week, and then simply rub off. Patience is the name of the game - shelling and peeling them straight after gathering is much harder.

▼ Pedunculate Oak

▼ Sessile Oak

▼ Holm Oak

Next, you need to leach out the tannins. One way to do this, and save a few pence on your water bill, is to put the peeled acorns in a muslin bag in your toilet cistern for a couple of weeks. Each time you flush, the water is changed. A quicker method is to blitz the acorns into a flour/meal, then hang them in a muslin bag under a slow-running tap for a few hours. The waste water will look like strong tea at first, and when it runs clear, the tannin is gone. Another quicker method is hot-leaching, where you boil the acorns and change the water several times, but you do lose more nutrients this way.

Used as flour, acorns impart a dark colour and intense malty flavour, so best used in combination with your usual flour at a ratio of 1:3 maximum. To make coffee, they should be roasted until light brown, ground, and boiled (1 heaped tablespoon to 1 litre of water) for 30 seconds, then left to stand for five minutes before drinking. They can also be chopped and roasted as a nut substitute, salted as a snack or used as an ingredient in nut roast or other recipes.

Holm or **Evergreen Oak (*Q. ilex*)** is an evergreen tree to 30m, with variable-shaped leaves – entire at the top of the tree, and more like holly (from which both its common and Latin names are derived) at the bottom, to deter grazing. The acorns are longer and more pointed than the two native British oaks. Introduced from southern Europe in the 16th century and now frequent in southern and eastern England, occasional in Wales and northern England, rare in Scotland but locally common near Edinburgh. Holm acorns typically contain less tannin than the other two varieties, but the bitterness of those I have found in south-east England is inconsistent, even for acorns collected from the same tree. There are reportedly two genetically distinct populations, the northern one having more bitter-tasting acorns. Use as native Oaks, but you may find they need less, or no, leaching.

▾ Perfect acorns

▾ Acorn flour

Sweet Chestnut (*Castanea sativa*) (!)

"To keep Chesnuts all the Year – After the Bread is drawn, disperse your Nuts thinly over the bottom of the Oven, and by this means, the moisture being dryed up, the Nuts will last all the Year; but if you perceive them to mould, put them into the Oven again."
(Hannah Woolley, 1675)

Sweet Chestnut is a deciduous tree to 35m with large, sharply toothed, lanceolate leaves, yellow-white flowers (late spring and early summer), and brown nuts in extremely spiky cases. Introduced by the Romans and common in most of the British Isles (though avoiding the most alkaline areas), the tree is native to the temperate zone of Eurasia, and widely cultivated in temperate zones worldwide. Horse Chestnut (p272) is unrelated. The further north you go in the British Isles, the less likely the trees are to produce edible nuts. In Scotland they usually either don't set seed at all, or the nuts are empty.

Gloves are required to safely de-case the earliest nuts (mid-autumn); they open on their own later in the season.

Chestnuts have been an important food source in the British Isles for over two millennia, at all levels of society, and in both sweet and savoury dishes. While technically edible raw, they are much nicer cooked. To roast, whether over fire or in an oven, they should be scored with a diagonal cross on the flat side, to allow the steam to escape – all except one nut. When the unscored nut explodes, the others will be ready to have their shells and skins removed. Alternatively, they can be boiled for a few minutes (again, score first) before shelling and peeling. They are much easier to peel when still warm than after they have cooled. This will give you a crumbly, parboiled chestnut – if you want it softer for puréeing then boil a little longer.

Peeled chestnuts can be frozen for storage, pickled, candied, crumbled for stuffing, dried and blitzed for gluten-free flour, puréed for sweet desserts, or 'devilled' – dried and fried in butter until golden, then sprinkled with salt and cayenne pepper.

Chestnut pudding (a sweet dessert with added sugar) was historically popular throughout Europe. In Tuscany, 'Castagnaccio' is still eaten – a dense savoury-sweet pudding made from chestnut flour. Chestnut leaves have been used to make tea, but for relieving coughs rather than because it tastes nice (Loewenfeld).

Chestnut was also historically important for its wood – the trees were coppiced in order to make posts, fencing, and the uncoppiced wood to make furniture, barrels and beams.

Castagnaccio (traditional Italian)

Ingredients:

300g sweet chestnut flour, 380g cold water, 4tbsp sugar (optional), 2tbsp olive oil, 40g raisins, 40g pine nuts, 40g walnuts, 2 sprigs rosemary, 1 pinch of salt.

Soak the raisins and toast the pine nuts. Preheat the oven to 180°C / fan 160°C. Mix the chestnut flour and sugar, then slowly add the oil and water and whisk to a batter. Add half the raisins raisins, pine nuts and walnuts and mix, then pour into a greased baking dish. Sprinkle on the remaining nuts and raisins, along with the rosemary and drizzle of olive oil. Bake for 30 mins or until small cracks appear on the surface, then cool in the dish before serving.

▾ Sweet Chestnuts. Also see photo on p30.

Betulaceae (Birch family)

This family of northern hemisphere deciduous trees and shrubs includes some important timber species, especially the exceptionally hard-wooded Hornbeam, which is very useful for making tools, such as digging sticks for uprooting edible roots and tubers. Its sap can also be tapped.

Birches (*Betula*)

Silver/Downy Birch (*B. pendula/pubescens*) are small trees to 25m, with diamond-shaped or triangular leaves that have double-toothed edges, which are more irregular in Downy Birch. Downy Birch shoots and leaf stalks are downy, Silver Birch have tiny warts instead. Younger trees have silvery-white, papery bark (smoother and browner in Downy Birch), older ones slowly turning darker and rough. They have catkins rather than flowers, and winged fruits. Common in acidic woodland throughout the British Isles, especially in colder areas of the north. Downy Birch can cope with very wet soil. A number of related alien species are commonly planted, and they hybridise.

Birch trees can be tapped for their sap in early spring. The window for doing this starts just as the trees begin to produce leaves and ends when the tree is in full leaf. There are various methods, but for me the easiest is to use a cordless drill to make a hole (slanting slightly upwards, so the sap drips out due to gravity), and put a plastic pipe in the hole (not too far in or you'll block some of the sap, just enough to secure it). The other end of the pipe goes into a large container such as a demijohn or bottle. You will need something to seal the hole when you are finished, to prevent

▲ Tapping Birch sap

further sap leaking out, or pathogens entering the tree via the hole. You can use a dowel, but it will need to be the exact right diameter to fill the hole. Or you can use a mixture of beeswax and cooking oil, either in conjunction with a dowel or on its own. This wax mixture can also be used to secure the pipe and seal the connection. The best trees for tapping are mature specimens with large crowns, and when these are in full flow you can easily fill a demijohn in 24 hours. The sap is mainly water, with a hint of sweetness and other flavours provided by the traces of nutrients present. It makes a cool, refreshing drink just as it is, or can be used to make wine (in place of water). You can boil it to make a syrup, but this requires a lot of sap and a lot of boiling. The sugar content is considerably lower than the sap of American Sugar Maples.

Tapping Birch trees can increase the chance of fungal infections which shorten their lives, especially if you repeatedly tap the same tree or make too large a hole. It has also been claimed that sealing the hole can cause more problems than leaving it open, so this practice may well become frowned upon in future.

The leaves and bark can be used to make tea, as can the twigs, which contain methyl salicylate, the flavour known as 'wintergreen'. To make birch twig tea you need young, flexible twigs, no longer than 20cm and preferably with buds, chopped into inch-long pieces – try to also chop them lengthwise to open up the bark. Pack these into a jar and cover with water that is very hot but not quite boiling, and leave to steep for several hours, then serve hot, chilled or iced, with optional honey. This tea can also be fermented into beer, and this has worked well for me with yeasts naturally present on the winter twigs. All you need to do is add a few tablespoons of sugar to each litre of tea, cover and leave for about 10 days until the mixture clears. The resulting fizzy, alcoholic brew should be served chilled. Another way to extract the wintergreen flavour is to put the twigs in a steamer, with the vegetable to be flavoured (eg peas) boiling in the water below.

The cambium is edible but very bitter and impossible to collect without permanently harming the tree. It is generally regarded as famine food, though for the Itelmen people of Kamchatka, Russia, it was a staple, served with raw fish eggs. The young catkins are another famine food, either ground to bulk out flour, or battered and fried. The very young leaves are edible, raw in salads or briefly cooked as greens.

Birch Wine (Elizabeth Moxon, 1741)

Take your birch water and boil it, clear it with whites of eggs; to every gallon of water take two pounds and a half of fine sugar, boil it three quarters of an hour, and when it is almost cold, put in a little yeast, work it two or three days, then put it into the barrel, and to every five gallons put in a quart of brandy, and half a pound of ston'd raisins; before you put up your wine burn a brimstone match in the barrel.

Hazels (*Corylus*)

Common Hazel (*C. avellana*) is a multi-stemmed shrub or small tree to 15m, with reddish, hairy twigs, roundish, toothed leaves with a distinct point at the end, and smooth, brown bark. It has long, yellow catkins in spring and hard-husked nuts in autumn. This species coppices itself naturally – older stems fall outwards and die, while new ones grow up from the centre. Hazel is native and common throughout Europe in woodland and hedges. **Cobnut** is a cultivar of wild Hazel, grown for its nuts. **Filbert (*C. maxima*)** is a native of south-east Europe, and very similar, but with a different (longer) nut husk covering.

The nuts are edible raw or cooked (nice toasted), or pressed to make a high-quality oil, usable in salad dressings as well as cooking, and also to make perfumes. Hazel has been cultivated for its nuts since prehistory, and were collected by the first hunter-gathering inhabitants of the British Isles.[*] Nuts picked fully green do not ripen, but can be eaten green (which is one way to beat the squirrels).

Once they've started to turn brown they will ripen after picking, though it may take a couple of months. Hazel catkins have also been used as flour-extending famine food.

Turkish Hazel (*C. colurna*) is a deciduous tree to 25m (the largest hazel) with a robust, upright trunk and relatively small branches. The nuts (known as 'Turkish nuts') are covered by a thick, very bristly (but soft) husk. Native to south-east Europe and south-west Asia, it is widely planted in Europe and North America in urban situations, especially as a street tree, due its architectural attractiveness and ability to cope with urban growing conditions.

The nuts are just as edible as those of other Hazels, but they are small and the shells are extremely hard – I can crack normal hazelnuts with my teeth, but there's no hope of doing so with these. This makes them commercially unattractive, but perfectly good quarry for a determined urban forager, especially as the squirrels seem to have a tough time with them too. The easiest method is to let them dry for a month, then smash them with a hammer.

▼ Common Hazel

▼ Turkish Hazel

* *Wild Food*, Mears, R, and Hillman, G, 2008, Hodder & Stoughton.

Juglandaceae (Walnut family)

This small family is of interest for its nut-producing trees, which include the non-European Pecan and Hickories.

Walnut (*Juglans regia*)

Walnut (also known as Common or English Walnut) is a deciduous tree to 35m with long (to 45cm), pinnate leaves with a terminal leaflet, catkins and a familiar brain-like nut in a hard shell surrounded by a fleshy green husk. The young bark is smooth and olive-brown, becoming silver-grey and fissured with age. Twigs are stout, green and curving. Walnut is reasonably common in the southern half of England, less so in the rest of the British Isles. Historically more abundant, but felled for its valuable wood. It is native to central Asia and southern and eastern Europe, and migrated north-west after the last ice age, with a complicated distribution history. **Black Walnut (*J. nigra*)** is a North American species, naturalised in a few locations in southern England and planted as an ornamental/crop elsewhere. The nuts have a stronger taste than native walnuts.

Foragers need no introduction to walnuts themselves, although they may not recognise the green fruits or know that the shells are edible, finely ground and used to stuff pasta. The green outer husk of the fruits is also edible, usually pickled, although it needs extensive processing to remove the bitterness. Walnut trees can be tapped like Birch and Maples in spring for their sap. Foraged walnuts do tend to go off – if in doubt, sniff before you bite. Keep them cool in an airtight container to delay this, or shell and keep in the fridge.

To preserve green Walnuts
(Hannah Woolley, 1675)

Boil your Walnuts till the water tastes bitter, then take them off, and put them in cold water, and pill off the bark, and weigh as much Sugar as they weigh and a little more water then will wet the Sugar, set them on the fire, and when they boil up take them off, and let them stand two days, and then boil them again once more.

Myricaceae (Bog-myrtle family)
Bog-myrtle or Sweet Gale/Gael
(*Myrica gale*) (!)

Bog-myrtle is an upright deciduous shrub to 2m with fragrant, simple, oval leaves up to 6cm long, and small catkins (in spring, before the leaves) and fruits (summer) that look a bit like tiny hops. It is native, can be found in acid bogs and wet heath and moor, and is common in Scotland and western coastal areas further south (especially the New Forest), but rare or absent elsewhere and declining.

This plant smells a bit like a fruity eucalyptus, containing a lot of terpenes and tannins. The leaves and fruits of Bog-myrtle were traditionally used to improve the flavour and frothiness of ales, and are still used in craft beers. It performs a similar purpose in soups and casseroles, and can also be used in a stuffing mix, to make tea or to flavour for soft drinks. The fruits have a waxy coating, which floats to the surface when they are boiled, and can be skimmed to make candles. Bog-myrtle is also used in combination with Lemon Balm (p410) to make midge-repelling preparations. Can cause miscarriages, so should not be consumed by pregnant women.

Bayberry (*M. pensylvanica*) is a deciduous shrub to 2m with rounder leaves and hairy twigs; native to North America, planted in northern Europe as cover for game birds or ornamental winter interest, and naturalised in parts of southern England. It is used in the same ways as Bog-myrtle.

Cucurbitales
Cucurbitaceae (Gourd family)

This is an important family for edible crops, including Cucumbers, Squash and Melons. Most (both wild and domesticated) are tropical/subtropical. White Bryony is the only native European species.

White Bryony (*Bryonia alba*)

White Bryony is a perennial herb with aggressively climbing/scrambling, anticlockwise-twining stems to 5m, 3-5 palmate-lobed leaves with toothed edges, long spring-like tendrils, green-white flowers and attractive berries that turn from green to red, to black. It is called 'white' after its white latex. It is common in south-east England in hedgerows, wood edges and scrub, preferring well-drained soil, but less common further north and west in England, and very rare in south-west England, Wales and Scotland. Native to most of Europe. When red, the berries can be confused with those of the unrelated Black Bryony (p114). All parts are poisonous, especially the large, tuberous root. Symptoms include severe gastrointestinal distress, dizziness and potentially fatal breathing problems. Forty berries can kill an adult human. One of the toxins (bryonin) has been used in herbal medicine as an emetic/cathartic.

Geraniales

Giant Honey Flower (*Melianthus major*) is an extremely poisonous member of this order (in the family *Francoaceae*). A native of southern Africa, it is grown as an ornamental in Europe. It contains cardiac glycosides, which cause severe exhaustion, violent gastric symptoms and rapid weak pulse.

Geraniaceae (Geranium family)

'Geranium' is both the Latin name of a large genus of plants commonly known as Cranesbills (none of which are of foraging interest) and the common name of the genus *Pelargonium*, most of which are native to southern Africa, but widely cultivated elsewhere. Most are strongly scented, and can be used to flavour white wine vinegar for use in vinaigrette dressing, or fruity desserts.

Herb Robert (*Geranium robertianum*)

Herb Robert is an annual or biennial herb to 50cm, with fragile stems, deeply cut leaves (five leaflets, sometimes only three near the top) and small, pink, five-petalled flowers. The whole plant is hairy, aromatic (unpleasantly so to some tastes), and tinged red ('Robert' is a corruption of '*rubra*' – Latin for 'red'). Native and common in woods and gardens and on walls, cliffs, roadsides, hedgebanks and shingle. The much rarer Little Robin (*G. purpureum*) is a coastal species of southern England, of unknown edibility (but unlikely to be poisonous).

The whole plant is edible, best when young. It's a bit hairy, but the flavour isn't bad, and it can work as a salad ingredient, or finely chopped into a vinaigrette dressing, or as a cooked vegetable. Also used to make tea. It is claimed in some circles to be highly nutritious.

Common Storksbill (*Erodium cicutarium*)

Common Storksbill is a rather variable annual herb with branched, hairy/sticky stems to 60cm, which can be prostrate, ascending or trailing, and stalkless, finely cut, pinnate leaves. The pale pink or lilac (rarely white) flowers are followed by seed pods supposedly shaped like a stork's bill. It is common on bare ground, dunes, arable land, short grassland and waste ground around most of the British coastline, and much of inland England (though absent in the south east). It is a bit like Herb Robert, but the leaflets are in parallel rows rather than coming from a central point. When not flowering, it might be mistaken for one of the smaller lacy-leaved umbellifers.

All parts of the plant are edible when young and fresh, and are reminiscent of parsley. Can be used in salads, but better cooked.

Musk Storksbill (*E. moschatum*) has much larger leaflets, and is sticky. It smells of musk when crushed. It is an introduced species, currently spreading in the British Isles from the south, and is also edible.

▲ Common Storksbill pods

▾ Musk Storksbill

▲ Common Storksbill

Myrtales

Myrtle (*Myrtus communis*, of the family *Myrtaceae*, order Myrtales) is a southern European species used as a flavouring and in wedding bouquets since antiquity.

Onagraceae (Evening Primrose family)
In addition to the species covered here, the very common Enchanter's Nightshade (*Circaea lutetiana*) is worth a mention. The name makes it sound toxic or magical, but it is neither, though it is sufficiently loaded with tannins to make it inedible.

Evening Primroses (*Oenothera*)

"The roots, when boiled, are very wholesome and nutritious, but have been little eaten as a table vegetable since the use of the potato became general. In former days they were taken with wine in the manner of olives, when, it is said, the name of the genus, signifying 'wine-trap', from the plant being used as a provocative to drinking. In Germany the roots are still eaten; they are sweet to the taste, somewhat resembling parsnips."
(C Pierpoint Johnson, 1862)

At least four species of Evening Primrose have been introduced to Europe from the Americas. The common name refers to a mistaken belief that the flowers only open in the evening. They are rather variable, readily hybridise and hard to tell apart (and for a forager it doesn't matter). The seeds can stay viable in the soil seed bank for 50 years, germinating when the area is disturbed. The mature seeds, which are plentiful and easily collected, are pressed to make an oil which is used both externally and as a food additive.

All are reputed to have edible roots – boiled, steamed or stir-fried and tasting like peppery parsnips – though there is conflicting information about quality and timing. Some sources claim the roots should be harvested before the flowering spike has begun to form (from the first autumn through to spring), others say the end of their second season and that younger roots should be boiled in a couple of changes of water to make them more palatable. In *The Forager Handbook* (2009) Miles Irving complains they caused an unpleasant irritation in the back of his throat and I concur. The edibility information about other parts of these plants is also inconsistent. Launert's *Edible and Medicinal Plants* (1981) warns "do not eat the leaves or any part of this plant except the root", but does not tell us why. Other sources claim the young shoots are edible and the flower buds can be eaten in salads, or pickled like capers. My own opinion is that the young shoots, leaves and flowers are all edible – they are mucilaginous and slightly peppery. The seed pods, which are also recorded as having been eaten by Native North Americans, are rather tough and soon become bitter.

Common Evening Primrose (*O. biennis*) is an annual or biennial herb to 1.2m, no sticky red hairs on the stem, lanceolate leaves to 20cm and large, bright yellow, four-petalled flowers and seeds in capsules. When biennial, it forms a low rosette of hairy leaves in the first year, and a flowering spike in the second. Found on dunes, waste ground, roadsides and railways, especially near the coast, frequent in most of England and coastal Wales, rare elsewhere in Britain. Introduced and naturalised in most of temperate Europe. **Large-flowered Evening Primrose (*O. glazioviana*)** is a biennial herb with stems to 1.8m with red glandular hairs, crinkly, twisted leaves to 15cm, a spike of large, bright yellow flowers and long seed pods. Inhabits waste ground, roadsides, gardens, preferring disturbed sandy soil, including dunes (where they are easy to uproot). **Small-flowered Evening Primrose (*O. cambrica*)** is very similar, but with red hairs restricted to the top of the stem. **Fragrant Evening Primrose (*O. stricta*)** has narrower, wavy-edged leaves.

Rosebay Willowherb
(*Chamaenerion angustifolium*)

Rosebay Willowherb is a colony-forming
perennial herb to 1.5m with upright pink
stems and alternate, stalkless, lanceolate
leaves (hairy topside, hairless underneath).
The magenta-pink flowers are borne
in large terminal spikes (summer), and
followed by fluffy seed pods (autumn).
Native to temperate and boreal regions of
the northern hemisphere, it was once rare,
found only on upland cliffs and scree. It
spread explosively after construction of the
railways, and is now common in a variety
of habitats, particularly disturbed waste
ground, derelict building and fire sites.
Take care not to confuse with toxic species
of Lily (p116).

The *young* leaves and stem (sometimes
peeled, and raw) and flower buds have been
widely eaten. The first spring shoot, while
still red, makes an acceptable addition to
a stir-fry, or boiled as a side vegetable. The
plant soon becomes more bitter, although
the pith of mature plants is edible – simply
split the main stem and scrape it out. It
tastes like cucumber and is usually eaten
as a trail snack. The fermented leaves of
slightly older plants make the king of wild
herbal teas ('Ivan Chai', once an important
Russian export). Though caffeine-free (it is
lightly sedative), it is the closest thing you
will get to a substitute for regular black
tea, and high in vitamin C. The flowers can
be used to make jam. The root can also be
eaten, usually roasted, though the taste is
not great.

Other Willowherbs (*Epilobium* spp.)

Several other Willowherbs are famine foods. All those mentioned here are perennials and they differ in having flowers that are scattered and held near vertical, whereas the flowers of the *Chamaenerion* species are held near horizontal, on a raceme. They are at their best for eating before the flowering shoot gets going. **Great (Hairy) Willowherb (*E. hirsutum*)** is frequently confused with Rosebay Willowherb, though it has hairier leaves and smaller, paler flowers, and grows in damp rather than disturbed locations. Young stems and leaves are edible, though with a slightly unpleasant (hot) aftertaste. The roots are also edible. There are some reports of toxicity or narcotic properties, but I eat them with no adverse effects. You can't make Ivan Chai with Great Willowherb, and internet claims to the contrary are the result of confusion with Rosebay Willowherb; it does not work. **Broadleaved Willowherb (*E. montanum*)** is a much smaller plant, and very common (can be confused with the edible Cornsalad (p467), which has lighter and less glossy leaves). Makes a respectable salad leaf before the flowering stem appears. **Hoary** and **Square-stalked Willowherbs (*E. parviflorum* and *tetragonum*)** are similarly edible.

▾ Great Willowherb

Ivan Chai (traditional Russian)

Ingredients:
Rosebay willowherb leaves (collected from the top half of the plant, before flowering or soon after), paeony flowers (p162), rose petals.

The leaves can easily be stripped from the plant by running your thumb and forefinger down the stem. Then they must be wilted. When collected, if you fold the leaf with the top surface inside, the main vein will snap with an audible crack. Leave them for about 24 hours, at which point the vein will no longer snap (this takes longer in some conditions, but do not allow them to dry out). Then roll them, no more than 3 or 4 at a time, between the palms of your hands. They will go dark green and remain loosely rolled into balls and spirals. The next step is fermentation. Place the leaves in a bowl, and then place a layer of paeony flowers, face down, on top. Cover securely and leave for another 24 hours. When fermented, remove the paeony flowers, add the rose petals, and dry, either in the sun or a low oven. The tea should then be sealed in an airtight container and will improve over the next few weeks.

Fuschia

Fuschias are ornamental shrubs, some of which are starting to naturalise in Europe. Both the flowers and berries of most species/varieties are edible to some extent, but the flavour is extremely variable, many are quite astringent and some are known to cause gastric upsets for some people. Some taste nice at first, but leave a weird, spicy aftertaste. The species reputed to have the best edible berries is the **Mexican Tree** or **Chilli Pepper Fuschia (*F. splendens*)** and in 2016 a new variety (called 'Berry') went on sale, which has been intentionally bred for its fruit.

▼ Mexican Tree Fuschia (*Fuschia splendens*)

Anacardiaceae (Cashew family)

The *Anacardiaceae* are a family of mainly tropical and subtropical flowering plants, including Cashew, Pistachio and Mango, as well as Poison Ivy and Poison Oaks.

Stag's-horn Sumach (*Rhus typhina*)

Stag's-horn Sumach is a deciduous shrub to 7m with velvet-textured red-brown branches (new Stag's-horns are velvety) and alternate compound pinnate leaves to 60cm, initially green but eventually turning spectacular fiery colours in autumn. It has dense, soft spikes of rich pink-red fruits. Native to North America, introduced to temperate areas elsewhere as an ornamental, often escaping and growing aggressively from suckers.

The fruits, which look more like flowers, should be picked when vibrant red, and not after a rainstorm, since this washes the flavour out. The easiest way to use it is to make a drink – 'sumacade' – which is high in vitamin C, although some of the lemon-like taste comes from oxalic and malic acids. Simply soak in cold water for 24-48 hours, and serve with a sprig of mint. If the fruits aren't ripe, or the water is warm/hot, the result will be bitter. Do not use from areas with high air pollution, as the flower/fruit heads absorb pollutants from the air (they are both hairy and sticky). The spice sumac is made from Sicilian Sumach (*R. coriaria*), but a similar equivalent can be made from Stag's-horn Sumach, though it is work-intensive. The berries must be removed from their twigs, and then dried and ground.

Two related species are introduced in the British Isles and naturalised in the south east. **Tanner's Sumach (*R. coraria*)** is native to southern European, the leaves and bark

▲ Stag's-horn Sumach

traditionally used in leather tanning, and **Shining Sumach (*R. copallina*)** is another American species. Both have larger fruits than Stag's-horn Sumach, and are used as a spice (dried), made into a drink, or even eaten in salads. Poison Sumach (*Toxicodendron vernix syn. Rhus vernix*) is found in damp habitats in eastern North America, and is a serious irritant to skin and mucous membranes, occasionally causing death by inhalation of the smoke from burning plants. It does not grow wild in Europe. The fruit heads are very different – white rather than red, and nothing like so tightly packed.

Sapindales

The citrus fruits are members of this this order, along with Mangos, Cashews, Lychees, Mahogany, and also Frankincense and Myrrh.

Sapindaceae (Soapberry family)
Horse-chestnut (*Aesculus hippocastanum*) (!)

Horse-chestnut is a large deciduous tree to 40m with sticky winter buds, large compound leaves with leaflets arranged in a radiating pattern, white flowers and seeds in a variably spiky casing ('conkers'). Red-flowered trees are a hybrid between Horse-chestnut and the American species *A. pavia*. Common in Europe, particularly in temperate areas as far north as southern Scandinavia, this species is native to south-east Europe (Pindus Mountains and Balkan Forests) but widely introduced elsewhere a long time ago. Do not confuse with Sweet Chestnut (p256), which is not closely related.

Conkers are loaded with saponins, making them slightly poisonous and very bitter – but they are sometimes eaten by children, regardless. Nothing worse than vomiting results, unless a very large quantity have been eaten – in which case they can cause paralysis and potentially death. They have been used as a coffee substitute, or dried and ground into a powder, after the saponins have been reduced to make them more palatable. This can be done by roasting slowly, or slicing and leaching in water, although this unfortunately also gets rid of most of the nutrients apart from starch. The leaves and bark are used to make a foul-tasting tea claimed to have medicinal properties for circulatory disorders. Both the leaves and seeds can be used to make a sort of soap. They should be crushed in water, releasing the saponins, which act as mild detergents. They make a perfectly decent laundry soap: peel, crush, dry, store, then soak a handful in water for three hours, strain, and use the liquid in place of laundry detergent.

Maples (*Acer*)

Field Maple (*A. campestre*) is a deciduous tree to 25m with five-lobed opposite leaves, yellow-green flowers and winged fruit. Common in southern England, especially on chalk, naturally much rarer further north, but widely planted as an ornamental tree. Native throughout temperate Europe and common in most places.

Sycamore (*A. pseudoplatanus*) is a deciduous tree to 35m with opposite, five-lobed compound palmate leaves, yellow-green flowers and winged fruit. It is widespread and common in Europe from the far south to southern Scandinavia, including the whole of the British Isles. It is native to central Europe and south-east Asia (not, as commonly believed, North America).

The sap of both these trees (plus several other non-native but self-seeding members of the genus) contains sugar, but is considerably more dilute than the American Sugar Maples. It can simply be drunk, or fermented into beer or wine. The cambium is edible, and the seed inside the Sycamore samara can be pickled or ground into flour. Some trees have lots of 'blanks', others have kernels but far fewer samaras.

▲ Field Maple   ▼ Sycamore

Brassicales

Along with the Cabbage family, the Brassicales include the tropical Papaya (*Caricaceae*) and Capers (*Capparaceae*). **Nasturtium (*Tropaeolum majus*)** of the family *Tropaeolaceae*, is an ornamental member native to South America, and does occasionally turn up naturalised in the British Isles and further south in Europe. The whole plant is edible: the flowers make a lovely addition to a salad and the leaves are very spicy (as are many plants in this order). The seeds can also be used in salads or pickles, or to produce an edible oil. See recipe on p482.

Resedaceae (Mignonette Family)
Wild Mignonette (*Reseda lutea*)

Wild Mignonette is a hairless biennial/perennial herb to 75cm, with sprawling, branching, ribbed stems, deeply cut leaves, and racemes of green-yellow flowers. It inhabits roadsides, grassland and waste/disturbed ground and is frequent in the east of England, much rarer in Scotland, Ireland and higher ground in England and Wales, and present in most of Europe. The young leaves are hot and bitter (not unlike Rocket), and the flowers and seed pods are also edible.

Weld (*R. luteola*) is found in similar habitats, especially on chalk, and has similar (but smaller) flowers, but is twice the size and more stiffly upright. Both were historically important dye plants.

▼ Wild Mignonette

▼ Weld

Brassicaceae (Cabbage Family)

The *Brassicaceae* are a large family, the internal phylogeny of which has proved difficult to nail down, and they also pose many identification challenges for foragers (though none are poisonous, and their uses are similar). Otherwise known as the crucifers (*Cruciferae*) because they all have 'cross-shaped' four-petalled flowers, followed by pod-like fruits which are key to identifying the species. The Cabbage family is second only in importance to the grasses for human agricultural production, including Cabbages, Kale, Cauliflower, Broccoli, Brussels Sprouts, Mustards, Radish, Horseradish, Rape, Rocket, Cress, Watercress, Turnip and Swede. The term 'cress' refers to various members of this family used as seedlings to provide a fiery kick in salads.

Species not covered in detail below include **Bastard Cabbage (*Rapistrum rugosum*)** – native to southern Europe but a naturalised weed of waste ground and increasingly arable land – and **Turkish Rocket** or **Warty-cabbage (*Bunias orientalis*)**, which is native to eastern Europe, introduced in the British Isles and naturalised on waste ground and rough grassland. Stems and young leaves of both species are edible (best cooked). **Woad (*Isatis tinctoria*)** was once a widely cultivated dye plant. The leaves are just about edible, but rather bitter. It is native to southern Europe, but can be found naturalised in a few locations further north, including the British Isles. **Gold of Pleasure** or **False Flax (*Camelina sativa*)** is an oilseed plant, similar to Rape in usage, but more closely related to Shepherd's Purse. Native to Europe and central Asia, it was first a weed of Flax fields, and then commonly

▲ Wild Cabbage in winter, growing on disturbed land by a newly built road.

cultivated in Germany and France, but now declining across much of Europe and rare or very localised in the British Isles, mainly from seeds imported as animal feed.

Brassica (genus)

Genetic sequencing has now shown that three diploid members of this genus – Wild Cabbage *(B. oleracea)*, Wild Turnip *(B. rapa)* and Black Mustard *(B. nigra)* – are the ancestors of three tetraploid vegetable and oilseed crop species – Rape *(B. napus)*, Indian/Chinese Leaf Mustard *(B. juncea)*, and Ethiopian Mustard or 'Texel Greens' *(B. carinata)*.

Wild Cabbage (*B. oleracea*)

Wild Cabbage is a hairless biennial to perennial herb, with a rosette of fleshy grey-green (sometimes with hints of purple) stalked leaves in the first year, and an upright stem with clasping leaves and a spike of four-petalled yellow flowers to 2m in the second and subsequent years. Older plants have a woody stem base, covered with leaf scars. Distinct cabbage smell, especially from the lower leaves. Prefers coastal areas, especially in calcareous regions in southern and western Europe, but escapes from cultivation elsewhere and I have seen it growing abundantly on more than one occasion on disturbed acidic, sandy loam. Widespread in the British Isles, apart from north-west Scotland and most of Ireland. Wild Cabbage could be confused with several other Brassicas, but no poisonous species. It is distinguishable from other Brassicas by having sepals pressed closed to the petals.

The leaves are edible, best cooked, and available in the winter. This is the wild ancestor not only of domesticated Cabbage, but also Broccoli, Cauliflower, Kohlrabi, Brussels Sprouts and Kale, as well as the 'spring greens' or 'collards' that resemble the wild plant. These different varieties of cultivated *oleracea* readily hybridise both with each other and wild plants, escapees quickly reverting towards the wild form, which doesn't make the identification of wild-growing Brassicas any easier.

According to Pierpoint Johnson, this was the first native plant to domesticated by "our own rude forefathers fresh from the Baltic pine-woods, or the ice-crowned cliffs of Norway ... The plant in its wild state forms a very wholesome vegetable, and was no doubt used for culinary purposes long before any attempt was made at its cultivation." (This was probably already happening in Saxon times.)

▾ Wild Cabbage flowering in May

Rape (*B. napus*)

Rape is a mainly hairless annual/biennial herb to 1.2m with grey-green, branching stems, obovate leaves thinner and less fleshy than those of Wild Cabbage, the lower ones with lobes and long stalks (and slightly hairy), the upper ones with clasping bases but no lobes or stalks. It has clustered, four-petalled yellow flowers at the stem tips which do not extend above the unopened buds, followed by long pods with a short beak. Common in much of the British Isles, less so in northern and western Scotland, and present but patchy in Ireland (naturalised in the south east), on arable and waste land, roadsides, ditches, and stream sides.

The leaves of this species are edible, but need to be cooked. They are similar to 'spring greens' (previous page), but rougher. The root can also be eaten as a cooked vegetable, and the grated root and unopened flowers can be used in salads.

Wild Rape is a natural hybrid of Wild Cabbage and Wild Turnip (overleaf). Domesticated Oilseed Rape is a subspecies (*oleifera*). There are records of Rape having been cultivated in antiquity, both in southern Europe and eastern Asia. However, the oil produced from wild varieties is bitter-tasting and causes cardiac lesions. It has become an important commercial crop only since cultivars were bred in 1973 that didn't suffer from either of these problems. Rape growing wild in Europe now is almost entirely an escape from cultivation. Today, a lot of what is sold as mustard in the UK is made from Rape seeds. Swede is descended from a hybrid of Rape and Wild Turnip.

▸ Rape growing on waste land

Black Mustard (*B. nigra*)

Black Mustard is an annual herb to 2m with an upright, hairy/bristly lower stem, and branches coming out near horizontal. Upper leaves stalked but unlobed, hairless, grey-green, lower leaves are lobed and hairy/bristly but not so grey. The four-petalled, bright yellow flowers are followed by upright pods with short beaks. Called 'Black' Mustard because the outer cases of the seeds are dark brown to black. Found on cliffs (including sea cliffs), riverbanks, waste ground and in other places. Frequent in England and Wales, especially in sandy coastal areas, rare in Scotland. Occasional in the south of Ireland, less so in the north. Either native to the British Isles or introduced from southern Europe by the Romans.

Roman writer Columella (4BCE-70CE) recorded that the leaves of this plant were pickled in vinegar. It wasn't until the 13th century that people started making mustard from the seeds, which have a stronger flavour than White Mustard, like Horseradish. The seeds contain a glucoside called sinigrin, which reacts in the presence of cold water to form a pungent mustard oil. Add cold water to ground seed (don't use warm water, sugar or salt, or the result will be bitter), and leave for 10-15 minutes. The sprouting seeds and very young seedlings can be eaten in salads or cooked, and the unopened flower heads used like a spicy version of broccoli. **Ethiopian Rape** or 'Texel Greens' (*B. carinata*) is a natural hybrid of Wild Cabbage and Black Mustard grown as cover for game, as well as a food crop.

▾ Black Mustard

▾ Black Mustard pods

(Wild) Turnip (*B. rapa*)

Wild Turnip or **Bargeman's Cabbage**
(*B. rapa* ssp. *campestris*) is very similar to
Rape, but the stalked lower leaves are less
grey and more bristly, and the flowers are
smaller, darker yellow and extend above
the unopened buds. Inhabits cliffs, canal
and riverbanks, disturbed/waste ground
and field edges. Probably not native, but
frequent in England, Wales and Ireland, rarer
in Scotland.

This is the wild ancestor not only of
domesticated Turnip (ssp. *rapa*) but also
Mizuna, Pak Choi, Napa Cabbage and Rapini
(all subsp. *oleifera*) and also some types of
Canola oil, which is used both for human
consumption and biofuel. It was in common
use (cultivated) in ancient Rome and Greece.
Pierpoint Johnson calls it "Navew or Field
Cabbage", because it is sometimes found at
the edge of arable fields.

The food uses are similar to Rape, but
especially the root of the pre-flowering
wild-growing plant, which may or may not
be swollen like domesticated varieties, and
may or may not be descended from them.
The leaves are usually too bitter.

Hoary Mustard (*Hirschfeldia incana* syn. *B. geniculata*)

Hoary Mustard is an annual or short-lived
perennial herb to 1.3m, roughly hairy at the
bottom, hairless at the top, with branches
closer to vertical than Black Mustard, lobed
leaves, yellow flowers and short, hairy pods.
Inhabits dry places, usually urban or coastal.
Frequent in south-east England, south Wales
and some parts of northern England, rare or
absent elsewhere in the British Isles. Native
to the Mediterranean.

The seedlings and young leaves are
edible raw or cooked, as are the seeds,
which can also be ground up and used like
Black Mustard to make a condiment.

▾ Hoary Mustard

White Mustard
(*Sinapis alba* syn. *B. alba*)

White Mustard is a hairy annual herb up to 80cm with pale green, deeply lobed soft leaves, all of which have stalks, including the stem leaves. The four-petalled yellow flowers are followed by bristly, beaked pods containing two pale-coloured ('white') seeds. A weed of arable land and waste ground, favouring calcareous soils. Occasional, more common in the south east of the British Isles, rarer as you go north and west. Native to the Mediterranean area, but introduced worldwide. Similar to Charlock (opposite), but with less hairy leaves that have deeper and more consistent lobes.

Once widely cultivated for the seeds, which were used as an ingredient in mustard. For this purpose, the seeds are ground up and added to cold water, which causes a chemical reaction to produce the pungent taste in about 15 minutes. Not as pungent as Black Mustard (White Mustard contains a different active chemical, sinalbin, which produces a much milder mustard oil). Its other uses are the same as Black Mustard. Can be planted as green manure.

Charlock or Wild Mustard
(*Sinapis arvensis*)

Charlock is a hairy or bristly annual herb with branched stems to 1m, with stalked lower leaves and stalkless upper stem leaves, all coarsely toothed and variably lobed. It has bright yellow four-petalled flowers in long spikes (summer) and cylindrical pods with long beaks. Habitat varies, but particularly waste ground, roadsides and any disturbed land, and historically a problematic weed of arable land. Introduced, but common everywhere but the far north-west of Scotland. Similar to White Mustard, but with stalkless stem leaves. Easily confused with Wild Radish, which has purple-veined flowers, and Chinese Leaf Mustard (*B. juncea*), an Asian species found in Europe as a birdseed alien.

The young leaves, which are edible raw, are recorded as having been sold in Dublin markets in the early 18th century, though in Ireland they were generally considered a famine food. Used as a spicy component of salads, or cooked as a pot-herb (sometimes as a substitute for nettles), or chopped and used in pâté or omelette. Opened flowers can be used as a garnish. Seeds can be sprouted, or used like White Mustard to produce a condiment/oil (contains sinalbin) and were a famine food in Scotland, used in gruel or to extend flour supplies.

Radishes (*Raphanus*)

"The seeds of the Wild Radish are very pungent, and form an excellent substitute for mustard; where the plant abounds, they are sometimes separated from the refuse corn, ground up, and sold for that condiment."
(C Pierpoint Johnson, 1862)

All *Raphanus* species have the distinctive radish smell when crushed.

Wild Radish (*R. raphanistrum* ssp. raphanistrum) is a hairy/bristly annual to biennial herb to 80cm, with irregularly lobed leaves (smaller and fewer-lobed near the top) and a large terminal lobe, four-

▾ Purple-veined 'White Charlock' flowers

▾ Wild Radish seed pods

petalled flowers that come in a variety of colours but always veined with purple, and ribbed/beaded pods (you can see where the large seeds are). Common in much of England, especially the south and west, less so elsewhere in the British Isles. It is usually found on arable land, where it can still be a serious problem weed. Also found on pasture, waste ground and roadsides. This is an ancient introduction from Asia, now present worldwide with a reputation for becoming invasive. Similar to Charlock and known as 'White Charlock' in south-east England, where the flowers are usually white.

The young leaves are a popular vegetable in the Aegean region, where they are typically cooked and served cold as a salad, with olive oil and lemon, or with pomegranate molasses, or mixed with eggs and fried, or used like Common Mallow in Khobeizeh (p311). Older leaves are tough and bitter. The flowers and young seed pods are also good salad items, though somewhat fiery, and the young seed pods can be pickled. Flower buds can be used like broccoli, steamed for five minutes. The seeds can be used like Mustards, and the root like Horseradish.

Garden Radish (*R. sativus*) sometimes turns up growing wild as an escape from cultivation. Its native range is unknown (maybe south-east Asia, in cultivation since at least 300BCE) but it is now present globally.

Sea Radish (*R. raphanistrum* ssp. maritimus syn. *R. maritima*) is a biennial to perennial herb with yellow (usually) flowers, and ribbed, long-beaked fruits that resemble a string of beads. Inhabits sandy or stony beaches, and other coastal habitats (but not salt marsh). It is native and common on British coastlines, apart from the east and north east of Great Britain. Uses are as Wild Radish.

▲ Wild Radish

▾ Sea Radish

▲ Hedge Mustard

Rockets (*Sisymbrium*)

Many members of this family have the word 'Rocket' in their name, presumably because of their fiery tastes, but it also refers to this genus. Confusingly, the salad plant you find labelled 'Wild Rocket' in supermarkets is neither wild nor a *Sisymbrium* (see Wall-rocket, p286).

Hedge Mustard (*S. officinale*) is an annual/biennial herb to 1m with purple-flushed, branching, upright stems (the branches distinctively come out of the main stem almost at right angles). The plant has large lobed/cut lower leaves, smaller unlobed (or fewer-lobed) upper leaves, dense racemes of tiny flowers and small pods. An ancient introduction from continental Europe, now very common in England and Wales as an arable weed, on waste ground, roadsides, by hedges and in urban areas, especially where it is dry. Less common in Scotland and rare/absent in the far north west of Scotland. Similar to Hoary Mustard.

This plant is cultivated in several northern European countries, for its leaves, shoots and seeds. The taste of the wild plant is very strong, and typical of this family – mustard-hot and bitter. The upper leaves are used sparingly in salads, lower leaves better cooked, and the seeds used as a spice (though not to make mustard).

▲ Eastern Rocket

▲ Eastern Rocket stem leaf

Eastern Rocket (*S. orientale*) is a hairy annual herb to 1m, with grey-green, deeply cut lower leaves with a large terminal lobe, upper leaves long and thin, large flowers and long seed pods. Occasional in England, rarer in Wales, very rare in Scotland and Ireland, inhabiting rough and waste ground, often urban. Native to southern Europe and Asia. The leaves are edible.

The rarer **Tall Rocket (*S. altissimum*)** is a tall perennial with longer leaves with lots of narrow lobes. Also edible, but unimpressive, and the same could be said of another member of the genus, **London Rocket (*S. irio*)**, which has one of the strangest distributions of any plant in this book. For several centuries it has been very rare everywhere in Britain except central/east London, where it has been common since the Great Fire of 1666. It is present in much of Europe, but only common in the Mediterranean south. In the south-western United States, where it is introduced, it is a well-established weed. Cultivated for its leaves and seeds in Asia, and known as 'Khubkalan' in India. **False London Rocket (*S. loeselii*)** is another edible member of this genus, slightly hairier with paler flowers, similarly rare in the British Isles and more more common in northern continental Europe.

Wall-rockets (*Diplotaxis*)

Both of these species could be confused with Ragworts and Groundsel (p425), though those species have an unpleasant smell and taste. The leaves are edible, usually eaten raw in salads, as are the seeds and pods, which can be added to pasta and pizza with a chilli-like effect.

Perennial Wall-rocket (*D. tenuifolia*) is a perennial herb to 90cm, with no basal rosette of leaves, instead having many grey-green leaves on the stems, with the familiar shape of domesticated rocket, and four-petalled yellow flowers. Fruit is a long pod with a stalk as long as the pod. Native to Europe, but probably an ancient introduction to the British Isles. Frequent in south-east England in a variety of dry locations (railways, ports, beaches, urban areas), rarer elsewhere. This is one of two species widely grown/marketed as 'wild rocket'. The other is the closely related *Eruca sativa*, which has purple-streaked flowers, and coarser leaves with wider lobes, and is a rare casual alien in the British Isles. Both species are native to the Mediterranean. The genuinely wild variety has a stronger flavour, and is available throughout the year, though the autumn leaves are particularly pungent and may need blanching for 30-60 seconds to make them more palatable.

Annual Wall-rocket (*D. muralis*) is a hairless annual or short-lived perennial herb to 70cm with a rosette of long-stalked, side-lobed leaves (few stem leaves, with smaller lobes but more obvious teeth), four-petalled yellow flowers and a pod-like fruit with a stalk much shorter than the pod. Frequent in England and Ireland, less so in Scotland and central Wales, in similar habitats to Perennial Wall-rocket. Introduced in the 19th century from southern Europe, slowly spreading. Similarly edible.

Sea Rocket (*Cakile maritima*)

Sea Rocket is a sprawling, hairless annual herb with succulent, branching, shiny grey-green stems and thick, deeply cut, hairless leaves and racemes of white, lilac or pale pink flowers which become fleshy seed pods. Frequent around all British and European coastlines on sand and pebbles, around the high-tide line.

This species is poisonous to some animals (damaging the heart muscle) but edible for humans. The whole plant can be eaten, apart from the mature seed pods, but it is not for the faint-hearted. Younger leaves are usable in salads, older leaves and immature seed pods are better cooked. The root is a famine food, and oil can be made from the mature seeds.

▼ Sea Rocket

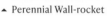 Perennial Wall-rocket   Sea Rocket ▲ Annual Wall-rocket

Watercresses (*Nasturtium*) ⚠

The 'green sickness' is hypochromic
anaemia, and Watercresses do indeed
contain useful amounts of both iron
and vitamin B6, deficiencies of which
cause anaemia.

**Watercress (*N. officinale* syn. *Rorippa
nasturtium-aquaticum*)** is a sprawling
perennial herb, with rather floppy, angular,
hollow stems (to 1m long) which root at the
nodes. It has glossy, succulent, purple-green
compound leaves (with a heart-shaped
terminal leaflet) and racemes of small white
or mauve flowers. The pods have two rows
of seeds. Common throughout the British
Isles, apart from in mountainous areas,
inhabiting ditches, ponds, streams and
water meadows. Often available during the
winter. Cultivated Watercress is genetically
identical to the wild plant, which was
not successfully grown until the early 19th
century. The older shoots are better for
eating than the younger ones, which are
comparatively tasteless. **Narrow-fruited
Watercress (*N. microphyllum* syn. *Rorippa
microphylla*)** is very similar, but with only
one row of seeds in the pods, and has the
same edible uses. Both plants could be
confused with (non-toxic) Fool's Watercress
(p471), although that plant tastes of carrots.
Neither should be confused with the familiar
(edible) garden flowers called Nasturtiums,
which belong to a different family. When
picking Watercress growing wild in
particularly fast-running water, or among
grass, there is the potential for confusion
with Water-parsnips (p491), although
those plants have much more sharply
indented leaves.

▾ Mature leaves

Watercresses must always be washed carefully, to remove small invertebrates. The leaves are used as a salad item or garnish, or made into a soup. Picked from the wild, the leaves can be repeatedly harvested and will keep growing back. Be careful when harvesting – do not eat raw downstream from anywhere there are livestock, or you run the very real risk of a nasty parasitic infection. Cooking destroys the parasite (*Fasciola hepatica*). The seeds can also be used like those of Mustard (grind, add cold water, then leave for 10-15 minutes). Also see recipe on p75.

Yellow-cresses (*Rorippa*)

These plants are closely related to Watercresses, which were members of this genus until quite recently. All of them inhabit damp locations. The young leaves and stems are usable in a similar way to Watercresses.

Great Yellow-cress (*R. amphibia*) is a hairless upright perennial herb with a stout stem to 1.2m with toothed, lanceolate leaves, yellow flowers and oval seed pods. Frequent and locally common in England and Wales on the banks of still or slow-moving freshwater bodies. Rare in Scotland, and probably not native. Frequent in much of temperate Europe, as far north as southern Sweden.

Creeping Yellow-cress (*R. sylvestris*) is much smaller (to 30cm), has deeply cut leaves, and is usually sprawling rather than upright. Frequent throughout temperate

▲ Great Yellow-cress

Europe in damp places. This is an excellent salad leaf.

Marsh Yellow-cress (*R. palustris*) is upright and taller (to 60cm). Frequent in British Isles.

Northern Yellow-cress (*R. islandica*) is another native, very similar to Marsh Yellow-cress, rare but becoming more common in damp places, especially near human activity.

▲ Creeping Yellow-cress growing by a waterfall

Shepherd's Purse (*Capsella bursa-pastoris*)

Shepherd's Purse is a very variable annual or biennial herb with a low rosette of lobed or undivided basal leaves and flowering stems (which can branch) up to 50cm high, with clasping leaves. The lobes point directly outwards (rather than backwards like those of Dandelion), although the shape of the leaves is highly variable. It has a loose raceme of tiny white flowers on thin stalks, and triangular, purse-like fruits. Very common in gardens, and on arable land, waste and disturbed ground. Native to eastern Europe and Asia, introduced in the British Isles.

This is a popular edible species in Japan and China, where it is both foraged from the wild and cultivated. It is often available in winter. The basal leaves before flowering are a good salad plant, or can be sautéed or used in soups and sauces. The seed pods can provide peppery flavouring in soups. Some North American sources claim the roots can be used like ginger, but I have found the taste to be mild.

Lady's Smock (*Cardamine pratensis*)

Lady's Smock is a rather variable perennial herb to 60cm, with variable pinnate leaves (1-7 leaflet pairs), basal/lower leaflets rounded with large terminal leaflet, and upper leaflets much narrower. The racemes of lilac, pale pink or white flowers are followed by long, narrow seed pods. It is common throughout the British Isles on roadsides, in ditches and other areas, usually near water, and preferring acidic soil, and native and common in most of temperate Europe (though listed as threatened in Germany). **Greater Lady's Smock (*C. raphanofolia*)** is a larger version of *pratensis*, with pinker flowers, native to the Pyrenees and mountainous areas of south-east Europe, introduced to the British Isles and now spreading. It is occasional in the British Isles, especially in south-west England, Wales and central and south-west Scotland.

The leaves, shoots and flowers are all edible, with a strong but very pleasant smell and taste. This makes an excellent component in mixed salads, and works perfectly with Three-cornered Leek (p134) and tomato, with a vinaigrette dressing. Also see see uses on p75 and p490.

Both of these plants are also known as 'Cuckooflower' because they flower when the cuckoos arrive in spring, but the same name has been given to several other plants for the same reason, so maybe it is better not to use it.

▶ Lady's Smock

▲ Greater Lady's Smock

Coralroot Bittercress (*C. bulbifera*)

Coralroot Bittercress is a rhizomatous perennial herb with unbranched, hairless stems to 70cm, lower leaves stalked and pinnate, upper leaves three-lobed, becoming simple. Pink flowers, similar to Lady's Smock, in short racemes. Rarely sets seed, but readily reproduces via distinctive purple bulbils in the leaf axils. Rare in most of the British Isles, at least as a native wild plant, though locally common in the Weald and Chiltern hills, and often grown in gardens, where it can become invasive and occasionally escapes. It is significantly more common in northern continental Europe. This species is named after its red roots, and both the roots and bulbils are edible, raw or cooked, as are the leaves. The flavour is similar to other members of the genus. The young leaves make a first-class salad ingredient, only mildly hot compared to its closest relatives. The bulbils make an interesting component of a salad. **Pinnate Coralroot (*C. heptaphylla*)** is a central European species with similar leaves, and a rare relic of cultivation in the British Isles.

Whorled Coralroot (*C. quinqefolia*) is from eastern Europe, cultivated in the British Isles and recently starting to naturalise. Both species are edible as Coralroot (though lacking bulbils).

▼ Coralroot

Other Bittercresses (*Cardamine* spp.)

Hairy Bittercress (*C. hirsuta*) is an annual or biennial herb with a rosette of pinnate basal leaves with up to 15 round leaflets, hairy flowering stems up to 30cm, a raceme of small, white flowers and explosive fruits. Habitat is very variable, but it particularly likes bare, disturbed ground and is an abundant weed in British gardens and throughout Europe, apart from the coldest parts of the north. The name seriously undersells this plant, since it is neither hairy nor bitter. It's a first-class edible species when young, especially the leaves, but the whole above-ground part of the plant is edible. It is typically used like watercress in salads, and is very useful because it is available throughout the winter.

Wood or **Wavy Bittercress (*C. flexuosa*)** is a biennial or perennial herb, very similar to Hairy Bittercress but larger and with a wavy stem. Common in damp woodland, and stream sides throughout Europe, and present in much of the rest of the world, especially in coastal areas. Even better as an edible.

Large Bittercress (*C. amara*) is a perennial herb similar to Hairy Bittercress and Lady's Smock, but larger (to 60cm) and with more oval-shaped leaflets than the former and purple-tipped stamens unlike the latter. Can be found in damp or wet places, and common throughout temperate areas of Europe, but absent in the far north. Frequent in much of the British Isles, rare in south-west England, Wales and north-west Scotland. Leaves and flowers edible as with other members of this genus, but not the tastiest member (rather bitter) so best used sparingly.

Narrow-leaved Bittercress (*C. impatiens*, not illustrated) is taller than the other members of the genus covered here (to 80cm), and annual/biennial, with narrower leaves and toothed leaflets. It is also much rarer in the British Isles, inhabiting damp limestone woods and riverbanks in a few localised parts of England and Wales. More common in the warmer areas of temperate continental Europe. Edible uses as Hairy Bitter-cress.

New Zealand Bittercress (*C. corymbosa*, not illustrated) is an antipodean species, similar to Hairy Bitter-cress. First recorded in the British Isles in 1985, it has become a problem horticultural weed (also in the Netherlands), especially in polytunnels, paths and rockeries. I've never seen or tried eating it, but it would be very surprising if it isn't edible.

▾ Hairy Bittercress

▲ Hairy Bittercress

▲ Large Bittercress

▲ Wood Bittercress

Field Pennycress (*Thlaspi arvense*)

Field Pennycress is a hairless annual herb to 50cm, with narrow leaves which clasp the stem, and a raceme of small, white flowers followed by the flat, circular seed pods, after which the plant is named. When damaged, the leaves smell of rotten garlic with a hint of turnip. Common in much of the British Isles (where it is an ancient introduction), especially England, on any type of disturbed ground, but particularly arable fields. Frequent apart from north-west Scotland and parts of Wales.

Young leaves are edible before the plant flowers, but even these can be rather bitter, as well as garlicky. The seeds can be used to season sausages,* ground into a powder and used as a mustard-like condiment, and sprouted for salads. This plant is currently being investigated as a potential source of biodiesel (oil from the seeds).†

* *Foraging in Eastern Europe*, Luczaj, L, 2021.
† *Turning a burden into an opportunity: Pennycress (Thlaspi arvense L.) a new oilseed crop for biofuel production*, Zanetti, F, et al, 2019, Biomass and Bioenergy, volume 130:105354.

Honesty (*Lunaria annua*)

Honesty is a very hairy upright biennial herb to 1.2m, with heart-shaped leaves (stalked and larger at the bottom, smaller and less-stalked at the top), purple or white flowers and distinctive membranous circular fruits (they are almost transparent, which is where the English name comes from). Native to the Balkans and south-west Asia, but frequent elsewhere as a garden escape, and increasing in woodland and on roadsides and waste ground, especially near human habitation. The seeds are edible, cooked or ground to make a mustard-like condiment. The roots of younger plants are also edible.

Dame's Rocket or Dame's Violet (*Hesperis matronalis*)

Dame's Rocket is an upright biennial or perennial herb to 1.5m, with hairy stems, alternate lanceolate leaves and fragrant white, pink or purple flowers. Frequent in most of the British Isles (less so in north-west Scotland) on riverbanks and waste ground, sometimes wood edges, and especially near human habitation. This is an ancient introduction to the British Isles, native to temperate and subtropical parts of Eurasia, but introduced elsewhere. Grown ornamentally as 'Sweet Rocket'. The young leaves are edible, usually chopped in salads, although predictably for this family they are rather strong-tasting. The sprouted seeds are also usable as a salad item, and can be pressed to make an edible oil. Flowers can be used in salads.

Lepidium (genus)

The best-known cultivated *Lepidium* is **Garden Cress (*L. sativum*)**, which isn't native to Europe but does occasionally turn up growing among rubbish. The leaves are edible, used like Watercress, and the roots and seed pods can be used as a Mustard-like condiment. The seeds can be pressed to make an oil, or sprouted and used in salads. This is one of the seven herbs required for authentic Frankfurter Green Sauce (p75 and p381).

Pepperworts (*L. campestre/ heterophyllum/ruderale*)

(Field) Pepperwort / Field Cress (*L. campestre*) is a slightly hairy annual to biennial herb with a basal rosette of leaves, and an erect, leafy, grey-green stem to 60cm. All leaves are oval-ish, with a slightly toothed margin, and forking off the stem are racemes of small white flowers, which turn into flat, oval seed pods. Frequent in lowland British Isles in a variety of habitats, including grassland, arable fields, waste ground and gardens, preferring sandy soils and dry environments. Present in much of the colder parts of temperate Europe, but not the far north. Native to Europe, probably an ancient introduction in the British Isles.

The young leaves and shoots are edible, usually chopped into salads or finely chopped in sauces (especially for fish, with capers, gherkins and olives). They can also be cooked, and taste hot, like all members of this genus. Changing the water a couple of times renders them more palatable. The immature seed pods are edible but very strong-tasting. They are usually cooked, as

▲ (Field) Pepperwort

a peppery addition to soups and stews, or pickled. The mature seeds can be used like peppercorns.

Smith's Pepperwort (*L. heterophyllum*) is very similar, but with floppier, less-branching stems. Frequent near the west coast of Great Britain and the east coast of Ireland, as a weed of arable land, also on shingle, heaths, and rocky, acidic soils. It is uncommon and scattered elsewhere in the British Isles, but present across most of Europe. **Narrow-leaved Pepperwort (*L. ruderale*)** has much more branching stems (to 40cm), and more bush-shaped, much narrower leaves, and a particularly pungent scent. Frequent in England, especially in the east, rarer elsewhere, in various man-made/disturbed habitats, particularly coastal and near salted roads. Edibility of both species are as Pepperwort.

Hoary Cress or Thanetweed (*L. draba*)

Hoary Cress is a rhizomatous, perennial, (usually) hairy herb with stout, upright, branching stems to 80cm, slightly toothed leaves which clasp the stem in the upper parts, and umbel-like racemes of small white flowers. It inhabits roadsides, open ground and arable fields, particularly in coastal areas. It is native to south-east Europe but abundant in south-east England, where it was famously introduced in 1802 (in Thanet), and slowly spreading.

The edibility of this plant is disputed. Many sources describe leaves and shoots as edible (raw or cooked) but there is also an unverified but widely quoted claim that they contain hydrogen cyanide. Young leaves, which are mildly peppery, are used sparingly to spice up salads, or can be used in mixed wild greens soups or terrine (p75). Unopened flower buds can be used like broccoli (though punchy). The roots are claimed to be usable like Horseradish (but were too fibrous when I tried it, with no strong taste), and the seeds used to make a condiment.

▲ Dittander ('Pfefferkraut') growing out of a pavement in Germany

Dittander (*L. latifolum*)

Dittander is an upright perennial herb to
1.5m, with a multiply branched stem, large,
ovate to lanceolate, slightly serrated leaves,
with panicles of numerous small racemes of
small, off-white (pale pink or purple) flowers
at the top, and oval pods. Naturally inhabits
coastal areas, but becoming more common
inland in environments such as waste
ground and beside roads and canals. Native
to southern Europe, rare in the British Isles
apart from some parts of East Anglia.

All parts are very hot raw, much milder
cooked, and were historically sometimes
soaked in water for 48 hours. Only very
young leaves can be used in salads. Older
names include 'Pepper Cress' and 'Poor
Man's Pepper'. It was once cultivated in
cottage gardens, but this had stopped
well before the mid-19th century. It was
used as a peppery condiment, but fell
out of favour because of cheaper
replacements, and also its tendency to
act as an emetic if consumed in quantity.
Available all year.

Swine-cresses
(*L. coronopus/didymum*)

(Greater) Swine-cress (*L. coronopus* syn. *C. squamatus*) is a sprawling annual or biennial herb with radiating stems to 35cm, with stalked, hairless, deeply cut leaves, and spikes of tiny flowers on the stem tips and in the leaf axils. The whole plant smells strongly of cress when crushed. Common in most of England and Wales, less so in Scotland and Ireland. Inhabits waste ground, arable land and pavements, often in damp and trampled places (such as gateways), and especially in urban areas. Introduced, probably in antiquity, from Europe. The leaves are edible, but very spicy and should be used sparingly.

    Lesser Swine-cress (*L. didymum* syn. *C. didymus*) is a smaller version of Swine-cress. Common in the southern half of England, coastal area of Wales and southern Ireland, also introduced a long time ago, from South America. Opinions differ on which, if either, is the hottest. I can't tell the difference: they are both too hot for me.

▾ (Greater) Swine-cress

Flixweed or Herb Sophia (*Descurainia sophia*)

Flixweed is a hairy (esp. towards the base), upright, annual or biennial herb to 1m with lacy, grey-green leaves and tiny flowers. It inhabits sandy waste ground, roadsides and arable fields. An ancient introduction, this species is occasional in most of the British Isles, more common in East Anglia, and absent from northern Scotland.

The seeds can also be ground into a flour, or sprouted. In Iran, these seeds are commercially available, under the name 'khakshir' ('Earthmilk'). They are used to make a thirst-quenching drink called 'sharbat', or sherbet, on hot days. The seeds should be steeped in cold water for 10-15 minutes, before adding sugar and rosewater and serving with plenty of ice. The young shoots and leaves are also edible cooked. They are slightly bitter and mustardy.

Horseradish (*Armoracia rusticana*)

Horseradish is a hairless perennial herb to 1.4m, with shiny, crinkled, dock-like (but toothed) basal leaves (can be 50cm long) and tall, leafy stems, wide clusters of white flowers, seed pods on long, upright stalks, and a very long tap root. It generally spreads by rhizomes rather than setting seed, so forms dense patches. It is found in fields, on riverbanks, roadsides, railway embankments and rough waste ground, often urban. Native to south-east Europe and western Asia but widely introduced in temperate areas elsewhere as a crop plant. Common in England, less so in Wales, rare or absent in Scotland, and in Ireland mainly southern and eastern.

This plant was well established in the British Isles by the 16th century and was commonly used to expel worms. Making a sauce from the roots was originally associated with the Germans, before being adopted by the British as part of our beloved roast beef dinner, replacing Dittander (p300). Horseradish sauce is also served with salmon or other fish. The peeled and grated young root is typically used (older roots are too tough), to make Horseradish sauce or as a flavouring in cold salad dishes (such as potato salad), and these are only worth collecting where the plant is growing in quite deep and rich soil. They are at their best in late autumn. The fresh roots contain sinigrin (see Black Mustard, p278), which gives the root its hot flavour. The roots can also be eaten very thinly sliced as flavouring in a sandwich and salads, or preserved in vinegar and citric acid, and stored in a fridge. The young leaves are used in salads or as a pot-herb, older leaves used to wrap fish before steaming or baking. The seeds can also be sprouted as a salad item. Also see recipe for pickled Elder buds and Rock Samphire (p482).

Scurvy-grasses (*Cochlearia*)

"Scurvy-grass, *Cochlearia*, of the Garden,
but especially that of the Sea, is sharp,
biting, and hot; of Nature like *Nasturtium*,
prevalent in the *Scorbute*. A few of the
tender Leaves may be admitted in
our Composition."
(John Evelyn, 1699)

Scurvy-grasses are small biennial herbs to
30cm, with clusters of tiny white flowers.
Three varieties are naturally coastal plants,
which were once used by sailors as a
treatment for scurvy (they have a high
vitamin C content), although they aren't
exactly tasty. They can be used sparingly
in mixed salads, or chopped into dishes as
strong flavouring. English Scurvy-grass is the
mildest tasting of the three. Historically also
used to make beer ('scurvy-grass ale').
     Common Scurvy-grass (*C. officinalis*)
is a plant of salt marsh and damp coastal
grassland, especially on the western coasts
of the British Isles and a few miles inland.
It has round basal leaves, with flattened
bases. **English Scurvy-grass (*C. anglica*)** is
more strictly found on the coast itself, in
the same habitats, mainly in England and
southern Ireland. Its leaves are larger, with
bases tapered into the stalk rather than
being flat, and variable ivy-like lobes/teeth.
Young fruits are edible. **Danish Scurvy-grass
(*C. danica*)** naturally inhabits rocky coastal
areas, including pavements and walls, and
has become the most common member of
the genus, due to its liking for growing near
salted main roads, including the central
reservations of motorways. Its basal leaves
are distinctly ivy-shaped.

▲ Common Scurvy-grass

▲ Danish Scurvy-grass

▲ English Scurvy-grass

Wintercresses (*Barbarea*)

"... it has been cultivated in our gardens for a long time as an early salad [...] the outer leaves are picked as the plant grows up, and the stems bearing the flower buds cut down as they appear, by which means leaves may be obtained from it all through the winter and spring. In Sweden the plant is boiled and eaten like cabbage ..."

(C Pierpoint Johnson, 1862)

(Common) Wintercress or **Yellow Rocket** (***B. vulgaris***) is a hairless biennial or perennial upright herb to 1m with shiny, dark green leaves, lobed with a large terminal lobe, and clusters of yellow four-petalled flowers. Pods near-upright and narrow. Native and frequent everywhere in the British Isles apart from the Highlands, especially near fresh water. This is the plant Johnson refers to. **Small-flowered** and **Medium-flowered Wintercresses** and **Land Cress (*B. stricta, intermedia and verna*)** are all similar, but Johnson goes on to say that "almost all the common weeds belonging to this well-marked group of plants would admit of such culinary use" (in winter salads, when garden vegetables are scarce) because they "are seldom destroyed by frosts". Only the young, winter leaves of the basal rosette are palatable raw, although even these are best used as flavouring, mixed with milder leaves. Boil older ones in a couple of changes of water. Traditionally this plant was blanched by covering, improving the taste. The flowering stems are also edible, before the flowers open (like Broccoli) and the seeds can be pressed to make an edible oil, or sprouted for salads. **Land Cress**, aka American Wintercress, actually came from south-west Europe and was already a frequent escape by Johnson's time. Once called 'Herb St Barbara' it was sown around her saint's day (4th or 16th December) and used like Mustard, all through spring and summer. The flavour is less intense than Common Wintercress. Historically it was used as an easier-to-grow substitute for Watercress (less water required), and recently came back into commercial use in mixed salads.

◄ Common Wintercress

Garlic Mustard (*Alliaria petiolata*)

"This is eaten by many country people as sauce to their salt fish, and helps to digest the crudities and other corrupt humours ingendered thereby; it warms the stomach, and causes digestion."
(Nicholas Culpeper, 1652)

"In Wales it is often fried with bacon or herrings."
(C Pierpoint Johnson, 1862)

"The white, tapering roots taste rather like Horseradish slightly flavoured with garlic and may be grated into salad or pounded with oil and vinegar into a good substitute for mustard or horseradish sauce."
(Jason Hill, 1939)

Garlic Mustard or **Jack-by-the-Hedge** is an upright biennial herb to 1.3m with glossy, cordate, coarse-toothed leaves (which smell of garlic when crushed). These form a basal rosette in the first year, followed by an upright, leafy stem in the second year, bearing clusters of small, white flowers and four-sided, beaded, pods. The plant has a very aromatic tap root, used rather like Horseradish. Habitat is very varied, but especially in moist hedgerows, wood edges and waste ground, usually in shady areas. Common throughout temperate Europe, apart from the far north. Abundant in the British Isles apart from northern Scotland and western Ireland. Native to Eurasia, invasive in North America.

Garlic Mustard has a long history of food use, usually eaten raw because cooking increases the bitterness and decreases the garlicky flavour. The young upper leaves of second-year plants, which are available from late winter, are the best part. The larger lower leaves, and the entire plant after flowering, become more bitter. It makes a superb sauce, for accompanying roast lamb or strongly flavoured fish. The classic Garlic Mustard dish is pesto, for which you will find hundreds of recipes online, though the name 'Garlic Mustard' confuses search engines. Some of these make use of the tap roots as well as the fresh leaves. The peeled roots of younger plants have a mild horseradish flavour, becoming more woody and less tasty as the plant flowers. The chopped leaves can also be used raw in salads, sparingly. The flowers and immature seed pods can be used in the same way. Seeds can be used like those of the Mustards, including sprouting them. There are some uses of the cooked leaves. They can be quickly fried into 'crisps', which works particularly well when mixed with nettle leaves. In Italy, they are used with spinach as a filling for ravioli (50/50 mixture), and also as a pizza topping. Some people stir-fry the tops until just before the flowers open.

Garlic Mustard Sauce

Ingredients:

Fresh garlic mustard leaves (best in spring, before the plant has flowered), olive oil, lemon juice (if the sauce is for lamb) or white wine vinegar (if it is for fish), salt, pepper.

Mix ingredients together and blitz. Serve with roast lamb, or strong-flavoured white fish.

Sea Kale (*Crambe maritima*)

Sea Kale is a perennial herb to 75cm with large, purple and grey-green fleshy leaves with lobed, wavy margins, and dense heads of white flowers on branching stems. Common along the south coast of England and west coast of Wales on shingle beaches, but globally rare (restricted to the coastlines of the British Isles, northern continental Europe and the Black Sea). The equally edible **Greater Sea Kale** (***C. cordifolia***) is native to south-east Europe, grown as an ornamental elsewhere.

Sea Kale is the king of wild vegetables, and was once so widely collected for this purpose that it became threatened. High in vitamin C, it was one of the plants used by sailors against scurvy, and was a popular garden vegetable in the 19th century. It is now becoming popular again, but the wild population remains vulnerable to large-scale gathering.

The stems and leaves make good eating, and are considered a delicacy when very young and still more purple than green. In this state they are even edible raw in salads (the young stems, peeled, are best), but are also fried, roasted, boiled in salted water for 20 minutes, or boiled for 10 minutes and then sautéed for 10 more in butter, with crushed and chopped garlic added near the end. The leaves become tougher and slightly bitter as they mature, but are still perfectly edible shredded and stir-fried. The unopened flowers are also first-class – sweet and crunchy – either eaten raw or briefly steamed. The freshly opened flowers smell richly of honey, and taste almost as sweet. The grape-like immature seed pods can be eaten raw or cooked. The roots are edible and nutritious, and are eaten by people who cultivate this plant as a vegetable. Rather fibrous, they should be peeled then boiled or roasted for 30 mins to soften them up, but there is no bitterness – they are sweet, salty and cabbage-flavoured. It is illegal in the UK to uproot wild plants, but you do sometimes find exposed roots where shingle has been washed away. Sea Kale was traditionally blanched, by piling pebbles over the emerging shoots, and it is worth having a look for stems that have been naturally buried by the action of waves on the pebbles.

Roasted Sea Kale Shoots

Wash 450g of sea kale shoots with unopened flower buds, then put in a small roasting dish with 1tbsp extra virgin olive oil. Roast for 10 mins at 200°C / fan 180°C, then turn and roast for another 8 mins. Season with 1tsp sea salt and serve immediately.

Crispy Fried Sea Kale

Wash and completely dry some large, but young, sea kale leaves. Thinly shred the leaves, discarding the midrib. Heat vegetable oil in a wok or pan until it is almost smoking, add the sea kale and stir-fry for no more than 30 seconds, optionally with a little salt and/or a splash of soy sauce. Drain, sprinkle with brown sugar, and serve immediately.

Sea Kale Salad (TF Garrett, 1892)

Cut the sea kale into small pieces, put them in a basin, cover with cream and a small quantity of tarragon vinegar, place a cloth over the basin, and leave all night. On the following morning trim some nice fresh lettuces and endive, wash them well, and cut into quarters. Arrange them in a salad-bowl, pile the sea-kale cream on the top, ornament tastefully with pieces of beetroot, and serve.

Malvales

There are deadly poisonous members of this order, in the family *Thymelaeaceae*. The berries cause burning to the soft tissues of mouth and throat, followed by coma and death. This includes two species native to the British Isles which are rare and confined to very alkaline soils in the wild, but also grown as ornamentals: **Spurge Laurel (*Daphne laureola*)** and **Mezereon (*D. mezereum*)**.

▾ Spurge Laurel

▾ Mezereon

Malvaceae (Mallow family)

"The smaller Mallows are prepared with garum, stock, oil and vinegar; the larger Mallows prepare with a wine sauce, pepper and stock."

(Apicius, 1ˢᵗ century)

"All the mallows yield an excellent fibre, capable of use for cordage, paper and textile manufacture. ... there is a tradition in Persia that Mohammed had once a garment made of it, with which he was so pleased that he turned the plant into the less useful but more showy geranium, as an acknowledgement of its Merits."

(C Pierpoint Johnson, 1862)

The Mallow Family is home to several important tropical crops, including Cocoa (*Theobroma cacao*) and Cotton (*Gossypium*). *Hibiscus* leaves and flowers can be used to make teas, and the flowers used in salads. The ornamental *Abutilon* species also have edible flowers, often available in winter. Another member is Okra (*Abelmoschus esculentus*), which is known for being particularly mucilaginous (slimy) – a characteristic also typical of the edible wild members found in colder regions: the Mallows. In addition to those covered here, **Chinese Mallow (*M. verticillata*,** not illustrated) is an annual herb to 1.7m with rounded palmate-lobed leaves, and white, pink or red flowers. Native to east Asia but naturalised (or at least occurs as a casual alien) in the British Isles, and common/ invasive in central northern Europe. This species is cultivated both as an ornamental and a salad leaf. A historically important food crop in ancient China.

Common Mallow (*M. sylvestris*)

Common Mallow is a hairy perennial, spreading herb to 1.3m with a branching stem, palmate-lobed leaves (stem leaves much more deeply lobed than the basal leaves) and purple-pink flowers with darker stripes, which grow in groups from the leaf axils. The segmented fruits are known formally as 'nutlets' and informally as 'cheeses' (which they resemble). Introduced in antiquity and common in the south of the British Isles (rare in the north) on roadsides and waste ground, and in fields and hedgerows, particularly in coastal areas. Common throughout Europe, apart from the far north.

The leaves and flowers can be eaten raw in salads, or cooked, whereby they take on a mucilaginous texture. They can be served as a side vegetable or used to thicken soups and stews. A related plant called Mulukhiyah (*Corchorus olitorius*) is widely used in southeast Asia and neighbouring parts of Africa to make a soup of the same name (the other main ingredients are chicken and garlic). The nutritious unripe seed cheeses are eaten raw in salads, used in place of peas in any recipe, or can be peeled and boiled with sugar to make a sort of meringue. The mature seeds are also edible, and high in protein and fat. The leaves have been used to make a tea, and a yellow or green dye. All parts of Mallow are rich in vitamins A and C, as well as important trace elements.

▲ Common Mallow

Sautéed Mallow With Onions
(Traditional Palestinian 'Khobeizeh')

Ingredients:
200g fresh mallow leaves (roughly chopped), 60ml olive oil, 1 large onion (chopped), 1 garlic clove (chopped), juice of one lemon, 1 red chilli (chopped).

Wash and drain the leaves. Fry the onion on medium heat for 4 mins. Add the garlic, cook for 30 seconds while stirring, then add the mallow leaves and a little bit of water. Cover and simmer on low heat for 15 mins. Add the lemon juice and chilli, and serve warm with rice or pitta bread, olives and yogurt.

Dwarf Mallow (*M. neglecta*)

Dwarf Mallow is a prostrate annual herb with stems to 60cm, leaves like common mallow but smaller, and white or pale lilac flowers. It inhabits waste ground, roadsides, beaches and walls, preferring dry, disturbed places. Introduced but frequent in southern and eastern England, rarer elsewhere on the British Isles. Common in most of Europe, apart from the far north. The leaves and stalks are good in salads, but can also be cooked like other Mallows. Flowers and seeds also usable as other Mallows. This is probably the best edible wild European member of the genus but known to accumulate high levels of nitrate from its environment.

Musk Mallow (*M. moschata*)

Musk Mallow is a perennial herb to 80cm with similar flowers to Common Mallow, but much more deeply cut leaves. It can be found in grassland, roadsides and fields, usually in dry locations. Native and frequent in England and Wales, rarer in Scotland and Ireland, and more common in the rest of temperate Europe. As with the other Mallows, the leaves are edible both cooked and raw, and the flowers and immature seeds are both also edible in salads. Historically used for its fibres, which are "very long and tolerably strong" (C Pierpoint Johnson, 1862).

▲ Dwarf Mallow

Tree Mallow (*M. arborea* syn. *Lavateria arborea*)

Tree Mallow is a shrubby annual, biennial or short-lived perennial to 2m (rarely taller), with velvety five-to-nine-lobed leaves, woody lower stems and terminal racemes of purple-veined dark pink flowers. Common, especially in exposed areas, on the southern and western coasts of the British Isles, the Atlantic coasts of France and Spain and throughout the Mediterranean. Very rare inland. The young leaves are just about edible, but the main foraging interest is the immature fruits (cheeses), which are sweet and juicy, eaten raw if very young, otherwise boiled, steamed or stir-fried. They taste like sweetcorn. Can also be pickled.

▲ Musk Mallow   ▼ Tree Mallow

(Common) Hollyhock (*Alcea rosea*)

Hollyhock is an annual/biennial herb to 3m with palmate-lobed leaves up to 20cm long and flowers that are pink, white or purple. Frequent in central and south-east England, typically on waste ground and roadsides. Probably native to south-east Asia but widely introduced elsewhere.

▼ Hollyhock

Historically grown for food in Egypt and Greece. The young leaves are usable as a pot-herb (too furry for salads) and the peeled stems are edible as a cooked vegetable, as are the starch-rich roots. The sweet-tasting, mucilaginous flowers can be eaten in salads, turned into fritters, or made into a tea.

Marsh-mallow (*Althaea officinalis*)

The roots are many and long, shooting from one head, of the bigness of a thumb or finger, very pliant, tough and bending, like liquorice, of a whitish-yellow colour on the outside, and more white within, full of slimy juice, which being laid in water, will render it thick as jelly.
(Nicholas Culpeper, 1652)

Marsh-mallow is a finely hairy perennial herb to 1.5m with slightly lobed, grey-green, oval-ish leaves and an irregular raceme of pale pink (or white) flowers, followed by a capsule fruit. Found in coastal grassland and brackish ditches, particularly drier parts of salt marshes just above the line of the highest spring tides. Native to the Mediterranean but introduced further north, including the British Isles, where it is uncommon, becoming very rare in Scotland. Present in most of continental Europe, but absent in Scandinavia apart from the south coast. Even though it is not native to the British Isles, it would be unfortunate if over-enthusiastic foraging were to harm its already small population levels.

You could be forgiven for believing the name 'Marshmallow' refers solely to an item of squidgy pink or white confectionery traditionally toasted in fires on the ends of

▲ Marsh-mallow

sticks. The plant's ethnobotanical history goes back to antiquity – it was used by the Greeks as a medicine for sore throats and other ailments ('Altho' means 'to cure' in Greek). The Egyptians were the first to make a sweet treat out of it by mixing the sap (probably of the root) with honey, nuts and seeds, and baking into cakes. Marshmallows as we know them can be traced back to 19th century France, where their rising popularity meant that using *A. officinalis* became impractical, partly because it wasn't that common or easy to get hold of, and partly because of how long it took to prepare the root for use. The modern confection contains no Marsh-mallow at all, the stickiness provided by gelatin, corn starch and gum arabic.

The Romans also used the leaves of this plant as a cooked vegetable, and it is still used as food in parts of south-east Asia. It has multiple uses for a modern forager. The leaves can be cooked as a pot-herb, but they are extremely mucilaginous and so should be used sparingly. They can also be eaten raw, but they can be quite tough, so need to be chopped. The root is edible, chopped raw, or boiled and then fried, or (as traditionally) dried, ground and used to make a sticky sweet in the spirit of the original Egyptian version. The immature seed pods ('cheeses') can be used in salads, and both the root and flowers can be made into a tea.

Common Lime or Linden (*Tilia x europaea*)

Common Lime (historically 'Line') is a large tree (to 30m). It is a hybrid of **Large-leaved Lime (*T. platyphyllos*)** and **Small-leaved Lime (*T. cordata*)**. Common – more so than either of its parent species – but nearly always planted rather than a natural hybrid. All of them have lime-green, heart-shaped leaves with asymmetrical bases. These trees often have a lot of twiggy growth around the base of the trunk. The uses are the same for all three. The fruits are woody structures called 'nutlets'.

The young leaves make an excellent base to a wild salad (very mild-tasting, like a slightly mucilaginous lettuce). They are at their very best when still curled and unopened. Older leaves can be stuffed like vine leaves, and you can use them to line the dish when making a wild greens terrine (p75), which helps to keep it in one piece. The leaves are an important famine food, widely used in France during the middle ages as a flour extender – a practice that was revived during World War II. To make Lime leaf flour you first need to dry the leaves (preferably in the sun) until they are crisp and crumbly, then break them up using a pestle and mortar and pass through a sieve. The resulting flour can be stored for several months in an airtight container, and can be used to make porridge or bread (ratio between 10:1 and 5:1 of wheat flour to Lime flour). You will also find the leaves are sometimes shiny, sticky and very sweet. This sweet coating is honeydew, excreted by aphids which have been feeding on the sap from the leaves. It is edible, and though it is rather off-putting to think of eating the waste product of aphids, there are ants that intentionally 'farm' aphids for this substance, and it also attracts honeybees, other insects and even some birds.

The young flowers are edible raw, or can be dried and used to make a herbal tea which is popular in eastern Europe. These have to be fully opened, but fresh – if they are too old then they can become slightly toxic. The flowers can also be cooked to make an interesting side garnish, which retains their delightful odour. Blanch in boiling water for 30 seconds, drain, then fry in butter for five minutes with salt, pepper and chopped chives. Mature fruits can be roasted and made into a coffee substitute. The sap can also be tapped in early spring, the flowers used in herbal smoking mixtures and the bark used to make rope.

Foraging legend has it that the flowers and immature fruits (before they go hard) can be ground together with grape oil to make into a chocolate-like substance, which only failed in marketing trials because of its tendency to decompose unless frozen. My attempts to replicate this have never resulted in anything that resembles chocolate in any sense other than taste and smell.

See pic of young leaves on p29.

▲ Lime leaves covered in honeydew

Caryophyllales

The precise relationship between the *Caryophyllales* and other flowering plants has long been debated. Some botanists consider them a sister clade to the Asterids, others place them within the Rosids or in their own Caryophyllid clade. The important Knotweed family is either a member of the Caryophyllales or closely related.

Pokeweed (*Phytolacca americana*) is a North American species sometimes cultivated in Europe, with fruit that look like elderberries on spikes and are poisonous raw, especially when unripe, but can be cooked and eaten in pies. Cacti are also members of this order, as are the carnivorous Sundew and Pitcher plants.

Polygonaceae (Knotweed family)
Rhubarbs (*Rheum*) are the best-known domesticated member of the Knotweed family (also sometimes named after Dock or Buckwheat). The green parts of Rhubarb cause nervous disorders, coma and potentially death. They contain several toxins, including large amounts of oxalic acid (the acidic taste in the edible stem is caused by malic acid). Rhubarb's closest native relative is **Mountain Sorrel (*Oxyria dignyna*)**, which has similar flowers to Common Sorrel (p322) but Rhubarb-like rounded leaves (though much smaller). This is a strictly northern/mountainous species, very rare outside the Highlands and north-west Wales, and can be used like Common Sorrel.

Wireplant (*Muehlenbeckia complexa*) is a native of New Zealand, grown ornamentally in Europe and naturalised on cliffs and walls in a few locations in south-west England. It escapes more commonly further south in Europe. The swollen flowers ('fruits') were traditionally eaten by the Maori.

Rumex (genus)

Rumex is split into two subgenera – *Rumex* (Docks) and *Acetosa* (Sorrels). Many are bitter, but the stems and leaves of the best edible species taste similar to rhubarb. The seeds and roots of various Docks have been ground and used as flour extenders. Docks aren't the easiest plants to identify to species, and if you're going to get serious about foraging them then you will need to learn about tepals. Botanically, these are the outermost whorl in a flower, especially where the petals and sepals aren't differentiated. The terminology alone is enough to put many people off, and this genus readily hybridises, making identification even trickier.

Many of our native Dock leaves are too bitter to consider eating unless you are starving (in which case you can boil them in several changes of water). The commonest (in a wide range of habitats) is **Broad-leaved Dock (*R. obtusifolius*)**, also known as Bitter Dock, which is all you need to know about its edibility. Its large, broad, red-tinged, cordate-based green leaves were once used to wrap butter. The very similar Northern Dock (*R. longifolius*) and our largest species – Great Water Dock (*R. hydrolapathum*) – are equally unpalatable. One member of the genus which absolutely must not be picked by foragers is **Shore Dock (*R. rupestris*)**, which is internationally rare, only known from a few locations in Wales, Cornwall and north-west France, where streams cross beaches. Its most similar common relatives are those on the opposite page.

Wood Dock (*R. sanguineus*)

Wood Dock is a perennial herb to 1m, with nearly straight stems, branches at a 30° angle (or more) to the stem, and no leaves at the top of the flower stem. It is common in moist lowland woodlands, and the young leaves, while still somewhat bitter, are less so than the previous species. A red-veined variety called **Bloody Dock (*R. sanguineus var. sanguineus*)** is cultivated both as an ornamental and a crop plant (as a baby leaf salad plant, or a cooked green vegetable as the leaves get a bit older). **Clustered Dock (*R. conglomeratus*)**, which is common throughout the British Isles and the rest of temperate Europe apart from the far north, is similar, but with wavier stems and small leaves running all the way up the flowering stem. Its leaves are more bitter, making it a poor edible species.

Curled Dock (*Rumex crispus*)

Curled Dock is a perennial herb to 1.2m. It has distinctive wavy-edged oblong to lanceolate leaves that are much narrower than they are long, with tapering to rounded bases, and a tall flower spike. It is common everywhere in Britain but the Scottish Highlands, particularly on disturbed ground and near the sea. Only the youngest leaves are eaten, before they get too bitter, and they are best cooked. The stems and seeds (raw, cooked or ground into a flour) are famine foods.

▲ Wood Dock
▼ Curled Dock

Monk's Rhubarb (*R. alpinus*)

Monk's Rhubarb or **Alpine Dock** is a rhizomatous perennial herb to 1m with very large (to 50cm long) oval to circular leaves, which have cordate bases, and flowers on a slightly branching, upright stem. It is an ancient introduction in the British Isles (native to Europe), found in nutrient-rich upland areas usually close to human habitation (at least historically). Frequent in some parts of northern England and eastern Scotland, rare or absent elsewhere in the British Isles, and almost entirely restricted to mountainous areas in continental Europe. Easily confused with Broad-leaved Dock, although it has rounder leaves which taste less bitter. Winter Heliotrope (p439) has similarly round leaves, but is much more bitter, and with no hint of sourness.

The leaves are edible, best cooked. They are tastiest in spring and autumn, becoming bitter during the summer.

Patience Dock (*R. patientia*)

Patience Dock or **Herb Patience** is a perennial herb to 2m with large, pointed, oval-lanceolate leaves, with truncate bases and toothless margins, lower leaves tapering to a stalk. Introduced and only occasional, mainly around London, usually on waste ground. **Greek Dock (*R. cristatus*)** is a similar introduced species (from central and southern Europe), and may be a subspecies.

The young leaves make an excellent Sorrel-like salad vegetable, and can also be cooked like spinach. They are the mildest tasting of any member of this genus, making much better for eating than most Docks, and very popular in south-east Europe as traditional Easter fare.

Alpine Dock Tart
(traditional Swiss, and delicious)

Ingredients:
Puff pastry for a 20cm diameter pie dish,
2tbsp jam, 3tbsp ground almonds, 300g
alpine dock leaf stems, 4tbsp brown sugar,
1 egg, 100ml cream.

Roll out the pastry and line the dish. Warm
the jam and spread over the base of the
pastry. Sprinkle the ground almonds over
the jam. Soak the stems in water (5 mins),
trim off any brown bits, then finely chop,
place in the pie and top with 2tbsp of
brown sugar. Beat the egg, cream and the
rest of the brown sugar together into a
custard. Pour this over the dock stems and
bake at 190°C / fan 170°C for 40 mins,
after which the pastry should be golden
brown and the contents starting to set.
Allow to cool before slicing and serving.

▲ Patience Dock

Lamb-Stuffed Patience Dock Rolls (traditional Romanian)

Ingredients:
2tbsp vegetable oil, for frying, enough patience dock leaves for 15 rolls (well washed), 300g
ground lamb, 2tbsp rice (washed), 1 small onion (chopped), dill (chopped), 3tbsp tomato
puree, ½tbsp lemon juice, seasoning, sour cream.

Fry the lamb, onion and rice on low heat, stirring until the meat isn't red, then add 100ml
water. Take off the heat and add dill and salt. Stir well. Bring a small pan of water to the
boil. In the meantime take each leaf and wash well, and separate the widest ones from the
narrower. Briefly dip the narrower ones in the boiling water (hold by the stalks), then use to
cover the base of a casserole dish, discarding stalks and thickest part of the main vein. To
make the rolls, take the widest leaves, similarly prepared, and roll up a tablespoon of the meat
mixture like stuffed vine leaves. Lay the rolls in the dish, covering the first complete layer of
rolls with another layer of narrower leaves before adding a second layer of rolls. Add a final
layer of leaves on the top, then add 300ml of water and bring to the boil. Boil 600ml of water
with tomato puree, salt and lemon juice, add to the dish, cover, and put in an oven at 185°C /
fan 175°C for 30 mins. Serve with the reduced liquid as sauce, and sour cream.

Sorrels (*Rumex* subg. *Acetosa*)

Common Sorrel (*R. acetosa*) is a perennial herb to 90cm with hollow stems which are usually upright and unbranched, long-stalked, alternate, arrow-shaped leaves (the lobes at the base point backwards/downwards), and whorled, usually leafless spikes of small red-pink flowers. It is common in grassland and open woodland, also sometimes cliffs and shingle beaches, avoiding calcareous soils. Native to Europe, and central and western Asia. There are four native subspecies in Europe, including the domesticated variety. Do not confuse with Lords and Ladies (see p112).

Sorrel has been cultivated for a very long time, for its fresh, sour, lemon-like taste. 'Sorrel' is derived from the old French 'surele', meaning 'sour', and before lemons were available in Britain, it was used as a flavouring in a similar way. It's at its best in spring, and available well before most other wild salad leaves. Also used in omelettes and soups (you will find many variations of sorrel soup online), or even to replace apples in turnovers. Also see recipes on p75 and p381. The buds, flowers, root and seeds are all also edible. Should be eaten in moderation due to its oxalic acid content.

Sheep's Sorrel (*R. acetosella*) is a perennial herb to 40cm with solid red stems and arrow-shaped leaves which are narrower than those of Common Sorrel, and have distinctive sideways-pointing basal lobes. Inhabits dry, acid grassland and heathland and is locally common throughout the British Isles and the whole of temperate Europe. **French Sorrel (*R. scutatus*)** is a native of the mountainous areas of continental Europe, only occurring in the British Isles as a very rare escape from cultivation. It has leaves a bit like a cross between Common and Sheep's Sorrel, and a branching stem. Both species are used as Common Sorrel.

> **Sorrel Sauce** (Jason Hill, 1939)
>
> Work a liberal amount of butter or preferably cream into a purée of sorrel, add pepper, salt and a little sugar and thicken with brown roux. A little strong stock is an improvement. A good accompaniment to veal, poached eggs, etc...

◀ Sheep's Sorrel
▶ Common Sorrel

Knotgrasses (*Polygonum* spp.)

The genus *Polygonum* used to be much bigger. Much taxonomic reshuffling has led to inconsistencies between common and Latin names. The genus *Persicaria* is often referred to with the common name 'Knotweed', but this is a source of confusion, given that the best-known plant bearing that common name belongs to another genus and several well-known members of the genus aren't called Knotweeds. 'Persicaria' is also in use as a common name. The word 'knot' in these names refer to the nodes along the stems of plants in this group, and another common characteristic is triangular seeds.

(Common) Knotgrass (*P. aviculare*) is an annual herb to 40cm with branching stems which can be upright or scrambling, lanceolate leaves and tiny white and pink flowers. It inhabits waste ground, paths and arable fields, especially in coastal areas, and is abundant throughout most of the British Isles, Scandinavia and the rest of temperate Europe. In northerly areas, including Scotland, the very similar **Northern Knotgrass (*P. boreale*)** is more common. **Small-leaved / Equal-leaved Knotgrass (*P. arenastrum*)** is also similar and can be used in the same ways. 'Knotgrass' also refers to several other *Polygonum* species, including one called 'Madimak' or 'Indian Knotgrass' **(*P. cognatum*)** that is both foraged for and cultivated in Turkey (very rarely naturalised in north-west Europe). The young leaves and whole plants are edible, raw, cooked or made into a tea. The seeds can be used like those of Buckwheat (opposite), but are rather small.

▸ Knotgrass

Buckwheat (*Fagopyrum esculentum*) (!)

No Buckwheat is any sort of Wheat or Grass – the name refers to the large, edible seeds, rich in carbohydrate. Preceded by 'wild', 'Buckwheat' generally refers to ***Fallopia convolvulus* (syn. *Polygonum convolvulus*)**, a plant that might be better called by its other common name of 'Black Bindweed', if that name wasn't also given to an unrelated poisonous plant with similar leaves and climbing habit: Black Bryony (p114). *Fallopia convolvulus* (which is locally common in the British Isles) was cultivated in the Bronze Age for its seeds, but they are small and difficult to process, as the seed coating must be removed before eating.

Buckwheat (*Fagopyrum esculentum*) is an annual herb to 70cm, with upright, hollow stems which are usually tinged red or purple, and dark green triangular leaves with cordate bases (lower ones stalked, upper ones stalkless). Dense clusters of cream flowers (often tinged with pink or yellow) are followed by triangular seeds, and the whole plant has a very rapid growth rate. Found in woodland clearings, on field margins, roadsides and tracks, and disturbed areas. Native to Asia, introduced in Europe as a food crop and now occasional in southern Britain, rarer further north, and naturalised but uncommon throughout temperate Europe.

Buckwheat was originally domesticated in south-east Asia, perhaps as early as 6000BC, and remains an important seed crop. It is cooked, sprouted for salad use, or ground and used like wheat flour. In Europe it has long been regarded as food for the peasantry or game birds, but has more recently become a trendy 'ancient grain' health food. The flour is suitable for gluten-free bread and pastry, and the leaves are mild-tasting and slightly mucilaginous, perfectly edible raw, but better cooked. Also used as green manure. Buckwheat can act as a photosensitising agent (when eaten).

▲ Wild Buckwheat (*Fallopia convolvulus*)

▲ ▼ Buckwheat

Knotweeds (*Reynoutria*)

Japanese Knotweed (*R. japonica* syn. *Fallopia japonica*) is a perennial herb to 3m with hollow red-green stems, oval, hairless leaves with a truncate/cordate base, and white flowers in large, erect racemes.
It grows in a variety of habitats, preferring to be near fresh water, and is common in the British Isles and much of northern Europe.

Native to Japan, Korea and China, where it grows on inhospitable rocky slopes. It was introduced to Europe as an ornamental, becoming the most feared of all invasive plants.

Japanese Knotweed grew in our garden when I was a child. I was aware of neither its edibility nor its reputation, but it was clearly a bit special. My parents called the shoots 'triffids', and every year they grew up through our terrace, and occasionally the concrete floor of our shed. It is now strictly illegal to transport or introduce anywhere, or to dispose of with normal garden waste. It can regrow from tiny fragments, even when deeply buried, sometimes appearing through the top of capped landfill sites. Eradication is a job for professionals and local authorities in the UK are obliged to remove it from public land. Unfortunately, the fact that it is so widely under attack with industrial-strength herbicides causes an obvious problem for foragers. The herbicides are systemic – they are applied to the leaves, but taken down into the whole plant in the hope the roots will die. The only way to be absolutely certain you are avoiding this problem is to contact the landowner.

Giant Knotweed (*R. sachalinensis*) is very similar but even taller, and with larger, more cordate leaves (and it sometimes hybridises with Japanese Knotweed). It is edible in the same ways. Also problematic (though scarcer), as is the smaller, and less cordate-leaved **Himalayan Knotweed (*Koenigia wallichii*)**.

◄ Japanese Knotweed growing by a mountain stream.

▲ Japanese Knotweed shoots in spring.

All parts of the plants are edible when young and tender, apart from the flowers (which are attractive to bees and make an excellent honey). The new shoots and stems in spring are the best, used as a substitute for rhubarb in fools and crumbles. The skin gets increasingly stringy with age, so you might have to peel the stems. The leaves are also edible, raw or cooked, as are the rhizomes. The seeds can be used like Buckwheat, although they are small. An extract of this plant is a popular alternative health supplement, the active ingredient presumed to be an anti-oxidant called resveratrol. No strong scientific evidence of efficacy exists at the time of writing.

Goes well in a crumble with Oregon Grape (see p161).

Japanese Knotweed, Almond and Orange Cake

Ingredients:
400g Japanese knotweed, 280g caster sugar, 225g butter, zest and juice 1 orange, 225g self-raising flour, 100g ground almonds, 1tsp baking powder, 3 eggs. Optional: dandelion honey (p433), primroses (p378) and sweet violets (p180).

Chop the knotweed stems into 1cm circles. Line a 23cm cake tin and heat oven to 180°C / fan 160°C. Beat the sugar, butter, orange zest and juice together in a bowl. Add the flour, almonds, baking powder and eggs, then beat again until smooth. Fold in the knotweed, then spoon into the tin and bake for 1 hour and 15 mins. When cool, glaze the top with dandelion honey and decorate with flowers.

Knotweed Fool

Ingredients:
300 ml double cream, 400g knotweed stems, 4tbsp caster sugar, gorse or broom flowers to garnish.

Chop the knotweed stems and stew in a little water until tender, then drain and add the sugar. Cool then blend to a pulp. Whip the cream, then fold together with the knotweed, and garnish with gorse or broom flowers.

Bistorts (*Bistorta*)

The name 'bistort' means 'twice twisted', a reference to the contorted growth habit of the edible roots. The leaves of several species have a distinct black blotch in the centre of their upper surface.

(Common) Bistort or **Snakeroot** (*B. officinalis* syn. *Persicaria bistorta*) is a rhizomatous perennial herb to 1m, with broad, triangular leaves with rounded edges, lower leaves with winged stems, and long, pink (occasionally white) flower spikes at the top of upright, unbranched stems. Common in northern England and Wales in water meadows and other damp places, especially on high ground, avoiding alkaline soils, and uncommon or rare elsewhere in the British Isles. Bistort is native to the British Isles, but many wild-growing plants are garden escapes. Only genuinely wild in north-west England. The roots have been eaten at times of scarcity. They need to be thoroughly washed and then soaked in water to leach out the tannins, before roasting and grinding for use as a flour substitute. The leaves can be eaten in salads when very young, but are more typically cooked like spinach, or used as a pot-herb, or in Easter Ledger Pudding.

Alpine Bistort (*B. vivipara* syn. *Persicaria viviparia*) is a slow-growing perennial herb to 15cm with erect stems, tiny white or pink flowers, and tiny purple bulbils below the flowers. Restricted to damp and rocky locations in mountainous areas in the British Isles, but locally common. Found throughout in the north of the European temperate zone, as well as the boreal and Arctic zones beyond. Usable as Bistort. The leaves are edible, raw in salads or cooked as a pot-herb. Seeds are also edible, but probably not worth bothering with. There are also starch-rich bulbils on the flowering stem which can be eaten raw.

▲ Bistort

Easter Ledger Pudding

Bistort is the key ingredient in an old northern English dish, which goes by a variety of names such as Dock, Lenten, Passion or Easter Ledge(r) Pudding. Traditionally eaten with lamb at Easter, or with bacon and sausages at other times, there are as many recipes for this dish as there are people who cook it. Which wild greens to include is a matter of personal taste, and great secrecy. For me, without bistort it isn't Easter Ledger Pudding, and young nettle tops and dandelion leaves (and maybe flowers) are also essential. I also include raspberry leaves (other people use strawberry or blackcurrant) and lady's mantle. I've also seen recipes calling for other docks (eg curled dock, redshanks), various wild mustards/cabbage, hawthorn, alliums, watercress and parsley.

Ingredients:

250g wild greens, one onion (finely chopped), 130g pearl barley, 50g oatmeal, 70g butter, four eggs, butter/lard/bacon fat for frying.

Wash, dry and finely chop the leaves, and mix in a bowl with the onion and the soaked and drained pearl barley, plus seasoning. Put the mixture into a muslin, seal tightly and simmer fully submerged for two hours in a saucepan (lid on). Hard boil and chop two of the eggs. When cooked, take the barley and wild greens and mix in a bowl with the butter, raw eggs, cooked eggs and oatmeal, adding more oatmeal if the mixture is too sloppy. Then shape into individual puddings (flat, circular) and fry for 2 mins on each side.

Other versions involve soaking the chopped wild greens with the pearl barley overnight, or baking for 45 mins instead of boiling and frying. Omitting the barley is not recommended, though this does allow you to skip the long boiling stage – just boil the greens on their own for 10 mins, then drain, before mixing with the other ingredients before frying.

▼ Alpine Bistort

▲ Water-pepper

Water-pepper (*Persicaria hydropiper*)

"The root or seed, put into an aching hollow tooth, takes off the pain."
(Nicholas Culpeper, 1652)

Water-pepper is an annual herb to 75cm with a branching stem, alternate, lanceolate leaves with tiny or no stalks, and a delicate, nodding spike of tiny green/white/pink flowers. Found in damp places and very shallow water, typically on muddy tracks. Common in the British Isles, apart from northern and eastern Scotland, and common throughout temperate Europe.

Also known as 'Arsesmart', which literally refers to its kick – it leaves you smarting. According to Miles Irving, this was derived from its use as a flea repellent in bedding, when the leaves occasionally found their way into places where the sun doesn't shine. It is cultivated in Japan, the domesticated variety being considerably less pungent, though still rather hot. Young leaves and stems are used like chilli peppers, especially to liven up seaweed dishes and sushi. It can also be used to make a dipping sauce, finely chopped into a mixture of soy sauce and rice vinegar, and the sprouted seeds are used as a spicy vegetable.

Small Water-pepper (*P. minor*) is native to Asia but naturalised in much of northern Europe, including some parts of the British Isles (notably Wales and south-west Scotland). Very similar but with smaller leaves, and inhabiting similar places (but much rarer), it is also cultivated for food in south-east Asia. **Tasteless Water-pepper (*P. mitis*)** is similar, but tasteless, and also rather rare (more common in continental Europe).

Redshank / Pale Persicaria
(*P. maculosa/lapathifolia*)

Redshank (*P. maculosa*) is an upright annual herb to 80cm, with lanceolate leaves and a cylindrical flower spike. A common weed, nearly always found near human activity, in grassland or disturbed/arable ground, often near water.

Pale Persicaria (*P. lapathifolia*) is a species complex, found in the same sort of habitats as Redshank. The two are very similar, with large dark blotches in the middle of their leaves (another name for Redshank is 'Jesus Plant'), and nodding flower clusters (Redshank flowers are pale pink, Pale Persicaria pale green).

The young leaves and shoots of both species are edible as cooked vegetables, and the seeds as a thickener for soups. Redshank is marginally the better for eating, and one of the possible components of Easter Ledger Pudding (p329). The closely related and visually very similar Vietnamese Coriander or Cambodian Mint (*P. odorata*) is a cultivated crop in south-east Asia.

Amphibious Bistort (*P. amphibia*) also has a blotch on the upper side of its leaves, but is very variable. Can be fully aquatic or terrestrial (though always in marshy or flood-prone areas). The leaves and seeds are edible, but unimpressive.

▾ Redshank

▲ Clove Pink

Caryophyllaceae (Pink family)

The *Caryophyllaceae* are a large (2,600+ species) family, better known as ornamentals than for their culinary value.

Clove Pink (*Dianthus caryophyllus*)

"Pickled Clove-Gilly Flowers for Sallets – Take the fairest Clove-Gilly-Flowers, clip off the whites from them, put them into a wide-mouth'd Glass, and strew a good deal of Sugar finely beaten among them, then put as much wine Vinegar to them as will throughly wet them, tye them up close, and set them in the Sun, and in a little while they will be fit for use."
(Hannah Woolley, 1675)

Clove Pink or **Carnation** is a perennial herb to 80cm, with grey-green leaves and sweet-smelling flowers which are a bright purple-pink in the wild form. Native to southern Europe, it has been cultivated for over 2,000 years, in a wide range of colours. Occasionally naturalises on old walls in the British Isles. They were a substitute for cloves when that spice was very expensive. Only the petals are eaten, with the bitter base cut away. 'Clove' historically meant the dried flower bud. 'Gillyflower' refers to any scented Carnation.

Thyme-leaved Sandwort (*Arenaria serpyllifolia*)

Thyme-leaved Sandwort is a biennial or winter annual herb to 30cm, with tiny, oval, opposite leaves and small white flowers. Locally common in dry habitats. Unevenly distributed – common in some parts of England and eastern Wales, but rare or absent in much of the British Isles.

There is disagreement about edibility. The Reader's Digest *Field Guide to the Wild Flowers of Britain* (1981) says "animals are deterred from eating the plant by the poison produced in its stem and leaves", evidenced by the observation that it often grows uneaten near rabbit burrows. G Kunkel's *Plants for Human Consumption* (1984) says the entire plant is edible as a pot-herb. It tastes bitter (raw), but that doesn't mean it is poisonous.

▼ Thyme-leaved Sandwort

Sea Sandwort (*Honckenya peploides*)

"In Iceland it is fermented, and in that state used as food, like sauer-kraut in Germany; the plant forms a wholesome vegetable when boiled."

(C Pierpoint Johnson, 1862)

Sea Sandwort is a sprawling perennial herb with simple, rounded, fleshy leaves and upright flower stems to 25cm, small green-white flowers, and fruits that resemble peas. Locally common all around the British coastline on beaches and dunes, just above the high-tide line. Present on coastlines of temperate and arctic regions of the northern hemisphere. Sea Milkwort (p377) is similar, but has more slender stems and greyer foliage. The inedible Knotted Pearlwort (*Sagina nodosa*) is also similar, but with sparser, smaller leaves.

Young shoots and leaves are edible, best cooked. A little sour and bitter, but perfectly edible when young, becoming tougher and unpalatable as the plant matures. Good for lactofermenting, but takes quite a long time. The small seeds are a famine food.

Campions (*Silene*)

Bladder Campion (*S. vulgaris*) is a perennial herb to 90cm with upright, usually branching stems, pointed ovate, opposite, grey-green leaves, white flowers (with **three styles**) and a purple-veined, balloon-shaped calyx (the 'bladder') behind them. Common in the south of the British Isles on open, waste and arable land, disturbed ground, roadsides and grassland, particularly on chalk slopes. Scarcer in the far south west, and the north. Present across the whole of Europe. This species can be confused with both White Campion (*S. latifolia*), which has **five styles**, and less pronounced bladders, and **Sea Campion (*S. uniflora* syn. *maritima*)**, which has very similar bladders, but is a smaller plant found exclusively in coastal locations (mainly western in the British Isles). Sea Campion is of similar edibility to Bladder Campion. White Campion and Red Campion (*S. dioica*) are too bitter to eat.

Bladder Campion is a popular plant in Mediterranean cuisine. It had fallen out of fashion, but in recent years people have started cultivating it again in Cyprus and Crete. The young leaves and shoots have a bitter-sweet taste when raw, and are used in salads, and the flowers are also edible raw (even sweeter, with a slight bitter overtone). In Spain the young shoots were traditionally used to make a dish with flatbread, called 'widower gazpacho' ('gazpacho viudo'), or cooked with scrambled eggs, or rice. Older leaves and shoots make a good green side vegetable cooked for 5-10 minutes, or chopped in omelettes. The Italians cook it in risotto, or make it into a sauce to serve with pasta. Bladder Campion is also native to, and traditionally eaten in, many Asian countries. It does contain some tannins, especially when older, so consume in moderation.

▾ Sea Campion

Bladder Campion Pasta Sauce (traditional Italian)

Ingredients:

300g bladder campion shoots/leaves, 50g pancetta (chopped), clove of garlic (crushed), 1 small onion (finely chopped), dash of dry white wine, olive oil, 500g can of chopped tomatoes, parmesan cheese (grated), pasta.

Start boiling the pasta. Sauté the pancetta, garlic and onion in oil for a couple of mins. Add the wine, and keep cooking until the liquid has gone. Turn down the heat very low, and put the bladder campion on top of the sauce. When it wilts, turn the heat off. When the pasta is ready, mix it in, add the tomatoes and heat through. Serve with parmesan. Alternatively, you can use fresh tomatoes, in which case they should be added with the wine, and the sauce cooked for 15 mins.

▼ Bladder Campion

Chickweeds and Stitchworts (*Stellaria*)

All of these species have white flowers with five deeply bisected petals, though some are tiny.

Common Chickweed (*S. media*) is a low-growing, sprawling, cool-season annual or biennial herb (typically germinating in the autumn or winter) with stems to 40cm and simple, paired, ovate leaves. The white flowers are clustered loosely at the ends of the stems, and the fruits are capsules. Very common throughout Europe on disturbed and waste ground, agricultural land, paths and gardens.

Chickweed is a first-class salad plant, its mild taste providing a backdrop for more pungent wild leaves. The more tender parts nearer the top are the best for this use. Can also be briefly cooked as a pot-herb or side vegetable, and you will find countless Chickweed pesto recipes online. Nutritious (rich in vitamin C), tasty and available all year. Can cause mild gastric problems if large amounts are consumed.

Greater Chickweed (*S. neglecta*) is very similar and equally edible, but much less common. There are many other lookalikes in this family, but Common Chickweed can be distinguished from them by looking closely at the stems. Chickweed has fine hairs on just one side of the stem, whereas the lookalikes have hairs covering the whole stem.

Do not confuse with the poisonous Scarlet Pimpernel (p377). The bitter Ivy-leaved Speedwell (*Veronica hederifolia*) is also sometimes mistaken by beginners for Chickweed. That plant is hairier, and as the name indicates, has ivy-shaped, rather than ovate leaves. The foul-tasting three-nerved Sandwort (*Moehringia trinervia*) looks similar, but with three prominent veins on the leaf.

▲ Greater Stitchwort

Greater Stitchwort (*S. holostea*) is a scrambling to ascending perennial herb (to 60cm) with long, thin leaves and conspicuous white flowers. It is perfectly edible, though more bitter than Common Chickweed. Common in temperate Europe, and most of the British Isles.

Lesser Stitchwort (*S. graminea*) is a low-growing perennial herb with thin stems, and smaller leaves and flowers than Greater Stitchwort. Usually inhabits grassland or roadsides, on neutral or acid soils. Common in the British Isles, and similarly edible.

The culinary status of the other European members of this genus is disputed, with different sources ranking them anywhere between excellent and inedible.

Chickweed, Sorrel and Ramsons Soup

Ingredients:

1.5l chicken stock, 5 ramsons plants (thin sliced), 150g of chickweed (chopped, any tough stems removed), plus 2 sprigs as a garnish, 30ml double cream, 8 sorrel leaves, 60g pearl barley, seasoning.

Boil the stock in a saucepan, and add the barley. Cook until soft, then add the wild greens and simmer gently for 15 mins. Allow to cool, then blend, season, and return to the pan to warm back to serving temperature. Stir in the cream and serve immediately.

▼ Common Chickweed

Mouse-ear Chickweeds (*Cerastium*)

Common Mouse-ear Chickweed (*C. fontanum* syn. *holosteoides*) is a low-growing, hairy perennial herb with runners and upright shoots bearing small white flowers. Frequent throughout the British Isles and the whole of temperate Europe, particularly liking wet meadows.

There are at least 10 other species of Mouse-ear (or 'Mouse-ear Chickweeds') in the British Isles, all of which have edible leaves and young stems, although the popular ornamental Snow-in-Summer (*C. tomentosum*) is not recommended. They are like Chickweed but smaller and with downy/hairy leaves, which make them rather less appetising. Mouse-ears are available as food throughout the winter.

▾ Common Mouse-ear Chickweed

▲ Corn-spurrey

Spurreys (*Spergula* and *Spergularia*)

Corn-spurrey (*Spergula arvensis*) is a sticky, hairy annual herb to 50cm, with weak but upright/ascending stems and whorls of long, thin, greyish-green furrowed leaves, and small white flowers (summer). Once common on sandy arable land, riverside shingle and coastal areas, now considered vulnerable in the British Isles. Present throughout temperate Europe and much of the rest of the world, especially near coasts. Corn-spurrey has historically been a pernicious agricultural weed, a bane not only of cereal farmers, but potatoes, carrots and other crops too. However, the seeds are rich in oil, and have been used as a food source since prehistoric times. They were certainly used as food by the Celts and Romans. Tollund Man, whose well-preserved body was found in a Danish peat bog in 1950, had eaten a meal containing Corn-spurrey seeds before being ritually strangled (4th century BCE). Corn-spurrey has also been grown for food in various parts of the world.[*] There are 17th century records of it being grown, notably in the Shetland Islands, where the seeds were ground into flour for bread-making. It is still cultivated as a fodder crop in South Africa. The leaves are also edible, but not tasty. Both leaves and seeds contain saponins and oxalates, so should only be consumed in moderation.

Greater Sea-spurrey (*Spergularia media*) is considered edible by some authorities[†] and the seeds of **Red Sand-spurrey (*Spergularia rubra*)** have also been used as famine food. I haven't tried eating them.

* *Nutritional assessment of the plant Spergula arvensis*, Sundarapandian, L, et al, 2016.
† *Wild Food*, Mears, R, and Hillman, G, 2008, Hodder & Stoughton.

Amaranthaceae (Amaranth family) ⚠

Most members of the Amaranth family (which now encompasses the old *Chenopodiaceae* family) are edible, including domesticated crops such as Spinach, Quinoa and Beets/Chards. The name 'Pigweed' has been used to refer to a number of different members of this family (as well as some relatives in the *Portulaceae*, see p362) mostly those belonging to the genus *Amaranthus*, but also Fat Hen (*Chenopodium album*). 'Pigweed' and 'Fat Hen' allude to the use of these plants as animal fodder, but they are nutritious and tasty enough to feed humans. In most cases the entire plant is edible. Massed heads of tiny flowers and seeds are a family characteristic, as are the red and yellow pigments we see in Amaranths and Chard. The seeds are high in energy, vitamins and minerals, and can be harvested by holding a container under the mature flower heads, and massaging until the seeds drop out, then passing through a fine sieve. They can then be ground into flour, popped like corn, or boiled into a gloopy paste.

Many plants in this family contain oxalic acid, and/or accumulate nitrates in nitrate-rich habitats, both of which can lead to problems if the foliage is consumed in large quantities. They can also cause increased photosensitivity if eaten raw, with multiple recorded cases of severe skin damage in eastern Europe during food shortages after World War II.

Amaranths (*Amaranthus*)

Four edible species native to the Americas (*A. palmeri, hybridus, blitoides* and *albus*) are established as agricultural weeds in Europe. They are a closely related group, and hard to reliably distinguish, especially considering that plants found growing wild in Europe are almost entirely descendants

▾ Common Amaranth

of domesticated varieties. Amaranth seeds are one of the 'ancient grains', and gluten-free. They are cultivated in parts of Asia as well as their South American homeland. In India they are called 'Ramdana', and the young leaves ('chaulai') are eaten as greens. The young stems and flower spikes work well cooked with chilli, garlic, olive oil and lemon. Older stems become too tough and stringy. The small seeds are usually roasted and ground, or sprouted and used in salads.

Common Amaranth (*A. retroflexus*) is an annual herb to 3m (though sometimes sprawling at first), with oval to lanceolate grey-green (sometimes reddish) leaves and a large, dense, bristly green flower spike. The lower stem is smooth, thick and slightly reddish, especially near the roots, the upper part rougher with dense short hairs. This adaptable plant can cope with different habitats and soil types, but is particularly fond of waste ground and agricultural land. Native to the American tropics, but introduced globally, it is occasional in parts of England (esp. East Anglia and the Severn valley), rarer elsewhere in the British Isles, more common in continental Europe.

Green Amaranth (*A. hybridus*, not pictured) is a very variable hairless annual herb to 3m similar to Common Amaranth but with fewer branches in the upper stems. Native to eastern North America, introduced and naturalised in Europe. In Britain most common in the south and east. Uses are the same as Common Amaranth.

Love Lies Bleeding (*A. caudatus*) is an annual (in temperate zones) herb to 2.5m, with ovate leaves, unmistakable long, drooping flower heads, which can be either brilliant red, or dull greenish-brown. Native to Andean South America, it is a widely planted ornamental that self-seeds and can be found in much of Europe as a garden escape. It is still cultivated as a food crop in Peru (where it is called 'kiwicha', and used in 'Day of the Dead' festivities). The seeds are popped and mixed with molasses to make a sweet treat, or used to fill out meatloaf. This is a great one for urban foragers to look out for, since the seeds of ornamental plants can be harvested after the plant has finished flowering.

▼ Love Lies Bleeding

Sea Beet (*Beta vulgaris* subsp. *maritima*)

"There is a *Beet* growing near the Sea,
which is the most delicate of all."
(John Evelyn, 1699)

Sea Beet is a hairless annual, biennial or
perennial herb with well-branched, straggly
stems to 1.2m, large (to 40cm), thick, glossy,
dark green, heart-shaped to triangular
leaves and long spikes of tiny, fleshy green,
red or purple flowers, which branch off
the main stem. Native and very common,
inhabiting the area between the high-tide
line of beaches (particularly shingle) and
tidal rivers, to slightly inland, especially in
nutrient-rich areas.

This plant is the wild ancestor of multiple
modern crops now classed as subspecies of
Beta vulgaris (though it has become so popular
with chefs that it is now also being cultivated).
The first to be developed, maybe 3,000 years
ago, were the leafy varieties, known as Chard
or Perpetual Spinach, and the young leaves of
the wild plant are much the same. Beetroot
and Sugar Beet came much later. It is not hard

to understand how this came about, because
the root of the wild plant is the sweetest of
any wild root I've tasted, apart from Common
Polypody (p87). And like Polypody it is
nauseating if you try eating more than very a
small amount of it. Sea Beet is also the ancestor
of a lesser-known root crop with the fantastic
name, derived from the German 'mangold',
meaning golden beet, and 'wurzel', meaning
'root'. Mangelwurzel was historically grown as
a winter fodder crop, only eaten by humans
during famines.

The leaves of Sea Beet are best in
spring, but available into autumn, the very
youngest edible raw in salads (especially on
plants nearest the high-tide line), older ones
needing to be cooked like spinach – remove
the midrib and discard or cook separately,
then steam or boil for a few minutes in a small
amount of water. Press to remove water before
serving with butter – traditionally this was an
accompaniment to bacon, pork, lamb or fish,
or sautéed with garlic and red onion.

Can also be chopped and mixed with
cheese and used to fill pancakes, or added
to quiches.

Sea Beet Soup (traditional British)

Ingredients:

450g sea beet greens, 2tbsp oil, 1 diced carrot, 75g diced celery, 150g chopped wild fennel (p480), 150g thinly sliced leeks (white part), 250g diced potatoes, 1.5l vegetable or chicken stock, 150g chopped tomatoes, 1tsp crushed fennel seeds. To taste: freshly grated nutmeg, freshly grated lemon zest, salt and freshly ground black pepper.

Remove the stalks off the sea beet leaves, and finely chop. Also chop the leaves. Put oil in a heavy-bottomed dish, with the carrot, celery, fennel, leeks and beet stems and cook for 8 mins, stirring frequently. Add the stock and potatoes, bring to boil then reduce the heat, cover and simmer for 20 mins. Use a masher to break up the potatoes, then add the beet leaves and tomatoes and cook for another 5 mins. Add the fennel seeds, nutmeg and lemon zest, season and cook for 2 mins. Serve with fresh, crusty bread.

▲ Good King Henry

Good King Henry (*Blitum bonus-henricus* syn. *Chenopodium bonus-henricus*) (!)

Good King Henry is a stout perennial herb to 70cm, with an upright stem (sometimes flushed red) and large (for this family) wavy-edged triangular leaves with large basal lobes. The leaves are mealy when young, becoming smooth and dull. The flowers (summer) are small and green, and arranged in a pyramidal spike. Easily confused with several relatives, especially Maple-leaved Goosefoot (p349), although that species has cordate leaf-bases. Occasional in most of the British Isles, usually on nitrogen-rich soils close to human habitation, also on roadsides, rare in northern and eastern Scotland and eastern and southern Ireland. More common in its native central and southern Europe.

Good King Henry was once widely cultivated, and probably introduced to the British Isles for this purpose by the Romans. The young shoots were eaten in spring, and the leaves taken sparingly in early summer, before they become too bitter. They can be eaten raw, but are better cooked, and even then inferior to the best members of this family. Historically they were blanched (by excluding light) to improve the flavour. The flower buds are used like miniature broccoli, and the seeds are also edible, but need to be soaked first to leach out saponins. High in vitamins B and C, iron and calcium. This is a useful permaculture plant – all parts are edible, it does well in shady areas, and makes good ground cover. Contains both saponins and oxalic acid, so should be consumed in moderation.

Strawberry Goosefoot (*B. capitatum*, not illustrated) is a North American species, naturalised in the wet mountain valleys of various parts of continental Europe, though not yet found growing wild in the British Isles. It has dense clusters of deep red berry-like 'fruit', and was used by Native Americans both as food and to make a red dye.

Chenopodium (genus)

Chenopodium was, until recently, a large genus commonly known as the Goosefoots. It has been shattered by DNA testing, but some of the departed species have retained the common name. Identification in this area is also complicated by the number of similar species and their variability. Goosefoots are also very easily confused with Oraches – see (p350) for distinguishing features. Fortunately for a forager, none are poisonous.

Stinking Goosefoot (*C. vulvaria*) has stems to 40cm and mealy grey leaves, smells of rotting fish and naturally inhabits drier areas of salt marsh, though also found on waste ground. It is an ancient introduction to the British Isles (from southern Europe), once quite common, now rare. This plant is edible, but the least attractive of the genus due to its smell. **Quinoa (*C. quinoa*)** can sometimes be found as an escape from cultivation in northern Europe, but it is rare. It is rather like Fat Hen (overleaf), except for the dense flower panicles and fruits, which can be white, red or black. **Giant Tree Spinach (*C. giganteum*)** is much larger but otherwise similar to Fat Hen, and with beautiful purple-flushed foliage. Native to India, grown in Europe as both ornamental and food, occasionally escapes in the British Isles but does not naturalise.

▾ Fig-leaved Goosefoot (described overleaf)

Fat Hen (*C. album*)

Fat Hen is an upright annual herb to 1.5m, with branching stems usually flushed red-purple, extremely variably shaped, variably mealy, grey-green leaves and globular clusters of tiny green flowers, arranged into spikes, which turn brown as the seeds mature. This is a weed of nutrient-rich agricultural and disturbed land (where it can completely take over for a while, before being replaced by less pioneering species), common everywhere in the British Isles apart from the Scottish Highlands. Its native range is unclear, but probably includes Europe, and it is widely cultivated in Asia (as it was once in Europe) and introduced worldwide. Extremely easy to confuse with other Goosefoots and Oraches, especially Common Orache (p351). **Swedish Goosefoot (*C. suecicum*)** is very similar to Fat Hen, but without the red-purple stem. It is an introduction from northern Europe and used in the same way.

▼ Fat Hen

Fat Hen is one of the best edible wild European plants. If it is possible for something to taste like it is really good for you, this is it. Think spinach but richer and tastier. The seeds are particularly nutritious – very high in vitamin A, phosphorus and calcium. The best parts for eating are the leaves, young shoots and the seed heads, all of which are usually cooked (either steamed or sautéed). Because it is so mild-tasting, it is an excellent base for combining with smaller amounts of stronger-tasting wild greens, especially those in the Cabbage family (p275). Some guides describe it as edible raw, but Fat Hen contains oxalates and should be cooked, especially if consumed in significant quantities, although it does not require long cooking. Boil or stir-fry for no longer than 4 minutes. It is grown as a winter crop in India, where it is known as 'Bathua', and you will find plenty of Indian recipes online. Useful in permaculture as a sacrificial crop to distract leaf-miners. See picture on p30.

Fig-leaved Goosefoot (*C. ficifolium*, pictured on previous page) is very similar to Fat Hen but smaller (to 1m) and the lower leaves always have three main lobes, the central of which is the by far the largest. The upper leaves are lobeless. It is an ancient introduction from south-west Asia. Common in the south and east of England on waste ground, disturbed land and arable land, especially in nutrient-rich areas, but doesn't like acidic soil. Rare in Wales, absent from most of Scotland and common throughout the central belt of Europe, rarer further north and south. Common in central northern Europe. This species is edible, used in the same ways as Fat Hen, but inferior.

▲ Fat Hen

Fat Hen Saag

This dish is popular in winter in north India, served as a main course with ghee-rich parantha or roti.

Ingredients:

500g fat hen, 3 small green chillis (chopped), 2tsp mustard oil, 1tsp garlic paste, 1tsp cumin seeds, 5 garlic cloves (peeled), 1tsp garam masala, salt, water.

Heat the oil in a frying pan until it starts to bubble, then add cumin seeds until they splutter. Add garlic paste and mix, then cook for a minute before adding the fat hen, chillies and salt. Then cook on a low heat until the oil starts to leave the sides of the pan. Garnish with garam masala and garlic cloves.

Red Goosefoot (*Oxybasis rubra* syn. *Chenopodium rubrum*)

Red Goosefoot is a sprawling or upright annual herb to 80cm with a slightly red-tinged stem, glossy (unlike the rest of the genus, which are more matt), alternate, irregular oval to triangular leaves which are also red or purple, and a red flower spike. Native and frequent in England, less so in Wales and Scotland, on waste ground, agricultural land and farmyards, especially near ponds and ditches and in coastal areas. Edibility much like the rest of this group, but a little more bitter. Not recommended raw.

Many-seeded Goosefoot (*Lipandra polysperma* syn. *Chenopodium polyspermum*)

Many-seeded Goosefoot is a bit like Fat Hen, but with square, reddish stems which have a greater tendency to branch and be prostrate. The leaves are non-mealy, unlobed, purple-edged and more consistently oval. Another ancient introduction, frequent in the southern half of England on arable or waste ground, especially near drying ponds. Edibility the same as the rest of this family, but inferior to the best of them.

▾ Red Goosefoot

▾ Many-seeded Goosefoot

Chenopodiastrum

Both of these ancient introductions, which are typically edible members of their family, could be confused with the poisonous Datura species (p418).

Maple-leaved Goosefoot (*C. hybridum* syn. *Chenopodium hybridum*) is an annual herb to 1m, with large grey-green, slightly mealy leaves which have widely spaced teeth, pointed tips and cordate bases; green-white flowers in clustered panicles at the end of branching stems. Native to central Europe, uncommon in the British Isles, mainly occurring in the south, usually on waste ground.

Nettle-leaved Goosefoot (*C. murale* syn. *Chenopodium murale*) is an annual herb to 70cm with oval to triangular slightly mealy grey-green leaves, similar to those of Maple-leaved Goosefoot but with more teeth (so nettle-like). Native to Asia, found on agricultural land and roadsides. Frequent in the whole of Europe apart from the north. Occasional on the coastlines of England and Wales, much rarer in Scotland (not recorded in Ireland).

▼ Maple-leaved Goosefoot

▼ Nettle-leaved Goosefoot

Oraches (*Atriplex*)

The Oraches (pronounced 'oraks' not 'orashes') are extremely easy to mistake for their Goosefoot relatives. The flower structures are an important distinguishing feature. Goosefoot flowers are bisexual (so there is only one type). Orache flowers are either male or female (so there are two types). Male flowers have green sepals and petals (which look very similar to each other). Female 'flowers' have neither sepals nor petals, but are enclosed by two bracteoles (like leaves, but arranged like hands together in prayer, triangular or diamond shaped). Because female flowers develop into fruits, then the fruits also end up enclosed by two bracteoles. Another difference is that while both Oraches and Goosefoots have opposite leaves near the base and alternate leaves further up the stem, Oraches have opposite leaves much higher up the stem.

All Oraches are primarily used as spinach substitutes. The mild-tasting leaves, shoots, flower heads and seeds are all edible, and should be cooked. The seeds are small and tricky to harvest, but can be ground and used to bulk out flour and thicken soups.

Grass-leaved Orache (*A. littoralis*)

Grass-leaved Orache is an annual herb to 1.5m, usually upright, and the only British member of this genus with lanceolate leaves (sometimes toothed, sometimes entire). Frequent in eastern England, in coastal areas, especially salt marshes, and along salted roadsides, very patchy elsewhere. On the menu at Noma in Copenhagen, so had to be included here.

▾ Grass-leaved Orache

▲ Common Orache

Common Orache (*A. patula*)

Common Orache is an annual herb to 1.2m with a variably creeping to upright stem, variably toothed/lobed, diamond-shaped leaves which taper into the stalk, and a terminal spike of green flowers. Never mealy. It is frequent on arable and waste ground throughout Europe, and other disturbed habitats, especially near the sea. Similar to Fig-leaved Goosefoot and Fat Hen (both on p347), and equally edible but not as tasty. Also similar to Spear-leaved Orache (p352), but less likely to turn up on beaches.

Garden Orache (*A. hortensis*)

Garden Orache is an annual herb to 1.4m with a green or red-tinged upright stem. Its lower leaves are triangular to heart-shaped with toothed margins, becoming lanceolate and toothless at the top, and with a terminal red/green flower spike. Leaves start mealy, becoming less so. This plant was more

widely cultivated until Spinach became popular. Probably native to Asia, frequently found as an escape from cultivation on arable and disturbed land, and occasionally shingle. Red Orache (*A. hortensis* var. *rubra*) is still a popular garden vegetable in much of Europe, and sometimes escapes.

▼ Red Orache, here growing in the middle of a roundabout with Fig-leaved Goosefoot.

Spear-leaved Orache (*A. prostrata*)

Spear-leaved Orache is a very variable annual herb to 1m, the stem creeping to upright, lower leaves triangular, all leaves slightly toothed and usually mealy, all parts sometimes becoming red. Very common throughout temperate Europe, apart from in mountainous areas. Naturally coastal (near the high-tide line) but also widespread inland in disturbed, damp places, especially near salted roads.

▾ Spear-leaved Orache

▲ Frosted Orache

Other Oraches (*Atriplex* spp.)

All of these are similar to Spear-leaved Orache.

Babington's Orache (*A. glabriuscula*) is always prostrate, always coastal, and strictly northern (from Brittany to the north coast of Sweden).

Frosted Orache (*A. laciniata*) is smaller and with 'frosted' foliage, and a creeping yellow or red stem. Found exclusively on sandy beaches, usually at the strand-line, where it is locally common on temperate European coastlines.

Early Orache (*A. praecox*) is also very similar, but rare (mainly Scotland).

Long-stalked Orache (*A. longipes*) is a red-flushed annual herb to 90cm, sprawling or upright, with narrow triangular lower leaves and stalks on larger bracteoles. Found with taller salt marsh vegetation. In the British Isles mainly recorded in south Wales, Somerset and Lancashire. More common on the coasts of Scandinavia and Brittany.

Sea Purslane (*A. portulacoides* syn. *Halimione portulacoides*)

Sea Purslane is a sprawling perennial herb with stems to 75cm and fleshy grey-green leaves. Frequent on temperate European coastlines, locally dominating in areas of salt marsh. Not to be confused with the tropical/southern species *Sesuvium portulacastrum*, also sometimes called 'Sea Purslane' as well as 'Shoreline Purslane' (although this is also edible).

This is a first-class wild food, but does need to be carefully washed. The best plants for eating are found closer to the top of their range, and the leaves are edible raw or cooked (stems are stringy/woody). Very salty raw and best used as a garnish, or made into pesto with pine nuts and olive oil. If cooked/pickled, it should only be blanched, because it quickly turns bitter. Can also be briefly stir-fried.

Pedunculate Sea Purslane (*H. pedunculata*) is a similarly edible but rare annual relative, confined to Essex in the British Isles but more common in northern France and southern Scandinavia. **Shrubby Orache (*A. halimus*)** is a shrub version of Sea Purslane to 2.5m with whitish, mealy leaves. Native to France and the Mediterranean but planted in southern England as a windbreak, and now naturalised in places and spreading. Edibility as Sea Purslane.

▾ Shrubby Orache

Pickled Sea Purslane (traditional British)

Ingredients:

700g sea purslane leaves, 600ml white wine vinegar, 400ml water, 300g sugar, 4tsp mustard seeds, 6 peppercorns, 6 cloves, slice of fresh ginger.

Bring a pot of salted water to the boil and blanch the sea purslane leaves for 2 mins, then allow to drain and cool. Simmer the spices in the vinegar for 10 mins. Place the leaves into a warmed jar, pour the spiced vinegar over it, and seal.

Seablites (*Suaeda*)

Annual Seablite (*S. maritima*) is a fleshy red-green annual herb, variably upright or prostrate, looking like a cross between Glasswort and Rosemary. Frequent around most of the UK coastline, usually in salt marsh. The leaves are edible raw (must be washed), cooked or pickled. Uses are like Glassworts (p358), with which they are often found, and they can be cooked and served together. The seeds are also edible raw or cooked.

Shrubby Seablite (*S. vera*) is much larger (a shrub to 1.2m), and rarer, mainly found in the south and east of the British Isles. It is also edible, and good. Young specimens can be distinguished from Annual Seablite by the cross-section of the leaves – semicircular in *maritima*, circular in *vera*. 'Blite' is an old English version of the Latin for Orache – '*Blitum*', which is now the genus name for Good King Henry (p344).

▲ Annual Seablite   ▼ Shrubby Seablite

Prickly Saltwort
(*Salsola kali syn. Kali turgidum*)

Prickly Saltwort is an annual herb with
a pale green (and usually red-striped),
branching, prostrate or semi-prostrate stem
to 60cm, and distinctive, stalkless, fleshy
leaves tipped with spines. The tiny flowers
appear in the leaf axils. Frequent around
most of the British coastline, just above
the high-tide line on sandy beaches, often
in disturbed ground. Native to northern
Europe. The leaves and stem are edible
when young, the prickles make older plants
less attractive as food, but can be removed
with sharp scissors. Eat raw (washed) or
cooked and served like spinach. The seeds
can be ground and used to thicken soups or
bulk out cereal flours.

▲ Prickly Saltwort

Summer-cypress (*Bassia scoparia*)

Summer-cypress or **Burningbush** is a
shrub-like annual herb with longer, thinner
leaves than most members of this family. It
is native to temperate Asia, and grown as
an ornamental in Europe but naturalised
in a few places, usually on waste ground.
In Britain it is particularly well established
around the Humber Estuary. Edibility
typical of this family. Used to make
brooms in Serbia.

▲ Summer-cypress

Annual Glassworts or Marsh Samphire (*Salicornia*)

Glassworts were used from the 16th century to make a poor quality glass. The process involved burning heaps of the plant, and combining the ash, which is rich in sodium carbonate, with sand. The name 'Marsh Samphire' is of more recent origin – see entry for Rock Samphire (p482).

Glassworts are annual succulent plants to 30cm consisting of thick, shiny green stems (turning yellow or red) and tiny leaves that look like stunted side-stems. The flowers are even smaller. Common in salt marsh and mudflats, especially in river estuaries, all around British coasts. Forms dense and extensive colonies. The number of species, hybrids or otherwise distinct varieties is a taxing problem for taxonomists, but they are all the same for a forager.

Young stems/shoots can be eaten raw – older stems have an inedible woody core. You can use your teeth to strip the edible exterior from the woody centres. They are at their best in the height of summer, and should be picked carefully. Don't simply rip them up – which is technically illegal, since it involves uprooting them. Rather, harvest the top two-thirds, leaving the base in place to sprout new shoots.

The best method of cooking is to steam for about 10 minutes, or simmer for less, and they can also briefly be microwaved with a knob of butter. Though lovely with nothing but a dash of hollandaise sauce, Marsh Samphire is the perfect accompaniment to fish, especially monkfish and flatfish, as well as strong-flavoured meats like kidney or duck. Also use in soups, adding near the end to avoid overcooking and retain

▲ Marsh Samphire

some texture. Some people recommend lactofermenting, which can be done very quickly, and gains you flavour at the expense of texture. The seeds are small, but yield a high-quality edible oil.

Perennial Glasswort or **Sheep's Samphire (*Sarcocornia perennis*)** is a perennial relative, and the only member of its genus native to northern Europe. Its stems grow to 30cm and are tougher and woodier than Annual Glassworts. Only the youngest growth is worth eating.

▲ Marsh Samphire   ▼ Sheep's Samphire

Montiaceae (Blinks family)

The biggest killer during the 1848-1854 Californian gold rush wasn't starvation, the cold or mining accidents, but scurvy. The miners took flour, dried meats and other non-perishable foods with them, but almost nothing containing vitamin C, and before long they started dying in their thousands. The cure, taught to them by the native tribes, was to eat a salad plant found in the mountains and coastal area of eastern North America. They called it 'Miner's Lettuce'.

Blinks (*Montia fontana*)

Blinks or **Water Miner's Lettuce** is an upright annual to perennial herb to 40cm with branching stems, fleshy spoon-shaped leaves and small white flowers. Inhabits ponds (sometimes with floating stems) and bogs, dark, damp woodland and muddy fields and tracks, especially on acidic soil. Locally common in Scotland, Wales and much of Ireland, less so in England apart from the south west. Present in temperate and subtropical zones globally. Do not confuse with the inedible Water Starworts (*Callitriche* spp.), which are found in the same sort of places.

This plant has traditionally been a highly rated wild food in the Iberian Peninsula, although also recorded as being eaten in other parts of Europe. The young stems and leaves are still widely consumed there raw, as a salad plant (after thorough cleaning, as is typically required for aquatic wild salad plants), served with a vinaigrette dressing. It must be harvested before it flowers, or it will be bitter.

Springbeauty, Winter Purslane or Miner's Lettuce (*Claytonia perfoliata*)

Springbeauty is an annual herb to 35cm with characteristic pairs of fused, succulent leaves, and small white (rarely pink) flowers. Frequent in England and locally common, especially in East Anglia, rarer in Scotland and Wales, on disturbed ground, especially sandy. Naturalised in western Europe since the early 19th century, when it was cultivated as a salad crop. Poisonous Spurges (p176) are occasionally mistaken for this species.

The young leaves are mild and crunchy. The roots are also edible – just pull up the whole plant and wash carefully. This is fiddly, but no more so than cutting the tops off, and the crispy roots add to the flavour.

Siberian Springbeauty or Pink Purslane (*C. sibirica*)

Siberian Springbeauty is an annual to perennial herb to 45cm with fleshy oval leaves (stalkless, but not fused) and pink (occasionally white) flowers. Inhabits damp woodland and stream banks, especially on sandy soil. Very common in south-west and north-west England, common in southern and eastern Scotland, occasional elsewhere. This plant is native to Siberia and western North America, but widely introduced in temperate zones elsewhere, and a problem weed in some places. Edibility is as Springbeauty.

▲ Springbeauty

▲ Siberian Springbeauty

Portulaceae (Purslane family)

Portulaceae is a much smaller family than it used to be, now consisting of just one genus, having lost 20 others.

Common Purslane (*Portulaca oleracea*)

Common Purslane is a succulent, mat-forming, annual herb with prostrate or upright red-green stems to 50cm, shiny, flattened, oval, almost-opposite ovate-oblong leaves and single yellow flowers, usually at the ends of the stems, which develop into off-spherical capsules. Occasional in parts of southern England, becoming rarer and absent further north in the British Isles. Usually found on arable land or waste ground, particularly liking vineyards. Common in warmer temperate parts of Europe and present throughout the tropical to warm temperate parts of the world. Native range is unclear due to widespread historical use by humans, but definitely includes southern Europe. Beware if you are picking this in the wild, because it is reputed to grow together with superficially similar poisonous species of Spurge (p176).

This species is cultivated (var. *sativa*) as a pot-herb, the older leaves being used for this purpose. The young leaves and stems can also be used in salads (works well in seaweed salads), or pickled with olives and capers, or in salted dry white wine. It is a traditional component of a Lebanese salad called 'Fattoush'. The seeds are also edible, raw, cooked or ground into flour.

Fried Purslane a la Milanaise
(TF Garrett, 1892)

Prepare the branches of Purslane, put them in a bowl, and cover with a mixture of lemon-juice, sweetened with caster sugar and flavoured with powdered cinnamon. Let them steep in this marinade for several hours; it is well to put them in the night before they are wanted, and leave them until the following morning. When ready, prepare a batter of eggs, milk, and flour, and add the marinade mixture to it. Put a large piece of butter into a flat stewpan, and place it over the fire until boiling; dip the branches of Purslane in the batter, then put them into the boiling fat, and fry until nicely browned. Drain them, put them on a hot dish over which has been spread a folded napkin or an ornamental dish-paper, and serve.

Aizozaceae (Dew Plant family)
Hottentot-figs or Ice Plants
(*Carpobrotus*)

▲ Hottentot-fig

Hottentot-fig (*C. edulis*) is a mat-forming perennial herb to 15cm high. It has creeping, fleshy stems (to 3m long) with a triangular cross-section, beautiful pink or yellow flowers and fig-like fruits known as 'sour figs'. This sea-cliff plant is native to southern Africa, but thrives in some coastal areas of south and south-west England (rare or absent in more northerly areas). It is also invasive in many coastal areas further south in Europe. The only thing you could mistake for this species are two similarly edible close relatives, called **Sally-my-handsome (*C. acinaciformis*)** and **Pigface (*C. glaucescens*)**, both of which are also invasive aliens.

The fruits have an outer seedy/salty layer and a sweet centre that smells like ripe banana. They are perfectly edible raw, and can be dried into something resembling a fig, but are most frequently pickled or made into a jam or chutney. They need to be very ripe – they should be harvested with a sharp knife when they have started to soften. The leaves can also be eaten, raw, cooked or pickled, though they are a little bitter.

'Hottentot' is derived from a colonial Dutch name for a traditionally nomadic tribe from south-west Africa, who ate the fruits. They call themselves 'Khoikhoi' – 'Hottentot' is a derogatory reference to their spoken language, which includes lots of click sounds.

Cornales

Order *Cornales* is considered either a sister clade or the most basal lineage of the large Asterid clade which occupies the remainder of this book. Hydrangeas are well-known ornamental members, which have been used as cake decorations but are toxic (causing vomiting, headache and muscle weakness).

Cornaceae (Dogwood family)

Common Dogwood (*Cornus sanguinea*) is a shrub to 4m with elliptical leaves, purple-black berries that I've seen described as both mildly toxic and edible but not worthwhile, and an oil can be extracted from the seeds. This plant is better used as a decoy in permaculture: birds like the fruit, so it can be used to distract them from berries we'd prefer they didn't eat. This species is native in calcareous regions of the British lowlands. The berries are frequently mistaken for elderberries by novice foragers and the occasional presenter on live breakfast TV.

 Dwarf Cornel (*C. suecica*) is a rhizomatous perennial herb growing to 20cm, opposite pairs of stalkless leaves, and small, tight umbels of dark purple flowers with four white bracts, followed by red berries. These are bitter but claimed to be an appetite stimulant. The plant is also rare (confined to the central highlands in Britain and far north in Europe), so should be left alone.

Cornelian Cherry or Cherry Dogwood (*C. mas*)

Cornelian Cherry is a deciduous shrub to 10m with opposite oval-oblong leaves, clusters of small yellow flowers and cherry-sized red berries. Inhabits woods and scrub on chalk/limestone. An occasional garden escape in Britain, though it has been here since the 16th century. Native to southern Europe and south-west Asia. The ripe fruit is edible, though rather astringent raw or unripe. It is best used in preserves or sauces, to make a cordial, or dried and used in muesli. The seeds can be pressed to make an oil.

Pickled Cornelians (Hannah Woolley, 1675)

Gather the fairest and biggest Cornelians when they first begin to grow red, and after they have lain a while, put them up into a Pot or Barrel, filling them up with Brine, as for Artichoaks, and put to them a little green Fennel, and a few Bay-leaves, to make them smell well, then stop them up very close, and let them stand for a Month.

Kousa or Japanese Dogwood (*C. kousa*)

Japanese Dogwood is a large shrub or small tree to 12m, with simple, opposite leaves and abundant white or pink flowers (it is actually the hydrangea-like bracts you can see, the flowers themselves are very small). It produces a crop (often also abundant) of distinctive red, compound berries. Native to eastern Asia, but widely planted as an ornamental elsewhere.

The berries are tasty, though the outer case is bitter and the large seeds aren't edible. The leaves are also allegedly edible, but too bitter for me.

The closely related **Bentham's Dogwood (*C.capitata*)**, native to the Himalayas and also grown as an ornamental, has similar edible fruits.

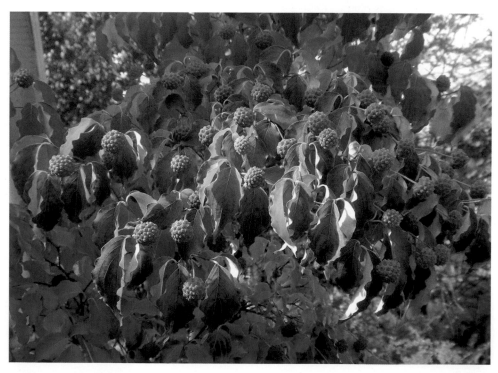

Ericales

The ornamental Perennial Phlox (*Phlox paniculata*) has edible flowers (use in salads and fruit drinks), as does another member of the Phlox family (*Polemoniaceae*) – Jacob's Ladder (*Polemonium caeruleum*). Jacob's Ladder is nationally rare as a native British wild flower, but is locally common in parts of Wales, Scotland and northern England, and also sometimes escapes from cultivation. It is more common in other parts of northern Europe.

Theaceae (Tea family)
Camellia spp.

Tea itself is made from the leaves of the strictly warm-climate *C. sinensis*, but the leaves and flower buds of most *Camellia* species can be used to make herbal teas. The seeds of **C. oleifera** are pressed to make a high-calorie oil known as 'Tea seed oil', used for cooking and seasoning (do not confuse with 'Tea Tree oil', which is poisonous and made from a completely unrelated plant). **Common** or **Japanese Camellia (C. Japonica)** is widely cultivated in temperate areas as an ornamental, but its flowers can be used as a vegetable. In Japan, Camellia leaves are used to serve sticky rice cakes called 'tsubaki mochi' in the early spring, but the leaves themselves are not eaten. Another well-known ornamental is the winter-flowering **C. sasanqua**, the seeds of which also yield edible oil.

▲ ▼ *C. sasanqua*

Balsaminaceae (Balsam family)
Balsams (*Impatiens*)

Impatiens refers to the explosive seed pods of this genus, as does the common name of the popular ornamental **Busy Lizzie (*I. walleriana*)**, which has sweet-tasting edible flowers.

Himalayan or **Indian Balsam (*I. glandulifera*)** is an annual herb with reddish stems to 2m, oval, finely toothed leaves with pointed tips, which have a distinctive musty smell when crushed, and pink/purple/white hood-shaped flowers. A common, invasive alien in England, Wales and lowland Scotland in damp places, especially on riverbanks and/or places with high nutrient levels.

The flowers, which can be picked in great volume with no fear of anybody complaining, can be made into jam. The young shoots and leaves can be boiled for 5-8 minutes and eaten in moderation (they contain oxalates, and can act as an emetic). It is the nutty, nutritious seeds that are of most foraging interest. The pods will explode into cupped hands, and the seeds can be eaten whole there and then (though be wary of eating large amounts raw). They can also be used in salads or in breads, pressed to make an oil, or popped – heat in a lidded saucepan, shaking like you would popcorn until most of them have exploded, then serve salted. The hollow stems can also be used as straws. The three other Balsams on the right have the same edible uses.

◄ Himalayan Balsam

▲ Himalayan Balsam pods

▲ Himalayan Balsam seeds

Orange Balsam (*I. capensis*) is an annual herb to 1.2m with large, dark-blotched, orange flowers with a bent double spur. Frequent in most of central England, and the centre of southern England near fresh water. Rare or absent in Kent, south-west England, Wales and Scotland. Native to north America, introduced in northern and central Europe, slowly spreading.

Touch-me-not Balsam (*I. noli-tangere*) is a native annual herb with an upright stem to 80cm and alternate, finely toothed, oval leaves. The large, yellow flowers have a distinctive spur bent at right angles. Native in some parts of the British Isles, but infrequent everywhere, in damp, shady places.

Small Balsam (*I. parviflora*) is an annual herb to 60cm with finely toothed leaves and small, pale yellow flowers with a straight spur. Inhabits dry or damp woodland and other shady places. Common in central southern England, East Anglia and parts of the Midlands, very rare in the south-east corner, south-west England and Scotland, occasional elsewhere. Introduced in the 19th century, native to Asia.

Ericaceae (Heather/Heath family)

Members of the *Ericaceae* prefer acidic, nutrient-poor soils ('Heaths'). In addition to those included below, the most foraging-relevant are the Rhododendrons, the flowers of which are eaten in their native Nepal, although some species are known to have toxic pollen and nectar (and leaves). These are a traditional medicine for lowering blood pressure, but also cause nausea and other unpleasant symptoms, possibly including coma and death. The grayanotoxins they contain disrupt the sodium ion channels of cell membranes. In Nepal, honey loaded with grayanotoxins is known as 'mad honey', and used as a recreational drug. Bog Rosemary (*Andromeda polifolia*), the leaves of which superficially resemble Rosemary, sometimes grows in among the edible species here, and also contains grayanotoxins. Common Wintergreen (*Pyrola minor*) has edible leaves, but they are quite bitter, and in the British Isles it is only common in Scotland (more common in the mountains and far north of continental Europe).

Heathers/Heaths (*Calluna/Erica*)

Heather or **Ling** is a perennial evergreen shrub to 80cm with rooting stems, tiny leaves and mauve or white flowers (the 'lucky' ones) in late summer. Very common on heaths and moors in much of the British Isles, less so in lowland areas of eastern England, and common throughout Europe. **Bell Heather (*E. cinerea*)** has longer leaves and fewer but larger flowers. It is very common apart from in lowland areas of central and eastern England. **Bog Heather** or **Cross-leaved Heath (*E. tetralix*)** is very similar. The shoots and flowering stems of all of them can be used to make tea, and to flavour mead and beer. 'Ling' is derived from the Anglo-Saxon 'Lig', meaning 'fire', because heather was once an important fuel.

▾ Heather

▲ Crowberry

Crowberry (*Empetrum nigrum*)

"The berries are slightly acid, and are sought for greedily by children in the extreme north of Scotland; the Russian peasantry also eat them, but they are not generally considered as of much value for food. In Kamtchatka they are used in great quantities to boil with fish, and form also an ingredient in some Kamtchatkan puddings."
(TF Garrett, 1892)

Crowberry is a dwarf evergreen shrub resembling Bell Heather, but with thicker leaves, which have a white stripe running along the midrib of the underside, small pinkish flowers, and shiny black berries in late summer (usually only sparsely produced). It is found in bleak, exposed, peaty, boggy or rocky upland and in northerly areas only, common in Scotland, but absent from lowland Britain. Present in the entire northern boreal zone.

There are reports that the berries cause headaches for some people, and they are certainly acidic. They can be used to make a jelly, or just served with game. Also used to make jam, or in fruit pies, or to flavour Schnapps. A traditional Kamchatkan use is in a dish called 'tolkusha', along with dried fish, fat from seals or reindeer, and edible bulbs, all pounded and ground together into a paste.

Crowberry Soup (traditional Icelandic)

Ingredients:

750g ripe crowberries, 1l water, 1 cinnamon stick, 2tbsp cornflour, 100g sugar, 100ml cold water.

Simmer the berries and cinnamon for 25 mins, and strain. Make a paste with the cornflour and cold water. Return the strained berries to the boil, add the paste, and stir while return to the boil again. Add sugar, and serve warm with zwieback (rusk bread).

Bearberry (*Arctostaphylos uva-ursi*) (!)

Bearberry is an evergreen, mat-forming shrub to 30cm high with creeping stems to 1.5m long, small shiny alternate obovate leaves with a distinctive network of veins on the lower surface, and without downturned edges, white or pink flowers, and shiny, red berries. Common in northern Scotland in free-draining moorland, absent from lowland Britain. Present in a north circumpolar fashion, and mountainous areas further south. **Arctic** or **Alpine Bearberry** (*A. alpinus*), which has purple-black berries, is strictly confined to mountains and the extreme north (Alps, Pyrenees, Scotland, northern Scandinavia).

The fruit of both these plants is dry and inferior to Cowberry, with which Bearberry is sometimes confused. They are better when cooked, in preserves or stews. As with other members of the group, the berries can also be dried, and the leaves used for tea. Native Americans smoked the dried leaves with tobacco.

Cowberry (*Vaccinium vitis-idaea*)

Cowberry, Red Bilberry or **Lingonberry** is a dwarf evergreen shrub to 35cm with upright shoots, and small, alternate, leathery, oval leaves, with turned-down edges and tiny black dots on their undersides. It has drooping clusters of pale pinkish-white bell-shaped flowers (summer) and red berries (autumn). It spreads via underground stems. Inhabits upland/northern areas, especially acid bogs and woodland, absent from lowland Britain. Common in the northern boreal zone and far north of the temperate zone. The fruits are very acidic,

and many people do not like them raw. Uses as Bilberry, to which it is similar, though evergreen and with larger fruits which are red rather than black. Bearberry has similar berries, but different shaped leaves.

▾ Bearberry

▾ Cowberry

▲ Bilberry

Bilberry (*V. myrtillus*)

Bilberry, Blaeberry or **Whortleberry** is a
deciduous, rhizomatous, dwarf woody shrub
to 70cm, with upright, ridged, green stems
and alternate, toothed, oval, bright green
leaves. The pinkish-red globular flowers
(summer) are followed by dark blue berries
(late summer and early autumn) with a white
bloom; inhabits bogs, heathland and acid
woodland, sometimes dominating entirely.
Native throughout Europe and common in
the British Isles apart from lowland areas
of central and eastern England, although
in many places it produces a very sparse
crop. The berries are a rare sight in south-
east England, though the plant is common.
The poisonous Herb-paris (p116) has been
mistaken for Bilberry.

The berries, which are rich in vitamins
C and D, can be eaten raw with cream, used
to make a first-class jam, dried and used in
muesli, or used to make wine. A good herbal
tea can be made from the leaves. A berry-
picker should speed up the collecting process.

Bog Bilberry (*V. uliginosum*) is a deciduous
upright or ascending shrub with brown
stems to 80cm, oval leaves, pendulous pale
pink flowers and dark blue berries. Found in
heathland and moorland on mountains, and
tundra in the far north. Common in north
England and north Scotland, absent from
lowland Britain. Uses as Bilberry.

▼ Bog Bilberry

Cranberry (*V. oxycoccus*)

Cranberry is an evergreen prostrate shrub with tiny, leathery, lanceolate leaves, white or pink flowers (mid to late summer) and red berries (mid-autumn to early winter). It inhabits areas with low nutrient levels, particularly among Sphagnum Moss in acid bogs. Locally common in Wales, northern England and southern Scotland, rare in northern Scotland and absent from much of the rest of Britain. It can be found throughout the cool temperate zones of the northern hemisphere. Close relatives include the smaller and rarer native **Small Cranberry (*V. microcarpum*)**, and the larger **American Cranberry (*V. macrocarpon*)**, which is naturalised in a few places.

Wild Cranberries can theoretically be used in the same way as the commercial crop, for making a sauce or jelly, or juiced. Both fruit and leaves are also used in/as teas. In reality, they are hard to find and collect in sufficient quantity.

Cranberry Kissel

"Typically allowed to cool and then served with manna porridge [semolina] or sweet cottage cheese."*

Ingredients:
3 cups cranberries, 150g sugar, 1tbsp potato starch, water.

Place the cranberries and 2tbsp of water in a small saucepan, and bring to the boil. Reduce heat and simmer 10-15 mins until the fruit is soft. Pass berries through a fine sieve with the back of a spoon. Add sugar and stir. Return to pan and bring back to the boil. Dissolve the potato starch in 1tbsp of water. Reduce heat and stir starch into fruit. Increase heat, and keep stirring until the mixture thickens and starts to boil. Remove from heat and pour into individual dishes when lukewarm. Refrigerate for at least four hours before serving.

* *Changes in the Use of Wild Food Plants in Estonia: 18th – 21st Century*, Sõukand, R, and Kalle, R, 2016, Springer Nature.

Shallon (*Gaultheria shallon*)

Shallon is an evergreen, suckering, thicket-forming shrub to 1.5m, upright or sprawling, with egg-shaped leaves with cordate bases, pinkish-white flowers and slightly hairy dark purple berries. Native to North America. Introduced to the British Isles in early Victorian times, naturalised since the early 20th century. It is usually planted in woods and heathland as cover and food for game birds, but is spreading and now becoming an invasive problem in some places, especially acidic heathland.

Historically it was an important food for Native Americans (this plant is known as 'Salal' in America). The berries, which taste rather like Blueberries, are best used in jams and jellies, though perfectly edible raw or dried. The berries and young leaves are widely claimed to be appetite suppressants.

Checkerberry or **Eastern Teaberry** (*G. procumbens*) is a dwarf shrub to 15cm, with bright red fruits with a flavour of wintergreen or mint. Native to eastern North America, planted as ground cover, and naturalised in a few northern European locations (mainly Scotland in the British Isles). **Prickly Heath** (*G. mucronata*), a compact shrub to 1.5m native to the mountains of Chile, is also naturalised in open woodland in a few places. The white or purple berries are an edible but tasteless survival food.

Strawberry Tree (*Arbutus unedo*)

Strawberry Tree is an evergreen shrub or small tree to 10m, with glossy, dark green lanceolate leaves with a serrated margin, large panicles of white (occasionally pink) flowers in autumn, and spherical fruits that look superficially like strawberries and take a long time to ripen, finally turning red the following autumn. Native to southern and western Europe, including western Ireland but not Great Britain, where it is usually planted. Introduced in the rest of Europe.

The fruits are edible, raw or cooked, and make an excellent jam. Sweet and soft, but with a rather gritty skin. Best when fully ripe (dark red, and just about to fall off the tree). This plant appears in the centre of Madrid's coat of arms. The Latin name is a reference to Roman writer Pliny the Elder supposedly saying of the fruit "*unum tantum edo*" – "I eat only one", although what he meant by this is unclear. I usually eat more than one if I come across a loaded tree, and our daughter couldn't get enough of them aged 2.

Primulaceae (Primrose family)

Marginally edible members of the Primrose family not included here are Water Pimpernel / Brookweed (*Samolus valerandi*) and Yellow Loosestrife (*Lysimachia vulgaris*), which is introduced from south-east Europe and usually found by rivers and streams (many members of this family like boggy habitats). The leaves of both are bitter but non-toxic. Ones to avoid are the houseplant Poison Primrose (*Primula abconica*), which has skin-irritating sap, and the mildly toxic ornamental *Cyclamen* species.

Scarlet Pimpernel (*Lysimachia arvensis* syn. *Anagallis arvensis*)

(!)

Scarlet Pimpernel is an annual herb with stems to 40cm which can be sprawling or upright, with opposite ovate leaves and flowers which are usually red, but sometimes orange, white, lilac or blue. Common throughout Europe apart from the far north (including north Scotland). Inhabits waste ground, dunes and grassland. The sap irritates skin and all parts of the plant contain toxins that are harmful if ingested. It has killed livestock, but fortunately it also tastes horrible, so is rarely eaten in quantity either by humans or animals. Could be mistaken for Chickweed (p336). The veins on Scarlet Pimpernel leaves run mainly from base to tip. Chickweed leaf veins multiply branch sideways. Yellow Pimpernel (*Lysimachia nemorum*), which is much larger, is similarly poisonous.

Sea Milkwort (*Lysimachia maritima* syn. *Glaux maritima*)

Sea Milkwort is a hairless, mat-forming perennial herb to 30cm with small, opposite, fleshy leaves and stalkless pink flowers. Usually coastal but sometimes found inland in very damp/wet and saline locations. Common in coastal areas in a variety of habitats. Could be confused with Sea Sandwort (p333)

A variety of this species (var. *obtusifolia*) was a food plant for Native Americans. Young shoots were eaten raw or pickled, and the rhizomes after long boiling, though consumption of large amounts are known to cause drowsiness and/or nausea.

▾ Scarlet Pimpernel

▾ Sea Milkwort

Primroses (*Primula*)

Common Primrose (*P. vulgaris*) is a rhizomatous perennial herb to 20cm with an almost-evergreen rosette of wrinkled, stalkless, ovate leaves, and large yellow or pink flowers (early spring) appearing singly on short stems. Found in short, grazed grassland, open deciduous woodland and hedgerows, and on banks and cliffs, throughout western and southern Europe

Cowslip (*P. veris*) is a rhizomatous, evergreen or semi-evergreen perennial herb with hairy, crinkly, ovate-oblong leaves (shorter than Primrose) and clusters of orange-yellow flowers smaller than those of Primrose and on taller stems (to 30cm). Inhabits grassland, open woodland, churchyards and similar habitats, particularly on chalk and limestone. Frequent in England and Wales, less so in Scotland and very rare in the far north west. Native to the temperate zones of Europe, but declining in many places. The rare **Oxlip (*P. elatior*)** is very similar, with larger, paler, more open flowers.

All of these plants are less common than they once were, partly because of historical over-picking by foragers, though they are making a comeback. The flowers make a highly regarded country wine, and can be eaten in salads, or used as a flavouring/decoration for desserts. You can also suck nectar from Cowslip flowers. The leaves are a little tough and a little bitter, but perfectly edible and available through the winter. They could be mistaken for those of the deadly poisonous Foxglove (p394), which are stalked and more pointed, as well as growing out of the stem instead of just from the base of the plant.

▾ Cowslip

▲ ▼ Primrose

Boraginales
Boraginaceae (Borage family)

Borage (*Borago officinalis*) (!)

"Borrage ... is an exhilarating Cordial, of
a pleasant Flavour: The tender Leaves,
and Flowers especially, may be eaten in
Composition; but above all, the Sprigs in
Wine, like those of *Baum* [Balm], are of
known Vertue to revive the *Hypochondriac*,
and chear the hard Student."
(John Evelyn, 1699)

Borage is a roughly hairy upright annual
herb to 70cm. The long-stalked basal leaves
are wrinkled, grey-green and oval with
cordate bases, and the stalkless stem leaves
are more lanceolate and wavy-edged, and
clasping. The star-shaped flowers are usually
bright blue, but can also be pink or white.
Introduced from southern Europe over 800
years ago, widely grown as an ornamental,
common in the wild in south-east England
on waste ground and roadsides, rarer
the further north and west you go. Easily
confused with Comfrey (p382), or much
more seriously with deadly Foxglove (p394).
Foxglove tastes very bitter, and the leaves
are a lot less hairy.

Popular in Liguria in Italy, especially
with pasta, and also Crete and parts of Spain.
This is one of the seven herbs required for
authentic Frankfurter Green Sauce (p75 and
p381). In Poland it is used to flavour pickled
gherkins. Only eat the leaves when young,
and then in moderation, in salads or cooked.
The flowers can be used as a garnish, in
drinks and salads. All parts taste of cucumber.
Borage seed oil is of medicinal importance,
containing the same active ingredients as
Evening Primrose oil (p378). An edible blue
dye can be extracted from the flowers.

Borage contains pyrrolizidine alkaloids.
Do not eat if you have liver problems, and
do not consume in large quantities.

Forget-me-nots (*Myosotis*) ⓘ

Forget-me-nots are small (to 40cm) annuals or short-lived perennials with hairy, oval leaves and familiar blue or pink (occasionally white or yellow) flowers. The most common species in the British Isles are the Field or Common Forget-me-not (*M. arvensis*), Wood Forget-me-not (*M. sylvatica*) and Water Forget-me-not (*M. scorpioides*). The only edible parts are the flowers, which are used as a garnish or decoration, on cakes or in drinks.

Frankfurter Grüne Soße (authentic German version)

This is a famous green sauce served cold with hard-boiled eggs or boiled potatoes. This 'authentic' version contains borage, chervil, chives, garden cress, parsley, salad burnet and sorrel (all of which are featured in this book). In times of scarcity, other wild herbs were used, including dandelion, greater plantain and even daisies, and a British version dating from World War II can be found on p75.

Ingredients:
300g herbs (equal amounts of each), 250g sour cream, mayonnaise or curd cheese, 2tbsp oil, 150g yogurt, 3 hard-boiled eggs, 1 teaspoon lemon juice (or vinegar), salt and pepper.

Remove thickest stems from the herbs, then wash and dry on a paper towel. Peel the eggs, and separate. Put the yolks, lemon juice, 200g of herbs, yoghurt and a pinch of salt into a bowl, and blend. Stir in the sour cream (or alternative). Add the remaining herbs (finely chopped) and egg whites (roughly chopped) and stir. Add salt, pepper and additional lemon juice or vinegar to taste. Rest in the fridge for an hour. Serve with eggs or potatoes.

A Tarte of Borage Flowers (from The Proper New Book of Cookerie, 1548)

Take borage flowers and parboyle them tender, then strayne them with the yolckes of three or foure eggs, and sweet curdes, or else take three or four apples and parboyle wythal and strayne them with sweete butter and a lyttel mace and so bake it.

Comfreys (*Symphytum*) ⚠

Comfreys are tall perennial herbs with untoothed hairy, oval leaves. The untoothed margins are important for distinguishing Comfreys from the deadly Foxglove (p394).

(Common) Comfrey (*S. officinale*) is a perennial herb to 1.4m, with (leafy) branching stems and tubular flowers which are cream or reddish-purple and grow in asymmetrical clusters on long stalks. The base of the leaf stem continues as a wing, down the stem, all the way to below the next leaf base. Native and common in most of the British Isles in woodland, stream banks and other moist, shady places. Rarer in the far north. **Russian Comfrey (*S. uplandicum*)** is a very common hybrid of Common Comfrey and (the non-European) Rough or Prickly Comfrey (*S. aspersum*). More bristly than Common Comfrey, and the flowers are variable in colour – pink, purple, blue, or a mixture. The wings extending from the leaf stem do not continue all the way down to the next leaf, and are narrower than in Common Comfrey. **White Comfrey (*S. orientale*)** is the only British Comfrey with pure white flowers.

Leaves are rounder than the other comfreys, and the leaf stems have no wings. The whole plant is hairy. Introduced from south-west Asia in the 19th century, but naturalised and frequent in lowland England. Rare escape elsewhere. **Tuberous Comfrey (*S. tuberosum*)** is shorter than Common Comfrey (to 60cm), and the stems (which turn purple) only branch towards the top. The lower leaves are stalked, further up not stalked, upper surface of the leaf has hooked hairs, and flowers are pale yellow. Inhabits damp, shady places. Frequent in the south and east of Scotland, uncommon in most of the British Isles, present throughout temperate Europe.

The mucilaginous leaves of all these plants have traditionally been eaten, and widely claimed to be nutritious. Perhaps for the same reason Comfrey makes good fertiliser and a useful permaculture plant – it brings up nutrients from deep down. They can be eaten raw, fried in batter, or dried to make a tea. The young shoots and blanched stalks are used like asparagus, either hot or allowed to cool for salads. The roots are also edible, either chopped and added to soups, or roasted like Dandelion and ground into a coffee substitute. The name is derived from the Latin 'conferre', meaning 'to bring together', because Common Comfrey roots were historically used in the setting of broken limbs. The roots were grated, and the resulting sludgy paste was then packed around the break, where it would set rather like plaster. They were also once used to make a gum which was used to treat wool before it was spun. Comfreys contain significant amounts of liver-damaging toxins, especially in the roots, and they act cumulatively, so it might be best to consume in moderation. There is disagreement about how dangerous this really is, but I don't personally eat it.

Comfrey Fritters (traditional German)

Ingredients:
Comfrey leaves (with stalks), 1 egg, 50g plain flour, 250ml beer or milk.

Wash the leaves, keeping the stalks, and dry well. Whisk together the flour, beer/milk and egg to make a batter, and leave to rest for 15 mins. Use the stalks to dip the leaves in the batter, and cook in hot oil until golden brown. Season and serve.

▲ Common Comfrey

▼ White Comfrey

▲ Russian Comfrey

▼ Tuberous Comfrey

Green Alkanet (*Pentaglottis semperivens*)

Green Alkanet is a bristly evergreen perennial herb to 60cm with oval basal leaves, thinner stem leaves, and brilliant blue flowers. Inhabits wood edges, hedges and rough ground, frequent in the British Isles apart from western Ireland and north-west Scotland. Native to continental Europe, introduced to the British Isles in the 18th century.

Alkanet has flowers that are edible but tasteless and only really used as decoration. The leaves can be eaten when very young, but aren't recommended. It tends to turn up as a plant that people have found near human habitation, placed in the right family, but then misidentified as Borage or a Forget-me-not. The flowers are brighter blue than those plants, and a different shape to Borage, and the leaves are bigger than those of Forget-me-nots. Can be confused with **Alkanet Oxtongue** or **Common Bugloss (*Anchusa officinalis*)**, another member of this family also sometimes called 'Alkanet', not native to the British Isles but occasionally found as a casual alien. It is common in much of the rest of Europe and has edible flowers (purple rather than blue) and leaves.

▼ Green Alkanet

▲ Viper's-bugloss

Viper's-bugloss (*Echium vulgare*)

Viper's-bugloss is a monocarpic (sets seed once then dies), usually biennial upright herb to 1m, with rough, hairy oblong-elliptical leaves, and pink buds that become blue flowers (summer). Inhabits grassland, cliffs, shingle and rough ground, especially in calcareous areas. Native to the British Isles and common in the south and east, and present across most of Europe.

The flowers have been used as a salad item, candied, and used to flavour cordial. There are anecdotal cases of mild poisoning of humans involving the leaves, which contain hepatoxic pyrrolizidine alkaloids capable of serious poisoning in cattle and horses.

Lungworts (*Pulmonaria*)

Common Lungwort (*P. officinalis*) is a hairy evergreen perennial herb to 30cm with pointed oval leaves with cordate bases and silvery green patches, and clusters of flowers that appear in late spring and change from red-pink to blue-violet. Native to the whole of Europe apart from the British Isles. Naturally inhabits open deciduous woodland, preferring nutrient-rich calcareous locations. In Britain it is more often found as a garden escape (in a variety of habitats, especially waste ground), although it has been naturalised since the late 18th century. The young basal leaves are edible, best cooked (boiled or steamed) since their texture makes them unappealing raw. They can also be battered and fried like Comfrey (p382). Even cooked they are a bit slimy, which is characteristic of plants in this family. The leaves are an ingredient in vermouth, a fortified wine, and the flowers can be used as a garnish or in salads. **Suffolk Lungwort (*P. obscura*)** is similar, but less hairy, less spotted and darker green. It is restricted to Suffolk in the British Isles, but common in Germany, Poland and southern Scandinavia. It also has edible flowers.

▾ Lungwort

▲ Oysterplant

Oysterplant (*Mertensia maritima*)

Oysterplant is a fleshy rhizomatous perennial herb to 60cm with sprawling, red-tinged stems, ovate leaves and plenty of long-stalked flowers (summer) which start out pink, then turn blue. It inhabits beaches (usually shingle), and in the British Isles is restricted to north-west Scotland, locally frequent but becoming rarer, and shouldn't really be taken by foragers at all. Present in much of the northern part of the northern temperate zone. The leaves are sometimes claimed to taste like oysters, but most people who've tried them disagree. They actually taste salty, like many other maritime plants, so the connection might have more to do with texture and shape than flavour. The flowers are also edible.

▲ Oleander

Gentianales

In addition to the Bedstraw family, order *Gentianales* includes four other much smaller families, of ornamental interest only, including the deadly Oleander (*Nerium oleander*) of the *Apocynaceae* (Dogbane family). Native to warmer parts of Europe and Asia, but grown for its showy pink or red flowers, very widely and for centuries. It has long, thin leaves, resembling an Olive tree. All parts are toxic, containing cardiac glycosides similar to those in Foxglove (p394), but serious poisonings are unlikely because of the plant's bitter taste.

Rubiaceae (Bedstraw family)

Rubiaceae is a very large (13,500 species) family, including the historically important dye plant **Madder (*Rubia tinctorum*)** and the tropical genus ***Coffea*** (source of coffee beans).

Sweet Woodruff (*Galium odoratum*)

Sweet Woodruff is a rhizomatous perennial herb to 50cm with hairless, unbranched, upright, four-angled, red-tinged stems, glossy, dark green, lanceolate leaves arranged in whorls of six to nine (the name 'ruff' refers to the whorls of leaves, after the item of clothing), and small white flowers. Inhabits woodland and other damp and shady places, especially on calcareous soils, and is an indicator of ancient woodland. Native to northern and central Europe, frequent in most of the British Isles and locally common, rarer in eastern England, north-west Scotland, and Ireland.

Woodruff smells of vanilla when crushed, because it contains coumarin, and is used as a flavouring in liqueurs and chilled white wine. In Germany, Belgium and northern France it is used to make 'Maitrank' ('May wine'), traditionally consumed on May Day. The young foliage is used before the plant flowers, added to a base of aromatised wine (such as vermouth), along with fruit (such as strawberries or orange) and a little sugar, and served chilled. Woodruff leaves can be used as a herbal tea, or to flavour game casseroles, and the flowers as a garnish. It is traditionally also used as a moth repellent. Reported to cause headaches if consumed in large quantities, and it reduces the ability of blood to clot so should not be eaten by anyone taking blood-thinning medicines.

Sweet Woodruff Syrup (traditional German)

Ingredients:

Sweet woodruff leaves (picked before flowering), 1kg sugar, 2l water, juice of 3 lemons.

Wash the woodruff and dry completely. Leave for 2 or 3 days for a stronger flavour. Remove the leaves from the stems. Boil the sugar and water for 10 mins, then remove from the heat. Add the lemon juice then the woodruff. Cover and refrigerate for up to 4 days (the longer you leave it, the stronger the flavour). Strain through a cheesecloth, bottle, and store in the fridge. Use as a cordial, on pancakes, on ice-cream or in cocktails.

Cleavers (*Galium aparine*) ⚠

"It is familiarly taken in broth to keep those lean and lank that are apt to grow fat."
(Nicholas Culpeper, 1652)

Cleavers (aka Sticky Willie, Goosegrass) is an annual herb with creeping/climbing, four-sided stems to 3m and lanceolate leaves arranged in whorls of six to nine. The small, white, tubular flowers (late spring) appear in the upper leaf axils, and the whole plant is sticky (like velcro, not glue). Abundant everywhere but particularly the coldest parts of Europe, in hedgerows, fields and other nutrient-rich environments, and a well-known garden weed.

This plant was considered useful in medieval times because it was available in late winter, even in the snow. The shoots and leaves are edible when very young, but though they are nutritious raw the texture is much improved by cooking for 10 minutes. Best used as a pot-herb, served with butter, made into soup, or cooled and added to salads. The seeds can be toasted to make a coffee substitute, and actually do contain a small amount of caffeine, and even taste mildly of coffee. For this purpose you should use the seeds when they are purple, not brown. Cleavers is still used as an ingredient in herbal slimming remedies (though whether it has any real effect is doubtful) and is sold in health-food stores as a lymphatic detoxification supplement.

Can cause contact dermatitis, and some people have an allergic reaction to ingesting it.

Lady's Bedstraw (*G. verum*)

"... it is called cheese-rennet, because
it performs the same office."
(Nicholas Culpeper, 1652)

Lady's Bedstraw is a hairless perennial herb
with branching, four-angled, scrambling to
upright stems to 1.5m, narrow, dark green
leaves arranged in whorls of 8-10, and dense
clusters of tiny yellow flowers. Native and
common throughout Europe in short,
grazed and unimproved grassland, by
hedgerows, and sometimes on cliffs
and dunes.

The name is derived from a traditional
belief that this species is a flea-killing
insecticide, and was included with straw in
mattresses, especially for women expecting
to give birth. Traditionally used to produce
yellow (stems and tops) and red (roots) dyes.
The leaves and flowers can be used to make
tea, and the seeds like those of Cleavers.
Culpeper's claim about milk-curdling (about
which some modern sources have expressed
scepticism) has recently been backed up
with scientific research.*

There are several other British members
of this genus known as 'Bedstraws', all of
which are marginally edible, but none good
enough to include here.

* *Expression, activation and processing of a novel plant milk-clotting aspartic protease in Pichia pastoris*, Feijoo-Siota, L, et al, Journal of Biotechnology, Volume 268, 2018.

Lamiales

The Lamiales are a large (24,000+ species) order, typically having flowers with four fused petals forming a tube. This taxonomic area has been disrupted recently, especially with respect to the Figwort family (*Scrophulariaceae*). Nearly all members of interest to foragers have been moved out, some of them into newly defined families, though the leaves and/or flowers of **Mullein (*Verbascum* spp.)** have traditionally been used as a tea to relieve coughs, and as the base of herbal smoking blends (40-50% of the mix).

Plantaginaceae (Plantain family)

The Plantain family has recently been much enlarged. The Plantains in question are not to be confused with unrelated cooking banana trees, which are tropical monocots with the same name, although both names ultimately refer to broad, flat leaves. A common feature of Plantains that all the leaves are produced from the base of leafless flower stalks.

Mare's-tail (*Hippuris vulgaris*)

Mare's-tail is a perennial, rhizomatous aquatic herb with stems to 30cm above the water surface (and to 1m below), dark green leaves in whorls, and tiny flowers. Locally common in most of the British Isles in shallow areas of still or slow-flowing fresh water. Rare in south-west England, Wales and the Scottish Highlands.

The young foliage is edible, best cooked. The texture of the frilly leaves isn't great for eating, especially raw. The best part is the stem. This plant was traditionally used by the Inuit in seal blood and cod liver soups.

▲ Great Mullein

▲ Greater Plantain

Greater Plantain (*Plantago major*)

Greater Plantain is an annual or perennial herb to 50cm with a rosette of near-hairless, broad, oval leaves with pronounced veins and long stalks, and tall spikes of tiny white flowers. It is abundant on disturbed ground, lawns, fields, paths and roadsides. Native to Europe, northern, western and central Asia, and introduced in much of the rest of the world. The young leaves are edible and nutritious, containing plenty of vitamins A, C and K, and calcium, though not a great culinary experience. They taste and smell a bit like mushrooms (something I hadn't noticed until pointed out by Miles Irving). Only the youngest are edible raw. Older, more fibrous leaves are better boiled for five minutes, even if destined for salad use. The seeds are also a useful food source, raw or cooked (ground into flour, or boiled like sago).

Hoary Plantain (*P. media*) is very similar to Greater Plantain, slightly smaller, with pinker flowers and leaves that are greyer and hairier, taper to a shorter and winged stalk, and form a more flattened, rosette-like structure. It usually inhabits damp calcareous grassland and is nationally rare, but can be locally common. Uses are as Greater Plantain.

Buck's-horn Plantain (*P. coronopus*)

Buck's-horn Plantain is an annual or perennial herb to 25cm with a low rosette of thick, toothed/lobed lanceolate leaves (vaguely resembling antlers) and small heads of flowers on spikes. Mainly coastal, infrequent but locally common on bare, sandy or rocky ground, especially liking car parks. In the British Isles it is mainly found in England. Native to Eurasia. This plant is a traditional component of the Italian 'misticanza' salad (mixed wild and domesticated greens). It has become very fashionable in speciality salad mixes, for which it is cultivated under the names 'Minutina' and 'Erba Stella' ('Star Grass'). The leaves can be stir-fried, or sautéed in butter, and are sometimes blanched before use in salads.

Ribwort Plantain (*P. lanceolata*)

Ribwort Plantain is a hairy perennial herb to 50cm with a rosette of grey-green lanceolate leaves (much longer and thinner than its relatives) with 3-5 pronounced parallel veins, and clusters of tiny flowers held high on tall flower stems. Habitat very variable (especially roadsides, waste ground, paths, unimproved grassland), but avoiding very acidic soil. Native and abundant throughout Europe. The young leaves are a bitter and fibrous famine food. Seed is usable as with other plantains. This plant is also considerably more effective than Dock at reducing irritation from nettle stings.

▼ Ribwort (top right) and Buckshorn (bottom) Plantains

Sea Plantain (*P. maritima*)

Sea Plantain is a perennial herb to 20cm with a dense rosette of narrow, fleshy leaves (untoothed or slightly toothed) and tall, white flower spikes. The leaves do not have the multiple veins/ribs of other members of this genus, just one groove down the centre. Primarily coastal, where it is frequent on sea cliffs, salt marsh and in short turf, but can also be found inland in damp and rocky locations in mountainous areas, and also sometimes by salted roads.

Native to most of Europe, and the entire northern temperate zone. Do not confuse with Sea Arrowgrass (p109), which has potentially poisonous leaves (narrower, with a deeper channel), or the marginally edible Thrift (Armeria maritima), which grows in the same habitat but has smaller, thinner leaves and pink flowers.

This is the best edible plantain, with a rich and pleasant flavour. It is best before the plant flowers, after which it toughens up. Blanch the leaves and serve with butter, or chop into salad. The seeds are also edible.

Ivy-leaved Toadflax (*Cymbalaria muralis*)

Ivy-leaved Toadflax is a perennial herb with straggly, creeping stems, glossy, ivy-shaped leaves (green with purple-tinged edges) and pale purple flowers like miniature Snapdragons. Abundant everywhere apart from the Scottish Highlands, on walls and in rock crevices, occasionally on shingle beaches or railway ballast. Native to Mediterranean Europe, introduced globally.

The flowers and small leaves can be used as decoration. The leaves are available all year as a salad item, but they are rather bitter.

Foxglove (*Digitalis purpurea*)

"In cases of accidental poisoning by Foxglove, after encouraging vomiting until the noxious matter has been removed from the stomach, its effects may be ameliorated by drinking strong green tea mixed with a little brandy..."
(Charles Johnson, 1856)

Foxglove is a biennial or short-lived perennial herb to 1.8m with long, hairy/ downy, wrinkled, oval-pointed leaves with a toothed margin, attached by short, winged stalks. Up to 80 white, pink or purple tubular flowers are produced on very tall stems. It forms a basal rosette in the first year, and a flowering spike in second and subsequent years. Very common throughout temperate Europe in woodland clearings, mountain grassland, moorland, heath and disturbed areas, sometimes sea cliffs, especially on acid soils.

This plant is extremely toxic. When not in flower, it could easily be mistaken for several members of the *Boraginaceae* (p380), and potentially for a whole bunch of other things, but because it smells foul and tastes bitter, the vast majority of historical fatalities were the result of medical rather than culinary misadventure. All above-ground parts contain glycosides capable of causing skin irritation on contact, as well as vomiting, dizziness, delirium and convulsions, headaches and cardiac arrest if consumed. Dosage is critically important for medical use, and individuals vary in their susceptibility to fatal poisoning.

Straw Foxglove (*D. lutea*), grown as an ornamental in the British Isles (native to continental Europe), is also poisonous, but not as deadly as Foxglove.

Brooklime or Water Speedwell
(*Veronica beccabunga*)

"They sometimes grow in small standing waters, but generally near water-cresses, and are sometimes sold for them in markets."
(Nicholas Culpeper, 1652)

Brooklime is an aquatic perennial herb with hollow creeping/rooting stems which sprawl to 60cm, short upright flowering stems, glossy and slightly fleshy oval leaves, and small, bright blue flowers. Native and common in streams, ponds and ditches throughout Europe.

The young shoots and leaves were once widely eaten as a salad plant, though they are bitter raw, and even more so cooked. They are at their best, and least bitter, in late winter and early spring, before the plant flowers. The rest of the **Speedwells (*Veronica*)** are also bitter, but the flowers are edible and are sometimes used decoratively.

Phrymaceae (Lopseed family)
Monkeyflower (*Erythranthe guttata* syn. *Mimulus guttatus*)

Monkeyflower is an annual/perennial herb to 80cm, very variable with small, opposite, pale green leaves and oversized yellow flowers, locally common in most of the British Isles, only absent in the Scottish Highlands. Usually found near water, especially streams, but not always. Introduced from North America in the early 19th century, this plant first spread itself around Britain via the canal network. **Hybrid Monkeyflower (*Mimulus x robertsii*)** is similar, but with red-blotched flowers.

Monkeyflower leaves were eaten by Native Americans and early European settlers in the Rocky Mountains, raw or cooked, though they are rather bitter.

▲ Monkeyflower growing as a self-seeded weed in a large pot.

Lamiaceae (Mint family)

Plants of the Mint family typically have square, or at least angular, stems. This can be an important identifying feature. They include a lot of familiar domesticated herbs, most of which are at their best just before they flower. The ornamental **English Lavender (*Lavandula angustifolia*)** isn't English at all (native to mountainous regions of the south-west Mediterranean), but can be used in small quantities as a flavouring in bakery. **Rosemary (*Rosmarinus officinalis*)** is an evergreen shrub native to southern Europe, but is widely planted in the British Isles as both a herb and an ornamental, including in public parks. **Hyssop (*Hyssopus officinalis*)**, planted as an ornamental in the British Isles and naturalised in a few locations, can be used (sparingly, chopped finely) to flavour sausages and stuffing. **Bodinier's Beauty-berry (*Callicarpa bodinier*)** is an ornamental shrub belonging to this family. It has vivid purple berries, which look misleadingly delicious. They aren't toxic, but they are very bitter, though some of their relatives are used for jam in North America. The above-ground parts of **Betony (*Betonica officinalis*)** were once used to make a popular tea with multiple claimed health benefits, and the leaves and flowers are used in herbal smoking blends. **Blue Bugle (*Ajuga reptans*)** is edible but not especially palatable (historically it was medicinally important). This family is also home to some plants with poisonous seeds. Ray Mears[*] was very ill after consuming the seed of **Hemp Nettles (*Galeopsis*)**, and the leaves are reported to have killed horses and pigs.

* *Wild Food*, Mears, R, and Hillman, G, 2008, Hodder & Stoughton, p284.

Dead-nettles (*Lamium*)

Dead-nettles look like Nettles, but don't sting – this is mimicry to deter would-be eaters of the leaves. The leaves and flowering shoots of all these species can used as pot-herbs, or in stir-fries, and when young can also be chopped raw into salads. The flowers can be used to make a herbal tea.

White Dead-nettle (*L. album*) is a hairy, rhizomatous perennial herb to 60cm, with upright stems, opposite, Nettle-like leaves, and whorls of white flowers. Common on verges, waste ground and other habitats almost everywhere in temperate Europe, though most abundant on dry, neutral soils in lowland areas. In the British Isles, common in England and Wales, rarer in Scotland and Ireland. Easily identified when flowering, otherwise could be confused with many other members of this family, as well as (visually) with true Nettles.

Red Dead-nettle (*L. purpureum*) is an annual herb to 30cm with reddish, hairy stems, toothed oval-cordate leaves (all of which are stalked) and pink-purple flowers. Very common throughout temperate Europe, apart from the coldest northern areas, inhabiting dry roadsides, field margins, forest edges and waste ground, especially in disturbed areas. Not native to the British Isles. This species can germinate at any time, and can often be found in an edible state during the winter. **Cut-leaved Dead-nettle (*L. hybridum*)** is very similar, but with more deeply toothed leaves. **Spotted Dead-nettle (*L. maculatum*)** is an occasional garden escape in the British Isles (native to continental Europe) with pink-purple flowers and a silvery-white blotch or line in the centre of the leaf. Both are similarly edible.

Henbit (Dead-nettle) (*L. amplexicaule*) is an annual herb to 25cm, with more rounded leaves with blunter teeth than Red Dead-nettle and stalkless upper leaves, fused together. Locally common in south and central England on various sorts of disturbed ground, also walls and pavements, rarer elsewhere in the British Isles. Native to southern Europe, but present widely in temperate and subtropical areas, probably accidentally introduced by humans as an arable weed. Milder flavour than most of its closest relatives. The very similar (and also edible) **Northern Dead-nettle (*L. confertum*)** is restricted to Scotland, Ireland, southern Scandinavia and the north of the Netherlands / Germany, though common there.

Yellow Archangel
(*Lamiastrium galeobdolon* syn. *Lamium galeobdolon*)

Yellow Archangel is a hairy perennial herb to 60cm, with creeping runners as well as leafy upright stems, stalked, opposite, oval-cordate toothed leaves and large, bright yellow flowers. Locally common in the south of the British Isles, rarer further north, inhabiting damp woodland and hedgerows, particularly on heavy soil. Common (and native) throughout temperate areas of Europe apart from the coldest parts of the north. There is a domesticated form with silvery leaves (subsp. *argentum*), which is increasingly present as an escape. Uses as Dead-nettles.

▲ White Dead-nettle

▼ Henbit

▲ Red Dead-nettle

▼ Yellow Archangel

Mints (*Mentha*) !

Mentha is a troublesome genus, even for botanists, due the variability of the species, and their tendency to hybridise and mutate. All are used in similar ways: teas and other beverages, sauces, flavouring for desserts and sweets, and also some rice dishes, and garnishes for food and drink. Mints are also used in smoking blends for their flavour. Their scent is their trademark – they all contain menthol – and the best means of telling you've got a mint rather than just a similar-looking member of the *Lamiaceae*. Scent also helps to distinguish between them, but defies detailed description.

While all mints are edible to some extent, they do come with a warning because they contain a compound called pulegone – the highest concentrations occurring in Spearmint, Peppermint and, most notoriously, Pennyroyal (see overleaf). It also occurs in Catmint (see p405). Pulegone is an insecticide, and in mammals can cause nausea and dizziness, and in large doses multiple organ failure and death. It is also an abortifacient, historically used as a contraceptive.

Water Mint (**M. aquatica**) is a common native perennial (to 60cm) found in damp habitats, such as ponds, streams and ditches. Leaves and stems are often purple-tinged (especially when young), flowers (summer) grow among leaves and at stem/branch tips, terminating with a round head. Young leaves and stem tips can be chopped into salads, used to flavour peas, or steeped to make tea. This species has been cultivated since antiquity. The scent is a mixture of 'normal mint' and something else which has been described as 'over-ripe Gorgonzola'.

Water Mint and Chocolate Chip Ice Cream

Ingredients:
200g caster sugar, 180ml water, 8tbsp chopped water mint leaves, 2tbsp water mint flowers, juice of 1 small lemon, 600ml double cream, small bar of very dark chocolate.

Heat the water in a saucepan. Add sugar and bring to the boil, stirring to dissolve the sugar. Add the lemon juice, mint leaves and half of the flowers (taken apart), blitz until smooth, then allow to cool. Stir thoroughly with a whisk when cold, add the cream and roughly chopped chocolate, stir again then put in a freezer until it has the consistency of slush. Stir thoroughly again, then return to the freezer. You can repeat this process two or three times, before leaving it to freeze hard. Serve with the remaining mint flowers as a garnish.

▸ Water Mint

▴ Corn Mint

▴ Whorled Mint

Corn Mint (*M. arvensis*), also known as Field Mint or simply Wild Mint, is another common native perennial herb to 50cm, with broad, usually hairy, opposite, rounded and serrated leaves and mauve flowers which appear only among the leaves, not at stem/branch tips. It is used as a medicinal tea for minor gastric ailments (nausea, flatulence). Historically a weed of cornfields, it is now more often found on woodland rides. This is the mint I see most often in southeast England.

Whorled Mint (*M. x verticillata*) is a common hybrid of Corn Mint and Water Mint, which is usually more similar to Corn Mint (including the scent) than Water Mint, though taller and more robust. Positively identifying it requires close attention to flower structures (exact calyx shape) beyond the scope of this book. You'll need a field guide and hand lens.

"The ancients entwined their wine caps with pennyroyal, and made crowns of it, which were placed on their heads during their repasts [meals], by the aid of which they hoped to escape the troublesome consequences of too copious libations [drinks]. On leaving the table, a small quantity of this plant was taken, to facilitate digestion."
(Alexis Soyer, 1853)

Pennyroyal (*M. pulegium*) is a highly aromatic, upright to prostrate, creeping perennial herb with stems to 40cm, resembling a smaller version of Corn Mint, but with a much stronger smell. It usually inhabits bare, sandy ground, near water. It has become very rare as a native wild plant in the south of the British Isles, and not much more common further north. More frequent in the southern half of Europe. Protected in the UK under the Wildlife and Countryside act 1981.

　　Corsican Mint (*M. requienii*) is a native of southern Europe, but introduced and naturalised further north, including a few locations in the British Isles. Though far smaller than other Mints, forming carpets, like Mind-your-own-business (*Soleirolia soleirolii*), it has similar properties to Pennyroyal, and is the flavouring used in Crème de Menthe.

▾ Corsican Mint　　　　　　▸ Pennyroyal

Spearmint (*M. spicata*) is one of the plants from which mint sauce is made, and the smell is unmistakable for anyone familiar with Spearmint chewing gum. It grows to 90cm tall, with paler and rounder leaves than most of its relatives, and distinctive spear-like flower spikes (though similar to Round-leaved Mint). Native to much of Europe, but not the British Isles, though it has been cultivated since antiquity and regularly escapes.

Gingermint (*M. x gracilis*, not pictured) is the sterile hybrid of Spearmint and Corn Mint, known as Scotchmint and used (commercially) for flavouring gum and mint sweets.

Peppermint (*M. x piperata*, not pictured) is the sterile hybrid of Spearmint and Water Mint, the rarer wild forms generally being less potent than the domesticated varieties. It has longer leaf stalks than most of its relatives, and a distinct smell of its own. Used in desserts – with chocolate, crème fraiche, butter icing, and sometimes mint sauce.

Round-leaved Mint (*M. suaveolens*) is a colony-forming perennial to 1m, that spreads by stolons. The leaves are light green, hairy/downy, with toothed margins. The flowers are in terminal spikes, similar to Spearmint. Native to southern and western Europe, but naturalised elsewhere. Inhabits damp places. It smells slightly of apple, and so is sometimes called 'Apple Mint' (but see below).

Horse Mint (*M. longifolia*, not pictured) is a wild European species which does not occur in the British Isles, with longer leaves than the other mints.

The name 'Apple Mint' can refer to Round-leaved Mint, hybrids of that species and Spearmint (*M. x villosa*, also known

▲ Spearmint

▲ Round-leaved Mint

as Bowles' Mint), and hybrids of Round-leaved Mint and Horse Mint (also known as *M. rotundiflora*). This is nowhere near a complete list of European Mint hybrids.

Calamints (*Clinopodium ascendens / nepeta*) (!)

(Common) Calamint (*C. ascendens*) is a tufted, hairy perennial herb to 60cm with aromatic, rounded-triangular, short-stalked leaves and pale pinkish-purple flowers with purple spots on the lower lip. Frequent in the south of the British Isles, on verges, hedgebanks and rough grassland, becoming rare or absent further north. The aroma and flavour is a mild mixture of mint, marjoram and thyme, and it is used to flavour stews.

Lesser Calamint (*C. nepeta* syn. *calamintha*) is similar, but with much more strongly scented stems and leaves, and looser, branching flower clusters. It is much scarcer (restricted to southern and eastern England in the British Isles). Leaves used as a flavouring in stews and soups, and to make tea. This plant is an important ingredient in Tuscan cuisine. Used sparingly, its strong flavour works well with fatty meats like lamb and pork, but also with game and wild mushrooms. Use in spicy sausages, pasta dishes or as a garnish for pizza. Do not consume if pregnant.

▾ Calamint   ▸ Lesser Calamint

▲ Wild Basil

Wild Basil (*C. vulgare*)

Wild Basil is a hairy perennial herb to 40cm, with straggly, upright, usually unbranched stems and shallow-toothed, oval leaves. Clusters of pinkish-purple flowers without stalks appear in whorls around the stem and open only two or three at a time. Locally common in southern and eastern England on dry, scrubby, unimproved grassland and hedgerows on calcareous soil, rarer elsewhere in the British Isles, and absent from much of Scotland and Ireland. Could be confused with Mints (different scent), Marjoram (less hairy, stalked flowers) or Woundwort (no smell). Dead-nettles have different shaped leaves. This is *not* the wild ancestor of domesticated basil (*Ocimum basilicum*), which is a tropical species. It has a different, much milder flavour, but can be used in similar ways – the leaves and flowering tips are edible fresh as a slightly aromatic component of salads.

Basil Thyme or **Spring Savory (*C. acinos*)** is not a particularly strong-scented plant, but can be used as a salad leaf or mild flavouring. Uncommon and vulnerable in southern and eastern England on dry, rocky or disturbed ground, rare elsewhere.

Catmint or Catnip (*Nepeta cataria*)

Catmint is a perennial herb to 90cm with upright stems and soft, grey, rounded Nettle-shaped leaves, which smell minty when bruised. Tall whorls of white to purple-pink flowers appear at the top of the stems. This is an ancient introduction, occasionally found growing wild in the south and east of England, on roadsides and verges, in grassland or near hedges, especially on chalk, rare elsewhere in the British Isles outside of cultivation.
Used to rub on meats before roasting. Young leaves can be used in salads, like mints. Older leaves only usable for their flavour (then removed before eating). Both leaves and flowers make good wild herbal teas (hot infusion of fresh herb works well). Flowers can be used sparingly as a spice in rice or pasta dishes. Contains pulegone (see p400).

▼ Catmint

▲ Marsh Woundwort

Marsh Woundwort (*Stachys palustris*)

Marsh Woundwort is a hairy perennial herb to 1m, with an unbranched or minimally branching stem and fine-toothed, opposite leaves. The pink flowers grow in loose spikes at the tip of the main stem, and in among the leaves. Resembles a Mint, but taller, with more pointed leaves and no minty scent. Native and locally common in marshes, wet meadows and stream sides. Very easily confused with Hedge Woundwort, but central and upper stem leaves are stalkless, and more lanceolate and the scent is much fainter when the leaves are bruised.

The young shoots are edible, but have an odour many people find unappealing. It is the tubers that are of most interest to foragers. Small but abundant, they are edible, raw or cooked, or dried and made into flour. They taste like sweet potatoes but retain their crunch when cooked, and work particularly well roasted with other root vegetables as part of Sunday lunch (only take 20 minutes in the oven). Widely used in medieval herbal medicine for healing wounds.

Hedge Woundwort (S. *sylvatica*) is similar, but has darker (purple) flowers, is found in drier locations and lacks the tubers. All leaves are stalked, and smell strong and unpleasant when bruised. It isn't poisonous, but does not make pleasant eating. Common in temperate Europe, including most of the British Isles.

▼ Marsh Woundwort tubers

White Horehound (*Marrubium vulgare*)

White Horehound is a densely hairy perennial herb to 60cm, with upright stems covered in white, felty hairs, grey, oval, toothed leaves with a crinkled surface, and dense whorls of white flowers in the leaf axils. Found in short grassland, open woodland, roadsides and waste ground, particularly in coastal areas. This plant is much more common in southern Europe than anywhere north of the Alps and Pyrenees. Uncommon in the British Isles and becoming rarer, though locally common in parts of England, especially the south. Black Horehound (*Ballota nigra*) has an unusably offensive resinous odour, longer and less felty leaves, and pale pink flowers.

The young foliage of White Horehound, well before flowering, is highly aromatic. It is easier to identify visually when in flower, though the smell is still a giveaway, even if not as intense. Used to make a medicinal tea, preferably as a fresh infusion in boiling water. Allowed to stand for an hour and serve with sugar. Historically used to make cough sweets and bitters (see p426).

▲ White Horehound (young foliage)

▲ White Horehound

White Horehound Candy (TF Garrett, 1892)

In the first place make a decoction of Horehound by putting 1oz of the dried leaves of the herb into a basin with sufficient water to cover them, and boiling for ten or twelve minutes. Remove the basin from the fire, cover it over, let it get cold, and press and strain through a fine sieve. Put this into a quart measure, fill up with water, pour it into a saucepan on the fire, and add 41b of granulated sugar and 1 teaspoonful of cream of tartar. Boil to the crack degree [about 150°C], pour the mass on to a slightly-greased marble slab, let it get nearly cold, turn in the edges, and cut the batch into bars by means of a cutter. When quite cold, the bars must be separated, and are then ready for use.

Ground-ivy (*Glechoma hederacea*)

Ground-ivy is a hairy, low-growing perennial herb with creeping non-flowering stems to 40cm, and much smaller upright flowering stems in spring and early summer. The small, stalked, dull dark-green, kidney-shaped leaves have rounded teeth, and the flowers are bright purple-blue. Very common and patch-forming in woods and hedgerows throughout the British Isles, apart from the high mountains, also found in grassland and the edges of arable fields. The leaves might be confused with Golden-saxifrages (p172), which grow in much damper habitats.

Ground-ivy leaves were once used to flavour and clear beer before being replaced by Hops for this use in the 16th century (Johnson tells us the old English name is 'Alehoof'). Before the plant flowers they are edible, but bitter. They are used as a herb, either finely chopped into omelettes or onto soft cheeses, or as a pot-herb. A tea made of the infused leaves and honey was once sold by street traders in London (known as 'gill tea'), and it is as a component of a mixed wild herb tea that it works best. This plant is also an effective remedy for Nettle stings. Just crush the leaves and apply the juice to the stung area. Poisonous to horses and cattle, with fatalities recorded.

Self-heal (*Prunella vulgaris*)

Self-heal is a patch-forming perennial herb to 30cm, with tough, upright and creeping/rooting stems, small, opposite, toothless, oval leaves and whorls of distinctive rectangular blueish-purple (rarely pink or white) flower spikes. Native and common in unimproved grassland, woodland edges, glades and paths, and roadsides, often in damp places.

The leaves can be used as a pot-herb, or in salads. The flowers are used to make a Chinese medicinal 'cooling tea' (leong cha). The leaves can also can be used to make tea, dried or fresh, using hot or cold infusion. As the name implies, this plant is historically of medicinal importance in other places than China. It has been used since antiquity to treat sore throats and mouth ulcers, along with many other conditions.

(Lemon) Balm (*Melissa officinalis*)

Balm is a perennial herb to 70cm with rounded, wrinkled, opposite, Nettle-shaped leaves and small, pale pink flowers in the leaf axils. It is easily identified by the unmistakable lemon-like scent released by the leaves when crushed. Frequent in southern England, on wasteland or near human habitation, usually in shade, rare or absent elsewhere in the British Isles. This is a Roman introduction from southern Europe.

Use to flavour cordials, chilled soft drinks or white wine, liqueurs (it is commercially used for this purpose), marinades, sauces, cakes and desserts. Very young leaves can be added to salads, older leaves are better cooked. Historically used to make a wine. Dried or fresh leaves can be used to make one of the very best herbal teas, for best results infuse the fresh herb in hot water for 15 minutes. Very attractive to bees, and sometimes planted in orchards to attract them as pollinators.

Bastard Balm (*Melittis melissophyllum*) is a rare native relative, restricted to south-west England, south-west Wales and Hampshire (more common further south in Europe). It contains coumarin, and can be used like Sweet Woodruff (p386). The visually similar **Gypsywort (*Lycopus europaeus*)** has leaves with bigger, more jagged teeth, and smaller white flowers and is common in damp locations. It is better known as a black dye plant, though the rhizomatous roots are recorded as a famine food.

▼ (Lemon) Balm

▼ Gypsywort

Wild Marjoram or Oregano
(*Origanum vulgare*)

Wild Marjoram is a slightly hairy, aromatic, rhizomatous perennial (in warmer climates) or annual (in colder climates) herb to 70cm with multiple branching, upright stems. It has opposite and oval leaves, and dense clusters of tiny pinkish-purple (occasionally white) flowers (summer to mid-autumn) on long stalks. Locally common in the south of the British Isles on dry, calcareous grassland, rare in the north. Probably a Roman introduction, but thrives naturalised in the British Isles. This plant has a weaker scent in the colder climate of northern Europe than it does when growing further south, but it is still an important identifying feature. Do not confuse with (Sweet) Marjoram (*O. majorana*) and Pot Marjoram (*O. onites*), which are native to the Mediterranean and unlikely to be found growing wild in northern Europe. Wild Basil (p405) is smaller and has stalkless flowers.

Wild Marjoram is the wild ancestor of some types of domesticated Oregano (other species are also used), and has a stronger smell and flavour. The dried leaves and flowers are used in the same way, especially with strongly flavoured meats such as lamb and game. The fresh leaves can be used similarly, and also sparingly in salads. The dried or fresh leaves, and the flowers, can be used to make a herbal tea.

Thymes (*Thymus*)

Wild Thyme (*T. drucei* syn. *polytrichus*) is a dwarf (to 10cm), woody, mat-forming, evergreen perennial shrub, with reddish stems, small, hairy, oval leaves in opposite pairs, and roundish clusters of small pink flowers (summer). Common on dry, calcareous grassland in south-east England, and cliffs and rocks, grasslands, dunes, and heaths in much of the rest of the British Isles. The foliage smells only faintly like domesticated **Garden Thyme (*T. vulgaris*)**, which is native to southern Europe.

 Large Thyme (*T. pulegioides*) is also perennial, larger than Wild Thyme (to 25cm), more upright and has less of a tendency to form mats, with longer flower heads. Most importantly it smells much more strongly of domesticated Thyme. It is locally common in dry, calcareous grassland in southern England, rare or absent elsewhere. Similar to Wild Marjoram, but half the size. Used as part of a bouquet garni mix, or as flavouring in soups and casseroles. If drying for use as a herb, this is best done shortly before the plant flowers. For tea, it works well as hot infusion of fresh herb. **Breckland Thyme (*T. serpyllum*)** is also sometimes called 'Wild Thyme'. It is very similar to Large Thyme, and present in the British Isles, but rare in the wild (probably restricted to East Anglia) and protected. Cultivated as an ornamental, and used like Garden Thyme.

▲ Wild Thyme

▲ Large Thyme

Sages / Claries (*Salvia*)

Wild Clary or **Wild Sage** (*S. verbenaca*) is a downy perennial herb up to 80cm tall with opposite, oval-oblong leaves with rather random 'teeth', wrinkled like sage, and whorled spikes of small purple-blue flowers. Native, occasional and locally common in southern England and East Anglia on dunes, dry grassland and roadsides, preferring alkaline soil and sunny locations. Rare/absent elsewhere in the British Isles. The leaves are like a mild version of Sage, and used as an aromatic herb in cooked dishes, the flowers raw in salads or as a garnish. Seeds used to thicken soups and stews. Also used in herbal smoking blends.

 Clary Sage (*S. sclarea*) is a native of southern Europe, but grown as an ornamental further north, and can be used as Wild Clary. **Meadow Clary** (*S. pratensis*) is a rare, protected native in the British Isles, much more common in continental Europe and historically used to flavour beer. The edible **(Garden) Sage** (*S. officinalis*), is primarily a Mediterranean species, and a rare

▲ Wood Sage

garden escape in the British Isles. The very common **Wood Sage** (*Teucrium scorodonia*) is not closely related. Its tough, unpalatable leaves contain toxins that cause liver damage, although they were also historically used as flavouring for beer.

Clary Water (TF Garrett, 1892)

A cordial composed of Clary-flowers macerated in brandy, with a small proportion of cinnamon and a little ambergris. After straining, the liquor is sweetened with syrup. The proportion of the ingredients used vary according to taste. Considered a good aid to digestion.

◄ Wild Clary

Orobanchaceae (Broomrape family)

The *Orobanchaceae* are parasitic plants, some of which are occasionally mistaken for fungi. 'Broomrape' (for *Orobanche* sp.) refers to the fact that the plant often parasitises Broom (p190). Broomrapes are mildly toxic (gastric symptoms). Other members of this family worthy of note are the Eyebrights (*Euphrasia*), some of which have been important medicinal herbs for treating eye conditions. The leaves are edible but bitter.

(Common) Toothwort
(*Lathraea squamaria*)

Toothwort is a native perennial parasite of trees, especially Hazel (p260). It has no identifiable leaves, only creamy white tooth-shaped scales and one-sided spikes of short-lived pale pinky-cream flowers. Locally frequent in damp locations, usually near streams in deciduous woodland. The peppery roots are edible sliced raw into salads, cooked as a pot-herb or in stir-fries, or dried and powdered for use as a seasoning.

(Common) Lousewort
(*Pedicularis sylvatica*)

Lousewort is a semi-parasitic biennial or short-lived perennial herb to 20cm, with multiple stems and short-stalked, opposite leaves with pinnate lobes and toothed margins, and a raceme of pink-purple flowers. Common on damp heathland and grassland throughout most of temperate Europe, though rare in much of England, especially the centre. The leaves of Lousewort were traditionally eaten in Galicia, Spain.[*] The flowers are also edible. All parts are used in smoking mixtures, for flavour and sedative effects. The much rarer Marsh Lousewort (*P. palustris*) is taller (to 60cm), with a single stem and far more flowers. It is declining, and should not be picked.

* *Ethnobotanical review of wild edible plants in Spain*, 2006, Tardío, J, et al, Botanical Journal of the Linnean Society. Vol 152, issue 1, pp27-71.

Oleaceae (Olive family)

Olives (*Olea europaea*) are strictly native to the Mediterranean. People do try to grow them in the British Isles, with rather limited success so far. This family is also home to the ornamental Privet (*Ligustrum*), which is native to southern Asia but widely naturalised/invasive. The black berries are toxic (containing syringin, which causes gastric and nervous symptoms, and potentially death).

(Common) Jasmine (*Jasminium officinale*)

Jasmine is a scrambling deciduous shrub to 10m with deeply pinnate leaves and clusters of strongly scented white (often tinged pink-purple) summer flowers. It is a popular ornamental, and sometimes self-seeds in the British Isles. Native range is unclear, though probably includes south-east Europe as well as parts of Asia. The flowers are used to scent tea.

Lilac (*Syringa vulgaris*)

Lilac is a suckering deciduous shrub or small tree to 7m. It has ovate leaves with cordate to truncate bases and strongly scented lilac or white flowers in terminal panicles. Native to south-east Europe, but widely grown as an ornamental and spreads through suckers. To capture the heady floral scent without the bitterness, Lilac can be used to make wine, cordial or 'champagne' (follow one of the many Elderflower Champagne recipes online).

Ash (*Fraxinus excelsior*)

Ash is a deciduous tree to 30m with smooth, grey bark and large pinnate leaves having multiple fine-toothed leaflets. It has thick twigs, distinctive black vegetative buds, flowers that appear before the leaves and winged fruits that hang in large bunches. Prefers damp and calcareous soils, where it is still very common at the time of writing, though under attack from a fungus called Ash Dieback. Native in Europe apart from northern Scandinavia and the southern half of the Iberian peninsula.

The mature seeds can be pressed to make an oil, and the cambium is a famine food, but the main food use is the immature samaras (or 'keys', because they dangle like a bunch of keys). Pickled Ash keys taste a bit like a cross between olives and pickled walnuts, and are used to accompany other foods. It took me several attempts to get these right. Firstly, they must be picked when very young – before the seed has started to form – any later and they get tough and stringy. Secondly, they must be properly prepared, which takes repeated simmering. Thirdly, wait at least three months before you open the jar, and preferably six.

Pickled Ash Keys

Ingredients:
800g ash keys (debris carefully removed), 1.5l white distilled vinegar, paprika, cayenne pepper, curry powder, whole peppercorns, mustard seeds, garlic, dried chillies, 3tbsp salt.

Simmer the ash keys in 4 changes of water, for 15 mins each time. Then add the salt and simmer for another hour. Meanwhile, put your three powdered spices in the vinegar and bring to the boil, then take off the heat and allow to cool. When the ash keys have finished their hour's boiling, strain again. Now return your spiced vinegar to the heat, add the ash keys and the four whole spices, simmer for 15 mins. Pour into sterilised jars.

Solanales

Solanaceae (Nightshade family)

The Nightshades include tomatoes, potatoes and tobacco, all of which are American natives that turn up as escapes and relics of cultivation. Tomato leaves are edible. **Cape Gooseberry (*Physalis peruviana*)** and **Chinese Lantern (*P. alkekengi*)** have edible berries, and also occasionally escape in the British Isles. Most of the native European members are poisonous and some are psychoactive – this family is known for its mythology and medicinal properties, sometimes verging on the magical.

Henbane (*Hyciscyamus niger*)

Henbane is an annual to biennial upright herb to 80cm, with sticky/hairy oval-oblong leaves and very distinctive lurid, purple-veined, pale yellow flowers. Very locally common on parts of the south and east English coast in dry, sandy, disturbed areas, but nationally rare. It is extremely poisonous, though rarely fatal, containing tropane alkaloids (see Deadly Nightshade, p419), but foul-smelling and very unlikely to confused with anything edible. The infamous Dr Crippen used this plant to poison his wife in 1910.

Thorn-apple (*Datura stramonium*)

Thorn-apple is an annual herb to 1.5m with upright, multiply branching stems, alternate leaves with an irregular margin and asymmetrical base, unmistakable trumpet-shaped flowers which are usually white, but occasionally pink or violet, and spiny fruits. Native to North America, introduced widely in temperate and warmer zones. In Europe it usually inhabits waste ground, roadsides and farmyards. Frequent escape from cultivation in parts of England, rare elsewhere in the British Isles.

All parts are toxic, especially the flowers and seeds. It was famously used to poison British soldiers who came to quell an uprising on Jamestown Island in Virginia in 1607 (none of whom died, but several 'went mad' for over a week). Thorn-apple has been used as a medicine, and might well be effective in some cases, but dosage is critically important, making it very dangerous to use. The effects are similar to Deadly Nightshade (see opposite). It could potentially be confused with some of the edible members of the *Amaranthaceae*, especially Maple-leaved Goosefoot (p349).

Deadly Nightshade (*Atropa belladonna*)

Deadly Nightshade is an upright perennial herb to 2m with multiply branching stems, alternate, entire ovate leaves, upright purple-brown tubular flowers and drooping, shiny, cherry-like berries that sit on a five-pointed base and turn from green through red to black. It inhabits hedgerows, often in damp and shady places. Frequent in England, apart from the far south west, uncommon or rare in the rest of the British Isles. Native to most of Europe, more common in the south. This plant would be considerably more common had it not been intentionally eradicated from many places by humans.

Deadly Nightshade contains a cocktail of toxins, primarily tropane alkaloids. It causes a wide range of symptoms associated with severe disruption to the nervous system, including hallucinations (victims may start talking gibberish or swipe at imaginary flying objects) and eventually death by respiratory failure. It also causes constipation, unusually for a plant toxin. This species was used in antiquity as poison for murdering humans, as well as for various medicinal and cosmetic effects (it causes pupils to dilate, from where the Latin name comes – 'beautiful lady'). It has been grown as a medicinal crop in more recent times, for extracting active ingredients to use as an antidote to some nerve gases and pesticides, and to the mycotoxin muscarine. The whole plant is poisonous. The foliage can cause skin irritation, and while the roots are the most poisonous part, it is the attractive berries that pose the greatest danger, especially to children. They have been mistaken for Bilberries (p373) by adults.

▲ Duke of Argyll's Teaplant or Gojiberry

Duke of Argyll's Teaplant or Gojiberry (*Lycium barbarum*)

The Duke of Argyll's Teaplant is a scrambling perennial shrub to 3m, with ovate to lanceolate leaves, pinkish-purple flowers and red berries (late summer to mid-autumn). It is native to China, introduced in Europe and primarily used as hedging, though also found on waste ground. More common in the south of the British Isles than the north, particularly in coastal areas. **Chinese Teaplant (*L. chinense*)** is another introduction, rarer, with larger flowers, but equally edible fruits.

When this plant was introduced to the British Isles in the 1730s by the 3rd Duke of Argyll, its label had been mixed up with a tea plant, and the unusual name stuck. More recently its berries have become a familiar health-food product. They taste better dried than fresh. I searched for a long time before I found any growing wild, eventually finding a few bushes a couple of miles from my home, perched perilously on the edge of an exposed cliff. Many seedlings had also taken root at the base of the cliff, but the berries were few and far between. Fortunately, the young shoots and leaves are also edible, cooked as a green vegetable.

Woody Nightshade (*Solanum dulcamara*) ⓘ

Woody Nightshade or **Bittersweet** is a scrambling/climbing perennial with woody-based stems that can exceed 4m, and heart-shaped or triangular leaves which sometimes have small lobes at the base. Loose clusters of drooping purple and yellow flowers in summer are followed by red berries in autumn. Common in woodland and hedgerows, also on walls, and especially near water, throughout the lowland British Isles. There is a prostrate, coastal variety (var. *maritimum*), with thicker leaves.

All parts of the plant are poisonous, especially the unripe berries. They are potentially deadly, though serious cases are rarely recorded, the toxin involved is presumed to be solanine (see Black Nightshade on p423). Symptoms of poisoning are typically nausea and dizziness. The name 'bittersweet' is a translation of the Latin dulcamara, and it refers to the taste of both the berries and the leaves. The toxin solanine initially tastes bitter, and then becomes sweet.

▾ Woody Nightshade on a sandy beach.

Black Nightshade (*Solanum nigrum*) (!)

Black Nightshade is an upright perennial herb/shrub to 80cm with ovate to heart-shaped, grey-green leaves, green-white flowers and purple-black berries which can be dull or shiny. Common in England and most of Wales in woodland, hedgerows, arable fields (where it can become a problem weed) and disturbed ground, rare or absent in most of Scotland. Black Nightshade lacks the woody stem base of Woody Nightshade, and the fruits are much darker. Black Nightshade also has berries arranged in bunches, rather than the singletons of Deadly Nightshade. There are similar introduced species. **Green Nightshade (*S. physafolium*)** has paler foliage and berries that ripen to yellow-brown. Introduced to the British Isles from South America in 1949, currently spreading (mainly East Anglia, on arable land).

I could find no reliable information about its edibility/toxicity. **Red Nightshade (*S. villosum*)** is native to southern Europe, and has yellow to red berries, which are edible like those of Black Nightshade.

It was from the unripe berries of Black Nightshade that solanine – the toxin in the green parts of potato plants – was first isolated. The berries become edible as they ripen, tasting mild and savoury, rather like tomatoes. It took over a century after their arrival from the New World to convince Europeans that tomatoes were edible, but their native relative has been subjected to an edibility dispute for much longer. Both the berries and leaves of this plant have been extensively eaten historically, both foraged and cultivated. The berries are particularly popular in the Volga German community, who call them Schwartzbeeren ('blackberries') and use them with coffee in a cake or to fill dumplings.

The green berries are certainly poisonous, especially raw. It is the cooked black berries and fresh foliage tops that are eaten. There are reports that some toxic alkaloids can be produced under certain soil conditions, and others that the toxicity of this plant varies quite widely, either because it is a species complex with some varieties more toxic than others, or for reasons currently unknown.

For maximum safety the berries should be cooked and used in preserves and pies, and some people recommend that the leaves should be cooked for at least 5 minutes before discarding the water. I have eaten the leaves and the ripe berries, uncooked, on several occasions with no problems, though I have never eaten a large amount in one go.

Black Nightshade, Courgette and Tomato Salad (traditional Turkish)

Ingredients:
500g black nightshade tops, 2 courgettes (sliced), 2 large ripe tomatoes, 3tbsp olive oil, 2 garlic cloves (grated), sea salt.

Bring a large pot of water to the boil and put in the courgettes and whole tomatoes. After 5 mins, remove the tomatoes and put the nightshade and courgette onto a serving plate. Skin the tomatoes, break them up with a fork and mix with the garlic, olive oil and salt and pour the mixture over the nightshade and courgette. Serve immediately (warm).

Asterales

The Asterales is a very large order of plants, most of which are small herbs. The whole order utilises inulin rather than starch as an energy storage molecule, which is rather indigestible and causes wind.

Menyanthaceae (Bogbean family)
Bogbean (*Menyanthes trifoliata*)

Bogbean is an aquatic perennial herb with thick, grey-green, fleshy leaves like Giant Clover (or Broad Bean), and spikes of unusual, hairy, white flowers. Locally common in most of the British Isles, in bogs, ponds and fens, rare in south-east England. Common in most of northern Europe, including the extreme north.

Bogbean tea, made from the leaves, is commercially available. Historically it was used in place of hops to flavour beer, and to improve the flavour of herbal cigarettes made primarily from Coltsfoot (p438). The roots are a famine food, but they require drying, grinding and washing to render them edible. Bogbean has also been used as a medicine for rheumatism, poor appetite and upset stomachs.

Fringed Water-lily (*Nymphoides peltata*)

Fringed Water-lily is a rhizomatous aquatic perennial to 1.5m, superficially similar to Yellow Water-lily (p102) but much smaller, and unrelated. The dark green floating leaves are up to 11cm across and the yellow flowers have a frilly fringe. Inhabits still and slow-moving water, up to 1.5m deep. Rather rare as a native wild flower in the British Isles, more common as an escape/introduction. Native and frequent in lowland temperate Europe, absent in mountains and the far north.

The flowers, leaves and peeled stems are all edible, although various sources rank them anywhere between delicious and poor. I have never tried eating any part of them.

Asteraceae (Daisy family)

The *Asteraceae* are the largest plant family, and their trademark is composite flowers. What we naturally assume to be a single daisy flower is actually composed of multiple flowers (or 'florets'). Many of these develop into hairy/fluffy parachutes (a 'pappus') for carrying seeds away on the wind. Relatively few have ever been important food. The only leaf crops are Lettuce (p444) and Chicory/Raddichio/Endive (p440). **Sunflower (*Helianthus annuus*)** is an important oilseed crop, native to America, which also has edible petals, and can sometimes be found growing semi-wild in Europe, most often on rubbish tips. **Jerusalem Artichokes (*H. tuberosus*)** are another American species in the same genus, the tubers of which will survive a long time without human assistance, but their quality rapidly degrades unless they are lifted and replanted in nutrient-enriched soil. **Artichokes (*Cynara*)** are a genus of mainly subtropical thistle-like plants that include two closely related crop species native to the Mediterranean: the **Cardoon** or **'Wild Artichoke' (*C. cardunculus*)** and the **Globe Artichoke (*C. scolymus*)**. Two other southern European species (***C. humilis*** and ***cornigera***) are also edible, more often foraged than grown. None of these are yet naturalised in the British Isles.

There are numerous marginally edible wild species. The young leaves of the **Bur-marigolds (*Bidens spp.*)** are edible (cooked), as are those of salt marsh/cliff plant **Golden Samphire (*Limbarda crithmoides*)**, which taste both bitter and salty. You can eat the leaves and flowers of native **Goldenrod (*Solidago virgaurea*)** and **Canadian Goldenrod (*S. canadensis*)**, which is naturalised in the British Isles. **Cornflower**

▲ Golden Samphire

(*Centaurea cyanus*) was once a very common weed of arable fields, but modern farming techniques have left it almost extinct in the wild. The flowers are edible, used in salads and also some tea blends, and were used in Poland to make a fermented drink. **Common Knapweed (*C. nigra*)** can be used in a similar manner. **Curry Plant (*Helichrysum italicum*)** is native to Mediterranean, but grown further north as an ornamental. It is used as a flavouring during cooking (like Bay leaves). ***Dahlia spp.***, native to Central America and widely planted as an ornamental, has edible flowers and (also tasty) tubers. **Pot Marigolds (*Tagetes spp.*)** have edible flowers (hence 'pot'). The young shoots of **Alpine Sowthistle (*Cicerbita alpina*)** were traditionally eaten, either raw or cooked in reindeer milk. This plant is restricted to northern Scandinavia and some mountainous regions further south in Europe, and is very rare and protected in the UK.

There are some very common toxic species. **Ragworts** and **Groundsels (*Jacobaea* and *Senecio* spp.)** contain a cocktail of pyrrolizidine alkaloids causing, among other things, irreversible liver damage and DNA damage to cells. These can be absorbed through the skin, so avoid touching them if possible.

Mugwort (*Artemisia vulgaris*) ⓘ

Mugwort is a hairy perennial herb to 2m with multiply branching upright stems, deeply cut leaves which are dark green and hairless on top and silvery-grey and finely hairy underneath, and spikes of tiny red-brown flowers. Common throughout Europe on waste ground, roadsides and hedgerows and beside paths. The smell is distinctive and some people find it unpleasant. **Chinese Mugwort (A. *verlotorium*)** is a recent introduction, becoming more frequent as an escape by the Thames in London and also parts of northern England. The leaves have darker upper sides than Mugwort and longer, narrower lobes. It has similar uses, and a stronger smell.

Mugwort leaves are edible, but should be used sparingly because the flavour is very strong. Traditionally used in Germany in goose stuffing. The peeled young stems can be eaten in salads. Mugwort jelly is an accompaniment to meats. Mugwort tea is commercially available dried, and the fresh plant works well as a cold infusion. Contains small amounts of thujone (see opposite). In Korea, a close relative known as 'Sssuk' or Korean Mugwort (*A. princeps*) is used to make a soup with fermented soy bean paste and flounder. It is traditionally eaten in spring, as the taste of both main ingredients is at their best in March.

Mugwort's name refers to its use in flavouring beer (in England), which used to be drunk from mugs rather than glasses. It is also used to make bitters – strong alcoholic drinks infused with aromatic plants, originally medicinal but becoming more popular as cocktail ingredients. Mugwort is often combined with Horehound (p407) to this effect: take 50g of Mugwort Leaves and 50g of Horehound leaves/buds and infuse them in a bottle of Madeira wine for two weeks, and decant before use.

Mugwort is reputed to make dreams more vivid, semi or fully lucid and memorable, either smoked or drunk as tea. Wild food experimentalist and educator Fergus Drennan has said he finds this more effective when the fresh plant is placed inside his pillowcase.

Wormwood (*A. absinthium*) (!)

"The leaves of wormwood are used in salad to make it more digestible and heighten the flavour. They are preserved in vinegar, and to season dishes. Lastly, they are considered by some persons as a remedy, and the frequent use of them to be indispensable for the preservation of their existence."
(**Alexis Soyer, 1853**)

Wormwood is a perennial herb to 1m, with deeply cut leaves which have blunt tips to their lobes, and small drooping flowers (summer). The whole plant is silvery-grey and silky-hairy, with a very strong scent. Ancient introduction, locally frequent in old quarries and gravel pits, and on other waste ground. More common in central England than other parts of the British Isles.

Wormwood was used to expel intestinal worms, and is allegedly the active ingredient of the French spirit absinthe. Absinthe was prohibited across Europe in the 20th century because of alleged psychoactive properties (Launert warns of its potential to cause "severe brain damage"[*]). No psychoactive ingredient but alcohol has ever been identified. Thujone, once claimed to be responsible, does not fit the bill, although its actual effects are still much debated.[†] The leaves of this plant therefore do qualify as edible (though bitter), but should not be consumed in pregnancy.

Sea Wormwood (*A. maritima*), reputed to have similar properties and uses, is a frequent find in temperate European salt marshes.

[*] *Edible and Medicinal Plants of Britain and Europe*, Launert, E, 1981, Hamlyn.
[†] *Thujone, a widely debated volatile compound: What do we know about it?*, Németh, ÉZ, and Nguyen, HT, 2020, Phytochem Rev 19, pp405-423.

▲ Wormwood   ▼ Sea Wormwood

Yarrows (*Achillea*) (!)

Yarrow (*A. millefolium*) is a sweet-scented, hairy perennial herb with stiff, unbranched, upright stems to 80cm, and alternate, very feathery bipinnate/tripinnate dark green leaves (the whole leaves are longer and thinner than Pineappleweed and the Mayweeds (pp432-433). It has dense, flat-topped, umbellifer-like clusters of white to pink flowers (midsummer to mid-autumn) and smells like Crysanthemums. Abundant throughout temperate Europe on disturbed ground, grassland, roadsides, sand dunes and open woodland.

Tender *young* (before the flowering shoots get going) Yarrow leaves and shoots are a passable component of a wild salad or stew, though somewhat bitter even then – they have been compared to Rosemary. The plant was used to flavour beer before the widespread use of Hops. Both the leaves and flowers are also used to flavour various types of stronger alcoholic drinks, as well soft drinks, and as a herbal tea reputed to be effective against fever (see Culpeper quote, left). Historically, it was used to staunch bleeding, possibly because it lowers blood pressure and has anti-microbial properties (the genus name is derived from the Greek god Achilles, who supposedly used it for this purpose after battles), and as a mild painkiller. In China, dried Yarrow stalks are used for I-Ching divination. Also used in herbal smoking mixtures. Yarrow can cause skin irritation in some individuals, and is mildly poisonous to dogs, cats and horses.

▾ Yarrow (leaves lower left are Silverweed)

▲ Sneezewort   ▼ Fernleaf Yarrow

Sneezewort or **European Pellitory (*A. ptarmica*)** is a slightly smaller plant with larger flowers, lanceolate-linear leaves and similar properties, though the flavour is rather stronger. It also induces sneezing. It is fairly common in the British Isles, though preferring colder and wetter places than Yarrow. Used sparingly in sauces, sausages and stuffing.

    Fernleaf Yarrow (*A. filipendulina*) is larger (to 1.3m) with rough, hairy, serrated, pinnate leaves and complex yellow flower heads. It has a very strong smell, and dries with an odour of mint mixed with curry. Native to Asia, grown as an ornamental in Europe, and sometimes found in abundance on roadsides. Uses are somewhere between Yarrow (opposite) and Tansy (overleaf).

Tansy (*Tanacetum vulgare* syn. *Chrysanthemum vulgare*)

"... in regard of its domineering relish, sparingly mixt with our cold *Sallet*, and much fitter (tho' in very small quantity) for the Pan, being qualified with the Juices of other fresh Herbs, *Spinach*, *Green Corn*, *Violet*, *Primrose-Leaves*, &c. at entrance of the Spring, and then fried brownish, is eaten hot with the Juice of *Orange* and *Sugar*, as one of the most agreeable of all the boil'd *Herbaceous* Dishes."

(John Evelyn, 1699)

Tansy is an aromatic, creeping perennial herb to 1.2m, with robust, upright stems tinged purplish-red and finely cut, frilly, pinnate leaves. The flat-topped golden yellow flower heads are more strongly scented than the leaves. An ancient introduction, much cultivated historically both as a herb and an ornamental, now frequent on riverbanks, roadsides, waste ground and rough grassland. More common in England and Wales than in Scotland, and uncommon in Ireland, but present in most of temperate Europe.

The finely chopped young leaves were once popular in France as a filling for omelettes, and also used as a spice in bakery, like cinnamon and nutmeg.

The leaves can be used in salads, but the taste is a bit overpowering. Flowers can be used as a garnish for food or cocktails, or for tea. All parts, but especially the flowers, can cause an allergic reaction which can be severe. Contains thujone (see Wormwood, p427), and should not be eaten during pregnancy, and only eaten in small quantities at any time.

Feverfew (*T. parthenium*)

Feverfew is a strongly aromatic perennial herb to 70cm with slightly hairy, upright, branching stems, deeply lobed, yellow-green leaves and Daisy-like flowers. An ancient introduction, frequently found as a more recent garden escape, usually on walls or rocky waste ground close to human settlement. In its natural range it inhabits mountain scrub.

The part most commonly used is the flowers, as a flavouring in bakery and pastries. They are also made into a herbal tea, traditionally used to prevent and relieve headaches.

Tansy Pudding (traditional English)

This dish was eaten at Easter and other spring festivals. Easy to make, and well worth trying.

Ingredients:
85g white breadcrumbs, 30g sugar, 15g butter, 2 eggs, 250ml milk, 3tsp of finely chopped tansy leaves.

Boil the milk and pour over the breadcrumbs, leave for 30 mins, beat the eggs, add the sugar, tansy and butter, then bake in a pie dish at 175°C / fan 155°C until set. Serve cold with double cream and more sugar.

Pineappleweed (*Matricaria discoidea*)

Pineappleweed is an upright annual herb to 35cm with finely frilly leaves with a strong pineapple scent, especially when crushed, that some people find unpleasant. The flowers lack petals. Late Victorian introduction from Asia which has become an abundant weed throughout temperate Europe, mainly found in disturbed or trampled ground and arable fields.

The flower heads can be eaten raw or cooked, or made (usually dried) into a pineapple-flavoured tea that was traditionally popular in Greece. Before the plant flowers, the leaves are edible in salads – slightly bitter, but otherwise tasting as they smell.

Scented Mayweed (*M. chamomilla*)

Scented Mayweed or **German Chamomile** is an upright annual herb to 60cm with feathery leaves and Daisy-like flowers. It is a locally common (esp. England and Wales) weed of arable fields and other disturbed habitats. Has a mild chamomile or apple aroma, especially when crushed. Ancient introduction to British Isles, native to southern/eastern Europe.

The young shoots can be used as a flavouring, but they are bitter. The flowers can be gently dried in a warm, sunny location to make a herbal tea (this is the plant used to make what is called 'chamomile tea'), and as a flavouring for sauces and desserts. Also used as a medicinal herb for gastric complaints and as a sleep aid.

The more common and rather variable **Scentless Mayweed (*Tripleurospermum inodorum*)** is similar, but scentless. **Sea Mayweed (*T. maritimum*)** has fleshier leaves and is only found very close to the sea. Neither of them have any food uses. **Common** or **Roman Chamomile (*Chamaemelum nobile*)** is native but uncommon to extinct in much of the British Isles (only common in coastal grassland in parts of the deep south) and while also used medicinally and for tea, is rather bitter for eating. More common further south in Europe. It smells of apple.

▸ Scented Mayweed

Gallant-soldier (*Galinsoga parviflora*)

Gallant-soldier is an annual herb to 80cm
with upright, branching stems, opposite,
slightly toothed leaves and flowers a bit
like Daisies but with very short ray florets. A
Victorian introduction from South America,
it is now locally common in the wild in
parts of England, mostly in urban areas (esp.
London) and man-made habitats, sometimes
arable fields and allotments. The leaves,
stem and flowering shoots are all edible,
raw or cooked, with a mild flavour by the
standards of this family.

▲ Gallant-soldier

    Shaggy Soldier (*G. quadriradiata*) is
similar but much hairier (introduced from
Mexico). It is also edible, and becoming
more common than Gallant-soldier, in
similar places.

Elecampane (*Inula helenium*)

Elecampane is an upright perennial herb
to 2.5m, with stout, finely hairy stems,
ovate stem leaves and large yellow flowers.
Native to Asia, ancient introduction in the
British Isles, once common as an escape but
rarer now as it is less frequently cultivated;
frequent in much of temperate Europe
(absent in northern Scandinavia).

▲ ▼ Elecampane

    The roots are made into a commercially
popular medicinal tea. Eaten by the Romans,
preserved in a mixture of water, honey and
vinegar, though it isn't clear whether this
was regarded as food or medicine.*
They are too bitter to be treated as a
normal vegetable.

* *Mediterranean Wild Edible Plants*, edited
by Sánchez-Mata, M, and Tardio, J, 2016.

**Sea Aster (*Tripolium pannonicum*
syn. *Aster tripolium*)**

Sea Aster is a hairless upright annual or
biennial herb to 1m, with stout stems
and fleshy, untoothed, dark grey-green,
lanceolate leaves (lower ones stalked, stem
leaves stalkless). The dense clusters of
flowers in late summer come in two colour
schemes. They all have yellow centres, but
the rays can either be pale purple-blue, or
also yellow. Locally common in salt marsh
and other coastal habitats all around the
British Isles and Europe.

Can be confused with Michaelmas-daisies
(*A. amellus*), which are introduced and
inhabit non-saline environments (usually waste
ground, sometimes riverbanks). Confusion of
young plants with Sea Lavenders (*Limonium*)
is also possible, though the flowers are very
different. Both are bitter but not poisonous.

Sea Aster leaves can be used raw in
salads or blanched as a side vegetable,
or pickled. Their interesting flavour and
firm texture have made them popular as
a gourmet treat (featured on the menu
at Noma), served blanched and buttered,
perhaps with garlic. Also used in stir-fries.

Oxeye Daisy (*Leucanthemum vulgare*)

"Daisy, *Buphthalmum*, Ox-Eye, or *Bellis-major*: The young *Roots* are frequently eaten by the *Spaniards* and *Italians* all the Spring till *June*."
(John Evelyn, 1699)

Oxeye Daisy is a rhizomatous perennial herb to 75cm with stiff, upright stems and large Daisy-like flowers. The stalked lower leaves are round or oval, with broad teeth, and the stalkless upper leaves have large, blunt teeth. Common throughout Europe, mainly in dry, grassy habitats, avoiding acidic soil.

Flowers can be used like Dandelion for wine. Closed flower heads are popular pickled like capers. Leaves and young shoots in spring can be used in salads, but best cooked – the taste is strong and interesting. As for the roots, they have the same pleasant taste but they really do have to be young to be classed as edible.

Common Daisy (*Bellis perennis*)

Common Daisy is a small perennial herb with a basal rosette of spoon-shaped leaves and flowers recognisable by everyone. Abundant in short grassland everywhere in Europe apart from the extreme north; persistent lawn weed.

The leaves and flowers can be used in salads, although they are rather bitter (less so when cooked). The unopened flowers can be turned into capers.

▲ ▼ Oxeye Daisy

▼ Common Daisy'

▲ Oxeye Daisy

Oxeye Daisy Greens with Onions and Garlic

Ingredients:

150g oxeye daisy (young greens and unopened flower buds, roughly chopped), 1 medium onion (chopped), 2 cloves of garlic (finely chopped), seasoning.

Fry the onion in olive oil until they start to go soft, then add garlic and fry for another minute, then add the greens and stir-fry for 2 mins. Season and serve.

Coltsfoot (*Tussilago farfara*) ⓘ

Coltsfoot is a perennial herb to 20cm with solitary yellow flowers similar to those of Dandelion, on purple-scaled upright stems. These appear in early spring, before the leaves, which are long-stalked, hoof-shaped, rounded-triangular and cordate, up to 30cm across. Locally common on waste ground, disturbed ground (especially landslips), steep slopes, arable land, dunes and cliffs, especially in coastal areas or near water. Common throughout temperate Europe. Can be confused with Butterbur, opposite, which is larger and has more rounded leaves, or Purple Coltsfoot (*Homogyne alpina*), which has kidney-shaped leaves and purple-red flowers, and is native to the Alps and Pyrenees but present elsewhere as an ornamental or rare garden escape.

Coltsfoot has been historically used as both food and medicine. The flowers and leaves have been eaten, raw and cooked, wine can be made from the flowers (like Dandelion) and an extract of Coltsfoot is a key ingredient of a 'regional heritage' type of confectionery from Lancashire, England, called 'Coltsfoot Rock'. This type of sweet was inspired by the use of this plant as a cough remedy in traditional western herbal medicine. It is also important in traditional Chinese medicine, for a variety of throat and lung disorders, including asthma and colds. The dried leaves were once smoked as a cure for asthma. There is conflicting evidence regarding its effectiveness for any of these purposes, but conclusive evidence that it contains carcinogenic pyrrolizidine alkaloids: it causes liver cancer. The unprocessed plant shouldn't be used, either as a food or a medicine.

Butterbur (*Petasites hybridus*) ⚠

Butterbur is a patch-forming, rhizomatous perennial herb to 50cm with pink racemes of flowers that appear before rounded, cordate leaves (like Coltsfoot but much bigger and with toothed edges) on long, hollow stalks. Frequent in damp ground, especially near rivers, in most of the British Isles, rare/absent in the Scottish Highlands. Frequent in most of temperate Europe. White Butterbur (*P. albus*) is a slightly smaller version, native to mountainous areas of continental Europe but introduced widely elsewhere. Giant Butterbur (*P. japonicus*) is an enormous plant, with leaves up to 1m across, native to Japan and planted ornamentally in Europe. Winter Heliotrope (*P. pyrenaicus*) is a semi-invasive naturalised alien (from the Mediterranean) with round leaves which might be mistaken for Monk's Rhubarb (p320), though the leaves are much smaller. It is bitter, but apparently non-toxic.

Butterbur gets its name from the traditional use of the leaves to wrap and store butter. The stems have been used as food, but it is much better known for its medicinal uses, which are similar to those of Coltsfoot and also for migraines and allergic rhinitis. However, as with Coltsfoot, Butterbur contains carcinogenic pyrrolizidine alkaloid, so only professionally produced extracts are safe to use.

Chicory (*Cichorium intybus*)

Chicory or **(Wild) Succory** is a slightly woody
perennial herb to 1.2m with stiff, grooved,
branching, upright stems and lanceolate-
oval leaves of variable shape (sometimes
unlobed apart from at the bases, sometimes
lobed all the way to the top). The flowers
resemble bright blue (occasionally white
or pink) Dandelions, on short, thick stalks,
in pairs. It has a large tap root. Introduced
in antiquity as a fodder plant, now found
growing wild or as a more recent escape,
on grassland, roadsides and waste ground,
especially on calcareous soil. Frequent in
England, rarer elsewhere in the British Isles.
Frequent to common throughout Europe,
apart from the far north. Native to eastern
Asia, introduced in Europe.

Chicory is the wild ancestor of
Radicchio and some types of domesticated
endive. Its primary use is as a salad
vegetable, the very young leaves in spring
being the best for this purpose, soon
becoming bitter. Wild Chicory is popular
in Italy, where it is cooked with salt, garlic,
chilli and olive oil, and served with pasta.
The leaves can also be used as a pot-herb.
In all cases they taste better if blanched by
'earthing up' to exclude light when they are
young. The flower buds, though bitter, can
be pickled like capers, and the uncooked
open flowers can also be used as a salad
ingredient. The first-year roots can also be
sautéed or roasted like parsnips, or used
to flavour soups and sauces. Slightly older
roots can be roasted until dry and brown,
then ground and used as a flavouring for
desserts or to make a convincing (at least to
non-coffee-drinkers like myself) caffeine-
free coffee substitute. It was once grown in
Europe to provide an illegal adulterant for
the real thing, so widely that it too became
adulterated with "sawdust, roasted beans,
dried horse liver, and other substances"
(C Pierpoint Johnson).

Nipplewort (*Lapsana communis*)

Nipplewort is an upright annual or perennial
herb to 1m, with multiply branching stems,
clear sap (not milky), and yellow flowers.
Lower leaves are hairy and pinnate with
a large terminal leaflet, upper leaves are
hairless and oval-diamond shaped; all leaves
are toothed. Common throughout the
British Isles, and the whole of temperate
Europe, apart from mountainous areas.

Young foliage is edible, becoming bitter
as it ages.

▾ Nipplewort   ▸ Chicory

Dandelions (*Taraxacum*)

"[The blanched leaves] may be had in winter by lifting large roots from September onwards and packing them, after cutting off the large leaves, in a box of light soil, sand or peat and putting this under the scullery table or in a warm cellar; the soil should be kept just moist and the leaves will be ready in about a month."

(Jason Hill, 1939)

Dandelions are perennial herbs sufficiently familiar to not require a description, although there are plenty of other members of this family which look rather similar (none of which are poisonous). Key identifying features are the low rosette of leaves with backward-pointing lobes, and bright yellow flowers on hollow stems. There are about 250 microspecies, all of which reproduce clonally.

Dandelion leaves are at their best when blanched (though this may reduce the vitamin content), and the best way to do this is a variation on Jason Hill's World War II method. You may be uprooting them from your garden anyway, in which case you might as well use all of the tap roots, but the best ones are the biggest and these make themselves known in late winter and early spring by being the first to produce flowers. Chop off all the existing leaves, taking care not to damage the top of the root, then put them in a container deprived of light (a plastic bag in a dark cupboard will do). Within 3 or 4 weeks, you will have a crop of sweet salad leaves. If collecting unblanched leaves from wild plants, you can soak them in water for 2 hours to reduce the bitterness. Dandelion leaves can also be served like spinach, just soak them first and cook longer than you would for spinach. The leaves have a high content of vitamins A and C. The flowers aren't bitter at all (the yellow bits), and can be pickled like capers, in vinegar or brine, when closed. They also make good wine, herbal tea and syrup. The cooked roots are perfectly edible before the flowering stem begins to grow (though slightly bitter and a little stringy). Both roots and stems can be made into Kinpara (p455), and the roots roasted to make a coffee substitute.

Dandelion 'Honey'

Ingredients:
100g dandelion flowers (green parts removed), 400ml water, half a lemon (sliced), granulated sugar.

Collect your flowers on a dry, sunny day. Discard the green parts, and put the yellow parts in a saucepan with the water and lemon. Bring to the boil then simmer for 15 mins, and leave to steep overnight. Strain the liquid and measure it, then add an equal amount of sugar (eg for 250ml liquid add 250g sugar). Bring to the boil and simmer until it thickens, and pour into a hot, sterile glass jar. It will thicken further as it cools.

Fried Dandelion Buds
(traditional British)

Collect unopened dandelion buds. Coat with a mixture of plain flour, salt and pepper. Put some butter in a frying pan and heat until bubbling, and quickly fry the coated flower heads, stirring so they are crispy all over. Serve immediately with a dipping sauce.

Squid and Dandelions

This is a traditional Burmese dish (Pyi-Gyi Nga Kazun Ywet).

Ingredients:
1tsp dried hot chilli flakes,1tbsp lemon juice, 2tsp light soy sauce, 1tsp brown sugar, 2tsp groundnut oil, 1 clove garlic (finely chopped), 500g fresh squid, cut into 1cm slices, 225g dandelion leaves only (halved).

Mix the chilli flakes, lemon juice, soy sauce, and sugar and stand for 15 mins, heat the oil in a pan and fry the garlic on medium heat for 1 minute. Add the squid and cook for another 2 mins, then add the chilli mixture and the dandelion leaves. Cook until wilted (about 2 mins). Serve warm as a starter or with other dishes.

Dandelion Roots with Soy Sauce
(traditional Japanese)

Ingredients:
250g dandelion roots, 2tbsp groundnut oil, salt to taste, 2tbsp soy sauce.

Scrub the dandelion roots clean then slice them very finely into rings. Heat the oil in a pan, add the sliced dandelion roots and fry until golden. Season with salt then add about 3tbsp water. Cover and cook gently until the dandelion is tender and almost all the liquid has evaporated away (about 8 mins). Season with the soy sauce then serve as a vegetable.

◀ Blanched Dandelions grown from tap roots.

Lettuces (*Lactuca*)

Garden Lettuce is classified as its own species (*Lactuca sativa* – 'sativa' means 'cultivated'). It was probably already in existence in the Old Kingdom of Egypt, 4,500 years ago. It is morphologically similar to a group of at least six wild *Lactuca* species, mostly adapted to the arid and rocky conditions of the Mediterranean basin and south-west Asia.

The closest of these to the domesticated form is **Prickly Lettuce (*L. serriola*)**, which is presumed to be the primary wild ancestor (they also hybridise to some extent). It's a biennial herb found in disturbed/waste ground, especially near the sea. It initially forms a rosette of leaves, before 'bolting' to 1.7m, with variable upright, thick, spiny, greyish-green leaves with a clear white midrib and arrow-shaped basal lobes. These produce abundant milky 'latex' when damaged. An ancient introduction to the British Isles, frequent and currently increasing/spreading.

Wild, Bitter or **Great Lettuce (*L. virosa*)** is rather larger (to 2.5m), more purple-flushed, the leaves with more rounded basal lobes, and not so upright. Frequent in the British Isles, especially in coastal areas, though spreading inland along roads. **Least Lettuce (*L. saligna*)** has similar properties, native but very rare in the British Isles apart from the south-east corner. All these species are considerably more frequent in the south of the British Isles than the north, becoming even more common the further south you go in Europe.

Historically, these wild lettuces were more important as medicine than food, although by the mid-19th century the flowering stem of the domesticated varieties was more widely used (C Pierpoint Johnson,

p144). The 'milk' is known as 'Lactucarium', and superficially resembles opium – it is a white liquid that can be reduced to a smokable solid, with alleged pain-killing, sedative and psychotropic properties. Scientific testing in the 1940s indicated that commercially available concoctions of Lactucarium had no detectable effect, but this may be because the active ingredients rapidly degrade. It regained some popularity in the hippy movement of the late 60s. The leaves and seeds have also been used in the past for their supposed medicinal properties.

For food, only the youngest shoots and leaves (in late winter and early spring, or when the plant is still in its rosette form) are edible. Even these tend to be rather bitter, especially those of *virosa*. The Anglo-Saxon author Ælfric of Eynsham (late 10th century) uses 'Wild Lettuce' as a translation of the bitter herbs Israelites ate at Passover.* They are still eaten in some parts of the Mediterranean, where their bitterness is diminished by boiling and discarding the water, and then offset by the use of complementary ingredients. The seeds have also been used to make an edible oil (for cooking).

Closely related **Wall Lettuce (*Mycelis muralis*)** is an upright short-lived perennial herb to 1.3m, with winged-stalked, lyre-shaped lower leaves with clasping bases. The leaves are thin and tinged maroon, and the flowers are small and yellow, in open panicles on stalks held at 90° to the main stem. Frequent in most of temperate Europe and probably native in the British Isles, locally common in England and Wales. Inhabits woodland and roadsides. Easily confused with Lettuces and Sowthistles. The young leaves are edible.

* *The Forager Handbook*, Irving, M, p48.

▸ Prickly Lettuce

Cat's-ear (*Hypochaeris*) and similar species

Many members of this family have Dandelion-like flowers. Working out which one you've found frequently isn't easy, and from a foraging point of view usually isn't worth the bother. Most can be eaten, but none are worth hunting for and none are poisonous either. At worst they are inedibly bitter.

Cat's-ear (*H. radicata*) is a perennial herb to 60cm resembling Dandelion, but with hairy leaves and solid, branched flower stems (and thus with multiple flowers for each main stem). The lobes on the leaves don't point backwards like those of Dandelion, and they are flattened to the ground, helping them to elude both grazers and mowers. The broken flesh produces a white latex. This is a well-known and troublesome lawn weed, but also grows on heaths and beaches. The leaves and young shoots are edible raw or cooked, and were traditionally gathered in several

▼ Bristly Oxtongue   ▶ Cat's-ear

Mediterranean countries.* Can be used in similar ways to Dandelion anyway, so confusion isn't a major problem.

Spotted and **Smooth Cat's-ears (*H. maculata* and *glabra*)** are similarly edible, but rarer.

Autumnal Hawkbit (*Scorzoneroides autumnalis*) looks a lot like Cat's-ear but is too bitter to eat. It produces no latex when broken.

Rough Hawkbit (*Leontodon hispidus*) is a perennial herb to 60cm much like Cat's-ear but with more upright and hairy leaves, and unbranched, hairy flower stems. The young leaves are edible (best cooked) right through the winter, and the roots can be roasted like Dandelion.

Lesser Hawkbit (*L. saxatilis*) is also similar, but with smaller flowers and less hairy flower stems, and the leaves are edible raw or cooked.

Hawkweed Oxtongue (*Picris hieracioides*) is an upright biennial to perennial herb to 1m with a stout, bristly, branching stem, short-stalked, clasping lower leaves and loose umbels of yellow flowers. Leaves and young shoots are edible. Common in temperate Europe as far north as England and Denmark, rare further north. Young shoots and leaves are edible, raw or cooked, though typically bitter for this family.

Bristly Oxtongue (*Helminthotheca echioides*) is an annual to biennial to 80cm, very similar but more densely covered with bristly blisters. Similar range, but extending south into Africa. Also edible, but no esculent.

The Hawksbeards (*Crepis*) can be used in the same ways as Cat's-ear.

---

* *Wild Food*, Mears, R, and Hillman, G, 2008, p302.

Sowthistles (*Sonchus*)

Three native Sowthistles are common garden weeds, found on waste ground, roadsides, arable field margins and disturbed ground anywhere. They have had much historic food use worldwide, and are particularly well known in Italy. The *young* leaves and shoots of all of them are edible, becoming considerably less so as they age and (apart from Smooth Sowthistle) develop spikes. Blanching in-situ works well. They make a decent salad item when young, older leaves require boiling for a couple of minutes to reduce the bitterness, and the rosettes and peeled stems of all species are best cooked (boil for 5 minutes and serve buttered). They work well as a stir-fry ingredient, since the midrib of the leaves retains some of its crunch even after pre-boiling for a minute or two. The flowers of all Sowthistles are also edible, as Dandelion.

In many parts of eastern Europe, there is a very commonly believed myth that Sowthistles are poisonous. It can be traced back to a 1975 Polish book called *Poisonous Plants* by Jakub Mowszowicz, which wrongly classifies them as containing toxic alkaloids.

Perennial Sowthistle (*S. arvensis*) is a rhizomatous perennial herb to 1.5m with branching, leafy stems, covered with sticky yellow glands at the top. Basal leaves are lanceolate with fine spiny teeth at the edges. Stem leaves have pointed lobes at their bases. Upper surface of leaves is shiny, flowers are bright yellow. Common throughout the British Isles and temperate Europe, apart from Scandinavian mountains.

Smooth (or **Common**) **Sowthistle** (*S. oleraceus*) is a perennial herb to 1.6m, upright, hairless, minimally branched stems, variable leaves with dull grey-green upper surfaces, uncurled margins and no spines, pointed lobes at the base of the clasping stem leaves, and clusters of pale yellow Dandelion-like flowers. Abundant throughout lowland British Isles and Europe, apart from the extreme north, especially on waste or arable ground.

Prickly Sowthistle (*S. asper*) is taller (to 2m), has upright, minimally branched stems which are hairless all the way to the top, very spiny leaves with green and shiny upper surfaces, rounded lobes at the base of stem leaves, and dark yellow flowers. The leaf bases clasp the rather angular, minimally branching stem. Distribution as Smooth Sowthistle.

Plume Thistles (*Cirsium*)

The Plume Thistles are typically tall plants with prickly leaves and dense heads of pink flowers which produce abundant nectar, making them ecologically useful for insect pollinators. 'Plume' refers to the feather-like structure of the hairs on their achenes. Often found on nutrient-rich but neglected land, they are edible and mild-tasting, but challenging due to the thin, fragile spines, which readily break off into flesh. Their stems are good to eat after soaking in water for an hour, and the de-spined leaves (especially the midrib) and flower buds are also edible, as are the sprouted seeds. The pre-flowering roots of larger species are usable like Burdock (p454). Flowers make a vegetable rennet.

Spear Thistle (*C. vulgare*) is a biennial or short-lived perennial herb to 1.5m, with stems which do branch, though the plant is usually tall and slim. The stems have discontinuous wings, the grey-green, allegedly spear-shaped leaves have deep lobes, and both have dangerous spines. The purple-pink flowers are usually clustered. Common throughout temperate Europe on roadsides, waste ground and ungrazed grassland. The long, thick tap root (to 70cm) is a good cooking vegetable. It can be boiled or steamed and served with butter, roasted, or thinly sliced and used in a stir-fry like water chestnuts. The main stem, young flower stems and heads are also edible after de-prickling. The flowers can be roasted in embers for 10 mins, which singes off the prickles while cooking the contents, making it easy to scoop out the edible parts (thanks to foraging tutor Marcus Harrison).

The similar **Woolly Thistle (*C. eriophorum,*** not pictured) is an upright biennial herb to 1.5m with unwinged, branching stems, and dark green leaves, which are deeply cut and armed with sharp spines at the lobe tips. Much of the plant is cobwebby, especially the flower heads. Found on rough, dry grassland, waste and disturbed ground, old quarries, and urban areas. Locally common in the southern half of the British Isles and the central zone of temperate Europe. Uses as Spear Thistle.

Creeping Thistle (*C. arvense*) is a creeping perennial herb to 1.2m with spineless, wingless, branching stems and tough spines on its oblong-lanceolate leaves. Unlike the other common members of the genus, this one has no basal rosette. Common in waste and disturbed ground, fields, and roadsides, where it spreads via creeping rhizomes, and is hard to eradicate if unwanted. The thin tap root is edible in the first year, after that it is too fibrous. The peeled stems and flower stalks are edible, but the leaves aren't worth de-prickling.

Marsh Thistle (*C. palustre*) is a biennial or perennial herb to 2m, with no hairs on top of the deeply lobed, purple-edged, spiny leaves, and stems with very spiny wings which run along the whole stem. Native and abundant in damp habitats throughout temperate Europe. Young leaves, shoots and flower stalks are edible, peeled, raw or cooked, though beware this plant has particularly vicious spines.

Cabbage Thistle (*C. oleraceum*) is a perennial herb to 1.5m, with sparsely branched unwinged stems, slightly lobed or unlobed leaves with slightly spiny edges, and yellow flowers. It is grown for food in Asia, native to continental temperate Europe. Usually found in the British Isles as an ornamental, but occasionally escapes. The young leaves are eaten (cooked), and the seeds used to make an edible oil.

▲ Spear Thistle flowers   ▼ Spear Thistle leaves

▲ Marsh Thistle   ▼ Creeping Thistle

▼ Spear Thistle roots

▼ Cabbage Thistle

Milk Thistle (*Silybum marianum*)

"Take the long Stalks of the middle Leaf of the Milky-Thistle, about May, when they are young and tender: wash and scrape them, and boil them in Water, with a little Salt, till they are very soft, and so let them lie to drain. They are eaten with fresh Butter melted not too thin, and is a delicate and wholsome Dish."
(John Evelyn, 1699)

Milk Thistle is an annual or biennial herb to 1m, with an unwinged stem and shiny, white-marbled leaves with sharp, spiny edges. The solitary reddish-purple flowers are protected by a collar of ferocious yellow spines on the bracts below. This plant is probably an ancient introduction (though possibly native to southern England) and once widely cultivated, mainly for medical use. Now an uncommon find, usually on rough grassland, arable fields or waste ground. Most frequent (in the British Isles) in East Anglia. Sometimes grows from bird-seed.

The visually attractive leaves of very young plants make a first-class, sweet-tasting salad item (slugs like them so much that I had to protect them like bean seedlings when I tried growing them). Slightly older leaves are edible only after the prickles have been removed, raw or cooked. The flower heads can be used like miniature artichokes, but the spines are hazardous. The sprouted seeds are good in salads and the roots are edible (as Salsify, p456). This plant can also be juiced, the juice then used to flavour cocktails. Known to accumulate nitrates under certain conditions, which sometimes poisons sheep and cattle.

Plumeless Thistles (*Carduus*) ⓘ

The Plumeless Thistles are less numerous and generally of less interest to foragers than their plumed relatives. Plumeless Thistles are reported to sometimes accumulate toxic amounts of nitrates.

Musk or **Nodding Thistle (*C. nutans*)** is an upright biennial herb to 1.2m, with a downy, branching, spiny-winged stem. Lower leaves have wavy edges, upper leaves deeply cut with long spines. Large, fragrant, solitary, drooping, purple-pink flowers surrounded by spiny bracts. Common in most of the British Isles on roadsides, waste ground and chalk grassland. The peeled stems are edible, and the dried flowers can be used as a curdling agent.

Welted Thistle (*C. crispus*) is a biennial herb to 1.1m with upright, spiny-winged, multiply branched stems, weak-spined leaves and upright pale red-purple flowers in groups of three to five. Occasional in England, rarer in the rest of the British Isles in open woodland, waste ground and other habitats, usually on calcareous soil. Native to south-west Europe. Young leaves are a famine food. Easily confused with Creeping Thistle (which is wingless).

▼ Musk Thistle

▼ Welted Thistle

▲ A young Greater Burdock

Burdocks (*Arctium*)

Greater Burdock (*A. lappa*) is a very large, upright biennial herb to 2m, with a multiply branched, red-tinged stem, solid-stalked lower leaves, and rounded or heart-shaped leaves which are hairy/woolly on the underside and as wide as they are long. It has globular, purple, Thistle-like flowers (midsummer to early autumn) and fruits covered in curved, hooked bracts which allow them to attach to fur and clothing (these can be hazardous if they get in your eyes or airways). This species is an ancient introduction to the British Isles, but common in the south, especially in hedgerows, open woodland, rough grassland, by rivers and roads, and on disturbed ground. There is a risk of confusion with the deadly poisonous Foxglove (p394). The side veins on the leaves of Foxglove run closer to parallel to the main vein of the leaves, which also have a more pointed tip. The side veins of Burdock leaves are relatively more perpendicular with the main vein. Young plants of poisonous Butterbur (p439) are also similar, but with rounder leaves.

The young leaves and stalks (of both leaves and flowers) are edible, but bitter, and only slightly less so when cooked.

The peeled young shoots make a decent Asparagus substitute and the stems can be lactofermented. The seeds can be sprouted and used in salads (but the sprouts are also bitter). It is the long tap root (can be over 50cm) which is of main interest to a forager. Greater Burdock is cultivated throughout south-east Asia for its roots, and is especially prized in Japan. Known as 'Gobo', the roots are boiled, or fried in soy sauce, sake and dashi (p47). They should be scraped first with a knife, to remove the delicate skin. Roots of plants in the first year are smaller, more tender and easier to dig up, and they are usually eaten in the autumn of year one, or at the very least before the flowering shoot is 20cm tall. Slightly larger, older roots are preferred by some, said to have more flavour, although they do eventually become too woody (although what might seem like too woody raw can sometimes be edible after cooking). The roots have a tendency to go an unattractive brown colour when exposed to air, and to stop this and also reduce the 'muddiness' of the flavour, they should be soaked in water for 5 to 10 minutes with a splash of something acidic like vinegar or lemon juice

Lesser Burdock (*A.minus*) is a smaller version of Greater Burdock (to 1.5m), but with hollow-stalked lower leaves, longer than they are wide, and with a sharper tip, and typically found in shadier places. It is common (and native) in the British Isles apart from northern Scotland, and throughout Europe. It is usable in exactly the same way, although the roots are smaller and used when the plant is younger. **Wood Burdock (*A. nemorosum*)** is extremely similar to Lesser Burdock, but with a more northerly skew to its distribution. **Woolly Burdock (*A. tomentosum*)** is an eastern European relative, the peeled stems of which are eaten in Estonia and northern Germany.

▲ Lesser Burdock in flower

Kinpara Gobo
(traditional Japanese side dish)

Ingredients:
1 large burdock root, washed and peeled, 1 small carrot (optional), 1 tbsp white sesame seeds (optional), 1 small red chilli pepper (optional), 1 tbsp vegetable oil, 2 tsp roasted sesame oil, 2 tbsp dashi, 2 tbsp light soy sauce, 2 tbsp sake (or dry sherry), 2 tbsp mirin, 1 tbsp sugar.

Peel or scrape the burdock root, cut into 2-inch-long thin strips. Then soak in water with a drop of vinegar for 10 mins. Optionally repeat, removing when ready to fry. Similarly slice the carrot and set aside. Heat the vegetable oil, fry the burdock for a few mins, add carrot and cook for a few more mins. Then add the dashi, soy sauce, sake, mirin and sugar. When most of the liquid is gone, add the chilli, sesame seeds and sesame oil.

Salsify (*Tragopogon*)

The names 'Salsify' and 'Goatsbeard' have been applied to both the entire genus *Tragopogon*, and individual species within it, and the former also to the southern European species *Scorzonera hispanica* (Black Salsify). *Tragopogon* are also known as 'Oyster Plant' (along with several other plants which supposedly taste/feel like oysters), and Jack-go-to-bed-at-noon, because their flowers close up around

▾ Meadow Salsify

lunchtime. 'Goatsbeard' is also the common name of the unrelated *Aruncus dioicus* ('Bride's Feathers'), which is usually found as an ornamental in the British Isles and has marginally edible leaves.

Goatsbeard or **Meadow Salsify (*T. pratensis*)** is an upright annual to perennial herb to 65cm with grass-like leaves to 30cm, blueish-grey-green with a white midrib, and sheathed at the base. It has solitary yellow flowers (summer) on long stalks at the ends of the stems. Inhabits grassland, waste ground, roadsides and sea cliffs. Native to the British Isles and frequent everywhere apart from north-west Scotland. Common in temperate Europe apart from the extreme north.

(Common or **Purple) Salsify (*T. porrifolius*)** is very similar, but a bit taller, leaves slightly wider at the bases, and with swollen stems just beneath the flowers, which are purple. Locally frequent in some parts of south-east England, rare elsewhere in the British Isles (where it is introduced). More common further south in temperate Europe, and in its native Mediterranean.

These are first-class edible species, with many uses. They were traditionally cultivated for their roots (harvested in the early autumn of their first year), which can be used raw when young (grated in salads, like carrots) or boiled and mashed with butter, fried in breadcrumbs, or roasted/baked for 30 mins at 190°C / fan 170°C. Older roots need cooking for 30 minutes in water with lemon juice or salt. The young leaves and shoots are also tasty, raw or cooked, as are the closed flowers, steamed and served with butter. The seeds can be sprouted, and the latex produced by the root can be used as chewing gum (leave it to dry on the side of a glass).

▲ Purple Salsify

Salsify with Parmesan Cheese
(TF Garrett, 1892)

Prepare the Salsify, cut it into short lengths, and boil it until tender with a moderate quantity of salt in the water. Put 1oz. of butter in a stewpan with 4 table-spoonful of flour and mix them over the fire, then stir in sufficient of the cooking-liquor of the Salsify to make the sauce, add 2oz. of grated Parmesan cheese, and stir it with a wooden spoon until thick and smooth. Put the Salsify on a hot dish, pour the sauce over, and serve.

Salsify Sauce
(TF Garrett, 1892)

Scrape the roots of Salsify, and put them out of hand into acidulated water. Put 2 table-spoonfuls of flour in a saucepan with a little salt, and stir in gradually 1 pint of water. Continue stirring it over the fire till boiling, then put in the roots of Salsify, and let them stew gently till tender.

When cooked, strain the roots, put them in a sauce boat with some butter sauce, and serve.

Campanulaceae (Bellflower family)

"The root is not used in physicke, but only for a sallet root boiled and eaten, with oile, vineger, and pepper."
(John Gerard, 1597)

It is believed that Gerard was referring to the native Nettle-leaved Bellflower (*Campanula trachelium*), which he calls 'Coventry Bells' (it is common near Coventry), but also mentions 'Canterbury Bells' (*C. medium*), which is native to south-east Europe. "They all be kinds of Rampion", he tells us, "and the roots eaten as Rampions are."

Rampions (*Phyteuma*)

'Rampion' is an ambiguous common name, referring both to a species of Bellflower and a genus of plants with beautiful and distinctive flowers which give no hint they are related to Bellflowers. The leaves, flowers and especially the roots of two edible species of *Phyteuma* were historically collected from the wild. Though edible, both species are far too rare in the British Isles for foraging here, but considerably more abundant in central continental Europe, especially in the mountains. Many English language sources claim that the edible salad plants coveted by Rapunzel's mother in the Grimm's fairytale were Rampions of some sort, but this is a case of mistaken identity. The confusion is due to 'Rapunzel' forming part or all of the German common names for several different plants – Rampions, Evening Primrose (p266) and Cornsalad (p467). It was the last of these that the Grimm brothers were referring to, although their story was derived from the older French/Italian fairytale (Petrosinella) and the original plant was actually Parsley!

Round-headed Rampion or **Pride of Sussex (*P. orbiculare*)** is the most widespread of the two, locally common on the South Downs.

Spiked Rampion (*P. spikatum*) is native to the British Isles, but restricted to a few sites in East Sussex and protected under Schedule 8 of the Wildlife and Countryside Act (1981). It's much more common in temperate continental Europe and naturally inhabits wood edges and rides, hedgebanks and meadows.

▼ Spiked Rampion

▼ Round-headed Rampion

Rampion Bellflower
(*Campanula rapunculus*)

"... much cultivated in France and Italy, and sometimes in Great Britain, for the roots, which are boiled tender and eaten hot with sauce, or cold with vinegar and pepper. At one time the Rampion was much used and highly esteemed as a vegetable in this country, but as the cultivation was superseded by other root crops, that yielded more satisfactorily (to the horticulturist), this root was neglected, and becoming scarcer, and consequently more expensive, was eventually discarded from the kitchen as being too costly as compared with its culinary value. This neglect is not altogether wise, for it may be grown in fields, and the leaves form an excellent food for cattle."
(TF Garrett, 1892)

Rampion Bellflower is a biennial herb with an erect, branching stem to 1m, with oval lower leaves and lanceolate upper leaves and pale violet-blue flowers arranged in a one-sided cluster. Inhabits woodlands, roadsides and dry meadows. It is not native to most of the British Isles, and only occasional as a garden escape, apart from parts of eastern Scotland, where it is a little more common, as it is in other parts of Europe. This plant was once widely cultivated in continental Europe for its leaves and sweet roots, which have been compared to radishes and turnips – 'rapunculus' has an etymologyical connection with 'Rape' and Turnip (*Brassica rapa*). They are better when younger, fiddly to clean, and typically boiled.

Nettle-leaved Bellflower
(*C. trachelium*)

Nettle-leaved Bellflower is a perennial herb to 1m with bristly/hairy, unbranched, sometimes reddish, sharp-angled stems, and alternate leaves. The long-stalked lower leaves are ovate to triangular with a cordate base. The stalkless, toothed upper leaves are ovate to lanceolate. It has a one-sided spike of violet (rarely white) flowers. Inhabits deciduous woodland, hedgerows, especially in humus-rich locations. Frequent in much of England and Wales, rarer in Scotland and Ireland, present in most of temperate Europe. The flowers are edible.

Other Bellflowers (*Campanula* spp.)

The flowers and young foliage of all Bellflower species are edible. This is not a complete list.

Adria Bellflower (*C. portenschlagiana*) and **Trailing Bellflower (*C. poscharskyana*)**

▾ Adria Bellflower

▾ Trailing Bellflower

are two rather similar 20th century introductions from south-east Europe. They are mound-forming perennial herbs with heart/kidney shaped leaves and purple-blue flowers. Both are already common escapes in urban areas of southern England, inhabiting walls and dry, rocky areas. Adria Bellflower has more tubular flowers and greener and less hairy leaves. Trailing Bellflower has a more upright habit, greyer, hairier leaves and paler, more star-like flowers (more widely spread petals). The flowers of both species are good to eat, the leaves passable.

Clustered Bellflower (*C. glomerata*) is a hairy perennial herb to 40cm, with upright, sparsely branching stems. Lower leaves are long-stalked, fine-toothed, oval-oblong with cordate bases, upper leaves are narrower and short-stalked, and the uppermost leaves have half-clasping bases. The clusters of stalkless, bell-shaped flowers are blue. Native, but also cultivated and often found as a garden escape. Locally common in open woodland and rough calcareous grassland in central southern England, rare or absent elsewhere in the British Isles. One of the best members of the genus for eating (all parts).

Creeping Bellflower (*C. rapunculoides*) is a perennial herb to 80cm with heart-shaped leaves and a long raceme of violet-blue, trumpet-shaped flowers. It is found in grassland, woodland, roadsides and agricultural land, usually in partial shade and nitrogen-rich locations. Occasional and scattered in the British Isles. Native to Europe and western Asia, invasive in North America. Creeping Bellflower has also been commonly referred to as 'Rampion Bellflower'. This is another species once cultivated for its roots, and the leaves and shoots are very mild.

▲ Creeping Bellflower

▲ Clustered Bellflower

▲ Peach-leaved Bellflower

▲ Giant Bellflower

Peach-leaved Bellflower (*C. persicifolia*) is a sprawling perennial herb to 30cm with hairless stems and narrow, pointed-lanceolate, fine-toothed leaves and large flowers. A traditional cottage garden plant, native to other parts of Eurasia, but now a reasonably frequent escape in open woodland, commons, grass verges and waste ground. Root is edible raw or cooked.

Giant Bellflower (*C. latifolia*) is a perennial herb to 1.2m, with hairy, fine-toothed leaves and solitary, short-stalked, purple flowers (paler than Nettle-leaved Bellflower). Native and locally common in the central section of Great Britain, rarer in northern Scotland and southern England, inhabiting woods and other shady locations, usually on damp, fertile soil.

Dipsacales
Adoxaceae (Moschatel family)

Moschatel is a small herb that smells of musk. 'Muscatel' is a type of grape that makes similar-smelling wines. Elder has the same scent, and both the flowers and fermented berry juice were historically used to "doctor" (Garrett, 1892) or "raise the status of" (Jason Hill, 1939) inferior wines.

Elders (*Sambucus*)   (!)

(Black) Elder is a shrub or small deciduous tree to 10m with arching branches and compound leaves having up to nine pairs of slightly toothed leaflets. Strong-scented clusters of white flowers in early summer are followed by dark purple berries. Common throughout Europe in woodland, hedges, scrub and other habitats, especially on nutrient-rich soil. There are cultivated forms with leaves that are darker, and sometimes deeply cut, which have the same uses. The poisonous Common Dogwood (p364) is frequently mistaken for Elder.

Red-berried Elder (*S. racemosa*) is a deciduous shrub to 6m with white flowers and red berries. Common in lowland Scotland, much less so in the rest of Britain. Closely related to Elder, it can be told apart by the shape of the flower clusters (flat topped in Elder, not so in Red Elder), and the colour of the berries. Native to continental Europe, inhabiting open woodland, particularly in mountainous areas. The berries are rather bitter, but have a high vitamin C content, and can be used to make preserves, with the same caveats about green parts as Elder.

Dwarf Elder (*S. ebulus*) is a central/southern European species complex with a long history of medicinal use, but questions about its safety and toxicity. As well as being considerably smaller than Elder, it can be identified by its **foul-smelling leaves**.

All of the green parts of Elder, and the roots, are poisonous, containing cyanide precursors and causing gastrointestinal problems, followed by weakness and in extreme cases coma. The thick young shoots of Elder were once peeled and pickled in Britain, and called 'English Bamboo'. They do indeed taste rather like bamboo when cooked, but they are no longer considered safe for consumption.

The fresh flower buds can be nibbled raw or pickled, and the open flowers used to make Elderflower wine, 'champagne', cordial, or dried and used to make tea. The flower heads are excellent fried in a light batter, or can be used to impart a musky flavour in jams or stewed fruit desserts.

For most uses, the flowers should be plucked off the stalks before use (some sources advise shaking them off, but I haven't found this to work very well). However, to make Elderflower fritters, it's easier to keep them attached – just make sure everyone knows not to eat the green parts. See p79 for flower fritter and cordial recipes.

Ripe Elderberries are best used to make jams, fruit pies (works well with apples), sorbets and wine, removing the seeds in the process. The juice can be mixed 50/50 with honey to make a spread. Again, the stalks should be removed. I have seen recipes using unripe (green) elderberries, for example to make 'capers' by preserving them in salt, claiming that the processing renders them safe. I can find no scientific basis for these claims, and advise against their consumption. The seeds of raw ripe berries are also slightly toxic.

Also see recipes on p64 and p482, and fruit introduction on p78.

Elderflower Wine

Ingredients: 1½ pints of stripped elder blossom, 2 lemons, 2 oranges, 2 knobs ginger, 3½ lb demerara sugar, 1 gallon boiling water, 1tsp yeast, 1tsp yeast nutrient.

Slice the citrus fruits and put them in a large pan or fermenting bucket with the elderflower, ginger and sugar. Add the boiling water, then the yeast nutrient. When it has cooled to tepid, add the yeast. Cover with a clean tea towel and leave to ferment in a warm place for 4 days. Strain, pour into a sterilised demijohn, and fit an airlock. Ferment for two months, then rack off to a fresh demijohn, seal, and leave for at least two more months. This recipe makes a rich, brown, almost brandy-like wine, and the longer you leave it (years), the better it gets. For a quicker ferment that requires less equipment, you'll find plenty of Elderflower Champagne recipes online.

▲ (Black) Elder

▲ Red-berried Elder

Elderberry Custard or Pie / Patina de sambuco
(Apicius, 1st century)

To make a dish of elder, hot or cold, wash the berries, remove the seeds, cook them in a little water, skim and strain. Grease a dish in which to cook the custard; crush 6 scruples [about 8g] of pepper with a little broth; add the elderberry pulp and another glass of broth, a glass of wine, a glass of raisin wine and up to 100ml of oil. Put the dish in a hot bath and stir. As soon as it is getting warm, break 6 eggs, whip them, use them to thicken the fluid. When thick enough sprinkle with pepper and serve up.

Elderberry and Bramley Juice Drink

Ingredients:
1.25 kg elderberries, 5 apples (bramleys work well), 0.5 litre water, 400g sugar. Wash and clean the elderberries thoroughly, removing the twigs. Wash, core and slice the apples. Put the berries, apples and water in a saucepan and simmer gently for about 20 mins. Strain through a muslin or fine sieve. Reheat the concentrated juice in the saucepan and add the sugar, heating and stirring until all the sugar is dissolved. Pour into bottles (sterilised if you want the juice to last) and keep refrigerated. Dilute to taste.

Elderberry Syrup

Ingredients:
500g elderberries, 500g caster sugar, 1 lemon (juiced), knob of ginger, 5 cloves, 1 cinnamon stick, 1 star anise.

Strip the elderberries, put them in a saucepan and cover with 1cm water. Add the ginger, cloves, cinnamon and star anise (these are optional – use what you like). Bring to the boil, then simmer gently for 15-20 mins until the berries have softened into a liquid. Leave to cool slightly. Strain through a fine sieve and measure the liquid, then add an equal amount of sugar. Tip back into the cleaned saucepan and add the lemon juice. Simmer until the sugar has dissolved and the mixture has thickened slightly (about 15 mins). Cool, then bottle or freeze.

Elderberry Ketchup (TF Garrett, 1892)

Put 6 pints of ripe berries without stalks into a jar, and add 3 pints of vinegar, 4oz. of ginger, twelve anchovies, four blades of mace, and 1oz. of whole pepper. Set the jar in a slightly-warmed oven and let it remain for ten or twelve hours. Strain off the juice into an enamelled saucepan, add the ginger, mace, anchovies, and a little pepper and salt, and boil until the anchovies are quite dissolved. Strain again, and when cold put it into bottles and cork down until wanted.

Guelder-rose (*Viburnum opulus*) (!)

Guelder-rose or **European Cranberry-bush** is a deciduous shrub to 4m with opposite, lobed leaves (one large lobe on each side), white flower heads resembling hydrangeas in the summer, and red berries in the autumn. It is common everywhere except northern Scotland, inhabiting woods and hedges, especially in damp areas. Frequently planted. It is native and common throughout temperate Europe.

The sour fruit is edible, best cooked in jams or jellies, or in porridge. It contains high levels of pectin, so is useful as a setting agent when mixed with other fruits. It is mildly toxic (causing gastric upsets) so best not consumed in large quantities, especially raw.

Wayfaring Tree (*V. lantana*) has similar flowers, unlobed, slightly hairy leaves, and berries which eventually become black, via red. These berries are slightly more toxic than those of Guelder-rose, and best avoided. Native only to the southern half of the British Isles, but widely planted further north.

Several other species of *Viburnum* are planted as ornamentals in parks. Their berries vary in edibility, none better for eating than Guelder-rose and none more toxic than Wayfaring Tree.

▲ Guelder-rose

▼ Wayfaring Tree

Caprifoliaceae (Honeysuckle family)

The Honeysuckle family has recently been expanded to include the old Valerian family (*Valerianaceae*). **Common Valerian (*Valeriana officinalis*)** has marginally edible seeds, leaves and roots, but is much more important as medicine than food. The leaves and roots of **Red Valerian (*Centrathus ruber*)** are also edible, but unimpressive. The distinctive white berries of **Snowberry (*Symphoricarpus albus*)**, which pop when squashed, contain saponins which pass safely through the human gut, but they taste soapy and can cause nausea.

(Wild European) Honeysuckle (*Lonicera periclymenum*) (!)

Honeysuckle is a deciduous or semi-evergreen woody climber to 7m with reddish stems, hairy, opposite, oval leaves and tubular, cream flowers and tight clusters of red berries. Native and common in woodland and hedges all over Britain, and throughout Europe apart from the colder parts of Scandinavia. Can only be confused with other Honeysuckles, all introduced and rare in the wild. The nectar can be sucked after picking an individual floret and nibbling a hole in the base. They are used in jam, to decorate cakes, as a fragrant garnish for drinks, infused in vodka or made into a rather nice white wine. The berries contain saponins which cause nausea.

Himalayan Honeysuckle (*Leycesteria formosa*) (!)

Himalayan Honeysuckle or **Pheasant Berry** is a deciduous shrub to 2m with opposite, dark green leaves and racemes of pendulous white/pink flowers and dark purple berries. Native to south-east Asia, but widely planted as an ornamental and naturalising (bird-sown) in some locations. The berries are edible and taste a bit like caramel when over-ripe. Before that point they are foul, though drying improves them. Can cause diarrhoea if consumed in large quantities.

(Common) Cornsalad (*Valerianella locusta*)

"The Tops and Leaves are a *Sallet* of
themselves, seasonably eaten with other
Salleting, the whole Winter long, and early
Spring: The *French* call them *Salad de Preter*,
for their being generally eaten in *Lent*."
(John Evelyn, 1699)

Cornsalad is an annual herb to 40cm, starting
as a low rosette, before producing brittle,
repeatedly forking stems with pairs of flat-
stalked, paddle-shaped leaves at each fork,
and tiny, delicate, pale lilac flowers (spring
and summer). Frequent to locally common
in most of the British Isles (though less so
in the north), in dry locations such as dunes,
grassland, rocks and walls, but also wheat
fields (hence the name). Present throughout
Europe, apart from Scandinavia, where
it is restricted to the southern coastline.
Commercially cultivated, usually under the
name 'Lamb's Lettuce'. Wild Cornsalad is
at its best in spring and autumn, when the
leaves and stems are excellent raw in salads.
The flowers can also be eaten raw. Several
similar and closely related plants are also
edible though not quite as tasty.

Apiales

In addition to the large and important Carrot family, the only family of interest in the *Apiales* is the Ivy family (*Araliaceae*). Ivy (*Hedera helix*) berries can cause gastric and respiratory problems, skin irritation and even coma, but are rarely eaten because the plant is so well known. Marsh Pennywort (*Hydrocotyle vulgaris*) might be mistaken for Wall Pennywort, although it is smaller and prefers damper environments, and the leaves are edible in small quantities anyway. Ivy and Wall Pennywort are pictured together on p167.

Apiaceae (Carrot family)

The *Apiaceae* are also known as Umbellifers (or *Umbelliferae*) after their characteristic umbrella-shaped flower heads. Cultivated members include Parsley, Celery, Caraway, Angelica, Cumin, Asafoetida, Anise, Dill, Fennel, Parsnip and Coriander. They tend to be aromatic, their seeds used as spices, and this is also true of many wild members. This family also contains some hazardous poisonous species.

There are many marginally edible species. **Burnet-saxifrage (*Pimpinella saxifraga*)** is a chalk downland plant, common throughout temperate Europe in that habitat, the root of which has been used to produce an aromatic flavouring. **Sanicle (*Sanicula europaea*)** is a woodland plant with distinctive shiny and firm-textured leaves, widespread in Europe but better known as medicine than food. **Root Chervil (*Chaerophyllum bulbosum*)** is native to much of northern continental Europe but not the British Isles. It was once commonly cultivated for its roots, though as a crop it is now obscure.

Cowbane (*Cicuta virosa*)

Cowbane is a perennial herb to 1.5m with ridged, hollow, purple-striped stems, triangular, tripinnate, sharply toothed leaves, and white umbels. Rare in most of the British Isles (locally common in north-west England and East Anglia) on the banks of lakes and other still or slow-moving freshwater, sometimes on floating mats of vegetation. Native to northern Europe and Asia. The edible species this plant is most likely to be mistaken for is Fool's Watercress (p471), although that species has once-pinnate leaves with smaller, blunter teeth.

This plant contains a potent neurotoxin structurally similar to oenanthotoxin, and the roots in particular are sufficiently poisonous to easily kill a human. There is disagreement about the smell – it is somewhere around Dill and Parsley – with some finding it pleasant, and others the opposite.

▾ Cowbane

Hemlock Water-dropwort
(*Oenanthe crocata*)

Hemlock Water-dropwort is a hairless perennial herb to 1.5m, with hollow, cylindrical stems, 1-4 times pinnate leaves, flowers in white umbels and finger-like tubers. It smells distinctive and unpleasant. Inhabits riverbanks, freshwater ditches and other damp places and is common in the south and west of the British Isles, less so further north, avoiding chalk. Common in most of western Europe, becoming rare or absent to the east.

In terms of actual poisonings of foragers, including fatalities, Hemlock Water-dropwort is the most dangerous wild plant in temperate Europe – other plants are more toxic, but they poison people less frequently. The most poisonous part is the root, and occasionally, when they become exposed near pasture, they kill cattle. The worst human poisonings also involve consumption of the roots, typically mistaken for those of Wild Celery (p472), which also grows near water and has similar leaves. The toxin involved (oenanthotoxin) causes convulsions and seizures, cardiac and respiratory failure, and also rhabdomyolysis leading to kidney failure. Human poisonings prove fatal in about 50% of cases. There are also several other types of Water-dropwort (*Oenanthe*), generally with narrower/finer leaves, all of which should be presumed poisonous.

▲ ▼ Hemlock Water-dropwort

Hemlock (*Conium maculatum*)

Hemlock is a hairless biennial herb to 2.5m, with a smooth, hollow stem, usually liberally spotted with purple, especially towards the base, finely divided leaves, and flowers in white umbels (summer). The whole plant smells strongly of cat urine. Common in the British Isles, apart from the Scottish Highlands, on roadsides, waste ground and both riverbanks and dry ground. Native to Europe, though possibly an ancient introduction in the north, including the British Isles.

There is some disagreement about the level of its toxicity, possibly because different populations have differing amounts of various toxins, the most dangerous of which is an alkaloid called coniine. There are records of food use in northern Europe, with more southerly populations possibly being more poisonous. At least one death is recorded in the British Isles from Scotland in 1854, the result of confusion with wild-growing Parsley (p477). Some sources state that young plants are much less toxic than mature ones (eg Charles Johnson, 1856), others (eg Miles Irving) say that the young leaves are the most poisonous part of the plant. Everybody agrees that the roots and seeds are particularly poisonous. The symptoms of coniine poisoning are entirely physical – starting with a dry and burning mouth, then paralysis from the legs upwards, eventually leading to the brain and heart being starved of oxygen.

Fool's Parsley (*Aethusa cynapium*) (!)

Fool's Parsley is an annual or biennial herb to 1m, similar to Cow Parsley (Wild Chervil, p474) but hairless, flowers are white umbels which have no bracts but do have clearly visible hanging bracteoles. The umbels are always at the end of a stem, opposite a leaf. Found in arable field margins, hedges, waste ground and gardens. Easily confused with edible lacy-leaved umbellifers, apart from its unpleasant smell when damaged. Common in the British Isles apart from north and west Scotland.

Fool's Parsley is certainly toxic, and though not as lethal as some older guides suggest, it must be considered potentially deadly if large quantities were to be consumed (contains coniine, especially the root). Most likely to be confused with wild-growing Parsley (p477), but the smell is different (unpleasant).

Fool's Watercress or Pie-cress (*Apium nodiflorum* syn. *Heloscadium nodiflorum*) (!)

Fool's Watercress is a perennial herb to 80cm, with hollow, prostrate stems and once-pinnate, blunt-toothed leaves. The white flowers (summer) are followed by egg-shaped seeds. Found in streams, ditches and other wet locations, especially on chalk and limestone. Frequent throughout much of Europe and in the British Isles apart from Scotland, where it is rare or absent.

This plant is sometimes alleged to be poisonous, but is in fact edible. It was historically eaten in south-west England "for cooking with meat in pasties and pies".* It is also more likely to be confused with the very similar Lesser Water-parsnip (*Berula erecta*), than Watercress. Lesser Water-parsnip can be distinguished by having bracts below its flower head, and has been condemned as toxic, though there are no reliable recordings of poisonings.

* *Field Guide to the Wild Flowers of Great Britain*, 1981, Reader's Digest, p181.

Wild Celery
(*Apium graveolens* var. *graveolens*)

Wild Celery is a robust biennial herb to 90cm with upright, solid, deeply grooved, branching stems, though sometimes sprawling sideways. It has shiny, green, once-pinnate, diamond or triangular leaves, divided into pairs of large, toothed leaflets, and the lower leaves have swollen stalk bases. Flowers (summer) are the typical yellow-green umbels of this family, and the strong celery smell is distinctive. Inhabits tidal marshland, or other moist soils with at least some salt present. Locally common in England, rarer further north in the British Isles. Frequent and locally common throughout Europe.

Do not confuse with the seriously poisonous Cowbane (p468, no Celery scent, hollow stem), or Hemlock Water-dropwort (p469, smells foul, hollow stem).

Also note that the leaves and stems even of domesticated Celery are slightly toxic raw. Wild Celery was originally gathered in ancient Egypt, as a pot-herb, and also its seeds as flavouring. It was probably domesticated by 3,000 years ago, and certainly by the time of Christ – the Roman name for it was 'Apium' and Pliny the Elder distinguished between wild and domesticated types. It was established as a stem crop by the early 17th century, although it needed extensive 'earthing up' to blanch the stems, a treatment not required by many modern forms. Celeriac is also descended from Wild Celery.

Unlike the cultivated crop, stems of the wild plant aren't the best part to eat, though usable in soups and stews. The leaves can be used in salads, but their strong taste makes them better suited as flavouring, and the same goes for the flowers and seeds. If you want to make Wild Celery soup, it is best to dry the

stems first, to reduce the overpowering scent. The cooked roots can also be eaten but again great care must be taken to avoid confusion with Hemlock Water-dropwort.

Sweet Cicely (*Myrrhis odorata*)

Sweet Cicely is a perennial herb to 1.8m, similar to Cow Parsley / Wild Chervil (see next page) but with a strong aniseed smell when crushed, and with paler, frequently white-blotched leaves. Found in hedgerows, roadsides and other grassy locations, especially on high ground and near human habitation. Introduced in the British Isles for culinary use – native to mountainous regions further south in Europe and present in most of temperate Europe. Frequent in the north of the British Isles, rare or absent in the south and in the Scottish Highlands.

    This is the best of the edible lacy-leaved wild umbellifers. The whole plant smells sweetly of aniseed. The leaves are the most commonly used part, and at their best before the plant flowers. Great raw in salads or cooked as an aromatic pot-herb. They can be dried and used as part of a herb mixture. They also work well in desserts, used in place of sugar when cooking tart fruits or rhubarb, or as a herbal tea. The roots are edible, both raw and cooked, until they become too tough, and are superb candied. Less bitter than most of their relatives, they are boiled and served as a side vegetable or allowed to cool and used in salads. The flower heads can also be made into fritters, like Elder and False Acacia (see p79). The seeds are used as flavouring, and can be eaten raw when green, becoming more like cloves as they mature. Historically this plant was used to polish oak furniture.

Candied Sweet Cicely Roots

Boil the roots for about 15 mins, until tender. Soak for an hour in a mixture of 50/50 water and golden syrup, with a dash of lemon or lime juice, then boil gently until the sugar candies. Drain any excess syrup and leave to dry in a warm place.

▲ Wild Chervil

▲ Wild Chervil roots

Chervils (*Anthriscus*)

Wild Chervil or **Cow Parsley** (*A. sylvestris*)
is a perennial herb to 1.5m, with unspotted,
hollow, grooved stems (sometimes purple,
but not blotched), finely lacy leaves and
umbels of white flowers in late spring. The
whole plant becomes very slightly downy
(the upper surfaces of the leaves of this
species are less hairy/downy than the
lookalikes listed here). Abundant throughout
the British Isles on roadsides, in woodland
and many other habitats, and frequent all
over Europe, although restricted to higher
altitudes in the south. Sometimes confused
with Wild Carrot (p476), although it lacks
the red flower in the middle of the umbel
and doesn't smell carroty. The most similar
poisonous species are Hemlock and Fool's
Parsley (p470-p471). The former is larger,
shinier and more purple-blotched, the latter
is smaller, and they both smell foul.
Wild Chervil is extremely abundant and

perfectly edible, if not the tastiest member
of this family. The whole plant is slightly
aromatic and slightly bitter. The leaves are
available in winter, though identification is
harder at this time. They can be chopped
into salads or used as a pot-herb. The
pleasant-smelling stems can replace celery
in stocks and soups, but if you are actually
going to eat them rather than merely
extracting flavour then you have to catch
them at just the right time – you need the
thickest stems, just before they start to get
brittle, and you only want the soft inner
flesh so they need to be carefully peeled
with a knife. The roots make an acceptable
roasted vegetable, though with a bitter
aftertaste. These can often be pulled
up without digging if the ground is soft
enough. You want roots about the size of
your finger – larger ones are more likely
to have inedibly stringy parts. While it is
illegal to uproot wild plants without the
landowner's permission, this one is arguably

▲ Bur Chervil

▲ Rough Chervil

a pest species in England, partly due to eutrophication and changes in management of roadside verges. It crowds out other species, diminishing biodiversity, and few people will complain if foragers remove it.

Bur Chervil (*A. caucalis*) is similar, but annual rather than perennial, hairless, smaller (to 70cm), with smaller umbels and more finely cut leaves. The seed capsules are covered with hooked bristles. Historically uncommon, apart from in East Anglia, the Severn Valley and some coastal areas, but now increasing as an arable weed. Used as Wild Chervil, with better texture and flavour. **Chervil (*A. cerefolium*)** is much smaller and more delicate, native to the mountains of south-east Europe. Spread by the Romans, a valued aromatic herb in French cuisine, an essential component of a herb mix called 'Fines Herbes', and one of seven herbs required for authentic Frankfurter Green Sauce (p75 and p381). Rarely naturalised in the British Isles.

Two other members of the Carrot family can be mistaken for Wild Chervil because they are its most common hedgebank/roadside relatives. The equally edible **Upright Hedge Parsley (*Torilis japonica*,** not pictured) is very similar, though the whole plant is rather more slender and has solid stems and leaf stalks. **Rough Chervil (*Chaerophyllum temulum*)** is a less edible lookalike, with hairier upper leaf surfaces, blunter ends to the lobes, and purple blotches on the stems, which have notably swollen nodes. It causes skin inflammation, gastrointestinal inflammation and other unpleasant symptoms, and has been known to kill grazing animals if consumed in large amounts (mainly pigs and cattle, with symptoms consistent with severe colic). These plants all flower at different times. Wild Chervil flowers first (late spring to early summer), Rough Chervil second (early summer to midsummer), and Upright Hedge Parsley last (midsummer to early autumn).

Wild Carrot (*Daucus carota*) ⚠

Wild Carrot is a hairy biennial herb to 1m with solid, ridged/striped stems and triangular, tripinnate leaves. The dense umbels of white flowers usually have a single reddish-purple flower right in the centre. The flower heads also have distinctive, finely divided, leaf-like bracts hanging down or sticking out, all the way around. Stems lack the purple flush of Rough Chervil (p475). Inhabits rough grassland, particularly near the coast, and in dry, chalky areas. Frequent in England and Wales, less so in Scotland. Frequent across most of Europe, apart from the extreme north, and introduced in temperate areas worldwide. There is a fleshier and less hairy subspecies called Sea Carrot (subsp. *gummifer*), locally common on western coasts.

Precisely how Carrots ended up being domesticated is something of a mystery, not least because of historical confusion with Parsnip. The older roots of the wild plant, as well as being white rather than the familiar orange of modern Carrots, are tough, spindly and rather bitter – not an obvious candidate for domestication as a root vegetable. It is probable that Carrots were originally domesticated, somewhere in central Asia, for the medicinal properties of their seeds and roots. Early cultivated forms had purple or yellow roots, the familiar orange variety not becoming widely available until the 16th century. Wild Carrot seeds were used as a contraceptive and abortifacient in antiquity, though attempts to scientifically verify its efficacy have so far proved inconclusive.

As food, the roots of Wild Carrots are best used as flavouring though it is possible to roast and grind older roots to make a

▲ Wild Carrot

coffee substitute. The seeds can be used as a mild flavouring (avoid if pregnant), and the flowers as a decorative addition to salads, or even deep fried. The leaves can cause hypersensitivity/photosensitivity to ultraviolet.

▲ Parsley

Parsley (*Petroselinum crispum*) ⓘ

Parsley is a hairless annual, biennial or perennial herb to 75cm, with shiny tripinnate leaves (which are flat, rather than curly) and umbels of yellow-green flowers up to 10cm across. The familiar scent is an important distinguishing characteristic. Native to southern Europe, occasional garden escape further north. Occasional in the British Isles, on walls, waste ground and cliffs and rocky areas near the coast, and sometimes in marshy locations. Do not confuse with Fool's Parsley, which smells foul when damaged, and has darker leaves. Probably brought to the British Isles by the Romans, and definitely in cultivation by the 8th century. The leaves and seeds can be used like domesticated forms, although these are also grown for their roots ('Root Parsley'). See recipes on p75 and p381.

Parsley is at its most aromatic shortly before flowering, after which it contains potentially dangerous levels of the toxin apiole, which causes organ damage and miscarriage. It has been used to treat menstrual disorders. Also contains myristicine, which is the psychoactive chemical in nutmeg.

Sison (genus)

Stone Parsley (*S. amomum*) is a many-branched, slender, upright, hairless biennial herb to 1m, with once-pinnate leaves and sparse umbels of white flowers, and a strong smell of petrol and nutmeg. It is frequent in grasslands on heavy clay in the south and east of the British Isles, rare or absent elsewhere. The aromatic leaves and seeds are used as flavouring, and the root is edible cooked.

Corn Parsley (*S. segetum* syn. *Petroselinum segetum*) has the same taste and smell as parsley, and can be used in similar ways. It is also the same size, with pinnate leaves (like Stone Parsley but smaller and without the strong smell) and tiny white flowers in sparse, irregular umbels. Historically a common arable weed, now rarer but locally frequent in the southern half of Great Britain, near coasts or further inland on dry chalk grassland. Very rare further north.

▼ Stone Parsley

▼ Corn Parsley

Pignut (*Conopodium majus*)

Pignut is a perennial herb to 45cm, with
stems that become hollow after flowering,
very slender, deeply cut, twice pinnate
leaves and umbels of small white flowers.
Frequent in old, non-calcareous woods and
grassland throughout the British Isles and
western Europe, apart from Scandinavia,
where it is restricted to southern
coastal areas. **Great Pignut (*Bunium
bulbocastanum*)** is very similar, but also
very rare in the British Isles, although more
common in central Europe. It is possible to
mistake various feathery-leaved members
of the *Asteraceae* for this plant (p433).
Burnet-saxifrage (p468) also has similar
foliage, but grows on more alkaline soils,
and usually in more open areas.

The tubers are excellent raw or cooked,
reminiscent of hazelnuts, but fiddly to
harvest. Each plant has only one tuber,
and it usually isn't directly below the point
where the stem emerges from the ground,
so you either have to carefully follow the
main root, or dig up quite a large area in
order to find it. Pigs were once used to sniff
out these tubers, like truffles. Attempts were
once made to cultivate and improve Pignut,
but it doesn't like ploughed land.

Caraway (*Carum carvi*)

Caraway is a biennial or perennial herb to 80cm, with a rosette of delicate, feathery leaves in the first year, and an upright, leafy, branching, flowering stem in the second, topped with white umbels often tinged with pink. In the British Isles this species is a rare naturalised escape from historic cultivation, apart from Shetland, where it is quite common on dunes. Its native range is unclear, but it is present across much of the rest of Europe (in grassland, woodland and waste ground), especially in the north and in mountainous regions. Cultivated (and foraged) for its seeds since antiquity, which are used as a spice, both raw and cooked, especially in breads, sauerkrauts, sausages, and casseroles with rich meats. The tap roots are edible, usually roasted like parsnips, and the leaves can be used both in salads and as a cooked vegetable. Related but with very different leaves, **Whorled Caraway (*Trocdaris verticillatum* syn. *Carum verticillatum*)** has similarly edible seeds.

▾ Caraway

▴ ▾ Shepherd's-needle

Shepherd's-needle (*Scandix pecten-veris*)

Shepherd's-needle is a perennial herb to 50cm, with leaves like a slightly frillier version of Pignut and very distinctive long, thin fruits (the 'needles' – Latin name means 'comb of Venus'). Found on arable and other disturbed land and waste ground, especially calcareous and/or coastal areas. This ancient introduction was once a common agricultural weed in the British Isles, now rather rare, usually found on disturbed ground or paths. Present throughout Europe, apart from Scandinavia. This plant has long been used for food (usually the tops of the stems), wild and cultivated, cooked and raw.

(Wild) Fennel (*Foeniculum vulgare*)

"The Stalks are to be peel'd when young, and then dress'd like *Sellery*. The tender Tufts and Leaves emerging, being minc'd, are eaten alone with *Vinegar*, or *Oyl*, and *Pepper*, and to correct the colder Materials, enter properly into Composition. The *Italians* eat the blanch'd Stalk (which they call *Cartucci*) all Winter long."
(John Evelyn, 1699)

Fennel is a hairless perennial herb to 2m, with a stem that is solid at first, becoming slightly hollow. The feathery leaves have a slightly blue tinge, and the flowers are in yellow umbels. It has a distinctive aniseed smell. Native to southern Europe, brought to the British Isles by the Romans. Mainly coastal (in the British Isles at least), where it is found on waste ground and roadsides. Frequent in the south, uncommon and scattered inland, rare in Scotland and northern England. Frequent in Europe, especially in the south and coastal areas, absent from the far north. Could be confused with Dill (as a garden escape), which has a different smell, as do various members of the Daisy family which have similar-looking leaves (see p433). **Giant Fennel (*Ferula communis*)** is a Mediterranean relative, grown as an ornamental in the British Isles and naturalised in a few places. It is known to be toxic to livestock and should not be consumed by humans.

The young leaves and stems of Fennel are edible, raw in salads or as a garnish, or cooked, and especially effective used as a bed on which to steam fish, to decorate a terrine, or pressed into shortbread biscuits. The flavour also works well with pork and lamb. Finely chopped leaves can be mixed into yoghurt or crème fraiche to make a sauce or dip. Seeds are used as flavouring, especially for curries, baked goods and pickles. The root is edible cooked. The younger roots are best, or the side roots of older plants, with a sweet flavour and a fennel overtone. Older roots are reminiscent of parsnips, but they have fibrous cores which must be pulled out or removed with a sieve. The flower heads are also good, best cooked. See recipe on p342. Fennel is also highly regarded medicinally, usually taken as a tea for a wide range of digestive disorders, and the seeds are chewed as a remedy for wind.

Another member of this family with feathery leaves is **Spignel** or **Baldmoney** (or '**Badmonnie**') (*Meum athamanticum*). This is a small plant (to 60cm) of northern/mountainous regions – very rare in the British Isles outside of the Scottish Highlands, and restricted to mountainous areas of continental Europe. The leaves and roots are edible, and used for their curry-like flavouring. Historically used in the manufacture of snuff.

Pasta with Sardines and Wild Fennel (traditional Sicilian)

Ingredients:
400g spaghetti or other pasta, 300g wild fennel stems and fronds (washed), 4 anchovies (chopped), 50g pine nuts, sea salt and pepper, 100g dried breadcrumbs, 50g sultanas, 5tbsp extra virgin olive oil, 2 cloves garlic (1 chopped, 1 whole), 300g fresh sardines.

Gently toast the breadcrumbs in a frying pan until golden, and set aside. Bring a pan of water to the boil and simmer the fennel for 10 mins. Meanwhile soak the sultanas in warm water for 10 mins. When tender, drain the fennel, reserving the water. Roughly chop the fennel and set aside. Cook the pasta in the reserved water until 'al dente'. Meanwhile, heat 3tbsp of oil and fry the garlic for 1-2 mins to soften (do not burn). Add anchovies and cook for 1 minute, then the sardines, pine nuts and (drained) sultanas. Stir, and add the fennel. Season and fry for 5 mins, regularly stirring. Drain the pasta (again reserve the water) and add to the frying pan, cook for 1 minute, stirring. Add a few tablespoons of the reserved water, 2tbsp of oil and the toasted breadcrumbs, and toss. Discard the whole garlic clove and serve.

(Rock) Samphire (*Crithmum maritimum*)

Rock Samphire is a spreading perennial herb to 45cm with triangular grey-green leaves composed of very fleshy segments and umbels of yellow-green flowers. Strictly coastal in the wild, inhabiting cliffs and shingle beaches, also sometimes walls and other man-made structures. Common on British coastline clockwise from Great Yarmouth to Galloway, in Ireland apart from the north, and the Atlantic and Mediterranean coasts of Europe.

Samphire is an etymological corruption of Saint Pierre or San Pietro. Pierre/Peter means 'rock', so this was 'St Peter's Herb'. This plant was for a long time simply known as 'Samphire', and was a popular snack in England, pickled in vinegar or even seawater. Over-collection and dwindling supplies led to it being adulterated with an unrelated but similarly fleshy salt marsh plant then known as 'Glasswort' (p385). Glasswort eventually usurped the name 'Samphire', so now we call it 'Marsh Samphire' and *C. maritimum* is usually called 'Rock Samphire' to avoid confusion.

Rock Samphire is a Marmite plant. Personally I like it when young, but plenty of other people find the taste overpowering and disagreeable – it has been compared to petrol and furniture polish. I'd say it is more like supercharged carrots. The leaves are best steamed and served with butter, usually with seafood or freshwater fish, and the seed pods are used in pickles. Dried Rock Samphire can be used in the same ways as Rosemary, eg in focaccia or sourdough bread, or roasted with potatoes. It also makes an unusual pizza topping.

The simplest way to preserve Rock Samphire is to dry it, which also removes some of the bitterness. Soak it overnight in salted water, then change the water, bring to the boil and simmer until it turns bright green. Drain, then dry in a low oven or airing cupboard, and when it is completely dry, seal in glass jars. It also works well as a strong-flavoured pickle, for which there are various recipes (see two below). Some Croatian recipes call for the Samphire to be soaked in seawater for three days before beginning the pickling process.

Pickled Samphire (Mary Eaton, 1822)

Clear the branches of the samphire from the dead leaves, and lay them into a large jar, or small cask. Make a strong brine of white or bay salt, skim it clean while it is boiling, and when done let it cool. Take the samphire out of the water, and put it into a bottle with a broad mouth. Add some strong white-wine vinegar, and keep it well covered down.

Pickled Samphire (TF Garrett, 1892)

Remove all the weeds from the Samphire, spread it out on a large dish, dredge it well with salt, and leave until the following day. Next put the Samphire in a colander and drain it. Put in a pan a sufficient quantity of white vinegar to cover the Samphire, with moderate quantities of mace, ginger, and pepper, and boil them. Wipe the Samphire dry on a cloth, put it into jars, and pour the boiling vinegar over. When the pickle is cold, tie the jars over with stout brown paper. The Samphire will be ready for use in about a fortnight's time.

Samphire Salad (TF Garrett, 1892)

Select some small not too ripe red tomatoes, mince some Samphire pickles, and lay them in alternate rows in a glass dish, placing here and there a few slices of pickled eggs; if the eggs cannot be obtained use pickled walnuts. Make a dressing with the beaten yolks of two eggs, oil, and the vinegar from the pickled Samphire, seasoning it to taste with salt and pepper, and pour it over the Samphire. This makes a pretty dish, the colours contrasting well.

Dried Samphire (TF Garrett, 1892)

Lay some green Samphire in a pan, sprinkle over 3 or 4 table-spoonfuls of salt, pour over sufficient cold water to cover it, and let it stand for twenty-four hours. After it has been steeped in water for the required time, drain it from the water and put it into a copper saucepan over the fire with 1 table-spoonful of salt. Take care that the fire be a very slow one. Leave the Samphire till it is quite crisp, then take it from the fire at once, for if allowed to become soft it will be spoiled; put it into a jar and when quite cold cover the jar air-tight.

Angelica

Wild Angelica (A. _sylvestris_) is a hairless, aromatic, perennial herb to 2.5m, with stout, hollow, purple-flushed, stems (downy near the base) and 2/3 times pinnate triangular leaves (far less finely divided than the lacey-leaved umbellifers) which have grooved upper surfaces. The large, domed white flower heads are followed by oval fruits. Common in the British Isles and throughout the temperate areas of Europe on various damp places, including stream sides, open woodland and cliff edges. Could be confused with Alexanders (p488), which has more rounded leaflets and yellow flowers.

Wild Angelica seeds are used as flavouring for sweet dishes, and the hot infusion of fresh herb makes a pleasant tea. The leaves and roots are edible but bitter. Some sources claim the stems can be used as an aromatic component of salads, but the flavour is very strong.

Garden Angelica (A. _archangelica_) is a rarer plant in the wild, introduced in the British Isles, but native to Scandinavia and central northern Europe. It lacks the purple colouring of _sylvestris_, has larger umbels and the leaf stalks are not grooved, but is otherwise very similar.

Garden Angelica has a milder taste than Wild Angelica, and is cultivated in parts of Europe. The leaves and stems are edible raw or cooked in soups and stews. As a side vegetable they may have to be boiled twice, discarding the first lot of water, to reduce bitterness. The stems were traditionally cooked with tart fruits and vegetables such as rhubarb or gooseberries, and the roots cooked and eaten or used as a component in a cordial. The roots, seeds and candied stems are used as a spicy

flavouring, including for alcoholic drinks such as Chartreuse. To candy the leaf stalks or stems, boil with sugar then store packed in sugar for a few days before boiling again, and then drying. These can be eaten as sweets, or used to decorate cakes.

To preserve Angellica Roots (Hannah Woolley, 1675)

Wash the Roots and slice them very thin, and lay them in water three or four days, change the water every day, then put the Roots into a pot of water, and set them in the embers all night, in the morning put away the water, then take a pound of Roots, four pints of water, and two pound of Sugar, let it boil and scum it clean, then put in the Roots, which will be boiled before the Syrup then take them up and boil the Syrup after, they will ask a whole days work very softly, at St. Andrews time is the best time to do them in all the year.

Angelica tarts (Mary Eaton, 1822)

Take an equal quantity of apples and [fresh] angelica [stems], pare and peel them, and cut them separately into small pieces. Boil the apples gently in a little water, with fine sugar and lemon peel, till they become a thin syrup: then boil the angelica about ten mins. Put some paste at the bottom of the pattipans, with alternate layers of apples and angelica: pour in some of the syrup, put on the lid, and bake them carefully.

◄   Wild Angelica

Hogweed (*Heraclium sphondylium*) ⚠

Hogweed or **Cow Parsnip** is a biennial herb to 2.5m, with thick, ridged, hairy, hollow, purple-tinted stems and variably shaped but usually once-pinnate and coarse-toothed, hairy leaves. The dense umbels are white, sometimes with a pink tinge, and the fruits are round and flat. Abundant throughout the British Isles and the whole of temperate Europe on rough ground, roadsides, grassland and in woodland. Can cause hypersensitivity to sunlight.

Do not confuse with young **Giant Hogweed (*H. mantegazzianum*)**. The fully grown plant is unmistakably enormous (to 6m), the foliage is shiny and much less hairy than Hogweed, and the lobes much more sharply toothed. Introduced from south-east Europe, usually found near rivers or canals, sometimes also by roads and railways, this plant contains photo-toxins capable of causing severe burns and blindness. The sap can pass through clothing when people are cutting it down.

A 1ˢᵗ century collection of Roman recipes ('Apicius') tells us that "Cow-parsnips are fried and eaten with a simple wine sauce". This is next to recipes for carrots and parsnips, so presumably it refers to the roots. They were also used by the Itelmen people of Kamchatka in a dish called 'Selaga' – a "mash of sarana [wild bulbs, usually identified as a type of lily], pine nuts, rosebay willowherb, hogweed and bistort roots, and wild berries, cooked in seal, whale or fish oil".*

Historically important both as animal fodder and human food, the roots, young stems, shoots, flower buds and seeds are all edible. In spring, the young leaf stems/shoots are a first-class cooked vegetable, either steamed, fried in plenty of butter (which it soaks up), made into tempura or soup. The Slavic dish borscht (Polish 'barszcz') was originally a Hogweed-based soup.† They are also excellent pickled, or fermented (same reference goes into quite some detail about this). They are at their very best before any leaves have uncurled. The flower buds can be used like broccoli, though the flavour is strong. The orange-flavoured seeds can be used as a spice, in pickles, or in biscuits and other baked goods.

Several authorities report that the stems can be tied in bundles and sun-dried until they turn yellow, and a sugary substance, considered a delicacy, forms on the stems. I have not been able to replicate this.

* *Steller's History of Kamchatka*, Engel, M, and Willmore, K, 2003, Fairbanks: University of Alaska Press.
† *Foraging in Eastern Europe*, Luczaj, L, 2021.

Hogweed and Ground-elder with Shredded Egg, Wine and Lemon

Ingredients:
400g hogweed shoots (very roughly chopped), juice and zest of one lemon, 30ml dry white wine, 25g chopped ground-elder leaves, 2tbsp butter, 1 hard-boiled egg, salt and pepper.

Blanch the hogweed shoots for 40 seconds in boiling, salted water, then immediately run under cold water to retain crispness. Drain and allow to dry. Force the egg through a sieve and fry in a pan in 1tbsp of butter. Add lemon juice and wine, bring to the boil, add the hogweed shoots, ground-elder and the rest of the butter. Season, cook gently for 2 mins and then sprinkle lemon zest and serve.

Alexanders (*Smirnium olusatrum*)

"The gentle fresh Sprouts, Buds, and Tops are to be chosen, and the Stalks eaten in the Spring; and when *Blanch'd*, in Winter likewise, with *Oyl*, *Pepper*, *Salt*, &c. by themselves, or in Composition: They make also an excellent *Vernal* Pottage."
(John Evelyn, 1699)

Alexanders is a (usually) biennial herb to 1.6m, with a solid, chunky stem and glossy, dark green, 2-3 pinnate leaves with stem-sheathing bases. The yellow-green umbels of flowers develop into black seeds. Common in coastal areas of England and Wales on roadsides, waste ground and other areas, particularly at the tops of coastal cliffs and downs, where it can displace all the native flora. It is much rarer inland and further north. In its native range further south it is not coastal – it is only coastal in Britain because these areas are less prone to frosts. Wild Angelica is the most similar umbellifer, but has more pointed leaves and is found in woodland or near fresh water. **Perfoliate Alexanders (*S. perfoliatum*)** is smaller, with yellowish leaves that strongly clasp the stem. Native to the Mediterranean, naturalised in a few places in England. Usable as Alexanders.

Alexanders was a Roman introduction, as food for both humans and horses. The British continued to cultivate it after they left, until it was eventually displaced as a crop by domesticated Celery in the 18th century. Alexanders is one of the few plants available to foragers during the winter (see photo on p31). It is at its very best in early spring as the strongest plants send up their first big flowering stem, though these soon become too tough to eat. It is the white heart of those primary stems, and their side-stems, that you want. Carefully rip off the green outer layers, then strip with a sharp knife or potato peeler, boil for a couple of minutes then steam for 5 to 10 minutes as preferred – the intensity of the flavour decreases with cooking, but the stems also become rather soft and squidgy. Serve with butter, salt and pepper, no complications needed.

The leaves when young can be added sparingly to salads, or chopped and used to flavour white sauce for fish – follow a recipe for Parsley sauce and use young Alexanders leaves in place of the Parsley. The flower buds can be cooked like broccoli (although they pack quite an aromatic punch) or pickled, but are best fried. The seeds can be used as a spice, added to pickles, or put in a pepper grinder for some seriously spicy seasoning. The whole plant can be used in stocks in place of celery. Alexanders pollen is also edible. Collect the flower heads, then place in a colander and knock the individual flowers off, which will fall through the holes. Then pass through a sieve to leave you with just the pollen. It has a strong flavour, and is used by Silo Restaurants in an unusual salad consisting of 50g salted cucumbers, 5g stonecrop (p168), 10g oyster sauce and a pinch of Alexanders pollen.

The roots can also be eaten, and though the taste is overpowering raw, they can work thinly sliced in the right salad. Cooked they can compete with the best wild root vegetables in this family, but the bitterness is variable. They do not need to be cooked for long – boil or steam for 5 minutes and serve with the inevitable knob of butter, roast like parsnips, or prepare like Burdock root, kinpara style (see p455).

A grand Sallet of Alexander-buds (Robert May, 1660)

Take large Alexander-buds, and boil them in fair water after they be cleansed and washed, but first let the water boil, then put them in, and being boil'd, drain them on a dish bottom or in a cullender; then have boil'd capers and currans, and lay them in the midst of a clean scowred dish, the buds parted in two with a sharp knife, and laid round about upright, or one half on one side, and the other against it on the other side, so also carved lemon, scrape on sugar, and serve it with good oyl and wine vinegar.

Lactofermented Alexanders Stems

Make a 2% salinity brine (20g salt per litre of unchlorinated water), peel and chop the stems, put into a glass jar (ideally a Mason jar or fermenting crock), cover with brine and use a weight or cabbage leaf to make sure they are all under the brine and not exposed to the air. Ferment at room temp for a week, 'burping' the jar twice a day, refrigerate and leave at least a couple of weeks before eating. Unopened, they will keep for months in the fridge or cold store.

Wine-battered Alexanders Shoots

Ingredients:
400g alexanders shoots, 150ml german white wine (chilled), 1 egg, 100g plain flour, béchamel sauce, oil for frying.

Chop and peel the shoots, boil in salted water for 6 mins, then drain. Beat the egg and wine, then sift in the flour and stir to make a batter. Coat the alexanders in more flour, dip in the batter and fry for 2 mins. Drain on kitchen towel and serve with béchamel sauce.

▼ Alexanders roots and seeds

For leaves, see picture on p31

Ground-elder (*Aegopodium podagraria*)

Ground-elder is a rhizomatous, patch-forming, hairless perennial herb to 1m, with grooved, hollow stems (no purple tinge), fine-toothed trifoliate leaves on long, grooved, hollow stalks, and umbels of tiny white flowers, usually in threes. A persistent garden weed most frequently found near human habitation, but also in woodland and on verges. Abundant in the British Isles apart from mountainous areas, and common throughout temperate Europe. Could be confused with Dog's Mercury (p177), which has finely hairy leaves.

Ground-elder was introduced to the British Isles by the Romans as a pot-herb and a cure for gout (another name is 'Goutweed').

Since this plant is both introduced and a problem weed, it is one of those that foragers can harvest to their heart's content. It is edible raw, but much better cooked. The young leaves and shoots are eaten before the plant has flowered, becoming less palatable as they age. The youngest, glossiest ones are the best, ideally before they unfurl. They can be cooked like spinach and served with butter (which rescues even the older leaves), or quickly fried, used to decorate quiches, or added to soups and savoury pies. They work well in a béchamel sauce to serve with gammon – just follow any recipe for Parsley sauce but substitute Ground-elder for the Parsley. This can be made more punchy by adding some finely chopped Lady's Smock leaves (p292). Also see p486.

Ground-elder Soup

Ingredients:
200g young ground-elder leaves, 30g butter, 30g flour, 1 small onion (chopped), 2 rashers of bacon (chopped), 500ml chicken stock, 250ml single cream.

Rinse the ground-elder leaves and sweat them off in the water remaining on the leaves for 1-2 mins, then remove from the heat. Cook the onion and bacon in the butter for 3-4 mins. Add the flour then slowly add the stock, stirring all the time. Add the leaves in and simmer for 5 mins, then blend. Add the cream, heat through and season to taste.

Wild parsnip (*Pastinaca sativa*) (!)

"Small, hard, woodie, and not fit to be eaten."
(John Gerard, 1597)

Wild Parsnip is a biennial or perennial herb to 1.8m, with a furrowed stem and rough, once-pinnate leaves (low rosette in first year, tall flowering stalk in subsequent years). The umbels of tiny yellow flowers are followed by flattened, near-circular fruits. This plant is easily identified by the strong parsnip smell. Native and common in central, southern and south-east England on waste ground, roadsides (especially roundabouts, it seems) and tracks, and in old quarries and fallow fields, favouring chalk and limestone. Rare/absent elsewhere in the British Isles. Frequent across Europe apart from the far north and the far south, most common in central northern Europe. Similar to Hogweed (p486) but smaller.

This plant was first domesticated for its alleged medicinal qualities, or perhaps as a sweet flavouring. Little is known about where and when it was domesticated, partly because Greek and Roman writers did not distinguish between Parsnip and Carrot. It was predated as a fleshy root crop by a related plant now almost entirely forgotten – the **Skirret** or **Water-parsnip** (***Sium sisarum***). Skirret originated in China, was grown in Europe in antiquity, and was popular in Britain in the 17th and 18th centuries, before almost entirely disappearing from the diet of Europeans. Its rare native relative **Greater Water-parsnip** (***S. latifolium***) has foul-tasting, poisonous roots, but the leaves have been cooked and eaten as a vegetable in Italy and the seeds are used as a spice in Scandinavian cuisine.

▲ Wild Parsnip

Wild Parsnips have less impressive roots, though they are bigger than those of Wild Carrot and were once used in Ireland to flavour ale. The leaves and young shoots are edible but must be cooked (work well in a soup) and the seeds can be used as flavouring (similar to Dill).

The sap causes hypersensitivity to sunlight. Do not collect with bare hands in bright sunlight, or if you have sensitive skin.

Scots Lovage (*Ligusticum scoticum*)

Scots Lovage is a hairless perennial herb to 1m (usually smaller) with stout stems, thick, glossy, bright green, twice trifoliate leaves and greenish-white umbels. Strictly northern and coastal (on cliffs and rocky beaches). In the British Isles only present in Scotland and Northern Ireland, and in continental Europe restricted to Scandinavia.

The aromatic flowers, shoots, leaves and roots are all edible, raw or cooked, and taste like parsley with a hint of celery. They go well with fish and game. The seeds are also used as flavouring, and have been compared to cumin and fenugreek. They can be used fresh while still green, or dried and ground once they've ripened to brown.

The related **Lovage (*Levisticum officinale*)** is a much larger perennial herb to 2.5m with shiny green or yellow-green leaves. Probably native to the Mediterranean, but was once a popular cultivated vegetable further north and may be naturalised in a few locations in the British Isles. Like Scots Lovage, it has a celery-like flavour, and is used in soups and casseroles, or wilted like spinach. The roots are also edible, sometimes grated into salads like carrots. Also the seeds are used to make an alcoholic cordial.

Sea Holly (*Eryngium maritimum*)

Sea Holly (pictured overleaf) is a small, bushy, branching perennial to 60cm, with grey-blue, holly-like, spiny leaves and beautiful metallic blue flowers (late summer) that look more like thistles/teasels than an umbellifer. Inhabits beaches, especially sandy but sometimes shingle, above the high-tide line, often on dunes. Occasional in the British Isles, apart from the far north. Much rarer than it once was, partly because it was once foraged unsustainably and partly because beachgoers dislike it because of its prickles. The whole plant is aromatic. Young leaves (minus the largest spines) and shoots are edible cooked, and were historically blanched by excluding light. The root was eaten boiled, roasted or candied. Take care not to confuse with the poisonous roots of Yellow-horned Poppy (p146).

Field Eryngo (*E. campestre*) has slimmer leaves with no trace of blue, and can be found in dry grasslands as well as dunes. It is very rare in the British Isles, which is at the northern limit of its range, and protected in the UK by the 1981 Wildlife and Countryside Act. The roots were historically used like Sea Holly.

‹ Field Eryngo

> **Candied Eringo Roots**
> (Hannah Woolley, 1675)
>
> Take your Eringos ready to be preserved, and weigh them. To every pound of your Roots take of the purest Sugar you can get two pound, and clarifie it with the whites of eggs exceeding well, that it may be as clear as crystal, for that will be best. It being clarified, boyl it to the height of Manus Christi [105-110°C], then dip in your roots two or three at once, till all be candyed, and so put them in a stove, and so keep them all the year.

Apiaceae (Carrot family) ~ **493**

Index

Page numbers in *italic* refer to images. Page numbers in **bold** refer to the main entry.

Glossary

Achene: a dry, one-seeded fruit which does not split open when ripe.

Anthers: the sac-like parts of a flower which produce pollen.

agg.: aggregate species – a range of closely related organisms.

Basal (leaves, rosette): growing from the lowest part of the stem.

Bipinnate: (of a pinnate leaf) having leaflets that are further subdivided in a pinnate arrangement.

Boreal: the climate and ecological zone between the Arctic and temperate regions.

Bract: a modified leaf that sits between the flower and the leaves.

Bracteole: a small bract on short stem (or pedicel).

Bulbil: a tiny plant (a clone) that is reproduced vegetatively from axillary buds on the parent plant's stem or in place of a flower.

Cambium: a thin layer of tissue beneath the bark of a tree which gives rise to new cells via division.

Clade: a complete group of living things descended from a single common ancestor.

Compound (leaf): composed of smaller leaflets.

Cordate (leaf): shaped like a spade symbol from a pack of cards, especially at the base.

Cosmopolitan (distribution): found in suitable habitats worldwide.

Cryptophyte: a plant that dies back each year to the ground.

Dioecious: a species that has separate male and female plants.

Diploid: a plant or species with two sets of chromosomes, one from each parent.

Double-toothed (leaves): has edges that have rows of smaller teeth, with occasional larger teeth.

Entire (leaf): having a smooth margin.

Herb: a non-woody plant.

Holdfast: the part of a seaweed that attaches to the substrate (usually rocks).

Intertidal zone: the area between the high and low spring tide-lines.

Interruptedly pinnate (leaf): larger leaflets interspersed with smaller ones.

Lanceolate (leaf): shaped like the head of a lance; tapering from a rounded base toward the apex.

Midrib: a large, strong vein along the midline of a leaf or seaweed thallus.

Oblanceolate (leaf): lanceolate with the pointed end at the base.

Obovoid/obovate (leaf): egg-shaped, with the narrow end at the base.

Panicle: a loose, branching cluster of flowers.

Palmate: having five or more lobes whose midribs all radiate from one point.

Petal: a modified leaf (usually coloured) that is part of a flower.

Pinnate: (of a compound leaf) having leaflets arranged on either side of the stem, typically in pairs opposite each other.

Polyphyletic: a group of species descended from more than one ancestor (so not a clade).

Raceme: a cluster of flowers with the individual flowers attached by short and equal stalks at equal distances along a central stem.

Rhizome: an underground stem which both stores nutrients and sends out the roots and shoots of new plants.

Sepal: a modified leaf (usually green) that encloses a flower.

spp.: abbreviation of species (plural).

Stamens: male parts in the centre of a flower

Stipule: a small leaf-like appendage to a leaf, usually in pairs at the base of the leaf stalk.

Style: a long stalk in the centre of a flower connecting the stigma (top) and ovary (bottom).

subsp.: a subdivision of a species.

subg. (subgenus): a subdivision of a large genus.

Sucker, suckering: a plant that sends up new stems from the roots.

Tepal: a modified leaf not easily classified as either sepal or petal (somewhere between the two).

Thallus: a plant or plant-like body that is not differentiated into stem and leaves and lacks true roots and a vascular system.

Tetraploid: a plant or species with four sets of chromosomes, two from each parent.

Tribe (taxonomy): the cladistic rank above genus but below family.

Trifoliate (leaf): has three leaflets.

Tripinnate (leaf): bipinnate leaflets that are themselves pinnately divided.

Truncate (leaf): ending abruptly as if cut off across the base or tip.

Tuber: a swollen storage organ, usually modified from the roots of plants.

Umbel: a flower cluster in which stalks of nearly equal length spring from a common centre and form a flat or curved surface.

Vascular (plant): composed of types of tissue called xylem (for structure) and phloem (for nutrient and water transportation).

Whorl(ed): a circular arrangement of leaves or flowers, around a point on an axis.

Photo credits and licences

11 Fertile Crescent map: Semhur, Creative Commons (CC) Share Alike (SA) 3.0 Unported

15 Black-banded ironstone: André Karwath aka Aka, CC SA 2.5 Generic

34 Iceland Moss: Tigerente, GNU Free Documentation v1.2

48 Wakame: Commonwealth Scientific and Industrial Research Organisation (CSIRO), CC Attribution 3.0 Unported (CC BY 3.0)

86 Maidenhair Fern: Marija Gajić, CC SA 4.0 International

90 Ostrich Fern: harum.koh: CC SA 2.0 Generic

90 Fiddlehead closeup: The Cosmonaut, CC SA 2.5 Canada

92 Monkeypuzzle female cone H. Zell, Attribution-ShareAlike 3.0 Unported (CC BY-SA 3.0)

102 Yellow Waterlily fruit: Kristian Peters, GNU Free Documentation v1.2

106 Sweet Flag flower: H. Zell, GNU Free Documentation v1.2

107 Arrowhead flower: Isissss, CC SA 4.0 International

108 Cape Pondweed: Cillas, CC SA 4.0 International

110 Flowering Rush: Christian Fischer, CC SA 3.0 Unported

111 Duckweed: Christian Fischer, CC SA 3.0 Unported

116 False Hellebore: 64, GNU Free Documentation v1.2

117 Autumn Crocus: Hedwig Storch, CC SA 3.0 Unported

117 Saffron Crocus: Zeynel Cebeci, CC SA 4.0 International

121 Solomon's-seal fruits: Agnieszka Kwiecień, Nova, CC SA 4.0 International

125 Wild Asparagus: Michel Gaubert, CC SA 2.0 France

126 *Allium carinatum*: Haeferl, CC SA 3.0 Unported

126 *Allium moly*: Dolly442, GNU Free Documentation v1.2

126 *Allium victorialis*: Florian Grossir, CC SA 3.0 Unported

126 *Allium sphaerocephalon*: Krzysztof Golik, CC SA 4.0 International

129 Field Garlic: Stefan Laefnaer, CC SA 4.0 International

131 Mouse Garlic: Kispál Zoltán CC SA 4.0 International

142 Great Fen Sedge: Krzysztof Ziarnek, CC SA 4.0 International

144 Common Club-rush: Kristian Peters, GNU Free Documentation v1.2

150 Baneberry: Аимаина хикари, CC CC0 1.0 Universal Public Domain Dedication

151 *Delphinium elatum*: Hanna Zelenko, CC SA 4.0 International

151 Pasque Flower: Magnus Manske, CC SA 3.0 Unported

153 Wolfsbane: Walter Starmühler, CC SA 3.0 Unported

158 Japanese Barberry: Alpsdake, CC SA 3.0 Unported

159 Barberry flowers: Stefan Lefnaer, CC SA 4.0 International

159 Barberry berries:H. Zell, GNU Free Documentation, v1.2

165 Blackcurrant: Rasbak GNU Free Documentation, v1.2

169 Rock Stonecrop: Anneli Salo, CC SA 3.0 Unported

171 Roseroot: User Alpsdake on Wikimedia commons, CC SA 4.0 International

172 Alternate-leaved Golden-saxifrage: Robert Flogaus-Faust, CC Attribution 4.0 International

173 Purple Saxifrage: Alistair Rae, Attribution-ShareAlike 2.0 Generic (CC BY-SA 2.0)

176 Caper Spurge fruits: Michel Chauvet, CC SA 4.0 International

189 False Acacia pods: (assumed) Bogdan, GNU Free Documentation v1.2

199 Heath Pea: Krzysztof Ziarnek, CC SA 4.0 International

202 Tuberous Pea: Franz Xaver, CC SA 3.0 Unported

209 Japanese Wineberry: Wouter Hagens, GNU Free Documentation v1.2

209 Salmonberry: pfly, CC SA 2.0 Generic

209 Cutleaf Bramble: meggar, GNU Free Documentation v1.2

212 Dewberry: Bjorn S..., CC SA 2.0 Generic

213 Stone Bramble: Simon Legner, CC SA 4.0 International

214 Cloudberry: Moravice, CC SA 4.0 International

217 Tormentil: Krzysztof Golik, CC SA 4.0 International

218 Water Avens: H. Zell, GNU Free Documentation v1.2

223 Magnus Manske: GNU Free Documentation v1.2

225 BotBln: GNU Free Documentation v1.2

231 Bird Cherry: Anneli Salo, CC SA 3.0 Unported

236 Juneberry: Eiku, CC SA 3.0 Unported

265 Musk Storksbill: Eugene Zelenko, CC SA 4.0 International

270 Tree Fuschia: Franz Xaver, GFDL, cc-by-sa

279 Wild Turnip: Rasbak, GNU Free Documentation v1.2

280 White Mustard: Ariel Palmon, GNU Free Documentation v1.2

280 White Mustard fruit: Meneerke Bloem, GNU Free Documentation v1.2

285 Eastern Rocket: Harry Rose, CC Attribution 2.0 Generic

285 Eastern Rocket leaf: Stefan Laefnaer, CC SA 4.0 International

290 Great Yellowcress: TeunSpaans, CC SA 3.0 Unported

296 Field Pennycress: H. Zell, GNU Free Documentation v1.2

298 Field Pepperwort: Fornax, CC SA 3.0 Unported

300 Dittander: Malte, CC SA 3.0 Unported

302 Flixweed: Stefan.lefnaer, CC SA 4.0 International

304 Common Scurvy-grass: Erlend Bjørtvedt CC, SA 3.0 Unported

310 *Daphne mezereum*: H. Zell, GNU Free Documentation v1.2

310 *Daphne laureola*: Gail Hampshire, CC Attribution 2.0 Generic

312 Dwarf Mallow: Luis Fernández García, CC SA 2.5 Spain

325 Wild Buckwheat: Olivier Pichard, CC SA 3.0 Unported

329 Alpine Bistort: Alpdsake, CC SA 3.0 Unported

339 Corn-spurrey: Rosser1954, CC SA 4.0 International

341 Common Amaranth: Stefan.lefnaer, CC SA 4.0 International

344 Good King Henry: Jerzy Opiola, CC SA 4.0 International

348 Red Goosefoot: Michael Becker, GNU Free Documentation v1.2

349 Nettle-leaved Goosefoot, Stefan.Lefnaer, CC SA 4.0 International

351 Common Orache: Matt Lavin, CC BY-SA 2.0

354 Shrubby Orache: Krzysztof Ziarnek, CC SA 4.0 International

357 Prickly Saltwort: Júlio Reis, CC SA 3.0 Unported

357 Summer Cypress: Rameshng, CC SA 3.0 Unported

349 Nettle-leaved goosefoot: Stefan Laefnaer, CC SA 4.0 International

349 Maple-leaved goosefoot: Hermann Schachner, CC0 1.0 Universal Public Domain Dedication

360 Blinks (both images): abalg, GNU Free Documentation v1.2

361 Pink Purslane: Rasbak, GNU Free Documentation v1.2

362 Purslane: Stefan Lefnaer, CC SA 4.0 International

364 Dwarf Cornel: Erlend Bjørtvedt, CC SA 4.0 International

365 Cornelian Cherry: Abdossamad Talebpour / R. Leysi, GNU Free Documentation , v1.2

366 Japanese Dogwood flower: Valérie75, CC SA 3.0 Unported

366 Japanese Dogwood berry: Wouter Hagens, CC SA 3.0 Unported

368 *Impatiens capensis*: Fritz Flohr Reynolds, CC SA 3.0 Unported

368 *Impatiens noli-tangere*: Björn S., CC SA 3.0 Unported

368 *Impatiens parviflora*: MurielBendel, CC SA 4.0 International

371 Crowberry: Ryan Hodnett, CC SA 4.0 International

372 Bearberry: Walter Siegmund, GNU Free Documentation v1.2

373 Bog bilberry: Maseltov, CC SA 4.0 International

374 Cranberry: B. Lezius, CC Attribution 3.0 Unported

383 Common Comfrey: Aiwok, CC Attribution 3.0 Unported

385 Oysterplant: Qwert1234, CC SA 4.0 International

399 Henbit: Anne Burgess, CC BY-SA 2.0, and by written permission

400 Corsican Mint: David Eickhoff, CC Attribution 2.0 Generic

404 Lesser Calamint: Wilfredo Rodriguez, GFDL and CC CC-BY-SA-2.5

404 Common Calamint: Jeffdelonge, GNU Free Documentation v1.2

418 Datura: Radio Tonreg (Gernot Molitor), CC Attribution 2.0 Generic

419 Deadly Nightshade (both images): GT1976, CC SA 4.0 International

424 Fringed Waterlily: KENPEI, GNU Free Documentation v1.2

434 Gallant Soldier: Olivier Pichard, CC SA 3.0 Unported

452 Cabbage Thistle: Franz Xaver, CC SA 3.0 Unported

458 Round-headed Rampion: Hans Hillewaert, CC SA 3.0 Unported

458 Spiked Rampion: Angela Duyster, GNU Free Documentation v1.2

461 Giant Bellflower: Vinayaraj V R, CC SA 4.0 International

461 Creeping Bellflower. Cillas, GNU Free Documentation v1.2

461 Peach-leaved Bellflower: Marinka kma, CC SA 4.0 International

465 Red berried Elder. Opiola Jerzy, GNU Free Documentation v1.2

469 Cowbane: Anneli Salo, CC SA 3.0 Unported

472 Wild Celery: Digigalos, CC SA 3.0 Unported

477 Corn Parsley: Liliane Roubaudi, CC SA 2.5 Generic

479 Caraway: Anneli Salo, CC SA 3.0 Unported

479 Shepherds Needle fruit closeup: G Hagedorn, CC SA 3.0 Unported